READER'S DIGEST

CONDENSED BOOKS

FIRST EDITION

THE READER'S DIGEST ASSOCIATION LIMITED
25 Berkeley Square, London W1X 6AB

THE READER'S DIGEST ASSOCIATION
SOUTH AFRICA (PTY) LTD
Nedbank Centre, Strand Street, Cape Town

Printed in Great Britain by Petty & Sons Ltd, Leeds
and Severn Valley Press Ltd, Caerphilly

Original cover design by Jeffery Matthews M.S.I.A.

For information as to ownership
of copyright in the material in this book see last page

ISBN 0 340 23951 4

Reader's Digest
CONDENSED BOOKS

TARA KANE
George Markstein

ELEPHANT BILL
J. H. Williams

THE BRENDAN VOYAGE
Tim Severin

A STRANGER IS WATCHING
Mary Higgins Clark

THE SPUDDY
Lillian Beckwith

COLLECTOR'S LIBRARY
EDITION

In this volume

TARA KANE *by George Markstein* (p. 9)

In the great days of the Klondike gold rush, a young
woman sets out to find her missing husband among
the thousands seeking riches in the inhospitable Yukon. High-spirited Tara Kane
encounters many a danger before she
reaches the astonishing end
of her quest. A vivid
and colourful story,
many of its larger-
than-life characters
and events are based
on contemporary
records.

ELEPHANT BILL
by J. H. Williams (p. 161)

One of the most remarkable animal
books of our time, *Elephant Bill* is
written with affection and great
charm by a man who spent more
than twenty years of his life working
with elephants in the teak jungles
of Burma.

He describes with humour and
warmth the varied personalities of
different elephants, tells of their
devotion to their mates and to their
young, offers surprising examples
of their intelligence, and gives a
memorable picture of the delightful
Burmese people who tend these
huge and lovable beasts.

THE BRENDAN VOYAGE
by Tim Severin (p. 217)

This is the epic account of a hazardous crossing of the Atlantic by leather boat, a skilfully made replica of the tiny craft used by Saint Brendan in the sixth century. An extraordinary true story of courage and high adventure, its excitements are heightened by outstanding colour photographs.

A STRANGER IS WATCHING
by Mary Higgins Clark (p. 345)

Steve Peterson's wife was brutally murdered; his small son witnessed the killing. A man faces execution and an attractive journalist is personally involved. Only one man knows the truth, a lurking stranger whose evil plan plunges them all into a living nightmare.

THE SPUDDY
by Lillian Beckwith (p. 459)

The haunting beauty of a Scottish fishing village is the setting for this tale of an unlikely trio: a lonely little boy, a disillusioned sea captain, and a friendless dog, each of them deserted by those he had most loved and trusted. A quietly memorable story of caring and courage.

TARA KANE

a condensation of the book by

GEORGE MARKSTEIN

Illustrated by Guy Deel
Published by Jonathan Cape

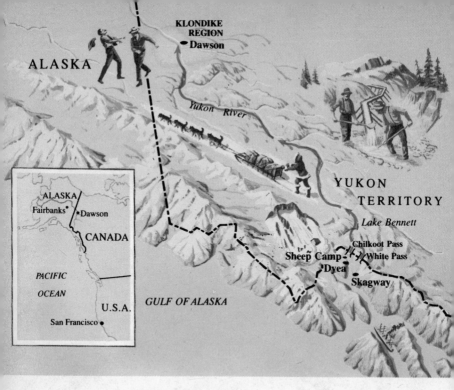

It is historical fact that, for a few short years at the height of the gold rush, the uncrowned King of the Klondike was an individual known as Soapy Smith.

That he met, and befriended, a handsome young woman, Tara Kane, is not so certain. But it's undoubtedly typical of what we know of the man and his methods.

Tara was searching in the sprawling shanty towns of the gold fields for her husband. It was a hard world, the climate merciless, the people rugged, picturesque, ungovernable. And Soapy Smith was, at best, a dubious ally. But Tara survived.

Much of the Klondike was then British territory. And in this exciting new book by a distinguished British author, it is brought to life perhaps more dramatically than ever before.

PROLOGUE

She made a strikingly attractive mourner. Black enhanced Tara Kane; it silhouetted her slim figure and complemented her deep auburn hair. Under the dark veil, tears ran down her pale cheeks. Her generous mouth, which like her large oval green eyes reflected her moods, was turned down at the corners. Hers was a private grief she could share with no one and all the sadder for its solitude.

The funeral of her nine-month-old daughter, Gabrielle, had taken place ten days earlier in San Francisco's Laurel Hill Cemetery. The gravedigger, who was scooping out fresh earth nearby, remembered her clearly. It had been a brief, austere burial with only two people present, the slender woman in black and the minister. No family. No husband. Afterwards she had walked off alone, and the gravedigger had wondered who the sad, elegant woman might be.

Now she was back, staring at Gabrielle's grave. Bending down, she placed a small bunch of flowers on the ground that covered the tiny coffin. For a moment she knelt silent, her eyes blurred with tears. Then, gathering her cloak around her, she stood up and walked off among the bending willows.

Tara looked back only once. At the cemetery gate she stopped, her eyes searching the rows of graves where, in the distance, Gabie lay. But the plot was already hidden from sight. She sighed. Tomorrow she would be gone from San Francisco, and there would be no one to visit the forlorn little grave. She turned, raised her head high, and walked out of the cemetery, her face set with determination. What she was about to do was the most desperate decision of her life, but there was no other course.

CHAPTER ONE

Tara had hired a hack to take her and her cabin trunk to the ship, but once through the dock gates movement was impossible. Across a sea of heads she could see the *North Fork* smoking from its three stacks. Even from this distance it looked what it was, a rusty and battered tramp steamer, more suited for the breaker's yard than a voyage to Alaska.

"Can't go no farther," announced the cabbie with finality as he dumped her trunk on the sidewalk.

"How am I going to manage?" Tara asked him despairingly.

"That's your problem," he replied as he jumped back into his hack. It was hopeless for her to try to move the trunk herself. None of the hundreds of jostling people took the slightest notice of her. KLONDIKE OR BUST someone had chalked on a warehouse wall, and that seemed to be the goal of all of them. She came near to panicking. She could visualize herself still trapped in this madhouse when the *North Fork* cast off in three hours' time. The ship sounded its steam whistle imperiously, and somebody almost pushed Tara down.

"Whoa!" said a man she was flung against. "Take it easy." He was large and muscular, and looked like a sailor.

"Oh, please," Tara gasped, "can you get my trunk to the ship? I'll pay you five dollars." She knew she was throwing her money away, but she was so near now that nothing would stop her.

"Let's try it," he said, picking up the trunk with a grunt and hoisting it on his shoulder.

Slowly he began to force his way through the dense mob. Tara followed and tried not to see the angry, desperate faces that flashed in front of her. People dug her in the ribs, stepped on her feet, jostled her. Grimly she kept a firm hold on her valise and handbag and forged on.

Suddenly, from behind her, came shouts of protest and howls of rage. She heard the cracking of a whip, and then a wagon began to force its way through, the driver furiously lashing people who blocked him. In the wagon Tara saw dozens of dogs chained

10

together, barking and snarling as they were driven to the ship.

The *North Fork* loomed over the pierhead, crowds of people already lining the rails. At the gangway, the man put her trunk down. "That's it," he said. "The rest is up to you."

"I'm so grateful to you," she said, pressing the dollars into his hand.

"Going to the Yukon?" he asked, smiling wryly. "Good luck! Hope you survive." Then he was engulfed by the crowd.

Close up, the soot-encrusted *North Fork* appeared even more squalid. "I'm a passenger," Tara shouted to a villainous-looking seaman blocking the gangway. "I need help with my trunk."

"Nobody more comes aboard," the man growled. "We're full."

"You have room for me," Tara cried. "I'm joining my husband." She held up the precious ticket for which she had queued for hours in a mile-long line of Alaska-bound prospectors trying to get passage north before the winter freeze-up.

"You're too late." The man grinned unpleasantly. "But maybe I can fix you up. For a little extra."

All Tara wanted was to get on that deck, and it was only a few yards away. If it needed a bribe, so be it. She took twenty dollars out of her purse and gave it to him.

"O.K., I'll get you on board." He turned and shouted to a sailor, "Hey, Rusky, get this trunk."

Tara followed the sailor up the long gangway, each step leading her into a frightening unknown. Yet she felt strangely elated. Despite all odds she'd got a ticket, was on the boat. Soon she would be on her way.

On deck, every inch of space seemed to be occupied. Neighing horses reared and kicked in wooden pens that had been erected as temporary stables. Rows of dog cages were roped to the deck, the animals inside snarling and snapping. Overhead swayed crates and other cargo being hoisted aboard. The sight of the crowd still pushing towards the gangway was frightening.

"I want to go to my cabin," Tara said to the sailor.

"The captain will fix you up." He nodded at a man with a walrus moustache standing nearby. Unconcerned about the chaos on his ship, the captain leaned against the rail and puffed at his pipe.

"Captain?" said Tara, walking up to him.

"Yes, ma'am, Captain Swain," he said, taking the pipe out of his mouth. "What's the trouble?" He had seen her wedding ring and the familiar way he eyed her made Tara's hackles rise.

"I want to know where my cabin is. I have a reservation."

"All by yourself?" There was something insulting about his manner. "There'll be a surcharge. One hundred dollars."

"Don't be ridiculous," she exclaimed. "I've paid my passage."

"Ladies on their own are a problem. Not easy to fit females into this vessel. We're not built for it. You can see for yourself."

"I've already had to bribe one of your men—"

"My men don't take bribes," Swain cut in. "If you don't like this ship, get off it. I'll have your luggage removed."

Tara was outraged. "If you put me ashore, I'll call the police!" she cried so fiercely that even he seemed shaken. "I'll have you arrested, the whole lot of you! You won't sail without me, I promise you, Captain Swain."

He sucked at his pipe, then asked, quite mildly, "What's your name?"

"Mrs. Kane."

"Well, Mrs. Kane, there's no need to fly off the handle. I guess we can squeeze you in. The only question is, ma'am, do you have the hundred bucks?"

By now she knew she had no choice. She wouldn't be able to get another ship for weeks, not in the middle of the gold rush, with men fighting for a passage to the Klondike. "All right," Tara agreed through gritted teeth as she counted out the money.

"Welcome aboard, Mrs. Kane." He smiled, stuffing the dollars into his pocket. "I'll have you shown to your quarters."

"I want my own cabin," Tara warned. "First class," she added, "I've paid enough."

"First class it is," the captain said. He ordered a seaman over. "Take this lady and her trunk to cabin four."

Tara turned and followed the man. The stench below decks was nauseating. Here, as everywhere else, soiled sawdust and wood shavings were strewn on the floor to soak up all manner of refuse. The smell was so overpowering that Tara felt faint.

"Here you are, cabin four," the seaman said, stopping before a door and kicking it open.

Tara stepped into what she had imagined would be her own cosy cabin. Instead it was what had apparently been a storeroom, now converted into a dormitory for four people. The woodwork was not painted, and the only light came from two oil lamps swinging from the low ceiling. It was shabby, rough and cramped.

"This can't be right," Tara cried as the seaman dragged in her trunk. "I'm travelling first class."

A broad grin spread across the sailor's face. "We ain't got first class on this tub. Unless this is it. You're lucky, ma'am. You got a bunk, and there's only four in here, being all ladies. The men are stacked ten to a cabin half this size. We got three hundred passengers and sleeping berths for only half that. So maybe you got first class." He closed the door, leaving an alarmed Tara looking around her new home.

The other occupants had already moved in. Flamboyant and garish clothes were strewn about, and Tara smelled the odour of cheap perfume. One bunk in the corner did not seem to have been claimed. A thin straw palliasse served as a mattress. There was no pillow, and the single blanket was so revolting that the thought of it covering her made Tara squirm.

From outside there was laughter, and then the door flew open. The two women who entered the cabin stopped still when they saw Tara. "What have we here?" asked the taller of the two. She was blonde, in her twenties, her face smothered with thick make-up.

Her companion was fat, and her eye shadow and red lipstick did nothing to enhance her sweaty face. The top of her dress was undone, and she carried a half-empty bottle of gin.

"I'll be sharing with you," Tara said, swallowing hard.

"Well!" said the blonde. "What do you think of that, Flo?"

"You'd better find somewhere else, honey," Flo hiccuped. "We're full up. There's no room."

Tara was at the end of her tether. "Believe me, I don't want to be here, but I'm staying," she said, sitting down on her bunk.

13

"What's your name?" Flo asked.

"Tara Kane."

Flo had spotted her wedding ring. "Married, are you?"

"I'm sailing to join my husband."

Flo sat down on the bunk beside Tara. "Well, Tara, you got to understand," she explained. "Seven of us use this cabin."

"Seven!" Tara echoed, horrified.

"Only me, Maggie, and Belle sleep here, but us and our friends will be using it. Connie, Lola, Pearl, and Frenchy. We need this shack for business. We got to earn our passage, honey."

Tara knew that if she gave up these few feet of space she was lost. "I can see your problem," she said quietly. "But this is where I stay."

Flo studied Tara. "O.K.," she said. "But don't say I didn't warn you, *Mrs.* Kane. The girls may not take it kindly."

"All right, Flo. Thank you for making it so clear. I will try to cause you and your friends as little trouble as possible."

Flo looked at her amazed. Her experiences on the Barbary Coast had not led her to expect politeness. She took a swig of gin, then stood up. "Let's go have a look round, Maggie," she said.

"The stuck-up little prude," Maggie hissed.

To Tara's surprise Flo turned on her friend. "Just leave it," she said. "She knows the score."

After they had gone Tara sat staring at the wall, utterly miserable. The prospect of long weeks on this ghastly ship had been bad enough, but how was she going to cope with seven whores in a floating brothel the size of a small storeroom? She sighed. One day at a time, she said to herself. Somehow I'll learn to live with everything.

She went up on deck to get some fresh air, but the confusion and noise were as great as ever. The ship's sirens shrieked, and underneath her feet the engines began to thump. The mooring ropes were released and then, suddenly, amid a great cheer, the *North Fork* slowly began to move. Gradually it edged away from the dockside, from San Francisco, out towards the Golden Gate, towards the ocean, towards Alaska.

Tara stayed at the railing for a long time watching the harbour front recede. Not even the thought that she had started the long journey to find Daniel could ease her melancholy. She opened her handbag to look for the little compass he had given her.

"Think of me, look at the needle," he had said. "It will always point to where I am."

As Tara held it in her hand the tiny needle quivered but, as always, its direction was northward. To the Klondike. To Daniel. To the future.

LIFE ABOARD the *North Fork* grew grimmer with every passing day. The weather was rough, and with the passengers packed like sardines, every wave caused the overloaded ship to roll unmercifully.

The ship's facilities were non-existent. Toilets were buckets, and washing had to be done in dirty tubs of seawater. Only when Tara stood on deck and the saltwater swept over the rails, dousing her, was there a moment of tangy, freezing freshness.

By the second week she had given up sleeping in the cabin at night because she was too often awakened as the whores conducted their business. She resorted to sleeping in her bunk during the day and walking around the deck at night. Even that was nerve-racking. Time after time Tara was scared by the men who stood in the shadows. Rough hands would reach out for her and she would run for a better-lit part of the ship.

Her experiences with Captain Swain and his crew made Tara abandon her plan to place her money in the care of the ship's purser. She secreted her roll of bills in a little pouch which she pinned to the inside of her bodice.

Flo noticed the pouch one day when Tara was changing her dress. "What do you keep in there, the family jewels?" she asked.

"Nothing," shrugged Tara, "just a couple of trinkets." She could feel herself blushing. She wasn't a good liar. Flo exchanged a look with Maggie but said nothing more.

Mealtimes on the *North Fork* were disgusting. The saloon also served as the dining room. Stew or hash were the order of the day; whichever it was tasted and looked foul. For several days Tara stayed away. Then hunger became too much. She nerved herself to face the ordeal and managed to find a seat. A plate of congealed stew was slung at her, but despite her hunger she could not bring herself to eat.

Sitting next to her was a bespectacled man in a crumpled city suit. He pushed his own plate away, then gave her a sympathetic smile. "Awful, isn't it?" He had a distinct foreign accent.

Tara nodded. He appeared to be in his late thirties and had a trim moustache and small sideburns. Tara liked him immediately, especially the laughter lines around his clear blue eyes.

"I wish I could force it down," she said, shuddering.

"I don't think we need go hungry," the man said. "Follow me."

On deck, Tara took a deep breath. "I know," commiserated the man. "I feel like that myself. Now close your eyes."

She studied him for a second, then shut her eyes.

"Open them!" he commanded. He was grinning when she looked at him. In his hand were two shiny green apples. "One for you, one for me."

She bit into the hard apple and it tasted delicious. Fresh fruit was a great luxury. "You're very kind," Tara said. "Thank you very much, Mr. . . ."

"Ernst Hart," he announced, giving a little bow. He finished his apple and tossed the core over the side. "You have not told me *your* name."

"Mrs. Kane."

"Oh. You are travelling with your husband?"

She shook her head. "No. I am joining him."

"In the Klondike?" He seemed surprised. "By yourself?"

"Mr. Hart, this is 1897, not the middle ages. Women can look after themselves quite well, you know."

He smiled. "You must understand. I am from Germany, and there a woman's place is in the kitchen and the nursery. Not on a ship like this. Why did you not go with your husband? It would have been simpler."

"I . . . I had to look after our baby," she explained falteringly. "She died. She had meningitis. It was so sudden, after he'd left. He doesn't even know."

"I'm sorry," Hart murmured. "Has your husband found gold?"

16

"I haven't heard. Knowing Daniel, I'm sure he's doing well."

"Good." Hart seemed pleased by her confidence. "I hope he becomes a millionaire." He paused. "Tell me, please. What made him go?"

"What makes any of them go?" asked Tara a little wistfully. He followed her glance. All kinds crowded the decks, clerks in city clothes, roughnecks from the slums, fresh-faced students, hard-bitten adventurers; each one counting the days until he would step ashore at Dyea and begin the trail. "Gold fever," she said simply.

Hart frowned. "He just left you and the baby?"

"It wasn't like that," Tara said firmly. "He provided for us, and he did what he thought was right. I wouldn't have dreamed of standing in his way. If it hadn't been for the baby, I would have gone with him then." Her lips trembled for a moment, remembering when Daniel had first told her he was going to get their pot of gold. She had been heartbroken at the thought of separation from him for at least a year. But he had pointed out that to achieve anything in life one had to make sacrifices. And what rewards that year would bring! They could buy a house. Gabie could have a private nurse, they could take trips to Europe. . . .

She pulled herself together and turned to Hart. "What about you, Mr. Hart? Are you off to make a fortune too?"

"No, Mrs. Kane," said Hart, his blue eyes twinkling. "I'm not interested in gold. I go looking for people."

He saw her puzzled expression.

"I am a photographer. I wish to record this madness for posterity. What Matthew Brady did for your Civil War with his camera, I want to do for this gold rush, so that people will always be able to see what it was like." He stopped, a little embarrassed. "It must seem foolish. Here is everybody out to become a millionaire, and all I want to do is take photographs."

"Not at all," Tara replied. "I think it sounds fascinating."

He glanced at her sharply. Then he nodded. "Yes. I think perhaps you do understand." He pulled out his watch. "Excuse me. I must see that everything is in order."

He had arranged, he explained, to store his equipment in the purser's office. He paid the man twenty dollars a week. But he checked every few hours, just to make sure.

They saw a lot of each other after that. They walked together on the deck, and if they found the space, they sat together and talked. He had secreted a little hoard of food, and he often produced delicious titbits for her—a bar of chocolate or even a piece of cheese.

Hart loved studying people. When Flo and Maggie flounced by, Hart looked at them intrigued. "*That's* what I want to photograph," he enthused. "When I get up to the Klondike I want to photograph the street girls, the saloons, the gamblers."

Tara smiled at him. "First, Ernst, we have to get there."

"What are you going to do when we do arrive?" he asked.

"Get to Skagway as quickly as possible. My husband is prospecting somewhere around there."

Hart's eyes opened wide. "But my dear lady, there is no gold at Skagway. To find gold you have to go to the creeks, hundreds of miles to the north."

For a moment Tara was stunned. "I always thought . . ." she began, then stopped. "Well, Skagway's where he made for, and I shall find him."

"I can see you love him very much," Hart said. "To come all this way, to put up with this terrible journey . . ." He stared down at the ocean. "One day I will find a woman like you. Until then, I suppose, I have my camera."

One morning a few days later Hart seemed to be preoccupied.

"What's the matter, Ernst?" Tara asked.

He glanced around nervously. "I don't want to frighten you."

Tara stiffened. "What is it?" she asked apprehensively.

He hesitated, then said, "Everybody on the ship is in great danger. We may all be blown sky-high at any moment. Last night I couldn't find a place to sleep. Two roughnecks had taken my bunk. There was no room on deck, but I managed to squeeze into one of the cargo holds. It was pitch dark, so I struck a match. I saw stacks of wooden cases. I took a closer look and they are all marked 'Danger—High Explosive'. Tara, we are sitting on hundreds of pounds of dynamite."

Tara stared at him. "What can we do?" she whispered.

"Nothing. We are trapped."

They both looked out at the ocean, where occasional pieces of drift ice heralded the distant northern shores, still days away. The *North Fork* rolled uneasily in the swell.

That afternoon, desperate for sleep, Tara made her way down to the smelly little cabin. Flo and Maggie were there with one of their friends, Frenchy, a dark-haired girl with narrow catlike eyes, wearing huge brass earrings.

They were all chattering, but when Tara entered they lapsed into silence. "You haven't met our lodger, have you?" Flo asked Frenchy. "Our Mrs. Kane."

"No. But I heard about you," Frenchy replied, giving Tara a cursory, unfriendly glance.

Tara squeezed through to her bunk, thinking how nice it would be if she could have a bath and curl up between clean sheets. But existence on the *North Fork* and a growing awareness of how primitive her new life would be were gradually teaching Tara to see as luxuries what she had formerly considered essentials.

She was just about to lie down when Frenchy started shouting, "Maggie, where did you get that?" She tugged at a thin gold chain around Maggie's neck, and the chain broke.

"Why, you lousy rat," Maggie screeched, and slapped the dark-haired girl across the face. They flew at each other, spitting and screaming. Frenchy grabbed the blonde's hair, and Maggie scrabbled for her face with long, clawing fingers. They staggered to and fro in the tiny cabin, squealing and cursing.

"For heaven's sake, stop it," Tara cried. "Flo, stop them."

Flo gave Tara a contemptuous smile. "If you're so bothered, why don't *you* stop it, Mrs. Kane?"

"All right, I will." Tara jumped off her bunk and grabbed the two struggling women, trying to separate them. Suddenly she found herself in a tangle of arms, legs, and bodies. Somebody hit her hard. Tara, in blind pain, struck out, and then realized that Flo had also joined in the fight and now she was struggling against all three women. Somebody kicked her, and somebody else knelt on her and was clawing at her bosom.

19

Then, as if by a signal, the fighting stopped. The women got to their feet. "O.K., girls, that's enough," panted Flo.

Tara slowly stood up. Her lip was bleeding. As she crawled onto her bunk, the three other women started drinking from a bottle and giggling. Now and then one of them glanced in Tara's direction, and then they all burst into ugly laughter.

"Let's go, Flo," Frenchy said.

"Yeah," Maggie agreed. "Leave Madame to cry herself to sleep." When they had gone Tara lay there, her whole body aching. She smoothed out her rumpled dress. Then, as if she had had a sudden electric shock, she sat upright. Her pouch was gone. Her money had vanished. She could see the rip in her bodice where the pouch had been torn away. They had planned it all.

Tara went at once to the bridge. "Yes, Mrs. Kane?" asked Captain Swain. He had been sweeping the horizon through binoculars.

"I have been robbed. All my money's been stolen," Tara told him, incensed.

"That is an extremely serious allegation," he said. "Who is supposed to have done this?"

"The women in my cabin."

"Have you any proof?" Swain asked.

"They've got my money," Tara insisted doggedly.

"You do get confused about such things, don't you, Mrs. Kane? I remember you wildly accused one of my men of extortion when you came aboard."

"Captain Swain, I remember very well what happened when I came on board," Tara said.

He cleared his throat. "Mr. Jensen," he shouted, "take over. I have some business to attend to. Come along, Mrs. Kane."

She followed him below to cabin four. Her roommates had returned. Flo was in her bunk, and Maggie was arranging her hair. "Do come in, Captain," Maggie said. "We are honoured."

Swain sat down on the only chair. "Your fellow passenger here is alleging that you ladies stole her money," he announced.

"Mrs. Kane, how could you?" Flo gasped, looking shocked.

Tara stood her ground firmly. "They are thieves."

"Mrs. Kane, kindly observe the basics of polite behaviour," Swain huffed. "These ladies are passengers on my ship."

"I want my one hundred and sixty-five dollars," Tara demanded. "It was torn from a pouch in my bodice."

Swain was impressed. He gave the whores a closer look. "That's a lot of money. Are you saying they attacked you and took it?"

"Not exactly attacked me. They staged a fight, and in the confusion—" Tara faltered. It wasn't easy to explain.

"She is telling a pack of lies," Flo interrupted. "The truth is that this woman drinks. When she is under the influence she becomes violent. It has made life very difficult for us, sharing this cabin. She attacked my friend, Maggie. She has the strength of three men, and we eventually had to use force. Now she is trying to get back at us."

Swain gave Tara a cold look. "Well? What do you say to that?" he said.

Tara shrugged her shoulders. "What's the point, Captain? You don't want to believe me."

"We are quite prepared to have our things searched, Captain," offered Flo.

He stood up. "I don't think that will be necessary. I am quite satisfied. But you listen to me, Mrs. Kane," he growled, "I'm evicting you from this cabin."

"I paid my passage," Tara cried. "It's my right—"

He cut her short. "You got no rights, lady. I make the decisions. These ladies are entitled to privacy, not wild accusations."

"Where am I supposed to sleep?" Tara cried.

He grinned savagely. "That's your problem now. I imagine you'll find a corner to bed down."

She controlled herself. "My trunk is here," she said coldly.

"You can leave it," Swain retorted.

Hart found her on deck, huddled against a horse pen, trying to find shelter against the bitter northerly wind. "*Gott in Himmel*, what has happened to you?" he asked when he saw her swollen lip.

"Oh, Ernst. My money's been stolen. Everything I have."

And then she told him the whole story.

Hart stood up. "You wait here." He was back after a few minutes with a small tin. He gently brushed her lip with some ointment, and then said, "Give me your hand."

Hesitatingly she held out her hand, and he pressed something into it. She opened it, and found he had given her thirty dollars.

"It's not much, but I haven't got a lot left."

"I can't take it," Tara protested.

Hart drew himself up stiffly. "The matter is closed," he said. "It is my pleasure and my privilege as a gentleman."

Even in her misery Tara had to smile at his stilted manner. "All right, thank you. It's very good of you. As soon as I meet up with Daniel, I will pay you back."

They had been at sea nearly three weeks, and although it was only the middle of September, the weather grew harsher and the cold more intense as they sailed north. Tara became one of the homeless, constantly on the hunt for some free space to bed down. When she had found a place sleep remained uneasy.

She felt filthy and uncomfortable and was ashamed of her appearance—her hair unwashed, her face drawn and tired, her eyes bloodshot from lack of sleep. Even cabin four seemed a haven compared to this nomadic existence.

"You can't go on like this," Hart said. "We must sleep together."

She didn't know what to say.

"No, no," he protested, reddening. "I do not mean like that. Do you think me to be so dishonourable as to take advantage of you? It's that you will not be molested if you are with a man. And we can keep each other warm. Don't worry."

That night they managed to find space between two snoring men in the passageway. Hart lay down, and she beside him. He leaned against her, and in a moment he was deep asleep.

Tara lay open-eyed, staring into space. "I love you so very much," Daniel had said. "Fate cannot keep us apart for very long."

"And I love you," Tara whispered into the darkness. Everything would be all right once this terrible voyage was over.

CHAPTER TWO

When at last, after four weeks, the Alaskan land appeared it looked inhospitable. Tara shivered as she surveyed the mountain-locked inlet of the Lynn Canal, just off the supply centre of Dyea, where the ship had anchored for the night. She had expected some kind of port, but there were no piers, no harbour front, only the beach and some tents and rough wooden shacks in the distance. She could hear dogs barking across the water.

Disembarkation was barred until daylight. "If you stay up here, you'll catch your death," Hart said, when he found a half-frozen Tara standing by the rail, looking at the bleak shore.

They went below, and found the saloon packed with people. For safety Tara pinned her purse to her dress. Bottles of whisky passed from hand to hand. Toasts were drunk to the future, to each other, to wealth and success, and to gold. Somebody produced a mouth organ, others started clapping in tempo with the tune.

Flo and Maggie were in their element. Flo's lipstick was smeared, and she was shrieking with laughter. Maggie was locked in an embrace with a thick-set individual, and Frenchy danced by herself, holding up her skirt for all the world to see her knickers.

Suddenly there was a scuffle. Two men were at each other, and one of them knocked against an oil lamp swinging from a hook in the low ceiling. It all happened so quickly that many people were not even aware of it.

Frenchy screamed, and Tara, horrified, saw the whore's skirt on fire, and then the rest of her flared up like a torch. The smashed oil lamp sent a stream of burning oil cascading across the sawdust.

Tara looked around for a blanket, a rug, anything to wrap around the pyre that had been the dark-haired Frenchy. But already people were screaming and falling over each other as they tried to escape the flames that had begun to spread.

Hart grabbed Tara and dragged her up the companionway to the deck. There was a wild stampede of people behind them, clawing and fighting to escape from the blazing saloon.

Tara vaguely heard a bell clanging, and then smoke began to swirl across the deck. "You have to get off the ship," Hart yelled at her. "You must swim ashore."

"I can't," she cried. "I can't . . ."

"Don't you understand?" Hart shouted at her. "*The dynamite.*"

He forced her to face the railing. All she could see was the darkness of the sea. "No, Ernst," Tara screamed.

Around them the ship had turned into bedlam, horses desperately kicking out, dogs howling, smoke pouring across the deck, and the ugly crackling sound of flames growing louder.

"Go on, jump," Hart shouted. "It's your only chance."

She stared at him wide-eyed, her legs paralyzed. Roughly Hart lifted her bodily over the *North Fork*'s rail. Disbelieving, she found herself in mid-air, plunging down into the black abyss. When she struck the icy water it was as if her breath had been cut off. She was numb with cold and panic. She started thrashing about in blind fear, and then she heard a thundering, roaring sound followed by a huge flash which lit up the whole sea. She tried to swim, but her legs would not move and she blacked out.

Tara never knew who it was that saved her. She never saw the boats that set off from the beach to pick up survivors, but for long afterwards she was haunted by the memory of the water around her lit by the blazing ship and the sound of terrifying screams.

The stinging pain of her face being slapped roused her. Hart, white-faced, soaking, was kneeling by her side. It was daylight, and she was lying in a freezing pool of water on a beach. "On your feet," he ordered, putting his arm around her and dragging her upright. "Walk. Keep moving. You're freezing to death."

Gradually sensation returned. She started hobbling along, supported by Hart.

"The ship?" she asked through chattering teeth.

"There is no ship. It blew up." He was staggering along, dragging his big camera case and other gear with him. "A boat came alongside, just before the explosion. I threw everything in."

She was still dazed. "How many were saved?" she asked.

He pointed to the few dozen survivors crouched around fires on the beach.

Slowly they trekked towards the little huddle of habitations that was Dyea. For weeks it had been the name that represented to Tara the gateway to the Klondike and the first step to Daniel. She had thought it would be a bustling, lively community. What she saw were clusters of tents a quarter of a mile inland and then groups of rickety-looking wooden shacks. The place was littered with rubbish, broken-down carts, and abandoned cabins. It was dreary and unwelcoming.

The people who had survived the *North Fork* straggled in the same direction, the lucky ones weighed down by belongings they had managed to salvage. All Tara had left was her purse with the little compass, thirty dollars of borrowed money, her mother's silver locket on a chain, and the icy, wet clothes she stood in.

Dyea had one main thoroughfare, a glorified muddy track, at one end of which stood a rough wooden sign proclaiming: TRAIL STREET. It was flanked by shacks that led to a frozen river. Beyond that was a narrow canyon that rose towards a pass.

"There's the route I'll take," Hart said. "The Chilkoot Pass."

There was one solidly constructed building on the street. GENERAL STORE read a notice over the entrance. Hart led the way up the wooden steps, Tara wearily dragging behind him.

Inside the store there were great piles of food and clothing. Two Indians leaned against the counter. Stacked against the walls were sleds and rolled-up camping equipment and in the centre of the floor there was an enormous stove with the chimney pipe going straight to the roof. They went over to the stove, holding out their hands.

A fat man in rubber boots and a checked shirt waddled over. "The lady needs some clothes," Hart said to him.

"Help yourself," he invited, indicating the store. "Got most things here. Better get some mukluks too."

"Mukluks?"

"Boots. Five dollars," he said.

"That's a lot of money," Hart said.

"Don't need to have 'em. Lose your toes instead. Up to you."

Tara selected some clothes from the stacked piles. "Where do I change?" she asked.

"Right here, lady," the fat man said. "Behind those sacks. No extra charge."

Tara felt herself go red. She grabbed the clothes and went to the corner, where cases and sacks came up to her shoulders. As quickly as she could she got out of her wet, dirty, torn dress. Wearing rough woollen longjohns and no corset felt strange. She emerged finally, her whole appearance changed. Except for her auburn hair, which hung damply to her shoulders, she looked boyish in a checked shirt, sweater, a parka trimmed with wolverine around the hood, and heavy flannel-lined trousers. She wore a pair of mukluks, heavy, watertight, and very comfortable, like overgrown moccasins.

"Fits you perfect," the fat man said. "Don't it?"

"How much?" Tara asked coldly.

"Well now, guess twenty-eight dollars will cover it."

As Tara counted out the dollar bills the fat man asked Hart, "Is she your woman?"

"Yes." Hart said.

She was aggravated until she realized why he had said it. In this land a woman had to be owned—or she was free game.

"Man ought to pay for his woman," the storekeeper said. "Otherwise somebody might jump his claim."

"Mind your own business," Tara said fiercely.

"We need a hotel for tonight," Hart interjected.

"Try the Klondike, down the street," the fat man said. "Beds twenty-five cents a night. Sort of rough, but it's warm and dry. No lice either."

The Klondike Lodging House was a two-floored timber building, across the street from the Ritz Bar. Its proprietor, Joe Gibbons, evidently did not believe in home comforts. The floors had no covering, the stairs were broken, the tables stained, the plates and cutlery bent and broken. The place had never seen a coat of paint.

Some kind of meeting was going on. Gibbons, a man who boasted proudly that he had not had a bath for twenty-one years, presided over it from a table in the centre of the room near the big stove, which was surrounded by spittoons. Spread on the table in front of him were boots, pots and pans, a sleeping bag, some field glasses. Rough-looking men were lolling about on chairs, drinking.

Gibbons hammered on the table with the butt of a pistol. "O.K.," he yelled, "what am I bid for these boots? We got to bury Tommy good and decent."

"Any blood on them?" called out a voice.

"You ought to know better." Gibbons grinned. "He wasn't shot in the feet. Fifty cents, anybody?" Tara wondered what had happened to the dead man, how he came to be shot.

Gibbons held up the dead man's sleeping bag. "Kept him dry and snug," he announced. "Clean too. No bugs."

To Tara's amazement Hart raised his hand. "One dollar, please."

"O.K. Going for a dollar once, twice. Sold."

"What did you buy that for?" Tara asked.

"You need a sleeping bag," Hart replied matter-of-factly.

Gradually Gibbons auctioned off the late Tommy's belongings. When everything had been sold Gibbons counted the money. "Well, fellows," he announced jovially, "I don't calculate there's sufficient to bury Tommy, but we got enough to adjourn and drink his health. On the house."

"They even cheat a dead man," Tara remarked bitterly.

"It doesn't matter to him," Hart said. "He's past caring, whoever he was."

Hart asked Gibbons for two rooms for the night.

"Rooms? Place is full up. But if you can find space, you can bed down on the floor. For two dollars each."

"The store said twenty-five cents for a bed," Hart protested. "What do you mean, two dollars to sleep on the floor?"

"Take it or leave it," Gibbons grunted.

That night, lying on the hard wooden floorboards in the dead Tommy's sleeping bag, surrounded by strange, snoring men, Tara made a promise to herself. She was going to survive. Tomorrow, for the first time in this new world, she would be completely on her own. She would be sorry to say goodbye to Hart and also a little afraid. Until she met up with Daniel in Skagway, ten miles inland, there would be no one to help, no one to protect her. The prospect made her feel apprehensive, but the challenge excited her too.

CHAPTER THREE

Tara could hear hymn singing. A drum was beating in time and someone was shaking a tambourine. A handful of voices croaked about our Lord in Ages Past.

When she emerged from the lodging house, the group was standing across the street, in front of the Ritz Bar. The singing had stopped and a tall, gaunt man was thumping a Bible in his hand. The big drum was strapped to a sad-looking Indian, and beside the tall man stood a buxom woman, her lips a thin, disapproving line. She was the one with the tambourine. Next to her stood another Indian carrying a banner reading: BISHOP BEAUCHAMP'S KLONDIKE CRUSADE.

Their audience consisted of two grinning prospectors, a trapper swaying slightly in an alcoholic haze, and another Indian. A few feet away was Hart, camera on tripod, cloth over his head and shoulders, photographing the group.

"The moment of salvation has come for you sinners," cried the tall man. "I have come to guide you to salvation, to bring the word of the Lord to these unfortunate heathens, and to return to them this fine land which is being corrupted by the men of Babylon and their painted harlots."

Bishop Beauchamp looked around challengingly. The prospectors chewed their tobacco undeterred. "You miserable pagans," the bishop cried. "You have joined Satan in pursuit of the evil yellow metal, but all the gold in the world will not buy your way out of the hellfire that is to come."

"Amen," the woman intoned.

"Today the crusade will depart for Skagway on the first stage of its great work," the bishop announced. "Travel with us and help us to raise the banner of the Lord in that den of iniquity."

Tara took a step forward. "I'll go to Skagway with you," she called out.

"A sinner repenteth," the bishop cried. Tara bristled, but she knew her great chance was here. These people would take her to Skagway.

28

"What's your name?" the grim woman demanded.

"Tara Kane."

"Welcome." The bishop smiled. "Perhaps you had to come here to see the light."

"What are you doing in Dyea?" asked the woman. She did not seem utterly convinced that Tara had seen any light.

"I'm joining my husband," Tara said. "But a woman travelling on her own in these parts needs respectable company."

The bishop's hard, fanatical eyes stared straight into hers. "We trust that you *are* truly seeking to do the Lord's work?"

Tara swallowed. "Of course."

"Then pack your things on one of the sleds. We leave at twelve," said the woman, who Tara gathered must be the bishop's wife.

Later, in the lodging house, Hart embraced her. "Look after yourself, Tara," he said. "You're a very special woman." He was quite moved.

Gently she released herself. "Good luck on your way north, Ernst." She kissed him and left him looking after her. He kept looking for a long while.

Three sleds were drawn up on Trail Street, each with a team of dogs. One of the sleds was loaded with wooden crates roped securely together. "We have a precious cargo," the bishop explained. "Holy Scriptures. Paid for by our benefactor in Skagway. He also built our mission hall there."

"He must be a very generous man," Tara remarked.

The bishop nodded. "Mr. Jefferson Smith is a gentleman. There are some left, even in this wilderness. Now, you will ride with Mrs. Beauchamp," he continued. "Matthew will drive your team."

Matthew, the Indian who had beaten the drum, stood behind them controlling the four pairs of growling huskies. The other Indian took the rear sled loaded with the crates and the luggage. The bishop drove the front sled.

"Mush!" yelled the bishop, and Tara held on as the little caval-cade shot off, the huskies yelping excitedly, whips cracking and the wind blowing in their faces.

It was a great moment for Tara, and she felt exhilarated. Hart had said the dogsleds could cover thirty miles a day, which meant they would be in Skagway in three or four hours—after all these weeks of waiting.

Mrs. Beauchamp interrupted her thoughts. "Does your family approve of your travelling in this wild territory?" she questioned.

"Both my parents are dead," Tara said.

"I'm sorry," Mrs. Beauchamp apologized. Then she pressed on, "Where is your husband? He's not a gold prospector, I trust."

Tara hesitated. "He's a Mountie. Up north," she lied. "In Canada."

Mrs. Beauchamp shot her a peculiar look. "But they're not allowed to marry."

"He's an officer," Tara said haughtily.

"Tell me, can you teach Sunday school?"

"Why, of course I can," Tara said.

"Good. Mrs. Constantine and I—"

"Mrs. Constantine?"

"I'd have thought you'd know *Inspector* Constantine's wife. He commands the Mounted Police detachment in Dawson. She and I have a great problem finding helpers. So, when the crusade reaches Dawson, maybe—"

"Mrs. Beauchamp," Tara said hastily, "I don't want to make a decision right now."

Mrs. Beauchamp lapsed into a frosty silence.

The convoy of sleds made good time over the hard, frozen snow, and in the bright sunshine even the cold seemed less harsh. For the first time Tara saw the aloof beauty of Alaska, snowcapped mountains and cascading waterfalls.

Suddenly they were in Skagway, heralded by huts and tents and timber buildings. It was a makeshift, rough sprawl inhabited by thousands of people. Quite orderly, however, the houses in neat lines. The main street was named Broadway.

Tara could see the landing stage, with a couple of river steamers at anchor. All around her the snow had been churned into mud by carts and wagons. There were innumerable tree stumps, standing beside the huts that had been built out of their timber.

Many of the signs were bizarre, EGGS FRIED IN BEER, $1.50 read

31

one. A log building had an old pair of trousers slung on a line in the front, with the word MEALS daubed on the seat in white paint.

The convoy came to a halt in front of a little wooden hut which had SKAGWAY MISSION painted on it. The hut was completely over-shadowed by a two-floored building next to it, a garish sign identifying it as THE PALACE OF FORBIDDEN DELIGHTS.

At the door of the mission stood a burly man in a black hat with a broad brim, and a thin string tie. As the sleds came to a halt, he walked forward, smiling, and greeted Beauchamp.

"The Reverend Charles Bowers," explained the bishop, introducing Tara. There was something suspicious about the man's glittering eyes, his smile. He was the last person she would have taken to be a clergyman; the last person she would have trusted.

"A great honour, ma'am," he intoned. "A gracious Christian lady come to beard Babylon." He turned to the bishop. "May I unload the precious cargo?" he asked.

"Of course." The bishop rubbed his hands. "Tell me, how is our benefactor?"

"Mr. Smith is well," Bowers said. He snapped his fingers, and the two Indians started to unload the third sled, piled high with crates marked FRAGILE—BIBLES. To Tara's surprise they didn't carry them into the mission hall, but marched straight through a back door of the Palace of Forbidden Delights. Tara grabbed her sleeping bag, stuffed with her belongings, and followed them.

The saloon inside was like a barn, with a long bar running the length of the room. A bull-like barman in shirt sleeves was counting out a wad of dollars for the two Indians, who had stacked the crates in front of the bar. Two other men began breaking them open. Each crate contained bottles of whisky—and no Bibles. But this aroused no curiosity. Evidently this was a normal delivery.

Around the saloon men were drinking and playing cards. "Won't you join me in a drink of mountain tea?" a soft voice asked.

Tara turned and saw Bowers standing beside her, grinning. His mournful demeanour had miraculously vanished. He fitted much better into this setting than in his role as a cleric. He slapped her on the back and signalled to the barman.

Tara didn't trust him, but she liked something about this rogue. He didn't pretend with her. "No, thank you. But can you tell me why they said our cargo was Bibles?" she asked.

"Bless you child," he said. "Don't you know hooch is illegal in this territory? We look to the good bishop to bring it in. He brings us all kinds of good things, unknowingly. Like you."

"My husband's here," Tara said coldly. "I've come to join him. Do you know a man named Daniel Kane?"

"Never heard of him," Bowers said.

"I'm sure he's here," Tara insisted. She turned to leave.

"Where are you off to?" Bowers asked.

"The U.S. Marshal," she replied.

When she entered Marshal Colson's office, the marshal had his feet on the desk and was filing his fingernails. "Are you the marshal?" Tara asked doubtfully. Perhaps he was just a deputy.

"Yeah," grunted Colson.

Tara cleared her throat. "I'm looking for my husband," she announced. "He arrived here early in August. On the steamship *Humboldt* from San Francisco. How can I find him?"

The marshal scratched his stomach. "I don't know. He'll have moved on, lady, most likely. Nobody stays in Skagway long."

"His name is Daniel Kane," Tara said. "He's about five foot eleven. Brown hair. Hazel eyes. Quite good-looking. . . ."

"He's prospecting for gold?"

She nodded.

"No gold around these parts, lady." He laughed. "The diggings are way north. Up the Yukon. Better make for Dawson."

"Dawson—where's that exactly?"

"Seven hundred miles north. Up the White Pass by Canada." Colson nodded at a map of the Yukon, vast and unpopulated.

Tara stood undecided. It was all going wrong. Daniel had never mentioned going to Dawson, he had always talked of Skagway. She had only the vaguest idea of the geography of this territory. She thought they found gold all over.

"Since you're on your own, you'll be looking for a bed for the night, I figure," said Colson, looking her up and down.

"I'll find one somewhere," Tara said, wishing that she was as confident as she sounded. She turned and walked out into the street.

The Indians called the town Skagus, which meant Home of the North Wind, and Skagway lived up to its name. In the weak afternoon sunshine it had seemed a city in the making, brash, but colourful and young. Now, in the gloom, it was suddenly unfriendly, the wind whistling around corners, the narrow paths full of shadows and lurking dangers.

Tara started wandering aimlessly in no specific direction, a nagging, unwanted thought beginning to grow. Suppose something had happened to Daniel? A fight? A robbery? She stopped eventually outside a window with SKAGWAY INTELLIGENCER—THE KLONDIKE'S BIGGEST LITTLE PAPER spelled out on the glass.

She went in and asked an old man behind a counter for the editor. He peered over the top of his glasses. "I'm the editor," he said.

"If anything happens in Skagway, you hear about it, don't you?" she asked.

The old man nodded.

"Have you heard of a man called Daniel Kane? I'm his wife. I've just arrived in town."

The old man looked at her sympathetically. "Well, Mrs. Kane, I don't think he's shot anybody or anybody's shot him. We haven't had any fights for a couple of months. And nobody's drowned lately. I don't think you need to worry about him having had a misadventure."

Tara's heart felt lighter. At least Daniel had survived Skagway.

She left the newspaper office. Now her immediate problem was securing a roof over her head, food and warmth. There was the mission hall, but she could not swallow more doses of the Beauchamps' brand of salvation.

Ahead of her was a sign. LOANS—CASH FOR ANY ITEM.

She tried to think of something on which she could raise a few dollars. She had only the little silver locket containing her mother's miniature. She hated the idea of pawning it. Yet she couldn't walk around Skagway all night.

She crossed the street and pushed through the swing doors. Waiting their turn in front of a counter with a grill like a bank-teller's window, were half a dozen haggard, shabby men, standing silently in line. This is the other side of the gold rush, she thought. These were the people who had failed.

The man behind the counter, a gun belt strapped around him, was called Sam; they all seemed to know him.

The man ahead of Tara waited, his hands empty. When it was his turn at the grill he took off his spectacles and handed them to Sam, who gave him a dollar. Then he added them to a collection of eyeglasses on a rack marked ALL ONE PRICE—$2.

"What's this?" asked Sam as Tara handed the locket across the counter. "This ain't worth a bent dime to me."

"It's sterling silver," Tara pointed out.

Sam ignored her. "You got any gold?"

She shook her head. Her face was drawn, pale with fatigue.

Sam seemed to feel sorry for her. "I'll tell you what," he said, pulling his ear. "I'll lend you five dollars on this."

"All right," Tara agreed reluctantly.

"No deal." It was a soft voice, with a southern drawl, but it had authority. She swung around.

Standing by the door was an immaculately dressed man. He was tall, in his mid-thirties, and across his black waistcoat was looped a heavy gold watch chain hung with charms. Above a well-trimmed moustache he had chiselled features. His eyes were grey, shrewd, alert and curiously piercing.

"Give it back to the lady," he ordered.

"Yes, boss," Sam said hastily. He thrust the locket at her.

"No," insisted Tara. "I want my money."

"My regrets, ma'am," the stranger said, shrugging.

"You keep out of it," she cried. "It's none of your business."

He smiled. "On the contrary, this is my business. I own it."

"Who are you?" she asked, staring at him with hostility.

"The name is Smith, Jefferson Randolph Smith."

"Mr. Smith, I need that money."

"May I?" he said. He took the locket out of her hand and looked at the painted miniature. "Very attractive. Is she your kin?"

"My mother."

"I should have guessed." He turned the locket over, looked at

35

the words inscribed on it. *To Tara*. He glanced up at her. "So tell me, Tara, what brings a looker like you to this hole?"

The bland way he appraised her was unnerving. "I'm here to find my husband," she replied coldly. "Daniel Kane. Have you come across him?"

"Should I have?"

Tara felt increasingly uncomfortable. His eyes did not leave her face. "Well?" she said. "Can I have my money?"

He shook his head. "Unfortunately this locket is worthless to me." He handed it back. He took out a cheroot, bit the end, and lit it. "We're interested in gold," he continued, exhaling a cloud of Havana smoke. "I'll tell you what I'll do. Jefferson Smith never lets a lady go broke. I'll make you an offer."

"For what?" she asked curtly.

"*That's* gold," he said, and pointed at her wedding ring. "I'll give you fifty dollars for it. Now that's a mighty generous offer. That's the going rate for three ounces of gold."

Her green eyes narrowed. "No."

"Can you afford not to?" Smith asked.

It was true that she couldn't. If she didn't get some money, what would she do? Freeze to death? Starve? Fifty dollars could take her a long way towards Dawson.

"Take it or leave it," Smith said carelessly.

Tara hesitated, then she slowly twisted the ring off her finger. She passed it over to Smith, the very symbol of her marriage vows. It had never been off her hand since Daniel put it there three years ago when they had exchanged rings.

"Pay the lady," Smith ordered Sam. Then, to her fury, he slipped the ring on the little finger of his left hand.

Sam counted out the money, and as Tara took it she said to Smith tersely, "It's only a loan. I'll get the ring back."

"It'll always be a pleasure to do business with you, Mrs. Kane," Smith replied, inclining his head.

Out in the dark, cold night air snow was falling lazily. Tara shivered. Next to a little store that sold cigars stood the wooden façade of the Mondame Hotel. It looked quiet, respectable.

The dingy hallway contained a bell marked VISITORS. Tara's

summons was answered by a polite Chinese couple. A single room would cost ten dollars for the night. For the comfort of a mattress, a pillow, and privacy, she thought it was cheap at the price.

After she had wolfed down a hearty meal served in her room, there was a knock on the door. The couple carried in a tub and a copper kettle of steaming water. The stove in the corner heated the room well, and she felt like Cleopatra as she sank into the tub. When she emerged she knew she could face anything.

She put out the lamp and lay curled up in the bed. It was bliss to be alone without fear of intrusion. It was only when she touched her bare finger and thought of her ring and the man who now had it, that the warmth and comfort felt less secure. She closed her eyes, but Jefferson Smith could not be shut out. He kept bowing mockingly, with a debonair, challenging smile.

When Tara came downstairs in the morning, the hefty figure of the Reverend Bowers rose from a wicker chair to greet her. "Good morning, Mrs. Kane. I trust you slept well."

"Yes, thank you," Tara said warily.

"Praise be," he said piously. "We were very anxious about your welfare. May I ask what your plans are?"

"Yes. I'm leaving for Dawson," said Tara brusquely.

"That is not a journey for a Christian woman on her own."

He could see that his clerical act was making no impression on Tara and dropped it suddenly. "You're not being very smart, are you?" he said. "If you stick around, I could fix you up with a good job. All it needs is a word to the boss. Mr. Smith can do anything for a girl. He's taken quite a fancy to you."

Tara looked Bowers straight in the eye. "You can tell your boss I'm not interested in anything he has to offer."

"Don't be dumb," Bowers said. "You're on your own. You need protection. He'll look after you."

Tara drew herself up. "I can imagine. And you can also give this message to your Mr. Smith. Tell him I'll get my wedding ring back." She stalked out of the hotel.

In the street something important was happening. A shouting mob of men swept by, half pushing, half dragging a terrified-looking man whose hands were tied behind his back. He made no sound, and his eyes were glassy. Leading the mob was Marshal Colson, carrying a shotgun.

The crowd formed a circle around a tall birch tree. Tara looked around at the screaming, distorted faces and saw nothing but crazed hate and eager anticipation. She knew this was a lynching.

The marshal stood on a crate and raised his hand to silence the throng. "This here execution is being carried out according to law, sentence of death having been passed by the citizens of this here community."

A roar went up from two hundred voices. The mob parted, and a horse was led into the centre. The white-faced man was hoisted on it.

"Cal Mason," called out Colson, turning to the man sitting rigid on the horse. "You're going to be hanged for the murder of Serena Bradley. Is there anything you want to say?"

The marshal didn't wait for an answer. He raised a coiled rope high above his head. It had already been knotted into a noose. He swung it over a bough of the tree. Tara felt sick. She turned and walked away from the crowd. Then she stopped.

Marching up the street towards her were six men, walking abreast, their faces set. Tara could see the high-necked collars of scarlet tunics under their fur-trimmed jackets, and a broad yellow stripe down the length of their blue breeches. Their bearing was upright, military, and they carried rifles.

The crowd around the tree were too preoccupied to notice them. Colson put the noose around the neck of the wretched man on the horse. "Let's get on with it," Colson yelled, raising his hand.

From behind the mob there was a shot. The Mountie sergeant had fired into the air. "Stop," he shouted.

The mob parted as Colson walked through to face the Mounties. "Keep out of this, Sarge," he rasped. "You've got no jurisdiction. This is United States territory."

"Release that man," said the sergeant.

"This is a legal execution," Colson bawled.

"It's a lynching," said the sergeant tersely. "Unlawful anywhere." The Mounties advanced, but the crowd closed their ranks. Colson smiled complacently. The mob at his back gave him confidence.

"Run 'em out of town," yelled somebody. From somewhere a piece of frozen snow was hurled, and hit one of the Mounties in the face. It was followed by a rock. Tara saw the crowd surge forward.

"No damn Canadian Mountie tells us what to do," Colson yelled. "I'm the U.S. Marshal, we mayn't be a state yet, but what I say goes. You got no rights in Skagway."

The Mounties ignored him. Slowly, deliberately, they advanced with their guns at the ready. Colson swung around, facing the mob. "Are you going to let these redbellies get away with it?"

"Marshal!" called out a commanding voice. Across the street a man had appeared on a white horse. Tara recognized Jefferson Smith. He cantered across the street until he was between the Mounties and the mob.

"Gentlemen," Smith declaimed. "Remember that we are all law-abiding citizens." He edged his horse through the crowd, which parted respectfully for him. He stopped next to Cal Mason. Leaning over, he lifted the noose from the man's neck.

Then Smith walked his horse to the centre of the throng and held up his hand. He was like a general commanding a rabble. His authority was unchallenged. He *does* own the place, Tara thought, as she watched Marshal Colson glowering at him resentfully.

"My friends, we are all proud of the way we run this town, and we must certainly co-operate with the officers here," said Smith.

"This ain't their territory," a man yelled. "Tell them to get back to Dawson."

"On the contrary, if these officers feel they have jurisdiction, it is not for us to argue."

"You're selling out, Soapy," shouted somebody from the back. "You're letting the Canucks take over."

A man pushed forward and went up to Smith. "Throwing your weight around, ain't you," he accused. "Trying to run the town your way. It's you they should arrest."

Smith looked down at him with contempt.

"I'm doing it by the book, Reid. Nice and legal," he retorted. "If you know what's good for you, you'll agree with me."

A wild-eyed man in the crowd addressed the prisoner. "You

39

murdering devil, Mason. You're not going to get away like this."

Smith edged his horse forward. "He isn't going to get away with anything, Matt," he said. "Take it easy."

"I want him strung up," yelled the man. "Serena was my woman."

"Sure," Smith said. "And Serena will get the best funeral money can buy, I promise you. But there'll be no lynching."

"You're yellow, Soapy," Matt yelled. "Six redbellies with popguns from the Yukon and you turn yellow.

There was stunned silence. Quietly, a dozen tough-looking individuals formed a protective ring around Smith. Two carried clubs and the rest had guns.

"Cal Mason killed my woman, and I'll get him, even if your whole gang is there," Matt cried.

"You'd better get out of town, Thatcher," growled one of two hoodlums who appeared suddenly behind Matt and twisted his arm until he bent double with pain.

Smith trotted back to the prisoner, who was still sitting upright, hands tied. He took the bridle of the horse and led it through the crowd, stopping in front of the Mounties. "Here's your man, Sergeant," Smith said. "He's your responsibility now. Get him out of town if you don't want a riot."

"We're hitting the trail to Dawson today," the sergeant said. He cut the rope tying Mason's hands and helped him down from the horse. He then gave a command, and his men formed around the prisoner. Without a second look at Smith or the sullen crowd they handcuffed Mason and marched him off.

"My compliments to Inspector Constantine," Smith called after them. Then, turning his horse around, he faced the assembly. "Gentlemen," he shouted, "drinks at my place. On the house."

Smith's gang gave a ragged cheer, and the rest joined in. They started drifting down the street in the direction of the saloon. Smith began to trot lazily after them. Just as Tara was turning to go, Smith spotted her. He cantered to her side, and took off his hat politely. "I'd be flattered if you'd join us, Mrs. Kane."

Without a word Tara turned on her heel. Smith rode off. He was smiling.

Back at the Mondame Hotel, Tara got some ink and paper. She

40

had little time, but this mustn't be botched. She began to write.

"My dear Tara," she wrote. "The Constantine household is in quite a tizz at the thought that you will be arriving here soon. I am dying to hear all the latest news from home. You have a long journey ahead of you, and since this is no easy venture for a gentle-woman on her own, your dear brother-in-law insists that as soon as you arrive in Skagway you approach the local post of the North-west Mounted Police, and ask them if they have a detachment proceeding to Dawson in whose company you might travel. They are *splendid* men, and we know they will take good care of you. We eagerly await your arrival. Your loving sister, Sarah."

Tara backdated the letter to June 30. She thought that, under the circumstances, she had done an admirable job. She knew from Mrs. Beauchamp that the commander of the Mounties at Dawson was an Inspector Constantine and that he was married. But she had no way of knowing whether Mrs. Constantine's name was Sarah, or if she had a sister. There was only one way to find out.

Outside the Mountie's post, four sleds were drawn up with their dog teams. Tara walked in, introducing herself, and told a startled Sergeant Campbell how grateful she would be for their help in getting her up to Dawson.

The sergeant stood by the stove reading the letter, a worried look on his face. "Nobody told me about this," he said.

"That's just like Sarah." Tara laughed. "She probably forgot. She must have taken it for granted you'd know."

"We got no orders, and without orders . . ."

"Sergeant, you can't just leave me here," Tara gasped.

"We have a prisoner," Campbell pointed out. "We ain't equipped to carry ladies. Not across the pass."

"I can look after myself," Tara said hastily. "I won't be any burden, I promise. And, Sergeant, think how angry my brother-in-law would be if you left me behind."

"I guess we could fit you on one of the sleds," Campbell conceded. "Where is your luggage, Mrs. Kane?"

"I've only a sleeping bag," she said. "Everything was lost on the *North Fork*."

Campbell chewed his lip. "I depend on you to sort it out with

41

Mr. Constantine if he gets mad at me for bending regulations."

"I'm sure he'll be more than grateful to you, Sergeant," Tara said. So far her plan to get to Dawson to look for Daniel had worked. Nothing else mattered.

CHAPTER FOUR

Tara admired the expertise with which Sergeant Campbell handled his team. He had a whip with a long braided sealskin lash that cracked like rifle fire, but he relied far more on his voice. It ordered, threatened, encouraged, and was always obeyed.

For hours after leaving Skagway they travelled across flat, frozen timberland, following a kind of primitive road, the route of thousands of travellers north. The snow fell steadily as the convoy began to ascend the White Pass, and the temperature dropped to twenty below zero. Tara felt pain in her nose; inside her nostrils the tiny hairs froze into sharp little barbs which, as she breathed in the biting air, drew blood.

They were now hundreds of feet up, travelling along a corkscrew trail which was dominated by ugly slate cliffs. Below the sheer fall, rocks were strewn with skeletons and the wreckage of wagons that had tried to edge their way along the track and failed. Tara clutched at the sled, pushing away fear.

The daylight was fading as they made camp behind some six-foot-high boulders. The dogs were unhitched, cooking gear unpacked, a tent pitched. Two Mounties gathered wood and began cutting it up. The dogs were fed first; that was a golden rule.

Inside the tent, the stove was lit, and everyone gathered around it. One of the men stuck a big lump of frozen snow on a branch. As the snow dissolved from the heat of the stove, the water was caught in a pan. The Mounties had supplies of beans, corned beef and potatoes, which they boiled in hot water. And there was steaming coffee. The meal was delicious, and Tara ate with vigour. They had taken off the prisoner's handcuffs. He was as silent as ever, staring into the glow of the stove as he ate his food.

Campbell took out a tobacco pouch and started rolling himself a cigarette. "If the weather holds, we'll make the post at Summit Hill in a day or so. If we stay lucky, I reckon we'll reach Bennett in four or five days. You got a rough time ahead, Mrs. Kane."

Tara was thankful for one thing. So far Campbell hadn't once asked her about her "sister" or the Constantine family. Sometimes, though, she thought she saw the lantern-jawed sergeant looking at her thoughtfully. Uneasily she wondered if he was growing suspicious of her. Outside, the wind shook the canvas, and Tara thought she could hear a wolf howling. Now and then the dogs whined. "Most important thing you can have here is a reliable dog team," the sergeant explained. "The dogs are your life. You can't look after them too well. And if you're starving, you can always eat 'em."

"*Eat* the dogs?" Tara made a grimace. "I'd rather starve."

"Hope you never run out of food," Campbell said quietly. He stretched himself. "I guess we'd all better have some shut-eye." He hesitated and looked at Tara. "Normally, Mrs. Kane, we all bed down in the tent. But seeing as you are a lady . . . I mean if you prefer . . ."

"Sergeant Campbell," Tara smiled. "Why don't we do just that? I've got my sleeping bag, and I'd feel much safer."

"That's dandy, then. You'll have that corner all to yourself, and I'll be right here." He was obviously relieved. He handcuffed the prisoner again, then turned down the oil lamp, but the red glow from the stove continued to illuminate the tent.

They broke camp early the following morning. It was a bright, hoary day, crystal clear and as sharp as a diamond. As the convoy progressed, Tara, for the first time, saw the price the White Pass demanded of those who braved it. They passed exhausted prospectors, moving at a snail's pace, short on supplies, whipping their tired, half-starved dog teams.

"Crazy fools," one of the Mounties said. "Greenhorns got no business in this godforsaken country."

They travelled on in silence. Suddenly there was a shot. Then another one. "Keep down," Campbell yelled. The prisoner, Cal Mason, sagged, face up, halfway out of the sled, and in the middle of his forehead was a neat little hole.

"Over there!" the sergeant shouted to two Mounties, pointing at a clump of trees. "I'll cover you."

Tara scrambled out of the sled and flung herself on the ground, feeling her heart pounding against the frozen earth. Three more shots whizzed past the two Mounties who were racing towards the trees. Campbell fired back from behind the sled. Two further shots rang out from inside the wood.

"You're surrounded, you don't stand a chance," Campbell yelled. "Come out with your hands up."

They waited tensely. Then a man emerged, holding his hands high above his head. He was dark-haired, dressed like a trapper, and seemed vaguely familiar.

As she scrambled to her feet Tara was shaking. She had seen a man murdered in front of her eyes.

"Is he dead?" the man asked, looking at Mason's slumped body.

"Dead as he'll ever be. What the hell's going on, Thatcher?"

"I swore I'd get him," Matt Thatcher said with satisfaction. "I trailed you from Skagway. He killed my woman," he added simply.

"I heard she was anybody's woman," the sergeant growled unfeelingly. He unlocked the dead man's handcuffs, and clicked them on Thatcher's wrists.

Before they moved off they buried Mason. One of the Mounties nailed a rough cross together, and they stuck it on top. CAL MASON they carved on it, DIED SEPT. 22 1897.

Mason's death had a marked effect on the sergeant. When they next made camp he remained aloof from the others. "He's got his hands full," one Mountie whispered to Tara. "You don't lose a prisoner, not in the Mounties."

They did not need to tell Tara when they were passing through Dead Horse Gulch. The snow in it was packed hard, the trail trampled by thousands who had relentlessly pursued the route north. The wailing of the sharp wind sounded to her like the screams of dying animals and the shrieks of desperate men who had met their end in this macabre graveyard.

It was thirty degrees colder than on the coast. She longed for warmth, not only a physical temperature, but something warm for the eye. Her surroundings were dazzlingly white, hard, cold; in

the shadows grey white; in the cold sun blue white; on the peaks in the distance silver white.

The final thousand feet to the top of Summit Hill was the worst ordeal Tara had yet had to face. To lighten the dogs' burden she and Thatcher had to make the climb on foot. She groped her way along, slipping and sliding, panic-stricken.

"You can have a rest when we get to the post," the sergeant said, trying to encourage her. "It's right ahead."

Four hours later it seemed no nearer. To Tara the police post at Summit Hill began to assume the image of a distant paradise. For the Mounties it was the official frontier, the border between United States territory and British Columbia. She looked forward to it with growing excitement. But all she saw, as they trudged on, was the same inhospitable landscape. She tried to think of Daniel struggling up this trail, gritting his teeth, each step heavier than the last.

At last she saw the sergeant's team halt. Tara's heart jumped. She could see a cluster of huts and two poles, flying the Stars and Stripes and the Union Jack side by side. This was the border. This was the Klondike District of British Columbia. This was not the end of the trail, but the beginning.

Once inside the post Tara was the centre of attention. The Mountie in charge, a sergeant called Grayburn, fussed over her like a mother hen. She was immediately given a berth in an empty bunkhouse. A tub of steaming water was brought to her, and she was invited to join the men for dinner in the mess.

She expected it to be a rough and ready affair. But the Mounties turned out in their scarlet tunics, buttons flashing, cavalry boots polished like mirrors, and they observed strict protocol. Every man remained on his feet until Tara sat down.

The food was coarse but good. There was caribou steak, pancakes, beans and fried potatoes, served all together. In this climate Tara was constantly hungry, and she consumed enormous helpings of food she would never have touched a few weeks ago.

Then came the moment that she had been dreading. "You lost your husband, Mrs. Kane?" Grayburn asked sympathetically. She was aware that Campbell, on her other side, was listening intently.

For a moment Tara did not know what to say. "Lost?"

"I notice that you don't wear your wedding ring," he said.

Tara tried to collect her thoughts. If she had to answer questions about her husband, her story about being Constantine's sister-in-law would collapse. "Oh, that." She dismissed it lightly. "I wear it on a chain around my neck. Where it's closest to me." She changed the subject. "Tell me, Sergeant Campbell, that man Smith in Skagway, does he rule the place?"

"Soapy?" Campbell smiled grimly. "He's town boss all right."

"Biggest bunko man in the territory," Grayburn snorted. He noticed her confused expression. "Con man, Mrs. Kane. Trickster."

"But why the name Soapy?"

"Some place in Colorado he sold shaving soap for five dollars a piece to anyone who believed his story that there was a twenty-dollar bill hidden under the wrapper. Made a small fortune out of the suckers."

"Guess he knows how to fool 'em," Campbell said. "He even laid a telegraph wire that only ran for six miles and got people to pay five bucks to send ten words anywhere in America."

"And when they found out?" Tara asked.

Campbell shrugged. "Mrs. Kane, folks have two rules about Soapy Smith. One, they don't argue with him. Two, they keep their eyes in the back of their heads when he's around."

So the elegant man who lorded it over Skagway with his smooth manner and soft drawl was just a cheap crook. Every time Tara felt her bare finger her anger rose. And yet . . . For some reason she was curiously intrigued by him.

They rested for twenty-four hours at Summit Hill, and Tara discovered that the border post was the end of the line of many a man's gold rush. As would-be prospectors came along the trail to cross into British Columbia, the Mounties checked each man's supplies. If he didn't have 1150 pounds of food, three months' supplies, he was turned back. Tara wondered if Daniel had passed this test.

Next morning they set off once more. Soon after the huts of the frontier post receded a blizzard struck. The Mounties, driving their teams, became strange, mute, frost-encrusted forms. The dogs' fur turned white, the sleds were thick with icy snow. The howling sleet and wind made the convoy look like phantoms. To protect them from frostbite their faces had to be completely covered. Tara realized that without the goggles Sergeant Grayburn had given her at Summit Hill she would have gone blind. As it was they kept frosting up, and she was unable to see most of the time.

They were only able to cover a few yards an hour. At intervals the wind was so violent, and the flurries of snow so thick, that they all seemed motionless, straining against an invisible wall. Despite the fury of the wind, Tara found herself nodding off once or twice. It was her first brush with the lure of the white death, the curious desire to fall asleep in the middle of the wilderness. Campbell saw her head nod and shook her shoulder roughly. People in blizzards who went to sleep rarely woke up again.

After a few hours the weather changed gradually. Tara was able to uncover her face and breathe properly once more. The dogs perked up and started moving faster. Now there was total and frightening silence enveloping them, and Tara wondered if she had become deaf. A group of caribou appeared in the distance. Up in the sky some geese passed in a ragged V, but they didn't make a sound. After the raucous wind of the blizzard it was eerie.

Three hours later they made camp. No one talked. They were too exhausted.

BEFORE THE GOLD RUSH, Lake Bennett, gateway to the Yukon River, had been one of the loveliest places in the territory. Now the lake was encircled by thousands of tents, large and small. There were dog tents, army tents, tent barbershops, and canvas saloons. The snow-covered lakeside echoed with the whine of saws, the blows of axes, the hammering of nails, the shouts of men warning of falling timber.

For now Lake Bennett was one giant boatyard. Everyone here was building boats to go up river when the ice thawed; boats that would have to be sailed, rowed, dragged through some of the most treacherous waters known to men.

After the loneliness of the White Pass, Tara found the sight of this swarming, canvas township cheering. Campbell thought otherwise. He looked around at the tree stumps, the stacks of felled timber. "They're tearing the guts out of the place, and they don't put anything back. Those trees took centuries to grow."

The Mounties pitched tents by the shore. Tara looked across the frozen lake at the river that reached beyond like a white highway. Along that river was their route to Dawson.

"But it's frozen," Tara exclaimed, dismayed, "How can we?"

"We travel on the ice," Campbell said. "It's easier in a boat but we haven't got time to wait for the thaw."

After resting for two days they followed the frozen river to the White Horse Rapids. Tara gazed down on a curtain of raging torrent where the waters never froze. They cascaded and thundered, a swift current of water spiked with sharp rock teeth lurking treacherously to rip the bottom off any craft. The walls rose sheer on either side of the foaming crest.

It took two and a half hours to manhandle the sleds along the two miles of cliff beside the rapids. They had to be dragged, pushed, and at one point even carried through tiny rock passages, up and down slippery trails, sometimes a few inches from a plunge to death. The dog teams, unhitched, had to be led step by step.

Tara's body ached, muscles she never knew she had hurt, and the sheer strain of dragging herself along the trail was so exhausting that all she wanted was to sink to her knees.

They stopped briefly at a mound of rocks. On it a primitive cross had four words only: HE NEVER MADE IT.

Who was the man who never made it? Tara wondered. Daniel must have come along this route. At the foot of the cliffs on the other side she could see more graves—tiny crosses, all of them men for whom this was the end of the gold rush.

A Mountie named Hennessy came to join her. "Guess I owe you an apology, ma'am," he said.

Tara looked at him. "What on earth for?"

"Well," he said scratching his head. "I told Sergeant Campbell this might be too tough for you. You proved me wrong. You can handle yourself O.K."

He could not have pleased her more. She knew that they had all been watching her and she had passed the test.

That night they camped near Lake Laberge. Tara warmed

herself over the fire, and Campbell handed her a mug of coffee. "How much longer to Dawson?" she asked him.

"Three, four weeks, maybe," the sergeant said noncommittally.

She sipped the coffee. "Sergeant, what's Inspector Constantine like?" It was out before she realized what she had said.

He looked at her blandly. "Your brother-in-law? Why, don't you know?"

"Not . . . not really. I don't know him very well."

"Hmm," Campbell said, and threw another piece of wood into the flames. "I guess he'll have a lot of questions to ask you."

Of course he had guessed the truth. He was saying as much.

"You know," she told him earnestly, "without your help I could never have made this journey. I don't know what I'd have done."

Giving Tara a curt nod, he left her to her thoughts.

Some days later, a few miles before Fort Selkirk, they met up with another Mountie patrol. Campbell conferred with the man in charge. Tara caught an occasional word, "sister", "letter", "expecting her". The officer walked towards her, and she knew that it meant trouble and more lies. He saluted her. "I hear you're on your way to Dawson to meet with your brother-in-law." He cocked his head on one side. "It's amazing," he said. "I never would have believed you're Alice's sister if I hadn't been told."

Alice! And she had signed the letter Sarah. "We're . . . quite different," she murmured.

"Anyway, I'm sorry you're in for a disappointment," he said. "Your sister's at Fort Constantine. Didn't she tell you?"

Tara avoided his question. "Isn't that near Dawson?"

"Not exactly. It's across the river from Fortymile. The empire's most northerly outpost."

She wasn't sure what to say. She had never heard of the place.

"Guess Mr. Constantine will have lots to talk about with you." He smiled. "I leave you in the sergeant's good hands, meantime."

Tara's heart was pounding as the officer walked back to his teams and Campbell started up the convoy.

"Guess Zac Wood knows your sister right well," he said genially. "He's a great guy. Nothing escapes him."

Tara had the uneasy feeling that Campbell was only too right.

CHAPTER FIVE

Only two years before, Dawson had been a wilderness at the junction of the Yukon and Klondike Rivers, a pasture for moose, unclaimed by men. Now thousands of prospectors were making fortunes, going bankrupt, gambling and drinking twenty-four hours a day. Deep in the heart of Yukon Territory, Dawson had turned itself into an American frontier town on Canadian soil. Nine out of ten men there were Americans, drawn by the gold, and the Stars and Stripes flew defiantly in the main street. Here a man who didn't have gold was worth less than a sled dog. Much less.

The handful of Mounties headquartered in a log cabin acted as a reminder that somewhere beyond this wild isolated town there was a Canadian government. A Union Jack hung outside the police cabin. As Campbell's patrol drew up in front of the ramshackle headquarters, Tara steeled herself for her confrontation with the inspector.

Inside the cabin Campbell indicated a wooden chair. "Wait here," he ordered. Then he went inside a door marked COMMANDING OFFICER. When he emerged a few minutes later he said flatly, "This way, Mrs. Kane."

She walked with him out of the headquarters building, around to the back, to a wooden hut. "In here," he said.

She found herself facing four cells. Thatcher sat on a bunk in one of them, his head in his hands. He looked up through the bars, puzzled, when he saw Tara.

Campbell held one of the cell doors open.

Tara stared at him. "In . . . in there?" she faltered.

"I'm acting under orders," Campbell said awkwardly.

She stepped into a bare cell with a bunk and one stool. She turned to Campbell, but he had already slammed the door and was locking it. She sank onto the stool in disbelief. She was in jail. Surely they couldn't do this without even talking to her.

Then she heard the door of the lockup open. An officer appeared and unlocked her cell. He was a sardonic-looking man, with a hook nose and a Vandyck beard. He didn't have to tell her he was Charles Constantine, the commander of the Mounties' Yukon detachment.

His eyes were unfriendly, and he studied her coldly. Tara braced herself. "Am I under arrest?" she asked.

He held out his hand. "The letter from my wife, please."

Nervously she pulled out the scrap of paper. He took it and glanced over the writing, then tore it up.

From his tunic Constantine took a folded piece of paper and handed it to her. "The bill, madam," he said frigidly.

"What bill?" Tara asked dully.

"You owe the government for transportation and food and shelter. Two hundred dollars will pay for the facilities you have obtained by false pretences and forgery."

"I haven't got the money," said Tara in a low voice.

"Of course not. That is why you are in here. Obtaining goods and services by deception is a serious criminal offence."

"I'm terribly sorry," Tara said contritely. "I was stuck in Skagway. So I told a story hoping—"

"A *lie*, madam."

"I don't make a habit of it. Please believe me."

He walked over to the bunk and sat on it. "All right," he said. "What the devil made you embark on your charade anyway?"

She told him, then waited anxiously for his reaction. It came like a cold shower. "Frankly, Mrs. Kane," he said, "you have little chance of finding your husband. Much of the Yukon is uncharted. He could be anywhere. You are friendless and alone. You should return home."

Tara lowered her head. "I'll find him," she insisted. "I must stay here and go on with the search. My mind is made up."

"Then so is mine," he said. "I'd give a man who cheated the government thirty days' hard labour. Since you won't remove yourself from Dawson, thirty days' hard labour it shall be."

She looked disbelieving as he walked from the cell, slammed the door, and locked it.

An hour later Sergeant Campbell appeared. "Come along, Mrs. Kane," he said. He took her arm and led her outside. He towered above her as they marched through the town.

"Where are we going?" Tara panted.

"Mrs. Miles's place," he said curtly. He avoided her eyes, and she knew her punishment had already begun. "Sergeant," she puffed, "I want to apologize for deceiving you."

He slowed down. "It doesn't matter," he said.

He steered her across the main street to a wooden, two-storey house. There was a NO VACANCIES sign on the front door. "In you go," Campbell ordered, and followed her inside.

The hallway had a smell which, at first, Tara couldn't place. Then she realized what it was. This place smelled clean. An Indian rug covered the floor. There was no sawdust, no spittoons. This was the first home she had been in since San Francisco.

"Mrs. Miles," called out Campbell. A severe-faced woman emerged from the kitchen in the rear, and Tara's heart sank. She was in her late fifties, with every steel-grey hair in place. Her starched apron creaked as she walked. She was the personification of a prison matron.

"Hello, Linda," Campbell said. "Can I have a word with you? In private?" A door closed behind them but not before Tara heard Campbell saying, "Mr. Constantine sent this letter. . . ."

A few minutes later Mrs. Miles came out with the inspector's letter in her hand, followed by Campbell. "Mrs. Kane," she said briskly. "Mr. Constantine has asked me to work you like a skivvy for thirty days. Now I need a domestic, but she has to be decent and respectable."

Tara's eyes smouldered defiantly. "I'll do the work. However, I would like to make it clear, Mrs. Miles, that I am not a trained domestic."

"By the time I'm finished, you will be," Mrs. Miles assured Tara grimly. She turned to Campbell. "But if she's no good, Mr. Constantine gets her back and be sure you tell him that."

"We appreciate that," Campbell said, beating a hasty retreat.

"Now, you and I have to get a few things straight," said Mrs. Miles, leading Tara through to the kitchen. "This is a respectable rooming house. You don't socialize with the lodgers. You don't go out in the evening without my permission. You are allowed no visitors. You don't whistle or sing. You will get up at six every

53

morning, and make up the fires, scrub the floors, clean the rooms, black the grates, and keep the place generally tidy. I do the cooking. At all times I shall expect you to be willing and cheerful."

"Of course," Tara concurred, her lips twitching.

"Well, come along, then. I'll show you your quarters."

Although it wasn't a cell, it was the smallest room Tara had ever seen. But she liked it. At long last she would have privacy. The small window actually had a tiny chintz curtain. As everywhere else in the house it was clean and neat.

"I think I'll be very comfortable," Tara said, and she meant it.

"If you need anything, tell me. But I don't want any mess in here," Mrs. Miles added gruffly, as if she was ashamed of sounding too nice. "Get settled in, and then we'll have a cup of tea."

Tara sat on the bed and tried to collect her thoughts. This wasn't how she had planned it. She had come thousands of miles, and now she was a domestic servant. She took out the little compass. The needle kept pointing to—where, she wondered. In San Francisco it had pointed this way. High up on the pass it had kept pointing. Always farther—to the beyond.

Tara went to the window and looked out at the street. This was where she had to begin her search, among the saloons, the stores. Here, somewhere, she would find news of Daniel. "That's right, isn't it?" she whispered to the compass, balancing it in her hand. "I'll find him, won't I?"

"Tara!" came a shout up the stairs.

In the kitchen she found Mrs. Miles surrounded by steaming pots and pans, preparing the evening meal. "They're hungry men, and there's got to be plenty for them." She eyed Tara's trousers disapprovingly. "You'll have to wear a dress, understand? I can't have you looking like that."

"I lost my clothes," Tara said.

"I don't call a female in trousers respectable. I'll have to find you a dress. Come along." She marched Tara up the stairs. From the cupboard she produced some black lisle stockings and a grey woollen dress with a high collar.

"There," she said, "these ought to fit you. They belonged to the last girl." Tara wondered about the last girl. Had Mrs. Miles

54

acquired her also from the ranks of errant ladies who had fallen foul of the law? "Wear this apron tonight to serve the supper," Mrs. Miles continued. "You'll eat in the kitchen, then clean up."

Tara got her first glimpse of the boarders when she carried the huge soup tureen into the dining room. Mrs. Miles was presiding at the head of the table, the five lodgers arranged on either side of her. There were the Bartlett brothers, who operated a successful freight-haulage business, Harry Robbins, the town's dentist, Eugene Brock, a storekeeper, and Joe Lamore, a sawmill owner who had turned timber into his own kind of gold mine.

Dinner was an unending succession of carrying in hot plates, taking out dirty dishes. At one point Tara caught the tail end of a conversation. ". . . this place could become another Skagway if we let him get away with it," the dentist was saying.

"That's the truth," Brock agreed. "I tell you, Soapy Smith is beginning to take over Dawson. Already he owns four saloons."

"So what's the law doing about it?" asked one of the Bartletts. "This is Canadian territory. We don't need to allow Yankee hoodlums in here."

"But ninety per cent of the people in Dawson are American citizens," Lamore pointed out. "What can a handful of Mounties do? They're outnumbered two hundred to one."

"They should have hanged Soapy Smith years ago," commented Robbins, but Tara missed the rest of it because she had to bring in the apple pie. In the kitchen, the words echoed in Tara's ears. Soapy Smith! His influence also here in Dawson?

Tara was up first thing in the morning doing chores. She began by scrubbing the hallway on her hands and knees.

"Where is Mr. Kane?" Mrs. Miles suddenly asked. "Or should I ask, is there a Mr. Kane?" She fixed her eyes on Tara's left hand. "After all, a married woman wears a wedding ring."

Tara held her temper in check. "Since you're so curious, there is a Mr. Kane, and I don't wear a wedding ring because I had to pawn it." Mrs. Miles eyes opened wide. "I had no choice," Tara went on. "I was starving, destitute and alone in Skagway."

Mrs. Miles softened a little. "I'm sure you had a rough time— but what were you doing in Skagway?"

Tara told her story yet again. Mrs. Miles shook her head. "How on earth do you expect to find him here? Do you know what it takes for a female to survive on her own in these parts? You're too soft. You're not up to it."

"Don't worry, Mrs. Miles, I'll make out. You managed all right."

Mrs. Miles grunted. "I was left with a broken wagon and a few supplies when my husband died in '95." She told Tara how she had got hold of a stove, baked bread, and sold it for fifty cents a loaf until she had earned three hundred dollars. Then she opened an eating place and served cheap meals. When she had enough capital she opened her lodging house.

"This is where I've made my stake, and it's all mine," she said fiercely. "I'm not beholden to anybody, and I know how to look after myself. Which is more than you can do."

"I've got this far," Tara said. She was gaining respect for Mrs. Miles. Dour and formidable she might be, but Tara found herself admiring the starched lady.

"You have, but on other people's backs." Mrs. Miles said it without rancour, more like a mother putting a daughter straight. "You haven't stood on your own feet. Anyway, all this talk won't get the housework done," she growled, turning to go.

"Mrs. Miles," Tara said, "I need some time off."

"Time off!" Mrs. Miles boomed. "You haven't even started working properly and you want time off?"

"I've got to start looking for Daniel."

"You mean wander round Dawson, talking to strangers, going into saloons all on your own?" Mrs. Miles was appalled.

"Yes. Stand on my own feet."

Mrs. Miles studied her hands, then looked at Tara sternly. "Very well. You can have an hour now and then. And you may call me Linda," she added, quickly disappearing into the kitchen as if embarrassed by her momentary lapse.

After their conversation Mrs. Miles seemed to think more kindly of her. She put a woven Indian blanket on Tara's bed and even smiled at her occasionally. When Tara fell into bed, dog-tired after sixteen hours' work, she knew she was proving herself capable, a quality Mrs. Miles respected.

THE MONTE CARLO SALOON was packed. Tara stood blinking, trying to adjust herself to the smoke-laden atmosphere and the deafening noise. Every man's path crossed the Monte Carlo, and here somebody could well have heard of Daniel. She mustered up her courage to begin inquiries at the bar.

"Let's have a whirl," a lumberjack said. He grabbed her and, without waiting for her reply, swung her around the dance floor, pressing her close. Suddenly Tara felt as if she had been struck by a giant; only the lumberjack's firm grip kept her on her feet. She looked around to see what had hit her. A gigantic woman was bear-hugging a man whose head reached only to her massive bosom. She must have weighed at least twenty stone. She wore a huge, sequined dress, which covered her body like a tarpaulin. The most disconcerting thing of all was her eye. She had only one, and it glared at Tara, bloodshot and furious. Where the other eye should have been was an empty socket.

"Watch your big feet," the woman snarled at Tara.

The lumberjack pulled Tara away. "Phew," he said. "The last girl that bumped into the Grizzly Bear lost her scalp. I'd rather tangle with an elephant."

"She looks pretty fierce," Tara said, mesmerised.

"Fierce? How do you think she lost her blinker?"

Tara shook her head.

"Buffalo Liz gouged it out with her nails over at Sam Bonnifield's place. The Grizzly broke three of her ribs. That was some fight."

The music stopped, and he dragged her to the bar. "I'll get us some bubbly." He thumped the counter. "Hey, Pierre, pint of fizz."

The barman produced a bottle and two glasses. "Thirty bucks."

The lumberjack brought out a thick wad of money. "Nothing's too good for any little lady I go with. And you've made two bucks, honey, haven't you?"

"Two bucks?"

"Hasn't Soapy told you? You get two bucks commission on every bottle of fizz the customers buy."

"Soapy Smith? What's he got to do with it?" Tara asked.

"He owns the joint. Aren't you one of his girls?"

Tara put the glass down. "I'm sorry. You've made a mistake."

The lumberjack gave Tara an evil look and shuffled off muttering. She turned to the barman. "I'm looking for a man called Daniel Kane. Do you know if he's come in here?"

"Kane? Wait a moment." Pierre went to the back of the bar, opened the cash register, and took out a small pile of chits.

Tara's heart jumped as he came back to her, holding one of the pieces of paper. "Yeah," said Pierre. "I remember the guy. He owes us forty-five bucks."

She looked excitedly at the paper. "What's that?" she asked.

"His marker. He gave us an IOU."

"Let me see," she said, reaching for the note. It was Dan's handwriting all right. At least she knew now that he had come to Dawson. "When was this?" Tara asked.

"Four, five weeks ago. What's he to you, anyway?"

"He's my husband," Tara replied quietly.

"Oh is he? Well then, in that case, lady, you'd better pay his debt," he said coldly. "The boss don't like cheaters."

"My husband doesn't cheat," Tara protested indignantly.

"Mort," Pierre yelled. A stocky man dressed in black came over. "Got a marker here for forty-five bucks. The guy ran out on us. Now his wife's showed up. She doesn't want to pay."

Mort nodded. "We got pretty strict house rules, lady, and the boss don't make exceptions. You'd better pay up."

"Tell Mr. Smith he can say that to my face," Tara retorted.

He looked at her dubiously. "You a friend of his?"

"Yes," Tara said. "I know him quite well."

"Well, in that case," said Mort, "we'd better leave it. The boss will be arriving in town in a couple of days. I'll tell him you're here."

He winked at Tara, who turned and pushed her way out into the cold air of Front Street.

"And how is Mrs. Kane doing?" asked a voice at her elbow. Sergeant Campbell stopped her as she came out.

"I'm being very law-abiding, Sergeant," said Tara.

"Not sergeant any more," he said, pointing at his sleeve. The three chevrons had gone. "Got busted," he sighed. "The inspector took the stripes away."

"Because of me?" It must be her fault. "Oh, I *am* sorry."

"No, not entirely." He gave her a little smile. "It's been a lousy deal all around. Thatcher strung himself up in his cell. Constantine was up all night writing the report. He's worried about jurisdiction. Maybe I should have left the other guy in Skagway."

"But you couldn't let him be lynched," Tara said.

"When you bend regulations you pay." He shrugged. "Have you found your husband yet?"

"I know he's been in Dawson. Now I'm looking around the town to see if anyone knows where he is."

"You just stay out of trouble, Tara," he said. "Find your husband, then get out."

"That's all I'm trying to do, Sergeant Campbell. . . ."

"Name's Andrew," he said. "Just watch yourself."

She watched the red-jacketed figure stroll off.

During the next few weeks, in her search for Daniel, Tara learned that in Dawson people lost their original identities. "Daniel Kane?" they asked her. "What's his name?"

At first she was at a loss for words. Then she began to understand. Phantom Archibald. Waterfront Brown. Limejuice Jim. These were the names men were known by, and that's what their friends put on their tombstones when they were buried.

"I'd like to help you, honey," a dance-hall caller told her. "But who'd call himself Daniel Kane? Doesn't he have a monniker? Frisco Dan? Faro Kane?"

Tara shook her head. And she had to admit that Daniel's description could fit one of a thousand men. And she didn't even know what he looked like now. Was his hair long? Had he grown a beard? But relentlessly she pursued her quest.

One day a few weeks later Mrs. Miles handed Tara a letter. She ripped it open as Mrs. Miles stood watching. It was a short note:

Dear Mrs. Kane, I may be in possession of some information which could be of interest to you. I look forward to the pleasure of your company tonight at supper. I will call for you at six o'clock.

Yours most sincerely,
Jefferson R. Smith

Tara's head was in a whirl. She passed the note to Mrs. Miles, whose face clouded over as she read it. "Well, that's out of the question," she decreed. "You can't go out with him."

"If he's got information about Daniel . . ."

"The man's a blackguard, and probably lying," exploded Mrs. Miles. "Good heavens, Tara, you couldn't think of accepting."

"I must, Linda. I'd have supper with the devil if he'd lead me to my husband. It is possible that he knows something. Why else should he bother? So I must go tonight. Will you give me the time off? I've served my thirty days."

"Please yourself," Mrs. Miles said coldly. "You're over twenty-one. But don't say you weren't warned."

The grandfather clock downstairs was striking six when Mrs. Miles banged on Tara's door. "He's come for you," she called out gruffly. "But he's outside. He's not coming into my house."

Tara's face was so pale that she pinched her cheeks to heighten her colour and smoothed her only dress. Mrs. Miles, busy in the kitchen, did not look up when she appeared. If she had, she would have seen a Tara who looked almost elegant, her luxuriant dark auburn hair swept up and carefully arranged. Here was a young woman who didn't need jewellery or furs to make her beautiful. Her natural loveliness was more than sufficient.

As Tara emerged from the house, Smith came towards her and raised his broad-brimmed hat. "What a pleasure to see you again," he drawled. "May I?" He bowed slightly and offered her his arm. She looked down. There on his little finger was her wedding ring.

"I must be back soon," Tara said coldly, ignoring his proffered arm. "I hope we're not going far."

"Hardly. And I promise to bring you back safe and sound."

They began walking down the street towards the centre of Dawson. "Where are we going, Mr. Smith?" she asked.

"Oh, a little place I have," he murmured.

It was called the Regina Café. Tara had noticed the four-storey building, the biggest in Dawson, under construction, without realizing what it would become.

When she stepped inside she was amazed. There was wall-to-wall deep red Brussels carpeting. Hanging from the ornate ceiling were glass chandeliers. The wood-panelled walls were decorated with gold leaf. No sawdust, and no spittoons.

"It will be Dawson's finest hotel," Smith said, looking around proudly. "Fifteen rooms, all steam-heated, all electrically lit. I'll get the power from a ship on the river. It's going to have class."

This was a new angle on Smith's operations. She associated him with rackets and cheap saloons.

Smith was well aware that she was impressed. He led her along a corridor and opened a door. Inside she saw a table laid for two. On it were candles in tall holders, already lit. At her place was a small silver vase with flowers in it. Bone china plates were on a snow-white tablecloth. The cutlery and crystal glasses shone and sparkled.

Smith tugged at a bell rope. There was a soft tap at the door, and a little Chinese entered. He handed Tara a printed menu. "I hope you're hungry," Smith said.

She couldn't believe such fare existed in these parts. There was *consommé à la jardinière*, Rock Point oysters, broiled caribou chops *aux champignons*, pears and peaches, and chocolate cake. And to drink, apart from the wine cooling in the bucket on a side table, there was a thirty-nine-year-old port and a Napoleon brandy.

Smith played the perfect host. He filled their glasses and then silently raised his, looking across at her. She was beginning to find his smooth attentiveness disconcerting.

When she took her first taste of the food, Smith watched her reaction closely. "What do you think?" he inquired. "The chef's on trial tonight. I've imported him from the Palace Hotel in Frisco. Now we're going to find out if he's worth it."

"Delicious," Tara said, and meant it. The mere fact that he could produce such luxuries so far from civilization earned her grudging respect for his ingenuity.

"You said you had some information which could interest me," she said, breaking a long and oddly intimate silence.

"There's plenty of time to talk about that," he protested.

"No," Tara said firmly. "This is not a social occasion, Mr. Smith. That's why I'm here."

He took a sip of wine. "I guess you've heard the most terrible

61

stories about this scoundrel Soapy Smith. How he runs all the rackets. Correct?"

"Why should I listen to stories about you, Mr. Smith? I've seen you in action. I know how you operate."

Now he was smiling broadly. "Sure. I'm a businessman."

Tara pushed her plate away. "Businessman? Selling people ten-cent bars of soap for five dollars? Rigging up fake telegraph lines? You call that business?"

"You really don't understand, do you? I'm a kind of educator. I teach people how easy it is for a sucker to be parted from his dough. I figure that's a public service. Now doesn't that appeal to you?"

Tara glared at him. "No. It so happens I'm honest, Mr. Smith."

He leaned back and looked at her cynically. "My, that's quite a statement coming from you. Yes, sir. I reckon you haven't much cause to preach me sermons. Any dame who succeeds in taking the Mounties for a ride the way you did certainly merits closer acquaintance."

Tara's green eyes blazed. "How dare you . . ."

He grinned at her. "Don't look so worried. I admire you. You're a good-looking woman all right but you got real talent as well. I have a feeling you and I sort of fit."

"I haven't, Mr. Smith," Tara said, an edge to her voice.

"One day you will, I promise you," he said softly.

"You flatter yourself," she snapped. "Now, what have you heard that could interest me?"

"Ah, about your husband. There's a rumour that a man called Daniel Kane from Frisco is prospecting around Fortymile. I'll take you there if you like."

Tara studied him suspiciously and was about to speak when the door burst open. Framed in the doorway was a stunning-looking woman. She wore a silver-fox jacket over a figure-hugging black gown, her dark hair piled on top of a good-looking, hard face with generous lips. Perhaps the most startling thing about her was the belt encircling her slim waist. It was made entirely of gold nuggets. There was a fortune there, and Tara gaped at it.

"Miss Cad Wilson," Smith said lazily, "Mrs. Tara Kane."

"I heard she was your new filly," Cad said insultingly, looking Tara up and down but addressing him.

"You know better than to believe everything you hear, Cad," retorted Smith, his tone mocking. "And now that you've met Mrs. Kane, I'm sure you have other matters to attend to."

Cad's glance swept the table. "My, my. Champagne, wine, candles. You *are* trying hard, Soapy."

"I don't like you calling me that, Cad." Smith said. They stared at each other angrily, the atmosphere between them full of unspoken threats. It was obvious that this was not the first time she had confronted Smith in such a situation.

Cad turned to Tara. "You don't belong in Dawson, honey. If I were you I'd get out, and that's good advice."

"Cad, it's time you were getting back to work," Smith said.

She leaned forward, picked up his wineglass, and poured what was left onto the white tablecloth. "Sweet dreams." She smiled, her eyes sharp knives ripping through Tara. At the door she blew a kiss to Smith and swept out.

Smith replenished his glass. "Well," he said, ignoring the interruption, "what do you say? Are you coming to Fortymile?"

"Why should I trust you?" Tara demanded. "I'd like to know exactly what you've heard about my husband."

"It's kind of thirdhand, but it sounds like Daniel Kane. From Frisco. Rumour has it he's a pretty sharp poker player too."

It could be Daniel. "And how did you . . . ?"

"I sort of kept a few ears open," Smith said airily.

"Why?" she asked sharply.

"Because he owes me money and . . ." he paused. "And because I am interested in you. So I put the word out. Just another public service. . . . I'll be leaving in the morning."

Tara stood up. "If I decide to join you, I'll be ready by then." She picked up her handbag and walked over to face him. "By the way, I'd like my wedding ring back, please."

"Ah," he sighed. He looked down at the gold band on his finger. "Despite what you might have heard, I'm a man of principle, and one of my strongest is never to mix business with pleasure. I'd hate to spoil a delightful evening by discussing sordid money matters. You're talking about a deal we made. Remember, Tara, you're at liberty to reclaim it at any time, but right now I guess the price is a little too steep for you."

"I could pay you by instalments, say two fifty a week."

Smith's eyes twinkled. "One hundred and fifteen dollars paid off at—"

"You only advanced me fifty," exclaimed Tara.

Smith felt in his pocket and pulled out a piece of paper. "The balance is made up by this," he said, unfolding Daniel's IOU. "Plus a surcharge for late payment."

"Of all the low, rotten—"

"Now, now, Tara. Business is business."

"One day," Tara said through gritted teeth, "you *will* give it back, and it might be·sooner than you think."

"That, Tara, is the day I'm waiting for. Until then I'll keep it in a safe place." He removed the ring from his finger and put it in his waistcoat pocket.

Smith insisted on walking her home. Tara noticed three men following them. "They're deputies," Smith said, wearing his arrogant smile.

"Your gang, you mean?"

He shrugged. "Somebody has to keep law and order. Businessmen like me have investments, and they have to protect them."

As they approached Mrs. Miles's house Smith said, "Tara, be careful. About Cad. Don't take any chances if she's around."

"Your lady friend?" said Tara coldly. "I really don't think we've much in common. I wouldn't worry about it."

"I know Cad," Smith said. "She can be dangerous."

They were outside Mrs. Miles's house. Tara pulled out her key. "Good night then, Mr. Smith. I'll think about Fortymile."

He shook his head. "You know something, Tara? You're the first woman I've ever spent an evening with who at the end of it still called me Mr. Smith."

"You forget," Tara reminded him, "that ours is strictly a business acquaintance." She turned her back on him and disappeared through the front door.

That night she lay in the darkness, looking at the ceiling. She

65

knew she would risk anything, even travelling alone in Soapy Smith's dubious company, if Daniel was at the end of the trail. In the morning she got up early and packed her few belongings, then sat down and wrote a note to Linda, explaining where she was going. She tiptoed downstairs and left it on the kitchen table.

CHAPTER SIX

They spoke little on the sled journey north. When they camped Smith prepared the food, made sure she was comfortable, but virtually ignored her. He was polite, correct, and just a little superior. All of which made him intensely annoying to Tara.

"That's Alaska over there," Smith said, pointing into the distance with his whip. "It's United States territory. And *that's* where we'll look for your husband."

Unlike Dawson, Fortymile did not even pretend to be civilized. It was a bleak and windswept settlement that had established itself at the junction of two frozen rivers, the Yukon and the Fortymile. In the middle of the Fortymile River was a small rocky island. To Tara's surprise Smith guided the team of huskies across the frozen river onto the shale beach of the island. A group of men ran over to them as Smith helped Tara out of the sled. Eagerly she scanned their faces. They were bearded, and wore a strange variety of furs, skins, and Indian anoraks.

"Greetings, General, welcome to Paradise," a white-haired man cried out, sweeping off his cap and bowing low.

"My friends," Smith called out, "this lady has come from Dawson. She is looking for her husband. Daniel Kane."

"Daniel Kane, did you say?" asked a man behind Tara. She swung around. He was a tall man in a scout's hat and buckskin jacket. "Sure I know him. Allow me to introduce myself. Colonel Lee, ma'am, at your service. Late Sixth U.S. Cavalry."

"You know my husband?" Tara stammered.

"Indeed, ma'am." The colonel walked her out of earshot. "He saved my life."

Tara looked at him, startled. "No. When was this?"

"Well," the colonel said, pulling his goatee beard. "We were cut off. Only me and Dan left. And, by jiminy, you know what he did? Killed six of the savages, got through to the fort, and brought the relief column. Custer was a fool, but with men like me and Dan, he would have survived."

"What are you talking about?" she stuttered. "That's not my husband. That's not Daniel Kane."

"Sure it is," the colonel insisted. "Daniel B. Kane, C Troop, 6th Cavalry. . . . Hey, wait a moment. Lord you're right. Come to think of it he got killed in '89. In New Mexico."

Tara didn't know whether to cry with rage or pity, she felt so let down. Smith, who had been walking among the men, slapping them on the back, laughing at their stories, looked at her inquiringly. "Any luck?"

"Luck?" Tara said bitterly. "Is *he* all the information you had for me? He's crazy. He's still with General Custer."

Smith shook his head sorrowfully. "That's what happens sometimes in the Klondike. It gets too much for some people."

"I don't think there is any point in going on with this charade," said Tara grimly. "Shall we go?" They walked to the sled, and by the time they drew up outside the one ramshackle building in Fortymile which passed for a hotel, Tara's anger was at boiling point. "You didn't really think I'd find out anything about my husband here, did you?" She faced him accusingly.

"Well, it *is* called Liar's Island." He moved round the sled to help her alight.

"Take your hands off me," she exploded.

"Please yourself," he said. "But we'll be staying here tonight."

Her eyes swept the seedy, uninviting hotel. "Looks delightful," she said scathingly. "I suppose you own this too. Another of your rackets?"

Smith burst out laughing. "Oh, Tara, you should just see yourself when you get indignant."

"I'm glad you find it so amusing, Mr. Smith, hoodwinking me into coming to this godforsaken place on a wild-goose chase." Smith saw her lift her hand to slap his face, but he grabbed her wrist and, holding her arms above her head, started to dance her around the sled, humming a lively polka. A group of bystanders laughed.

"Stop it," she cried, helplessly. The crowd gave a cheer.

"Why, Tara, I had no idea you danced so well." Then, as abruptly as he had grabbed her, he stopped dancing and kissed her on the lips. The men whistled and applauded. Smith turned and bowed.

"Come on," he said, seizing her hand. He half pulled, half dragged her into the shabby building, up the rickety staircase to the landing. He kicked open the door at the top, dragged her across the room, and threw her down on the bed. It almost knocked the breath out of her.

"Now you stay there until I get back," he said mildly.

She got off the bed and stood, panting. "How dare you?"

"Dare?" he looked at her, amused. "I dare anything, Tara, believe me." Smith looked at his watch. "High time I did my collection. Part of my public duties here includes running the post office. Every month I have to collect the takings. Tomorrow we return to Dawson. While I'm out, do not leave this room. Understand?" He went out, gently closing the door.

Tara, shoulders heaving, cried with the disappointment and injustice of it all. She hated herself for being such a gullible fool. Smith had played a cruel hoax on her; to cap it all, he had publicly humiliated her.

Gradually her tears subsided. She sat up and became aware for the first time of the room she was in. Her lips tightened. Smith's things were neatly arranged on the chest of drawers; a shaving mug and brush, a stick of soap, a razor. This must be where he usually stayed on his visits to Fortymile.

There was a closet too. Inside hung male clothing, obviously Smith's. Fury engulfed her. "All right, Mr. Soapy Smith," she said. "You want to play games. We'll play games."

The window overlooked the unpaved thoroughfare that passed as Fortymile's main street. Tara tried to open it. It was frozen shut. She smashed the glass. She took the shaving mug and the beaver-bristle brush and threw them out. Then she took a fur jacket from the closet and flung it out, followed by Smith's trousers and shirts. Under the window a little group had now gathered, fascinated by the barrage landing around them.

Tara spotted a leather Gladstone bag on the other side of the bed. There were papers inside, a box of Havana cheroots, and a silver hip flask. Tara bombarded the street with them, item by item. Finally the Gladstone bag, with JRS embossed on the calf hide, went out of the window.

The crowd below had grown to thirty or forty people, and they were loving it all. "Hey, lady," somebody yelled up at Tara, "are you going to throw Soapy out too?"

She waved, but she wasn't finished yet. She went over to the bed and looked under it. Yes, there it was, the chamber pot. Triumphantly she carried it to the window like a trophy, then grandly flung it to the crowd below.

The sight of Soapy Smith's chamber pot sailing into Fortymile's main street was heralded with a burst of whistles and applause. Tara grinned. That was the most satisfying of all. They were laughing at Soapy Smith. The King of the Klondike would never be respected quite as much again.

Suddenly she spotted Smith striding purposefully through a barrage of cheers and catcalls towards the hotel. Tara rushed to the door and locked it. She heard him thundering up the stairs.

"Let me in, Tara," he yelled, rattling the door handle.

She smiled complacently. For the first time since she'd met this arrogant joker she had got the better of him.

Then, with a splintering of wood, the door gave way. "What the hell—" began Smith, looking wildly around the room.

"Excuse me," Tara said serenely, and tried to push past him.

He grabbed her arm. "You're not going anywhere."

"Mr. Smith, there are a lot of people outside. If you don't let me pass, I shall scream."

His eyes were blazing. "Just how do you expect to get back to Dawson?"

"I'll manage," Tara replied, pushing past him.

She came out into the street to find the crowd still standing around. They parted, almost reverently, to let her through. A man called out. "Hey, lady, just a moment." She turned. He was a young man in a stiff collar and necktie. "I'm a reporter on the *Nugget*. What was that all about at the hotel?"

"I don't want to talk about it. Excuse me," she said.

"If only that German photographer had been there," said the reporter sorrowfully. "I can still see that chamber pot—"

"What photographer?" Tara asked.

"Herr Hart. He's crazy about shooting things as they happen."

"Is he here? In Fortymile?" she demanded in excitement.

"Sure. He's set up just behind the general store. Taking portraits of everyone in town."

She rushed off. Hart, here in Fortymile. She couldn't believe her luck. A familiar face at last. She found his tent. YOUR PICTURE TAKEN FOR FIVE DOLLARS read the notice hanging from it.

Just then Hart's head popped out of the flap of the tent. When he saw her his eyes opened wide. "Tara," he gasped. He kissed her on both cheeks and drew her inside.

"Ernst," Tara said, "how have you been?"

He raised his hands. "Fantastic. You would never believe it. I have hundreds of photos. What an exhibition I will make." Then he stopped. "Have you found Daniel yet?"

She shook her head and told him what had happened since they had parted in Dyea. He was attentive and understanding. When she described the scene at the hotel he laughed.

After she had finished, Hart said firmly, in his correct, Germanic way, "I shall take you back to Dawson. I have finished my work here anyway, so there is no problem."

"Can you manage it? Have you got the room?" She looked anxiously around the tent, littered with boxes and chemicals.

"I've always got room for you, Tara," Hart said.

Before she left the town, she went to the District Claims office. There was no word of a gold prospector called Daniel Kane.

When they arrived in Dawson, Tara and Hart parted company. He looked crestfallen at losing her so soon, but Tara promised to come and see him when he had set up shop in Dawson.

"Oh. It's you," was Mrs. Miles's greeting when Tara walked into the lodging house. "It was a wild-goose chase, wasn't it, and now you've got nowhere to stay?"

Tara nodded.

Mrs. Miles sniffed. "Well, I'll take you back as a servant. I'll pay you five dollars a week, but that's all. You have disappointed me."

"Linda," protested Tara, "Smith never . . . If you'll only listen to what really happened."

Mrs. Miles shot her a quick glance. "I looked after you like my own kin. And you thank me by going off with that—"

"Please don't lecture me," Tara cried. "I got my just reward in Fortymile. I paid for the way I behaved."

Mrs. Miles's manner softened. "Very well." She nodded. "Just do your work, and we won't talk about it again."

The following day Tara was alone in the house when she heard someone knocking at the front door.

To her astonishment, there stood Smith's woman, Cad Wilson, wrapped in a magnificent fur cape with a hood. "Good morning, Mrs. Kane. Aren't you going to invite me in?"

She stepped into the hall, and Tara closed the door. "Yes?"

"I've come here because I've found out something about your husband, so I thought I'd pass it on."

"All right," Tara agreed warily. "Come into the parlour."

"Thank you," murmured Cad. "I have something I want to show you." She opened her handbag and gave Tara a wrapped object.

Tara looked at her mystified, and then unwrapped the piece of cloth. It was a man's silver watch. She stared at it in disbelief. It was the watch she had given to Daniel. There were the words she had had engraved in it: *To my darling husband Daniel, with eternal love from his devoted wife Tara Kane 1897.* "Where did you get this?" Tara whispered.

"Your husband sold it," Cad said. "He needed money for supplies. I understand he's teamed up with a man called Jake Gore. They've got a digging."

"Where?" gasped Tara.

"Oh, a hundred miles north of here, in Hell's Kitchen. It's a tough journey—up in Tagish country."

"What is it? A town?"

71

"A hole. The end of the line."

"How did you come by this watch?" asked Tara.

"Jake's brother bought it from your husband, then he had bad luck at faro at the Monte Carlo. So he paid his debt with it. I saw the name and asked him how he came by it."

"There's one thing I don't understand," said Tara, turning the watch over in her hands. "Why are you trying to help me?"

"Listen, Mrs. Kane. I don't want you around Jeff. Is that clear enough? He's my property. We belong to one another."

Tara stared at her. "Believe me, Miss Wilson, you're welcome to him. If I never see him again, I'll be happy."

Cad drew on her sealskin gloves. "For the life of me I don't know what the hell Jeff sees in you. You know where your man is now. Find him and get out of the territory."

After Cad left, Tara rushed to her room. She pressed the watch to her cheek. At last a tangible clue to Daniel's whereabouts. Hell's Kitchen, she mused. Only a hundred miles from Dawson. It couldn't be all that bad, not if Daniel was there.

Her requirements were simple, she decided. She needed a sled, a dog team, supplies, and a map. She thought of the lodgers. She was sure she could get a sled and team from the Bartlett brothers; weren't they in the haulage business? Then Mr. Brock the provision merchant might advance her sufficient supplies for the journey. As for a map, who better to approach than Hart?

Tara hurried to the temporary studio Hart had set up in the centre of town. Even after she had shown him the watch and explained what Cad had told her, he seemed unconvinced. He described the terrain she would have to cover. It was no place for a woman on her own. So, in the interests of a photographic record of the Klondike, he would accompany her.

"Well, if you really want to come . . ." said Tara.

"Of course. You don't think I would let you go alone? I will close shop and prepare my equipment for the journey. There will be room enough on my sled for you too."

"It's all right. I can hire my own team." Tara smiled at him. "With the watch and my compass, and you to guide me, I know we will find Daniel."

CHAPTER SEVEN

Early the following morning Tara trudged with the Bartlett brothers to their depot, where she picked up a sled and team. From there she went to Brock's store and collected supplies. Then, with a certain amount of trepidation, she drove the sled to Hart's studio. He was already waiting for her.

"Well, Mrs. Tara Kane," he said, going over to his sled and picking up the reins, "let's get going and find your husband."

The hundreds of miles she had travelled in other people's sleds, watching them handle their dog teams, had not been wasted. For the first few miles she was frightened, but then she realized the dogs were travelling the way she wanted, obeying her.

They were circling Lousetown, on the trail north, when she noticed a horseman following them. He was galloping furiously, and Tara tightened her lips when she recognized Jefferson Smith.

To Tara's annoyance Hart slowed down his team. Smith pulled up alongside them and looked down at her. "There's a rumour you're going north, Mrs. Kane. It's no place for a woman."

She stared straight through him.

Hart cleared his throat. "You need have no worries about Mrs. Kane. She will be well protected."

"Listen, mister," Smith said menacingly. "You look after her well. Because I'm telling you fair and square, if anything happens to her"—he reached out and grabbed Hart by his coat collar—"I'm going to hold you responsible."

Tara had never seen Smith like this. For the first time she realized that he actually cared what happened to her.

Smith released Hart and turned his horse to Tara. "Since you won't change your mind you'd better have this." It was a stubby pistol, a tiny .22 Derringer, beautifully made, with an engraved mother-of-pearl handle. "If anyone gets too close for comfort, use it." He swung his horse around and galloped off.

Tara looked at the pistol. It fitted her hand perfectly. Inscribed along the squat barrel was: *A Sure Thing from JRS*.

"What are we waiting for, Ernst?" Tara said, putting the pistol in her bag. It was as if she had communicated her sense of urgency to the dogs. They streaked through the snow, moving ahead of Hart's sled. She felt as she'd never felt before, free, completely in control of her destiny, no longer beholden to somebody else.

When they camped Tara set up the stove while Hart collected firewood. She melted snow as she had seen the Mounties do, and made sure that her dogs were fed. She was like a woman of the Klondike.

She saw Hart watching her. "Why are you staring at me?"

"Because you've changed," he said. "You're not the innocent, shivering orphan I met on the ship."

"What am I now, then?"

"You're a woman who can look after herself," he said, a little grudgingly. "You'll survive, no matter what."

During the night Tara stirred uneasily. She opened her eyes and then sat up, stifling a scream. A man with shoulder length hair and earrings was standing over her, a hideous grin on his face and a pistol in his hand.

"Howdy," he said genially. He stuck his pistol in his belt and hauled her to her feet.

Stupefied with fear, Tara watched wide-eyed as his ugly face came nearer. She turned her head in a feverish effort to escape his repulsive embrace.

The man grinned malevolently and dragged her from the tent. "Look what I found, boys," he announced triumphantly.

Two other men with rifles stood by the sleds. Hart was lying motionless on the ground.

"Ernst!" she cried, rushing towards him. She knelt by him and took his head in her hands.

His eyes flickered. "Tara," he gasped. "Are you all right?"

The three men were standing around laughing. The other two were as forbidding as their companion with the earrings. One had a black eye patch and was dressed like a trapper. The other had a red beard and brutish face.

"What do you want from us?" she demanded.

"You'd never guess," said the one with earrings.

"I'm sorry, Tara," Hart apologized. "They crept up on me, and then somebody hit me."

"He's O.K." said the man with the eye patch. "Hank never hits 'em too hard."

Hank was the one with the earrings. He grabbed Tara's chin and turned her head towards him. "She and me fancy each other," he said. "Ain't that right, sweetheart?"

"Keep away from me," she spat, kicking out at him.

"Where are you making for?" asked the man with the eye patch, who seemed to be in charge.

"We're going north," Tara said.

"Got any gold?"

Tara shook her head.

"She's lying, Duke," Hank said.

"So what's on the sled?" Duke asked. "Supplies?"

"Equipment," replied Tara. "Mr. Hart is a photographer."

They stared at her disbelieving. Then Hank went over to Hart's sled and pulled back the tarpaulin covering the cases and boxes. Duke picked up a box of plates and looked at it curiously. "What kind of pictures do you take?"

"I take portraits of famous people," Hart said, groping in the snow for his spectacles. "Important people."

"We should get our pictures made. You willing to picture me and the boys?"

"You'll have your own portfolio. I'll do you in a group and then individually," Hart said eagerly, struggling to his feet.

Tara wondered if this display of enthusiasm was genuine, or merely an attempt to get them out of a tight spot.

"We got a little hideaway," Duke said. "We'll take you. The rest of the boys there will want to be took too."

"What about her? Who gets her?" demanded red beard.

Hank swung around. "I do."

"Like hell you do—"

"Keep your hair on," intervened the man with the eye patch. "There's plenty for all of us."

Tara was petrified. She wondered wildly how they could escape.

"Where is this place?" Hart demanded.

"Mister, you ask too many questions," Duke said coldly.

Little was said once they were on the trail. Duke had a sled with a pack of dogs as villainous as the trio. Hank and the red-bearded man, whose name was Shorty, trekked along on snowshoes beside Tara and Hart who were driving their own sleds.

Daylight came. The landscape provided no clue to where they were going. It was more barren, more deserted, than any terrain Tara had seen so far. In the distance were great mountains, their summits obscured by frozen mist. Eventually they halted, and Hank approached Tara. A great uneasiness swept through her.

"Relax, sweetheart. I ain't going to harm you." He tied a blindfold securely over her eyes.

"I can't drive the team like this," Tara objected.

"That's O.K.," Duke said. "Hank'll take over. You can ride like a lady."

She could hear Hart protesting. "My glasses. I need my glasses," and then Shorty: "You don't need nothing, mister."

She had no idea how long they travelled nor in what direction. Then a shot rang out.

"It's O.K.," called out Hank. "Nothing to worry about." Three more quick shots followed, fired from just behind.

"Whoa there!" Hank shouted, and the sled pulled to a halt. "You can look now," he said, roughly pulling the scarf off.

She blinked, her eyes unaccustomed to the sudden brightness. The sleds had pulled up in a clearing, surrounded on all sides by high cliffs. There were a few tents and two rough wooden shacks.

Duke was talking to a tall man wearing the scarlet jacket of a Mountie. When Tara looked more closely she saw that most of the brass buttons were missing and there was a hole, edged by a stain, where the Mountie's heart had once been. Behind him stood three other men.

"How much do you want for her?" the man dressed as a Mountie asked Duke.

Duke shook his head. "She's not for sale. She belongs to us, Blue. Me and the boys found her, so she's ours."

Tara stared straight ahead, trying to conceal the raw fear she felt in the pit of her stomach. "Where is this?" she asked.

76

Blue smiled. "Some call it Hell's Kitchen. You've fallen among thieves."

"Hell's Kitchen," she repeated slowly. She glanced at Hart, who was shaken as she was to discover they'd reached their intended destination. "I am Daniel Kane's wife. From San Francisco."

"So?" asked Blue. It meant nothing to him.

"Where's Jake Gore, his partner?"

"You know Jake, eh?" said Blue. "Fancy that." He turned to one of the men behind him. "A friend of yours, Jake?"

Jake was a sallow-faced man with long black hair tied at the nape of his neck. He had a shoulder holster, but instead of a gun it held a knife sheath. He wore a gold ring on every finger. Tara stared at him incredulously. This was Daniel's partner?

Jake turned to Blue. "I think she and me got some private business," he said.

"You ain't doing any claim jumping while I'm around," Hank threatened, his hand going towards his gun.

Jake shrugged. He turned as if to walk away; then, with the speed of a rattlesnake, he whirled around and threw something. Hank sank to his knees, Jake's knife protruding from his chest. He slumped forward and lay still.

Slowly Jake walked up to Hank's lifeless body, turned it over with his foot, and drew out the knife.

"One moment, please!" shouted Hart, carefully sidestepping Hank's body. "I would like to take a picture."

"What for?" Jake growled.

"To photograph you. Here on the spot. As it happened."

Hart's cold-bloodedness shook Tara. He unloaded his sled, set up his camera, posed Jake Gore by Hank's body, disappeared under his blanket, and exposed the first plate.

When Hart had finished the men applauded and cheered. He told them he was photographer to the crowned heads of Europe, and available for anyone wishing to have his portrait taken.

Jake Gore went up to Tara, who was standing by pale and numb from what she had seen. "Come on, let's talk," he said, leading her to a tent. Inside there was only a bearskin rug. "So, you're Dan's wife?"

She nodded.

"Who told you I was here?"

"Cad Wilson," Tara said, reaching in her bag and bringing out the watch.

He looked at it, then again at her. "Yeah, that's his."

"Where is he?" she asked.

"Camped a few miles from here. At the claim."

"Can we leave now?"

He shook his head. "Weather don't look good. First thing in the morning, Mrs. Kane."

Once outside, Tara hugged herself with excitement. She had to find Hart. From the direction of a cave in the rock she could hear men shouting, so she went toward it.

The interior of the cave was illuminated by a roaring log fire and oil lamps hanging from the walls. The place was packed; obviously this was Hell's Kitchen's night-time haunt. Hart, oblivious to everything, was adjusting his camera on its tripod.

"Ernst," said Tara urgently, "I'm meeting Daniel in the morning."

"I don't think I have any pictures," Hart grumbled. "This light is too dim."

"I'm joining Daniel in the morning," Tara repeated. "He's camped a few miles away. He's got a claim."

"That's wonderful," he said, but he didn't sound enthusiastic. "I'm so happy for you." He didn't look at her. "I know you think I am a cold-blooded fish, yes? Here you are all excited, and I am only interested in taking pictures. But you see this is my mission out here."

She kissed him on the cheek.

"Jake Gore and I start at dawn."

Hart regarded her gravely. "He is a very bad man."

"He knows where Daniel is. He's taking me to him. That's all that matters."

"Wait until I can come with you."

"Oh, Ernst, you don't think I can *wait*, do you?"

"No, perhaps I do not." He sighed. "You are always impetuous, Tara. Your trouble is you won't change your mind."

78

CHAPTER EIGHT

It was not only the sounds of revelry and drunkenness that kept Tara awake most of that night. It was the thought that by this time tomorrow she and Daniel would be together again. It filled her with a strange combination of excitement and apprehension. Excitement at seeing him, of being in his arms, kissing him; apprehension at what he might have become.

Towards dawn she packed away her few things, put the gun in her pocket, and hitched up her team. Jake was waiting beside his sled. "Follow me," was all he said. There was no blindfold this time.

They travelled through a narrow ravine, then back down a bumpy trail. Finally they emerged onto open ground. She wanted to ask how long it would take, but Jake's sled kept too far ahead. All the time she hoped for some sign of their destination, but white emptiness stretched for miles on all sides.

Four hours later Tara saw, in the distance, what looked like a frozen lake, partly encircled by some scraggy pine trees. Pitched by the edge was a tent. Her excitement grew and she lashed away at the dogs, urging them to go faster in the biting wind. "Is that it?" she yelled, as she drew level with Jake's sled.

Jake nodded.

Tara felt a sense of triumph. She had found Daniel.

As she drew nearer she could see snow heaped against one side of the tent, where winds and blizzards had drifted it. She brought her sled to a halt a few yards from the tent and rushed forward, tumbling through the snow in her eagerness.

"Daniel! I'm here!" she called out, her eyes shining as she pulled aside the tent flap. The tent was empty.

For a moment she stood stunned. She could see enough to know that this was somebody's quarters. Some clothes were lying about, and there were cooking utensils, mining tools, a parka.

She stood puzzled, then, slowly, she turned and went outside. Jake's sled stood beside hers. "Where is he?" demanded Tara. "Where's Daniel?"

"This way," Jake said.

She followed him around to the back of the tent.

"There he is," Jake announced, stepping aside. A few feet in front of her was a little mound. Stuck on the top of it were two pieces of wood, tied together into a cross.

Tara stood, staring with disbelief, the blood draining from her face.

"No," she whispered. "No."

"That's him," Jake said. "Say howdy."

Her whole body felt numb. This could not be. Daniel buried here in the frozen ground, alone, abandoned? No, never.

"That's how I got his watch, see," Jake said. "He never was a willing giver."

She looked at him, her face a mask of horror.

"I guess you're a widow woman now. But don't worry." He smiled. "You ain't going to be lonesome." He reached out and grabbed her.

"No!" she shrieked, clawing at his face. He swung a fist. Stars flashed in her head and she could feel herself falling. Then, for a moment, everything went black.

When she came around, a few seconds later, she was on the ground, his full weight on top of her. He was tearing at her clothes, ripping them.

"I'm going to have you," he snarled. "Then I'm going to kill you, just like I told Cad."

She turned and twisted and he didn't even notice her pulling the gun from her pocket. She rammed the stocky muzzle against his head and without hesitation squeezed the trigger. Jake went rigid, his eyes opening wide. Then his body went limp.

"Oh God!" she screamed. With all her strength she pushed Jake off her body. He lay on his back, his sightless eyes staring up at the greying sky.

Tara couldn't believe that Jake was dead. She stared at him, sobbing like a child. She was alone, with a dozen dogs, a dead man, and a grave for company. She did not know where she was; she had no idea in what direction they had travelled. The tent billowed soundlessly in a cold wind whispering across the snow.

There was the grave. A voice in her head insisted it could not be Daniel's. Like a sleepwalker, she slowly got to her feet. She had to know who was in that lonely mound.

She grabbed a pickaxe from the tent, and ran to the grave. With the strength of a lunatic she started hacking away. The frozen outer layer began to crack. Now she could see the outline of a body. She fell to her knees, and with her bare hands started clawing at the frozen earth. She had to see his face. She was almost hysterical, mouthing prayers, as she brushed away the last veil of soil.

She was looking on the hard-set face of a middle-aged man. His eyes were shut, as if he were sleeping. Sleeping with a hole through his heart. He had been murdered. But he was not Daniel Kane.

"Aaah!" she screamed, jumping to her feet, her eyes wild. "He's not dead!" she cried to the vast emptiness around her. "Jake Gore lied! He lied!" She stood in the raging wind, snow swirling around her, laughing hysterically.

Gradually her elation receded, and she became aware of the snow and the frenzied yapping of the dogs. Her teeth began to chatter. She recalled what the Mounties had said: once you start freezing, you're finished.

She quickly gathered some wood, lit the stove in the deserted tent, and prepared coffee to warm herself. As she drank the scalding liquid she looked around the tent.

There were some canned foods, a few tools, and some clothes. She took off her torn jacket and shirt and put on a large parka. Then she saw a tin deedbox in the corner of the tent.

Tara lifted the lid. There were five dollars, a rabbit's paw, a necklace with an Indian pendant. None of these meant anything to her. There were also several stained letters. She threw them aside impatiently. Then she spotted handwriting she recognized. "Mrs. Tara Kane, 110 Fulton Street, San Francisco, Cal., USA," read Daniel's script. Her mind reeling, she tore open the envelope.

My own most dearest Tara, I do not know if you will ever receive this. Yet I must write to you, because I miss you more than words can describe. Things have not gone well so far and the only thing that keeps me going is the thought of you and our daughter. I love you, Tara.

This is a dismal hole and I am not at all sure I am on the right trail. Supplies are low and I have developed an irksome cough. The worst thing is the isolation. I have not seen a human face for days. But take no notice. We shall all be rich. One way or another. Isn't it insane how useless gold is, though? You cannot eat it. Out here it doesn't even keep you warm. Why do we worship it? What good is it? One thing, though, I do know. I will come back to you, Tara. In this world, or another. We will never be parted, you and I.

Her eyes were brimming with tears as she finished reading the letter. "Oh, Dan," she sobbed. "Dan."

Through her tears she tried to reason it out; the letter looked months old, but how had it got here? How had Jake Gore got hold of Daniel's watch? And how did Cad Wilson fit in?

Tara vaguely recalled something Jake had said before she killed him. Then it came back to her; his words about killing her as he'd told Cad he would. Could it be that Cad was so insanely jealous of her that she had hired Jake Gore to lure her out here to kill her?

She could hear the dogs snarling. They hadn't been fed for hours. There was some dried moose meat packed among her things, but she was frightened. A terrible gale had started up, and the sound of the wind, the howling of the dogs, and the two dead bodies filled her with foreboding. But she had to feed the dogs. Without them she wouldn't get back to civilization.

She pocketed Daniel's letter, and battled her way out to the sled and unwrapped the meat. She picked up her whip and went over to Jake's mangy malamutes. As she approached they growled at her, so she cracked the whip.

"Down!" she cried as one beast snapped at her ankles. Quickly she unwrapped the meat, and then unharnessed them. She had forgotten the golden rule: each dog had to be fed individually and unharnessed one at a time to eat.

As she returned to her own sled, where the tethered dogs were getting restless, Jake's team, free from their traces, streaked across the snow like a pack of wolves. "Come back!" Tara yelled, but they took no notice. Then she saw what had caused the stampede. The dogs were tearing, biting, ripping Jake's body.

Tara's own team responded by yapping and snapping with excitement, straining at their harnesses in their eagerness to join in. For Tara it had become a hideous nightmare. Her stomach turned over, but fear of what this maddened horde might do next overwhelmed her disgust.

She knew she had little time. If the malamutes turned on her, she was finished. She ran over to Jake's sled and, with shaking hands, untied his rifle from the handlebars. She pushed back the safety catch and, aiming as best she could through the snow the wind hurled against her, pulled the trigger.

She kept firing until the rifle clicked, its magazine empty. She had killed two of the dogs and wounded another. Then, like a grizzly epilogue, two of the survivors launched themselves at the crippled dog and sank their teeth into his body. The third watched for a moment, and then flung himself into the mêlée.

"Oh my God," Tara sobbed, as the frenzied animals fought each other. Their primitive lust to kill didn't last long. The dogs lay strewn around, dead or dying. Jake's pack had destroyed itself.

She dashed to her sled and, without a backward glance, she cracked her whip and urged her team ahead. They pulled the sled willingly. They were hungry, and a ravenous dog made a willing worker.

The swirling snow made visibility bad, and she didn't know in which direction she was going. Although she had no map, she decided she had travelled north. She had to get back to Dawson, which lay to the south. She rifled through her bag and took out the compass, but it was a pitiful aid to navigation.

She continued travelling through the night. Like a phantom team, the dogs pulled through the darkness, and she relied on them to keep travelling along the right track. In her delirious condition she thought, at times, she was lying safely in bed and all this was a dream. Then she would realize where she was. Once Tara screamed so terrifyingly that the dogs turned their heads and stared at her, their eyes puzzled.

"Somebody please help me! Save me!" she yelled dementedly to the empty landscape. "I don't want to die."

Then she saw it. She watched, awestruck, as an indescribable yellow light sprang from the whiteness of the snow to the heavens above. An unearthly golden glow spread across the sky, streamers of brilliant, dazzling colours dancing along the horizon, bathing the sky in a divine firework display.

The lights, vivid reds and yellows and blues, imbued the whole firmament and spread before Tara's hypnotized eyes. After the blackness, the greys, the whites, the monotones, this darting stream of colour was like the promise of another land.

Tara had never seen, but she had heard of the northern lights. Standing there, a lone human figure witnessing the sky on fire, she was enraptured by its beauty and hidden meaning. It was the omen that made all the difference.

"Thank God," Tara sobbed. "Oh, thank God."

Those glorious rays reflecting all the brightness of all the hopes of the Yukon, more dazzling than all the gold in the Klondike, gave her faith as nothing else could have.

It was a sign from heaven. There was hope.

She turned her back on the phenomenon and faced the direction she now knew was south. Although she was consumed by fatigue, she thrust the sled forward, determined to make it to Dawson.

CHAPTER NINE

The woman who staggered, robotlike, into Dawson three days later had no memory of her long, delirious trek. She stumbled down the main street, driven by the inner compulsion that had kept her travelling through the snowy wastes.

Suddenly she stopped. She was holding on to a hitching post, staring blankly at the wooden frontage of the Monte Carlo Saloon.

Dizzily, she realized that before her was the place where Cad Wilson worked. She was the only one who could tell Tara the truth.

She slowly mounted the wooden steps, pushing open the swing

doors of the saloon. With unseeing eyes she walked towards a man behind the bar. "Where is Cad Wilson?" she croaked.

The man raised his eyebrows. Tara's clothes were torn, her hands caked with dried blood, her face weather-beaten, her lips covered with scabs. "Miss Wilson's upstairs."

Clutching the bannister, Tara slowly climbed the stairs. Below, the man stood watching her, uncertain. She made her way down the corridor, looking for Cad in each room in turn, leaving angry whores in her wake. Finally she reached the last door.

Inside was a large and ornately decorated boudoir. Tara floated across a sea of thick carpet towards a chaise longue on which Cad Wilson reclined, dressed in a multicoloured kimono.

Cad stood up. From miles away Tara heard her gasp, "You!"

"He didn't kill me," Tara said.

"I don't know what you're talking about," Cad retorted.

"What happened to my husband?" Tara asked in a low voice.

"Don't tell me you didn't find him, Mrs. Kane."

Tara slapped her across the face. Cad fell back on to the sofa, staring up at Tara.

"You knew Daniel wasn't there. You used his watch to get me out of your way," screamed Tara. "You hired Jake Gore to kill me, didn't you? Only it didn't quite work out the way you planned it, because Jake Gore is dead."

Cad looked at her fearfully. "You're crazy!"

"I killed him!" Tara shrieked. "Now just tell me where my husband is." She grabbed Cad by the shoulders and shook her like a rag doll. "Where is he?" she sobbed.

Cad escaped her grip and ran to the door. "Get out before I have you thrown out."

Tara turned and looked at Cad standing beside the open door. Beyond her, a gaggle of whores crowded the corridor. She started through them, her head ringing. At the top of the stairs she fainted, falling down the entire flight and collapsing in a heap on the saloon floor.

She never heard the uproar. Smith had entered the saloon in time to see Tara crash down the stairs. He dashed to where she lay and carefully turned her over.

"What happened?" he demanded, still kneeling beside Tara.

Cad rushed forward. "Oh, Jeff, the poor woman came to my room raving, and when I told her she was sick she went quite wild, ran out of my room and you saw the rest."

"Mort!" shouted Smith, getting up. "Get some blankets. I'm taking Mrs. Kane home."

The sight of Jefferson Smith walking down Front Street carrying the seemingly lifeless body of a woman wrapped in blankets was unusual even in Dawson. But he ignored the gaping passers-by, mounted the steps, and knocked on Mrs. Miles's front door.

She gasped when she saw Tara limp in his arms.

"Mrs. Kane has collapsed," Smith said quietly. "She's very ill, Mrs. Miles. She needs your help."

Mrs. Miles's mouth was grim. "This way," she said.

They mounted the stairs in silence, Mrs. Miles leading the way to Tara's room. She hovered while Smith gently laid her on the bed. "Now leave my house. I don't want to see you here again."

"Of course," he agreed amiably. On the steps he paused. "Before I go, ma'am, I want to assure you that anything you may require will be at your disposal. I will arrange for the doctor to stop by. If I can be of—"

She slammed the door on him before he had time to finish.

After the doctor had examined the unconscious Tara, his face was grave. The fall down the stairs had been the last straw. She was suffering from exposure. She had bronchitis, which could be turning into pneumonia, and she was half starved.

Day and night Mrs. Miles nursed Tara like her own daughter. She attended her every need, sitting hour after hour by her bedside, watching her toss and turn, delirious with fever.

It was several weeks before the doctor announced that Tara could go downstairs for the first time. Mrs. Miles lit a huge fire in the parlour. There Tara spent the next few days, her mind becoming clearer and her body stronger. Slowly her eyes grew brighter, the scabs cleared from her lips, her skin began to glow once more.

Her gradual improvement was partially due to her decision that the nightmare events at the grave belonged to another world.

Tara wanted to tell Linda Miles what had happened, but she couldn't face the thought of having to admit that she had murdered. The terrible memories began to recede, but each time she dozed, frenzied images haunted her dreams. She often reread Daniel's desperate letter, wondering where he had written it, who he had given it to, where he had gone after sealing it.

One day there was a peremptory knock on the front door. Mrs. Miles was out shopping, having left firm instructions that Tara should stay in the fireside armchair.

The knocking sounded again, hammering urgently. Tara's legs still felt shaky as she opened the front door.

"Hello, Tara," said Sergeant Campbell. He was in uniform, and Tara noticed that he had been given his three stripes back.

"Andrew," Tara held out her hand, then led him into the parlour. "How have you been?"

Campbell seemed ill at ease. "This is official business, Tara."

"What about?"

"An allegation has been made." He paused. "I am following up a report that a man was murdered up north, near Hell's Kitchen. Is there anything *you* want to tell me?" he asked.

"About what?" she mumbled, clenching her hands.

Campbell hesitated. "Tara, did you kill a man?"

"Kill a man," she repeated dully. The nightmare turned into reality again. "Yes," she croaked. "I killed a man."

"Jake Gore?" prompted Campbell.

She was trembling. "I didn't want to . . . He tried to . . ."

"Was it self-defence?" asked Campbell.

Neither of them heard Mrs. Miles come in. "What's going on?" she demanded.

"I'm investigating a killing," said Campbell. "There's a man in town by the name of Arne Gore, who says that Tara killed his brother Jake."

"I don't believe you," exploded Mrs. Miles.

"Gore's threatened to whip up feeling against her and get the whole of Dawson on his side if we don't do our duty as law officers." He turned to Tara. "Did Jake try to assault you? Was he going to kill you?"

"Yes," she screamed, the tears pouring down her face. "Yes!"

"Oh, my dear," said Mrs. Miles, putting her arm around Tara's shoulders. "Why didn't you tell me? Oh you poor thing."

"Tara, you'll have to make a formal statement," said Campbell. He turned to Mrs. Miles. "Please try to understand that I can't afford trouble. I've got to do it by the book. Otherwise the Citizens' Committee or the Miners' Court might take the law into their own hands." Campbell went to the door. "Bring her over to the post as soon as she's fit, and I'll take a deposition."

After he had left, Mrs. Miles led Tara upstairs and helped her into bed. She sat beside her and took her hands. "Why don't you tell me about it?" she said very softly.

Tara looked at her, and then, her voice choked with emotion, her green eyes pools of sadness, told Mrs. Miles the whole story.

CAMPBELL had not been exaggerating when he said that Gore was stirring up bad feeling in Dawson. The next night men carrying flaming torches gathered in front of Mrs. Miles's house, shaking their fists and yelling. Tara couldn't make out what it was they shouted, but it was an ugly sound.

Mrs. Miles came into her room. "Get away from that window," she ordered. "Don't let them see you." For the first time Tara could hear the words the mob were yelling. "Tara Kane, we've come for you. Tara Kane!"

"What do they want from me?" she whispered.

The mob pressed closer to the house. They were being waved on by a tall, lean man with long hair. His blazing brand illuminated sharp features, an ugly snarling mouth. What she could see in the flickering light reminded Tara of the man she could never forget. Jake Gore.

"We're coming in to get you," the man yelled.

Mrs. Miles rushed from the room, Tara following her. The lodgers had gathered in the hallway. They were all armed.

Fists hammered on the front door. "Open up," came a voice. "We want the Kane woman. Orders of the court."

"It's the Miners' Court," Lamore, one of the lodgers, said.

Tara froze. This was the reckoning. As Sergeant Campbell

had predicted, the Miners' Court had decided to settle the matter themselves.

"She's sick," Mrs. Miles told them through the door. "Leave this business to the Mounties."

The only reply she got was a furious pounding, then they heard a window smash upstairs. One of the lodgers ran past Tara. "The first man that tries to come in, we'll blow his head off," he yelled from the first-floor window.

"What are we going to do?" asked Lamore. "They won't give up. They'll burn the house down."

"Linda! Open the door!" Tara said, hardly recognizing her own voice. "There's no other way. They've a right to hear the truth, and I want to tell it to them."

Reluctantly Mrs. Miles unlocked the door. As it opened, Tara saw a three-man deputation standing on the steps, and behind them a sea of torches.

"There she is," yelled the tall man, holding his torch high and pointing at her. "There is the woman who killed my brother."

Tara drew back but one of the three men took her arm. "Where are you taking me?" she asked, looking around for a familiar face, but the lodgers and Mrs. Miles were lost from sight. She was alone.

"Courtroom," grunted the leader, escorting her down the steps.

Tara found herself marching with the three vigilantes. The whole town appeared to have turned out for this grim procession. In the glow of torches she caught glimpses of hard faces, set grimly. Leading the way, his blazing brand held aloft, ran Jake Gore's brother.

Halfway down Front Street, the Reverend Charles Bowers suddenly appeared at Tara's elbow. Under his black coat a gun belt was visible. It was the first time Tara had seen him since Skagway.

"Keep your powder dry," he whispered urgently. "Plead 'not guilty', whatever they say, see?"

He merged back into the throng marching behind them. The procession halted on the steps of the Eldorado Saloon.

"Here she is," Arne Gore yelled. "Why don't we get a rope now and save a lot of time?"

The vigilante leader had his finger on the trigger of the rifle.

"Stand aside, Gore," he commanded. "This is all going to be done according to miners' law."

Gore wavered for a moment, then grudgingly stood aside, and the throng rushed forward, propelling Tara through the doors.

Inside, the saloon had been transformed into a crude courtroom. A table had been dragged in front of the bar; opposite it, on the dance floor, was another table; to its right, a lone chair. At the back, rows of chairs lined the walls. Now people stampeded wildly, pushing each other out of the way to get a good seat.

The vigilantes marched Tara to the vacant chair. "Sit there," ordered the leader.

Tara looked around. Cad Wilson, dressed in a magnificent silk dress, was in the front row, sitting between the fat one-eyed Grizzly Bear and Diamond-Tooth Gertie, one of Dawson's toughest saloon queens, whose vixenish grin bared an enormous diamond fixed between her two front teeth.

Tara clenched her hands, willing herself to keep calm. She couldn't believe that this was happening to her, that she was actually on trial for her life in this parody of a court of law.

A white-haired man appeared at the table in front of the bar and held up his hands. "Quiet!" he yelled. "Silence in court."

The buzz of conversation ebbed. Through the swing doors a man entered in a wheelchair. Gold-rimmed glasses perched on his nose, his skin was grey and pasty, his thin lips tinged with blue.

Slowly he manoeuvred the wheelchair between the bar and table, facing the crowd. His piercing eyes fixed unblinkingly on Tara while the white-haired man declaimed, "This court's now in session. The Honourable Judge Elmer Rickless presiding."

"Court's ready," the judge said, rapping for order with a hammer. "Where's the jury?"

Twelve men immediately stood up and trooped behind the bar. They sat down on high stools, facing the saloon. They looked almost identical, tough, villainous, shifty.

The judge nodded at the white-haired man, who appeared to act as court usher. "O.K.," he said. "Let's start. Who's prosecuting, and what's the charge?"

Arne Gore was on his feet. "I am, your honour, and the charge against this woman is murder." He pointed at Tara. "She killed my brother."

"O.K." The judge nodded. "What's your name?" he wheezed, staring at Tara.

"Kane. Mrs. Tara Kane."

"Are you pleading guilty or not guilty?"

"Not guilty," replied Tara quietly.

"You got a defence counsel?"

"I'll defend myself."

"O.K. It's your neck. So, Mr. Prosecutor. Tell us how she killed your brother."

"Your honour," Gore said, "she hired Jake up in Tagish country as a guide. Then out on the trail she shot him for his money. She's a hustler down on her luck. Jake had sixty dollars and three ounces of gold dust."

"Did you witness the murder?" the judge asked.

"No, your honour."

"Then how do you know she did it?" he queried.

Arne Gore grinned. "Miss Cad Wilson will testify to that."

The judge opened a book he had brought into court with him. He began thumbing the pages, then he looked up. "Without a body you don't have a murder. So who's seen the body?"

"I have," said Gore. "I went looking for my brother, and I found what was left of him. She'd set the dogs on him." There was a rustle in the saloon, and Tara could feel the hostility.

"O.K.," said Judge Rickless. "Let's hear from your witness."

Gore looked over to the spectators. "I call Miss Cad Wilson."

"Hold it!" yelled the judge, turning to the usher. "Where's the witness stand? A courtroom's gotta have a witness stand."

The usher dragged a wooden crate from behind the bar and put it in the middle of the floor. "How's that?" He beamed.

"Better," growled the judge. "Makes it decent and formal. O.K., Miss Wilson. You take the stand."

"Thank you, Judge." As she stepped on the crate she looked elegant, glamorous, and completely at ease.

"You swear to tell the truth, the whole truth, and nothing but the truth so help you God?" intoned the usher.

"On a stack of Bibles, Judge," Cad demurely agreed.

"Just tell 'em what you know," urged Gore.

Cad moistened her lips and took a deep breath. "She's a fortune hunter. She heard that Jake had struck it rich, and she asked me how to locate him. Later on I heard that she and a friend set off for Jake's camp. When she returned to Dawson she told me she'd killed Jake Gore. Then she threatened me, saying that I'd be the next person she'd kill."

"Hmm," said the judge. He looked across at Tara. "You want to ask her something?"

Tara stared at Cad, horrified. "She's a liar. There's no point in my asking her anything."

"Gentlemen, I appeal to you." Cad cried angrily. "Ain't a lady entitled to some protection from that murderess?"

The judge banged for order with his hammer. "I can't have witnesses yelling like that. You are excused, Miss Wilson."

Cad returned to her seat.

"Mrs. Kane, take the stand," ordered the judge. Tara sat paralyzed with fear. As she looked around, not one single face in this mob seemed remotely sympathetic. There was no sign of a scarlet tunic. Even Bowers had forsaken her. It was up to her to win over this kangaroo court, and her only defence was that she was the one person who knew the whole truth.

Tara stood and slowly climbed onto the crate vacated by Cad Wilson. In a low voice she repeated the promise to tell the truth.

"So what happened?" asked Judge Rickless.

"I killed Jake Gore, but I had to kill him because otherwise he would have killed me."

"Are you saying it was self-defence?"

Tara nodded. Cad Wilson emitted a high, sneering laugh.

"O.K.," said the judge. "If a woman says she killed a man in self-defence, that makes it justifiable homicide," he told the jury. "But she's got to prove it. Explain to the court, Mrs. Kane."

Tara swallowed and, white-faced, her voice shaking, she told the whole terrible story. At the end tears were streaming down her cheeks. She looked up, and for the first time noticed Jefferson Smith standing to the side of the crowded room. He was watching her closely and there was nothing mocking in his expression.

Tara concluded in a trembling voice. "I didn't even know he had any gold. The dogs tore his body to pieces. Do you think I'll ever forgive myself for taking a human life? Do you think I'll ever be able to wipe from my memory what I've been through? But Jake Gore had taken many lives and he would have taken mine."

Tara pointed at Cad Wilson. "That woman planned it. She hired Jake Gore to kill me. His only mistake was that he tried to assault me first."

"She's lying," screamed Cad.

"Order, order," hammered the judge. His bleary eyes blinked at Gore. "Prosecution wants to cross-examine the accused?"

Arne Gore smiled coldly. "Hell no, judge," he said. "She don't even deny she killed Jake. I say she's a murderess and I want justice for my brother's death. I went to the Mounties, and you can see what they did about it. They couldn't care less if a Yank gets killed. It's your duty as true Americans to see that I get it. I say we should hang Tara Kane!"

"O.K., Gore. You've made your point," the judge intervened. He paused as footsteps echoed around the silent saloon. Jefferson Smith had come forward and stood near the front row of tables, his arms folded.

Judge Rickless cleared his throat. "Now there's two sides to every story. The accused here says Jake assaulted her and she shot him. Does her credit. What kind of woman is it who lets a man do that? Arne Gore says it was robbery and murder, and she says it was self-defence. Now it's up to you jurors to say who's telling the truth. Go away now and consider your verdict. Court's recessed."

The men behind the bar didn't bother to move. One of them, in a tartan shirt, stood up. Tara got the impression that they hadn't even consulted each other.

"O.K., Judge," he said. "We're decided."

"So what's the verdict?" asked Judge Rickless.

"Not guilty."

There was pandemonium in the saloon. Many people applauded, others booed. Tara sat slumped, thanking God that they had believed her. Perhaps there was such a thing as divine justice.

94

An aromatic perfume pervaded the air. Glancing up, Tara saw Cad Wilson standing in front of her. "You'd better get out of town," warned Cad. "Fast."

"You're late for work, Cad," interrupted a cool voice. Smith had appeared by her side. "Get going."

Cad glared at Tara, her mouth curling with contempt, then sauntered off.

"Drinks on the house," shouted Smith. He walked over to the bar, where the jurors were standing in a group. "Gentlemen," he declared, "you've served the town well." They laughed as Smith poured champagne and raised his glass with them. Suddenly the Eldorado Saloon was its old self again, the piano tinkling away, the faro wheels clicking, people laughing and shouting.

Tara was exhausted and yearned for the peace of her own room. She started edging through the celebrating crowd when, unexpectedly, she came face to face with Arne Gore. A hush descended over the festivities, and Tara shrank back from the venom in his eyes.

"You!" spat Gore. "You're dead."

"That's enough, friend," intervened Smith. He reached out and grabbed Gore by the collar, pulling his face close to his. In various corners of the saloon armed men, who were Smith's shadows wherever he went, began to move forward. "You get out of here and keep walking. Don't come back." He hurled Gore against a nearby table.

Gore tottered, his eyes shifting uneasily. Then he turned and slunk towards the doors of the saloon.

"Mr. Gore," Smith called out. "You forgot something." His eyes had become chips of ice. "You forgot to apologize to the lady."

A nerve twitched in Gore's face as Smith eyed him lethally. "I'm sorry," Gore said through gritted teeth. Without another word he turned and walked out.

"I haven't had the chance to congratulate you, Tara," drawled Smith. "You had every man in the room on your side."

"I only told the truth," she said quietly.

"I know. And it won you the day, as it should have. Now I'll escort you home." He took her arm and propelled her through the saloon.

They walked in silence until they reached Mrs. Miles's house.

On the steps he faced her. "Tara, can't we at least be friendly?"

"I don't think we've enough in common even for that."

She closed the door, but Smith did not move for a long time. He stood, staring after her. Then, slowly, he made his way into the dark town. There was a smile on his face.

CHAPTER TEN

The next morning Tara entered Inspector Constantine's office. If she had expected sympathy for her ordeal, he quickly disillusioned her.

"I was hoping you'd have quit looking for your husband," he said. "You might not be so lucky next time."

"So you would have let me hang?" Tara asked.

"You weren't in any danger," he said frostily. "It was a carnival, and you took the starring role."

"What on earth are you talking about?"

"Nothing was going to happen to you. It was all staged."

"Staged? By whom?" asked Tara incredulously.

"The man who rigged the jury. Your protector, Soapy Smith."

"I don't believe you," gasped Tara.

"Please yourself," Constantine shrugged. "They got well paid, so I understand."

"No," breathed Tara. "That isn't so. That wasn't why."

"Oh no?" He smiled coldly. "They were on the rampage. They wanted blood. So why the change of heart to let you off so easily then? You're lucky you got that sort of friend."

Tara winced. "I . . . I didn't know," she said quietly.

"Mrs. Kane, I want you out of Dawson. Out of the Yukon. Since you've been here you've been nothing but trouble, and I don't need it or want it. And remember, your benefactor may not always be around."

"Damn him!" Tara said fervently and stormed out. She marched to the Monte Carlo, where the bartender told her Smith was in his office in the Regina Café. She strode through the town and into the Regina. The two men behind the desk were hardly hotel managers. Both wore guns. "I'm looking for Mr. Smith," Tara said.

"Sure, Mrs. Kane," said one. "I'll take you up." She followed the man up a staircase. He stuck his head in a door and said, "Mrs. Kane, boss."

Tara marched into the room. Smith rose from behind his desk, flashing her a welcoming smile. "Tara, my dear," he said, delighted to see her. "Please come in."

He pushed an ornate chair forward for her. The office was certainly not the sort Tara expected a racketeer to have. On one wall was a framed map of Alaska and a portrait of President McKinley. In a corner, on a flagstaff, was the Stars and Stripes.

Tara sat stiffly, but before she could say anything, Smith waved a hand. "How do you like my office?"

"I didn't come to see your office," she said coldly. "I've come to tell you I think you're contemptible. You think you can bribe and corrupt, buy anything and anyone with money. Even your kangaroo courts."

He reached into a bottom drawer, brought out a bottle of brandy and two cut-crystal glasses. He poured two and pushed one across to Tara.

"Tara," he said gently, "I didn't fix that trial. Cad Wilson did. She bribed the jury to find you guilty. So I bribed those twelve men not to let themselves be bribed. That pretty neck of yours deserves a better fate. As for Cad, she's leaving Dawson."

He took a drink and set the glass down. "Truth is you handled it beautifully. I'm proud of you. You didn't need anybody's help."

Tara glared at him, hating him and yet believing him.

"Tara, I've been thinking, you got guts. No screams, no hysterics. A mighty proud lady. Only one trouble. You don't know how to look after yourself."

"You've no need to worry about me, Mr. Smith."

"But I do," he said gently, sipping his brandy. "If I'm not around you . . . you get into big trouble. Figure out if you can afford it."

"Afford what?"

"To be without me," he said simply. He lit a cheroot.

"You mean I need a protector," Tara suggested.

He didn't rise to that. "I have plans, Tara. Big plans."

"More saloons, bigger and better rackets?"

Smith grinned. "I'm not interested in penny stakes, Tara. I'm talking about politics. The railroad that's being built from Skagway to the Yukon. The future of Alaska. I'm returning to Skagway. I'm going to put that little place on the map in a big way. It needs me, and I need a first lady . . . Governor of Alaska." His eyes were lost in his own vision. "Sure, it sounds crazy, but a man can do anything he sets his mind to, provided he's got the right woman beside him."

"Alaska a state?" she asked, amused.

"I'm going to add that star to the flag," promised Smith. He raised his glass. "Here's to great days," he proposed.

She hesitated. There was a plea in his eyes. She picked up her glass. "To great days," she toasted.

"So," went on Smith, as if it had all been decided. "I want you to come to Skagway with me. How about it?"

She looked him straight in the eyes. "All right. I'll come to Skagway if you'll help me to find Daniel."

He threw back his head and laughed. "I talk about opening up the world, and you just talk about him. Now listen. I'll do anything for you, Tara, but that's one job you got to do on your own."

He downed his drink, his eyes never leaving her face. "Well," he said. "Are you coming to Skagway with me?"

"No," replied Tara.

"I play long odds," he said.

"There are no odds, Mr. Smith."

He grinned. "I'm a born gambler, Tara. And I never lose."

So it was that just when Dawson could boast two banks, two newspapers, and five churches, as well as the biggest saloon district outside the Barbary Coast, Jefferson Randolph Smith decided to sell out.

Tara heard people say that Smith couldn't have chosen a better time to depart. His rich pickings were over. The railroad from the coast was becoming a reality. Slowly, mile by mile, it was going to forge northward, and its arrival would mean a different Dawson, a civilized Canadian city where Smith would find his buccaneering more restricted, fast communication curtailing his scope.

Also any move to make Alaska a state would have to start at Skagway, where the Stars and Stripes already flew. And it was there that Soapy Smith was now heading.

MEANWHILE Tara borrowed a horse and rode out to the creek land of the Klondike, Indian, and McQuesten rivers to look for Daniel.

The sheer effort of scouring eight hundred square miles of gold claims was daunting. In whatever direction Tara looked, tents dotted the landscape, fires burned to thaw out the ground, and men hacked at the frozen earth and streams so that they could pan the gravel. Tara found something eerie in these miles of creek land—the will-o'-the-wisp fires burning day and night, the men silently looking, searching, panning, the remoteness of it all.

Some of the friendlier sourdoughs talked of the gold lore: how gold water had its own flavour, how you had to stay on the right side of the Yukon, no good going upriver and looking for gold where the moose roamed. Trees had to lean the right way, they said—trees at a wrong angle meant no gold.

For days Tara rode through the claims, asking if anyone had seen or heard of Daniel Kane. But most men she spoke to either eyed her suspiciously or shook their heads.

It's hopeless, she thought, as she paused at the foot of Cheecha-koo Hill, by a tree on which had been hammered a primitively carved notice:

> TO WHOM IT MAY CONCERN!
> I do, this day, locate and claim, by
> right of discovery, five hundred feet,
> running upstream from this notice.
> Located this 17th day of August 1896.
>
> G. W. Carmack

So this is where it all began, she thought. On this spot, less than two years ago, Carmack and his partners had found the nugget that started the gold rush.

Tara returned to Dawson, despondent. She returned the horse to the livery stables. As she began trudging back to Mrs. Miles's house, a sign near the barbershop caught her eye. PHOTOGRAPHS! it proclaimed. ALASKA VIEWS. PORTRAITS. ERNST HART.

Her heart began to pound. So much had happened since she had last seen her friend. She rang the bell and went inside. Hart emerged from behind a curtain. "My dearest Tara." He held her close. "I only just returned to Dawson and heard what terrible things you have been through. I blame myself, I should never have let you go off alone with that man Jake."

"Dear Ernst," she said softly, "it's over. None of it matters now. The important thing is that Daniel is still alive."

"Of that you're sure?" he asked.

"Of course, Ernst. I know he is. I don't quite know where to go from here, but I'll find him."

"Of course you will," he agreed, patting her hand. "By the way, I've finished processing my photographs of my trip around the territory. Please, will you look at them?"

As Hart spread each print in front of her, it was as if Tara were looking at the whole of the gold rush unfolding in one long panorama. He had effectively recorded the vast and sweeping views as well as the small and personal. There were photographs of a weary gold prospector who had fallen asleep as he panned, a man gnawing at a frozen slab of bread, a good-time girl brazenly lifting her skirt to show her legs. Hart, Tara realized, was a sensitive artist, using his photographic plates like a canvas.

"I've never seen pictures like these. They're superb, truly marvellous. What are you going to do with them?" she asked.

"Take them back to the States, show them in exhibitions. A pictorial history of the gold rush."

Hart had stacks more photographs. She saw his views of prospectors, of Mounties, of Indian guides, of snow-covered shacks, of lonely graves . . . . Tara stopped. She stared at a photograph in her hand. "Where did you take this?" she asked very quietly.

"Oh, that one, at Sheep Camp, on the Chilkoot Pass. Why?"

"That man," she said, her hand shaking.

"What about him?" He looked at the picture again. The man was in front of a tent, perched on a crate, his right leg stiffly extended. He was holding a crude crutch. A dog team sat beside him.

100

"That's Daniel," she exclaimed. "I'm sure it's Daniel. When did you take this?"

"A few weeks ago. At the end of January. I did not take his name. I photographed him because I thought he looked like a man marooned. He'd broken his ankle. He couldn't continue up the Chilkoot until the bone had set. I felt sorry for him. The gold rush was passing him by."

"Ernst, he must be there now." Her eyes were shining with excitement. This was Daniel, no doubt about it. His eyes, his mouth. Despite the straggly beard, she could tell it was her husband. "I have to get to Sheep Camp as quickly as possible." She took Ernst's hand. "You've found him," she said, her eyes filling with tears of happiness. "You've found him, alive."

Tara told Mrs. Miles her plans the following morning. "You won't be coming back, then," Mrs. Miles said sadly.

"No," Tara said. "It's goodbye to Dawson. There's nothing more for me here. Daniel's at Sheep Camp, and the thought of being with him again is all that's kept me going all these months. And your kindness, Linda. Without you I don't know what would have happened to me."

"You would have survived," said Mrs. Miles. "I didn't think that when I first saw you, but now I don't worry."

"I wish I felt half as confident," said Tara.

"You know, over the past few months I've seen you gradually turn into one of us," Mrs. Miles reflected. "You belong now. I've watched you deal with the hardships of this place, and yet you've remained very much a woman."

"Thank you," Tara said as Mrs. Miles fussed over the coffeepot, embarrassed by what she had said.

Later that day Mrs. Miles went into Tara's bedroom and found her poring over a map Hart had given her. "How do you plan on getting to Sheep Camp?" Mrs. Miles asked.

"I'll take a dog team and make my way down to the lakes and through the Chilkoot Pass. Sheep Camp is a few miles on the other side, in Alaska."

"But you should wait till the river is thawed," cautioned Mrs. Miles. "There'll be dozens of prospectors leaving Dawson then."

101

"*Wait!*" exclaimed Tara. "*You* wouldn't would you?"

"No, I suppose not." Mrs. Miles knew that once Tara had made up her mind, it was pointless to argue. "All right. I'll go over to Mr. Brock's store and talk about getting your supplies at cost."

Before she departed, Tara went to say goodbye to Sergeant Campbell. Early the next morning, when she and Mrs. Miles arrived at the store, the sled and team Tara had hired from the Bartletts waited, piled high with equipment and provisions. Tara tucked in her sleeping bag filled with her belongings, and then turned to Mrs. Miles.

"Linda, you've got me enough stuff to last a lifetime. How can I begin to thank you?"

"Don't begin," Mrs. Miles said, tears in her eyes. They embraced. "Godspeed, travel safely."

She pressed Tara's hand reassuringly. Tara walked to her sled and picked up the whip. She turned and waved to Mrs. Miles, at the same time shouting, "Mush!" The dogs moved off.

CHAPTER ELEVEN

Sheep Camp—so named because, it was said, hunters had once camped there seeking mountain sheep—lay in a deep basin scooped out of the surrounding mountains, the last staging point beyond Dyea, and four miles south of the treacherous Chilkoot.

The White Pass had been terrible, but the Chilkoot had a cold, fearful majesty all of its own. An endless line of men climbed its slippery slope, draping the steep incline to the summit of the mountain like a human garland. They were going north, to the destiny they were all dreaming of, the gold fields of Dawson, Eldorado, Bonanza. Tara's route was in the opposite direction, south over the pass, and down to the outpost they called Stone House. Near there was the spot Hart had photographed Daniel.

A thick blanket of heavy snow blinded Tara as she slipped and slithered down the steep gradient. It became impossible to guide the dog team, and she had had to leave the animals to make their own way. At times she fell on her hands and knees but, finally,

102

exhausted and freezing cold, she reached the settlement at the foot of the hill. Although she was only a few miles from Sheep Camp, the threatening sky told her that she couldn't go on. She found a protected spot, made sure the dogs were safely fastened, then rigged up the tent and crawled inside.

When the blizzard came it charged with the ferocity of a tornado. The wind howled, gusts tore at the guy ropes and pummelled the canvas. After what seemed like hours, the howling eased. In the sudden quiet she thought she heard one or two distant rumblings that sounded like faraway artillery fire, a ghostly bombardment.

When she emerged from the tent the next morning it was curiously calm. The sky was clear, and there was a hint of sunshine. Hastily she fed the dogs, dug out the sled, and loaded up her tent and supplies.

The going was slow, the new snow so soft that the dogs and the sled sank into it. After an hour, in which she only covered a few hundred yards, she heard the same dull rumblings as the night before. This time they seemed louder, threateningly sinister. She urged on her dogs.

Gradually, spreading a few miles in front of her, was the sprawling sea of tents and shacks that was Sheep Camp. Hart had told her the place was a madhouse of nearly fifteen hundred people. On the far side, on the slopes leading down to it, were other dwellings. That was where Hart had photographed Daniel.

Once more the ominous rumbling echoed in the muffled stillness.

She entered Sheep Camp, driving her dogs along the slushy camp road leading up to the slope a mile away where she would find him.

"Thank God," she whispered, eyes riveted on the mountainside.

Then it happened. She could feel the tremors under her as the rumbling thunder crescendoed in a tremendous roar. Before Tara's disbelieving eyes the top of the mountain she was heading towards slid down and enveloped everything in its path—huts, tents, the specks of life on the slope. Tara screamed as she saw the people sucked under the white tide. The avalanche roared on, blanketing the slope encampment under thirty feet of snow and ice—crushing, suffocating those entombed under its weight. It was April 3, 1898, the date of one of Alaska's worst disasters, when sixty-three persons died in an avalanche on the Chilkoot trail.

In the eerie silence that followed Tara stood numb with horror. All over Sheep Camp people came rushing out of shacks, saloons, and shabby tents. They stood gaping at the awful spectacle of the avalanche's destruction. Then they rushed towards the slope.

Daniel was the only thought that pounded through Tara's head. I've got to get to him. I must get him out before it's too late. She joined with the crowd, which was stampeding forward wildly, carrying spades and pickaxes. By the time she got to the slope people were already digging frantically. They were standing on tons of snow, sinking into it, with who knew how many people buried beneath it, some dead, some slowly suffocating.

Tara grabbed a gold pan and, almost possessed, began digging at the frozen layers. They could hear a man's voice coming from the depths. They all stopped and listened, then began attacking the snow with renewed vigour. When, finally, they lifted him out they were too late.

More corpses were gradually dug out and laid in long, straight lines. Tara counted the bodies, studying each face. None was Daniel's. She lost count of the number of eyelids she closed, the frozen faces she covered with blankets. She tried group after group of rescuers, who were now digging by the light of hurricane lamps. "Has anyone come across Daniel Kane?" she demanded. They were too busy to answer. "Oh, please," Tara cried, tears streaming down her face. "Somebody help me find my husband!"

Then a hand shook her. "You!" barked a gruff voice. "We need you." A black-bearded man yanked her to her feet. "There's a woman we just dug out over there about to give birth. Get her down to Sheep Camp before it's too late."

"I'm not leaving until I find my husband!" Tara shouted. "Get somebody else. Why doesn't her husband look after her?"

"He's down there," the man said, pointing at the snow, "just the same as yours is." Unexpectedly he put his arm around her. "I know what you're going through, lass. We'll try to find your husband. You can help her. Come on."

Tara followed him. The woman, about seventeen or eighteen, had been covered with a fur pelt, but Tara could clearly see the outline of her swollen belly. She was pale, with blue-tinged skin stretched over prominent cheekbones. She gave a cry of pain and clutched Tara's hand. "My baby," she whimpered, "my baby."

Compassion flooded through Tara. Amid so much death, this woman was going to give life.

Tara wearily called to three bystanders to strap the woman onto a sled. She held the woman's hand as the three men gingerly negotiated the slippery descent to Sheep Camp. There they took the woman to a tent and lifted her onto a pallet.

Tara turned to the men. "I need plenty of hot water. Get me a stove, pans, extra blankets, a sharp knife. And I'll want a crate or a drawer, something to put the baby in."

Then she knelt down by the woman. "Everything will be all right," she said, trying to sound reassuring.

The woman opened her eyes. "My husband," she whispered.

"They're looking for him, don't worry," Tara said. "What's your name?"

"Suzanna Lacey. The baby isn't due for another two weeks. We thought we could make it to Dawson. Then the avalanche." Suzanna groaned. "I'm going to die."

"That's nonsense. You're going to have a beautiful baby, and I'm going to help you."

Suzanna looked beseechingly at Tara. "Promise me," she said, "until they find John, promise me you'll take care of the child."

"I promise."

"Thank you," sighed Suzanna. "I'm not worried anymore."

The men returned with the items Tara had requested. She began melting snow on the stove, all the while trying to remember her little practical knowledge of childbirth.

Suzanna's labour pains had started again, and Tara soothed her as she tossed and turned. Waiting for a new life to make its appearance, Tara remembered that first glorious moment when they had put Gabrielle in her arms. The way Daniel had smiled at both of them—the happiest moment in her life.

"Stay with me," sobbed Suzanna.

"Don't worry, I'm not going to leave you," Tara said quietly.

The pains were coming faster now. Suzanna gave an agonized cry. "Try to help by pushing, Suzanna," Tara said. "It's coming, push harder."

Very quickly the child was delivered. "It's a boy," Tara announced, bundling the baby in a blanket.

"Look," she said, placing the infant in his mother's arms, "hold your son. Isn't he perfect?"

Suzanna smiled weakly as she cradled the child, but she was too exhausted to speak. Suddenly she began to haemorrhage. Tara tried to staunch the flow, but it was hopeless. She made the woman as comfortable as possible, willing herself to believe that the inevitable would not happen.

"Please," came a whisper from Suzanna. "Love him for me."

Tara nodded, too full of emotion to speak. She bent closer to hear what Suzanna was trying to say. It sounded like "John". "Always," she whispered. "Always keep him, no one else."

"Please don't die," pleaded Tara, clutching Suzanna's hand. But Suzanna's head fell to one side. As Tara stared down at her she stopped breathing.

A terrible fatigue swept through Tara, making it impossible to keep her eyes open. She collapsed on the floor.

She was brought back to consciousness by someone roughly shaking her shoulder. The black-bearded man and another man peered down at her. "What happened?" the bearded man asked.

"I did everything I could," Tara whimpered, "but she's dead."

"What about the baby?"

"A boy. Have you found the father?"

"That's what we came to tell you," the other man said. "We found him, close to where we dug her out. He's dead. Crushed by the snow."

She looked at him, her unspoken question evident. "No," he said. "There's no news of your husband." Then he told her her sled had apparently been stolen.

Tara got up and went over to the baby. "Don't worry, John," she said. "You'll be safe. I promised your mother."

Perhaps this was what fate had intended all along. She had been robbed of her own child; she had failed to find Daniel. Everything seemed to have been taken from her. Until now.

She picked up the baby and rocked it. "We've got one another," she told him. "We need one another."

THE RESCUE OPERATION continued. Silently people from Sheep Camp waited, although every hour that passed lessened the chances of anyone being brought out alive. There was still no news of Daniel. In the tent Tara cradled the baby. He was asleep, but soon he would need milk and she had none to give him. She was determined about one thing: little John was going to be a survivor. Not just because of a promise she had given a dying woman, but because she had been given a second chance, someone to love.

For the first three days she boiled snow, added sugar, let it cool, then soaked a piece of linen in the liquid. John suckled hungrily at the syrupy cloth. But milk was essential. With the baby bundled up in blankets inside her parka, Tara ventured out to find some.

The catastrophe overshadowed the entire camp. People stood in groups, talking in subdued tones. Some of them were gathered around a log cabin, staring at a newly painted sign nailed to the door. It read, simply, CORONER. She had not realized that officials from Skagway were already in Sheep Camp.

Tara entered the cabin. Inside was a trestle table, on which lay a thick ledger, an inkwell, and a stack of papers. Behind the table sat Soapy Smith.

"Tara!" he gasped. Then he glanced down and saw John Lacey's head protruding from her coat. "Who is that?"

"That's no concern of yours," she replied. "I'll come back when the coroner is here."

"But he is, Tara." He stood and bowed. "I'm sort of acting coroner from Skagway for the Chilkoot division of the territory."

"Self-appointed, I suppose?"

"Of course. Somebody had to take on the task of safeguarding the victims' valuables until we locate the next of kin. But, Tara, I want to hear about you. What happened? And who is that?" He peered down at the top of the baby's head. "Sit down and tell me all about it."

Tara sank into a chair. "His name is John Lacey. His father was killed in the avalanche. His mother was dug out, and I delivered the baby, but she died." She stopped, then stared Smith straight in the eye. "He needs milk, and he needs it quickly. He won't survive if he doesn't get some soon."

Smith contemplated her. "Fortunately, in my official capacity, I'm not only the coroner but also registrar of births and deaths." He opened a ledger and wrote in it, and then on a form.

"Do you have to do that now?" Tara sighed.

"It won't take a minute," he said smoothly. "This makes him legal." He handed Tara the form.

She stared at the printed birth certificate. The name of the child was listed as John Jefferson Randolph Lacey.

"What are these names, 'Jefferson Randolph'?" asked Tara.

"Well, after all, I am his godfather," Smith said. Tara stared at him, amazed that he was serious. "It's quite customary for a child to have a godfather, you know. And it's a proud Southern name. My father was an officer in the Confederate Army."

"A godfather," Tara pointed out, "looks after his godchild's spiritual and moral welfare. I wouldn't have thought you were much up to that kind of responsibility."

Smith grinned. "Maybe that'll be your department. But I've got a few talents he'll find useful, believe me."

Tara wished that she could tell him that neither she nor the baby needed his help. But it wouldn't be true. She felt relieved that some of the responsibility for John's survival was being shared, even if it was with Soapy Smith.

Back in the tent, she wondered if she was deluding herself. Despite misgivings, she was placing a certain amount of faith in Smith's ability to help her. The baby's hungry crying could no longer be placated by her soothing voice and comforting arms.

The flap of the tent was pulled aside, and Smith stood there holding a piece of rope. On the other end of the line was a goat. "Here's the milk."

"How do I get it?" Tara asked, eyeing the animal timidly.

"You milk the goat," Smith replied. "How else?" He tied the animal to a peg outside the tent.

"Here," Tara said, handing him John. "Hold him firm."

Smith took the baby somewhat gingerly and then sat down, keeping a very straight face, while Tara gathered up a crate and saucepan and went outside. As best she could she emulated the pastoral paintings she had seen of rosy-faced milkmaids. She put her hands on the udders and pulled. When, half an hour later, she had managed to fill the saucepan full of milk, she felt triumphant.

Smith picked up his hat. "I'll be back, my dear," he said.

Tara began to feed the baby. "Thank you, Jeff, for the goat."

He stopped at the tent doorway. It was the first time she had ever thanked him for anything, and the first time she had used his name. But if he felt a triumph, he showed no sign. Instead he went over to her, knelt down beside her, and said, very gently, "Tara, somebody has to look after you."

"I'll be all right."

"You can't bring up an infant in this shanty-town." He paused. "I want to get you both to Skagway. To make sure you've got a decent roof over your heads, to make sure you get what you need." He knelt closer. "I beg you," he said.

"Why, Jeff? You don't need us. You've got money, power. Why do you want to do this?"

"I think you know, Tara." The rest remained unsaid.

"Are you going on with the search for Daniel?" he asked after a little while. "Because I don't think there's any point. The bodies still out there are twenty feet down. Many won't be found until the thaw."

She looked at him, her eyes filling with tears. "I don't even know if he's among those still buried on that slope, or if he'd left here before it happened."

He put his arms around her. "In any case, Tara, you and the baby can't stay here any longer. You must come with me."

Tara did not resist the comforting warmth of his body. He held her tight, and she felt him stroke her hair, then his lips brushed against her cheeks. He was more comforting, more kind, more reassuring than she would have thought possible. She and John would have to go with Jefferson Smith. Fate had decided for her.

And she found that now she allowed herself to wonder about a possibility, the shadow of which she had always before shut away. Supposing Daniel was dead? Had she been sentenced to a grey future without her husband's love?

CHAPTER TWELVE

When Tara had arrived in Skagway in 1897 Smith had been the unchallenged town boss. But during the first three months of 1898 industry and commerce began to make their mark, encouraged by the town's designation as the starting point for the forth-coming rail link with Whitehorse, in the Yukon.

With the completion of the first stage of the track future prospectors would be able to reach the summit of the White Pass by train. So thousands of sourdoughs thronged the trail from Dyea to Skagway, to prepare for their journey to Dawson via this easier route. The sidewalks teemed with prospectors, trappers, and traders, and, for the first time in the Yukon, a new class—businessmen, with city clothes peeping out of their parkas, who were reaping healthy profits from the spending power of lucky strikers.

Since Tara had been away, the amenities of Skagway had improved to keep up with its growth. The town's residents were now provided with better entertainment, better hotels. And, as the respectable element prospered, they became increasingly critical of the likes of Soapy Smith and his men.

It had taken Smith and Tara three days to reach Skagway from Sheep Camp. Tara had sat in the sled driven by Smith, young John warmly wrapped up in her arms. As they neared the end of their journey Smith was in high spirits. But if he had expected a welcoming committee, he was in for a shock. During his absence at Sheep Camp some of the townsfolk had decided it was time to clean up the place. They had printed a notice:

WARNING

All con men and other objectionable characters are notified to leave Skagway immediately. Failure to comply with this warning will be met by prompt action.

As Smith stood in front of the first poster he came across, there was the sound of hoofs from behind them, and Tara turned to see a man galloping towards them. "Hi, boss," the Reverend Charles Bowers called out. "And good day to you, Mrs. Kane," he said, eyeing her and the baby with a look of surprise. "The boys will be glad to know you're back in town."

"Where's Colson?" Smith asked without ceremony.

Tara remembered the U.S. Marshal, who had led the lynch party and who was jokingly referred to as Skagway's law.

Bowers leaned forward. "He's dead. He got shot at Fay's place."

"What happened?" Smith asked.

"Well, boss, a guy called McGrath walked into the saloon. Put down a bill for a drink, and Fay wouldn't give him change."

"So?" Smith shrugged. "What's wrong with that? Local custom, ain't it?"

"Yeah. But McGrath started a ruckus, and Colson rushed in. Fay kind of lost his head and Colson got his."

"Ah, well," Smith sighed, "guess we'd better get ourselves a new marshal.

"Sure, boss." Bowers galloped off.

"You see what happens when I turn my back?" remarked Smith.

"The baby and I need a place to stay," Tara said coldly, ignoring this latest evidence of Smith's racketeering.

"Sure," he agreed. "Got to get the important things done first."

Half an hour later Smith had installed Tara in a log cabin. It was neatly furnished: bright Indian rugs covered the rough floorboards, there were curtains at the windows, a roomy wooden bed, and a cooking range. To Tara it was a small palace.

"Whose is this?" she asked, looking around.

"Yours," Smith said. "My men will bring you wood, food, and supplies, and I'll get a basket for John." Smith paused. "This is O.K. for you, Tara, isn't it?"

"It's the nicest place I've been," she smiled. "Thank you."

"I've got things to do," he said, pulling on his gloves. "You'll be safe here, Tara. I promise." Then he was gone.

A couple of hours later Smith's men arrived with food, cooking utensils, kerosene lamps, linen, and every household item she

111

could possibly want. As she was putting it all away she heard someone hammering outside the cabin. A poster had been nailed to the cabin wall:

PUBLIC WARNING

The men who have been usurping civic authority are hereby notified that any overt act committed by them will promptly be met by the law-abiding citizens of Skagway. The Law and Order Society, consisting of over three hundred citizens, will see that justice is dealt.

Jefferson Smith, The Law and Order Society

Soapy Smith had declared war. It hadn't taken him long to warn Skagway that he commanded an army of followers, and that he ruled the town again. Tara ripped down the handbill, tore it in pieces, and threw them to the wind.

Even the luxury of lying on a feather-filled mattress, between crisp sheets, didn't help Tara sleep that night. She knew she had to tell Smith that her acceptance of his kindness did not indicate approval of his lawlessness.

The next day Smith turned up at the cabin with a basket. "This should be safe and snug for Johnny-boy."

Tara pushed in a pillow for a mattress and gently placed the baby in it. "It's exactly right," she said.

"Got another surprise for you," cut in Smith, disappearing outside and immediately returning with an Indian woman. She was young, her thick black hair in two long plaits. She smiled at Tara.

"Here's your milk supply," Smith said. "Her papoose died. Meet Lydia. She'll help take care of John."

"Do you speak English?" asked a startled Tara.

"Not a word," intervened Smith, "but she's perfect with the baby talk. Now you introduce her to John."

Lydia cooed with delight as she and Tara bent over the basket. Then Lydia picked the baby up, and he gurgled happily.

"There you see, they get on perfect." Smith beamed. "And there'll be somebody here, so I can take you out."

"I don't remember saying I was going out," Tara said stiffly. "I think it's time you and I had a serious talk."

"My pleasure," said Smith, "but now there's business I've got to attend to. I'll be seeing you soon."

Tara was left staring at the closed cabin door. Then she saw a white envelope lying on the table. Inside were fifty single-dollar bills and a note with just one word: "Housekeeping".

Tara held the money, at first undecided what to do. There were things she needed to buy for the baby. Material to make John clothes, proper napkins instead of torn towels, and ointments.

"All right." Tara put the money in her pocket. "I'll take it because John needs things, but, my goodness, Jeff Smith, don't think fifty dollars can buy me."

That afternoon Tara went out shopping, accompanied by Lydia, with John on the Indian girl's back wrapped up like a papoose. The excitement she felt at gazing in shop windows lifted Tara's spirits. So many stores had opened since she had been away. There were milliners, dress shops, and even a Viennese pastry shop. By the end of the day she had five dollars left.

Soapy Smith's posters were much in evidence. The people who gathered around appeared hostile as they discussed them. She shuddered as she heard one man complain to another, "Damn blackguard. Must think he owns the place."

"He'll get his come-uppance soon," prophesied the other.

After purchasing all the items John needed, they returned to the cabin. Within a few minutes there was a knock on the door and three men staggered in carrying a bath loaded with boxes and a folding rosewood screen upholstered in damask. "Compliments of Mr. Smith," puffed one of them, handing Tara a small envelope. Without further ado they all left.

She opened the envelope and read the card inside. "This isn't meant as an insult, just pamper yourself," Jefferson Smith had written in his neat script.

She undid the boxes and gasped as she took out an extravaganza of feminine luxury. There were jars of bath salts, bars of soap, several bottles of scent, and enormous white Turkish towels. "I don't know if you're hinting, Jeff Smith"—Tara smiled, pressing a soft towel to her face—"but this bath will be a treat."

And it was. Tara washed and scrubbed her sore and tired body,

113

feeling the grime of the past weeks float off her. Afterwards she tingled from head to foot with pleasure as she dropped into the soft bed. Her last thought before falling asleep was that tomorrow, when she put on her freshly laundered clothes, boiled by Lydia, she would look like a different woman, one ready to confront Jefferson Smith.

The following morning Smith called for her. "I'm taking you out," he announced. "So we can have that serious conversation you wanted."

With evident pride he walked her through the centre of Skagway, stopping at a restaurant with a white, immaculate façade. This was Jefferson Smith's Oyster Parlour, his seat of power in the town. He held open the door, and Tara entered a bar-room, complete with flags of American states, a big mirror over the polished mahogany counter, and, to Tara's astonishment, electric light.

Next door to the bar was the restaurant with fretwork screens and artificial palm trees. Unbelievably there were waiters in boiled shirts and white bow ties, their appearance somewhat spoiled by one or two of them having blackjacks in their belts.

Smith and Tara were greeted by a sinister, soft-spoken man in a blue suit, with diamond cuff-links. There was something about him that reminded Tara of Jake Gore. "Yeah Mow," Smith said to him, "This is Mrs. Kane. Anything the lady wants, she has. Understand?"

"Sure, Mr. Smith," said Yeah Mow diffidently.

"What did you say his name was?" Tara asked, following Smith to the back of the parlour.

"Yeah Mow. It's Chinese," Smith told her, leading the way upstairs. "Means wildcat. He bodyguarded some Tong lords in Frisco—the only American who used an axe better than the Chinese. Guess Frisco got too hot for him."

Smith opened the door to his office. It was even more palatial than the one in Dawson.

Tara looked around at the map of the North American continent, the framed copy of the Declaration of Independence, and the bust of Julius Caesar on a shelf.

114

Smith ushered her into a huge leather armchair in front of his desk. "Well, my dear, what is it you want to talk about?"

"Jeff," Tara said falteringly, "I want you to know I'm very grateful for the help you've given me with John, for your thoughtful gifts and your friendship, but I don't want you to think that because I might appear helpless at the moment and without funds that I approve of the sort of man you are or the things you do."

"And tell me, my dear, what sort of man is it that you think I am?" he asked softly.

"I think you're a crook. You take advantage of innocent people."

Smith laughed. "You know what the trouble is with you? You want it all ways, and however I play it I can't win. If I'd left you in Sheep Camp to fend for yourself, I'd have been a scoundrel. If I provide you with a roof over your head, which I can easily afford, it's so I can woo you into a lawless way of life."

She looked at him. "Why did you help me, then?"

"Because I wanted to," he said quietly.

"I don't believe you, Jeff, because I don't believe you've ever done anything without an ulterior motive."

"What a pity that such a kindhearted woman has so little faith," he mused. "I bow to your superior knowledge. But before you go I'm going to put you straight about me. If you think owning faro games is my ambition in life, you're as wrong as if you think you came to these parts to find that missing husband of yours."

"So what am I here for?"

"You ran away to find yourself, to learn something you would never have found out back in San Francisco. That you can stand on your own feet and own the world."

Tara was taken aback. "I have no interest in owning the world. That's your desire, not mine."

"We'll see," said Smith. From a drawer he brought out a heavy piece of rock into which was set a brass plate. It was engraved, Jefferson Randolph Smith, Governor of Alaska.

"Another sure thing?" she asked acidly.

"Exactly," he said. "Alaska, the Yukon, the Klondike. All under one flag. The richest slice of real estate in the world. And I aim that the whole territory will belong to the United States."

"And to you?"

"Sure. A few acres will. Commission, so to speak."

"And just how do you intend to go about this mighty mission?"

"I've already begun," he said softly. "I know the most important thing already. As much as you hate to admit it, you believe in me, Tara, and that's fine for starters. And I'm going to offer you a job, a chance to earn clean money. Be my right-hand woman, my assistant. Help me achieve a decent future for this godforsaken territory. Help me set the record straight."

His eyes were bright as he spoke. Tara was lost for words.

"If you're the woman I think you are, Tara, you'll accept my challenge. That way perhaps you'll stop being ashamed of having a friend in Jefferson Smith. That way we can help one another, because there's one thing I haven't got. And you can give me."

"What's that?"

"Class," he replied. He laughed a little wryly. "You can make me respectable."

He went to the door and opened it. "Think over what I've said. Don't give me your answer straightaway. Consider my proposition carefully, but let me know soon."

In a daze she moved out of the door.

Tara felt strangely stimulated by Smith's words. Was it because he had offered her an opportunity to prove herself? She brooded over what Smith had said about her coming to the Yukon to find her identity. He seemed to have taken it for granted that she had given up her search for Daniel, but that wasn't true.

If Daniel had survived Sheep Camp, then he must be in the territory somewhere. There was only one way for him to get back to San Francisco and that was by sea. He would have to pick up a boat in Juneau, Dyea, or Skagway, the only ports serving the gold rush. Gradually a plan began to form in Tara's mind, and the key to it was the Skagway *Intelligencer*.

She hurried to the newspaper office. Like the town it served, it had grown. Behind the counter men were pounding furiously at typewriters, the presses were clattering.

116

Tara shouted over the din, "I want to place an advertisement."

Eventually one of the men glanced up and came over to her. "What do you want to say?"

"'Daniel Kane' in big letters across the top, and underneath, 'A reward will be paid to anyone knowing his whereabouts. Contact his wife urgently care of box number,' et cetera. Does the paper sell in Dyea too?"

"Sells all over," the man replied. "I've seen them read the Skagway *Intelligencer* as far afield as Dawson, so don't expect an instant reaction. It could take months."

"That's all right. I'll still be here. Please keep running it until I tell you to stop."

That afternoon, Tara wrote a letter to Jefferson Smith.

Dear Mr. Smith,

With reference to your offer of employment, I am writing to advise you that I would be happy to accept the post of assistant to yourself, provided the following terms are agreeable:

I understand that my exclusive employer will be yourself, Jefferson Smith, and that I won't have to deal with any business appertaining to Soapy Smith. I would require a remuneration of one hundred dollars per month with free board and lodging for myself and John. I can commence working for you when it suits you.

Yours faithfully,

Tara Kane

Tara sealed the letter and went back to the Oyster Parlour. She handed it to the barman saying, "Please give this to Mr. Smith."

She went back to the cabin and waited nervously.

"TARA, you're incorrigible!" were Smith's first words when he walked into the cabin, holding her letter. "There's only one problem."

"What's that?" she asked anxiously.

"Money. I intend to pay my assistant a minimum of two hundred dollars a month."

Tara's eyes opened wide. "Two hundred dollars?"

117

"You'll have to be my hostess when necessary, and be available to work whenever I say. This is strictly business. I'm willing to pay for the additional socializing required. You need a job. I need somebody I can trust to be around me, to keep my books, and to do my letters."

"Well," said Tara slowly. "I can do your accounts. I'm a reasonable book-keeper, I suppose."

"Sure, and you'll make a fine hostess at a business function." He rose and smiled. "Well, Mrs. Kane, you're on the payroll now." He pulled out a bundle of notes. "Get yourself a dress and a decent coat," he said, pressing the money into Tara's hand. "You start at nine o'clock tomorrow morning. At the Oyster Parlour."

Without a backward glance he left.

CHAPTER THIRTEEN

Smith barely noticed Tara's arrival at the Oyster Parlour the next morning. Like a theatrical producer of a gala performance, he was busily instructing Yeah Mow on the wine that was to be served at a dinner party that evening.

Tara watched for a while, then mounted the stairs to Smith's office. A small writing table had been placed opposite his desk. On the desk was a box, and on top of that lay a newspaper with an item circled in blue crayon. Her advertisement in the Skagway *Intelligencer* had caught Smith's eye.

"You'll never give up, will you?" Smith remarked, going over to his desk. Tara glanced up. She hadn't heard him come in.

"No. Not while I believe there's a chance."

"If you want my opinion, you're wasting your time and money."

"I don't recall requesting your advice." Smith didn't answer. "What's in the box?" she inquired.

"A dress. I want you to wear it tonight."

"I'm quite capable of buying one myself, thank you," she said.

"Don't let's argue. Wear it," he instructed. "You'll look stunning, and I aim to cash in on it."

Tara glared at him.

"Here's the menu," he went on, handing her a sheet of paper. "I want you to do four copies of it, then do the place cards. I'll be out for the rest of the day. You sort out any problems here then go home and change, but be back by six thirty sharp. I don't want any hitches tonight. I'm negotiating an important business deal, and this dinner may well clinch it."

While she wrote out the place cards Tara wondered why "Sir Thomas Tancrede" and "Mr. Michael J. Henney" warranted such extravagant consideration.

Once home Tara undid the dress box and took out a sensational black taffeta evening gown with a plunging neckline. Quite out of the question. It struck Tara that Smith had given her a splendid opportunity. It was her public duty not to distract Smith's guests with such a décolletage. He would learn that Tara Kane was not a woman to dazzle the suckers while he conducted his shady deals. She laughed to herself and returned the exotic evening gown to its box.

She took painstaking care with her hair, sweeping it up but leaving wisps to frame her face. Then she put on the old trousers and shirt she had worn on the trail. When she finally entered the Oyster Parlour she was well aware she was twenty minutes late.

Without knocking she opened the door of the private dining room and stepped into the candlelit room. Smith, who was wearing evening dress, looked around, but not a flicker on his face betrayed his surprise at her appearance.

"Ah, Tara," he said smoothly, his diamond cuff-links twinkling in the subdued lighting, "you're just in time."

He turned to the two well-dressed gentlemen standing in front of the fireplace. "Gentlemen, may I present Mrs. Tara Kane." She smiled brilliantly.

"This is Sir Thomas Tancrede," he went on, indicating a beanpole of a man with a sardonic smile.

"Enchanted, my dear," said Sir Thomas in a clipped English accent, proferring his limp hand.

"And this is Mr. Michael J. Henney." Smith glanced at him. "Known as Big Mike to his friends." The granite-faced man did

119

not smile but nodded curtly. "These gentlemen are on the board of the railroad," explained Smith.

Now she knew why he had gone to so much trouble over the dinner. This was the get-together at which he intended to make his bid for a share of the Canadian White Pass and Yukon Railway.

"My goodness, Jeff, you should have told me," Tara said, not the slightest bit sorry for having messed up his well-laid plans. "If I'd realized this was going to be such an important occasion, I would have dressed more formally."

Smith did not blink an eyelid. "Mrs. Kane is a real pioneer lady," he said, turning to his guests. "She is more at home with a rifle and a dog team than with the frills of the salon. As you forge your railroad into the interior, you'll meet more of her kind in the settlements. Don't let their sex fool you. They're as tough as nails."

"I wouldn't say tough, Jeff." Tara laughed. "It's just we're more used to dealing with the practicalities of life than to being treated as pretty ornaments."

Smith's eyes raked her, then he reached for the bellpull. "Shall we eat?" He smiled coldly at Tara. "We're a little late, but you probably had to feed the dogs first."

"Jeff, how you exaggerate!" She turned to Sir Thomas. "Why, you'll have your guests believing everything you say."

They sat down at the large oval dining table, resplendent with crystal glasses and silver cutlery. Throughout the four courses Tara acted the perfect dinner companion, keeping up a spirited conversation, all the time stopping Smith from getting down to the business at hand. But he went along with her—attentive, amusing, very much a gentleman at ease.

When they reached the brandy stage, and the cigars came out, Tara started to leave. "No, Tara," Smith said firmly. "I'd like you to stay."

There was political talk. Of the war in South America with Spain and how long it would last. In the United States Teddy Roosevelt was raising a band of volunteers to fight in Cuba. They discussed the probable scale of the war.

Then Sir Thomas cleared his throat. "Why don't we get down to business? People say you're interested in our railroad, Smith. Is that right?"

"Damn right," said Smith. "I know a good investment when I see one."

"What exactly is your proposition?" Henney asked.

Carefully Smith knocked the ash off his cheroot. "We all have a dream, gentlemen, to make this territory a great land, a land which can make more money for all of us than anyone has imagined. The key to that land is the railroad. Open up the territory, and you shrink it to a manageable size. Cut the distances, and you've conquered it."

"I say"—Sir Thomas winked at Tara—"he can dress up things, can't he?"

"Well?" cut in Big Mike, unimpressed.

"The point is, Mr. Henney, I'd like us to be partners." Smith beamed at them. His watch chain and diamond cuff links danced in the candlelight.

"Sorry," said Henney gruffly. "No deal."

Smith remained unruffled. "But you haven't heard me out."

Sir Thomas sighed. "Mr. Smith, we're an Anglo-Canadian consortium. We don't want American involvement. No offence, of course."

"We're businessmen, all of us," Smith said. "Since when hasn't some extra capital been useful? You got big costs coming."

"Maybe," grunted Henney. "But we don't want you in, Smith. We don't want your kind of money."

"So you don't think my dough's good enough," said Smith very quietly. "You only like nice clean capital." He laughed mirthlessly. "Tell me, Sir Thomas, did your folks never ship any slaves? Never conquer any colonies?"

"We don't need lectures from a brothel owner," spat Henney.

Smith's eyes blazed. "Gentlemen, maybe you forgot a couple of things. You need a lot of supplies, a lot of men to build that one hundred and eleven miles of railroad. You haven't got them."

"Right now, Smith," Henney said triumphantly, "ships are on their way to Skagway with everything we need."

Smith nodded. "Of course. And within twenty-four hours of their arrival you'll start laying the track," he said smugly.

Henney's eyes narrowed. "What are you getting at?"

"I have a certain, let's say, influence on the waterfront. The men listen to me. I dare say, gentlemen, that if I didn't get a look into your railroad, they might not unload your ships."

Henney pushed back his chair unceremoniously and stood up. "Now you listen, Smith," he snarled. "Our railroad has the blessing of the authorities. You try to stop us unloading, you start your bullyboy tricks, and we'll have a battalion of United States Infantry in Skagway so quick you won't know what hit you."

He glanced at Sir Thomas. "I think it's time we went."

The Englishman stood up and bowed to Tara. "I do apologize, dear lady," he said. "Business can get so tedious."

"Business, Sir Thomas," she replied, smiling politely, "is never tedious. It interests me enormously."

"We'll see ourselves out," Sir Thomas said, nodding at Smith.

For a while Tara and Smith sat in silence. It was perhaps the first time she had known Jefferson Smith not to have the last word. She felt rather sorry for him. "Well?" she asked at last.

"I'll get my way. It might just take a little longer than I'd thought." He sipped his brandy. "What do you think, Tara?"

She looked at him in surprise. "Do you care?" she asked.

"Yes I do," he said. "Very much."

She looked into his eyes, and she knew it was time for her to be his friend. Perhaps she had the power to guide him.

"What are you thinking about, Tara?"

"I was wondering if I could help you."

"Well," he said accusingly, "what about this evening? Why didn't you help me, then? Look at yourself. Some hostess. What stopped you wearing the dress?"

"Jeff, I will not be an ornament. I didn't wear it because you only wanted me to be a pretty doll. That's not me. I'm not Cad Wilson. I'm not a plaything. It didn't make any difference anyway. They'd made up their minds before they got here. You know that."

Smith lit another cheroot, exhaled the smoke, and paused. "All right," he said at last. "If that's the way it's got to be." He gave his twisted grin. "Kind of expensive lesson. That dress cost me two hundred and fifty bucks." He became serious. "You and me got a lot in common. So let's share it."

As he told her of his various schemes to secure control of the railroad, Tara became increasingly uneasy. For she began to realise that if he did not achieve his means peacefully, he would do it by force. If he couldn't use a dock strike to win a say in the railroad, he would bring in his hired guns. Skagway would be ripped apart by bloodshed.

"You'd be surprised what can go wrong when you lay tracks, Tara. Accidents. Landslides. Explosions." He smiled. "Believe me, a few armed men and a load of dynamite, and they might find it cheaper my way."

"Jeff, if you try to stop them—they'll kill you."

"Maybe I've got a little more experience at that kind of game."

"No," Tara said. "That's not the way, Jeff. Violence never solves anything. Where would it end?"

"It's the only way. What alternative have I got?"

"To give in."

Smith laughed derisively. "You crazy?"

"Jeff, if you're serious about achieving your political ambitions —really becoming governor—you must prove now that you're after the best for Alaska, not just the best for Soapy Smith. If you allow the railroad to go ahead without a fight, you'll gain confidence. You'll be looked on as somebody worth voting for. Bring in gunmen, tear the town apart, and you'll be despised. And when you get killed, as most certainly you will, they'll all cheer."

Smith sighed wearily. "O.K., I'll do it your way. They can build their railroad. But, I'll get what I want . . . eventually."

She was surprised at how readily he'd agreed. Then that crooked, disarming grin of his appeared. He came over to her and put his hands on her shoulders. "Tara, maybe your way is the right way. And if that's your price—"

"I don't have a price," Tara whispered. "I don't ask anything. Only I don't want to see you with a bullet in your back."

He kissed her, a sudden, warm embrace, holding her tight.

124

Then he stepped back and smiled.

"I've got to be careful, Tara. If I don't watch it, you'll be educating me."

OVERSHADOWING the talk in the bars, the barbershops, the stores, was the war in South America. It was far removed from Alaska, didn't touch the life of the gold miner, but as the news filtered through, patriotic fervour grew. In the Oyster Parlour miniature Stars and Stripes sprouted everywhere, even in the artificial-palm pots. Uncle Sam posters appeared. A picture of Teddy Roosevelt hung prominently over the bar.

"I got to get into this war," Jefferson Smith told Tara.

"Are you volunteering?"

"Maybe," he said thoughtfully. "And there's more than one way of volunteering."

When she arrived at his office a few mornings later she stopped dead in her tracks. The door had been forced, and inside it was chaos. Drawers had been pulled out of his desk, a metal deedbox had been jimmied open, letters were strewn all over.

Tara started to tidy up the mess, trying to sort out what had been taken. But nothing seemed to be missing. The cashbox had been opened, but the money had not been touched.

Smith appeared in the doorway. "What the hell—" he began, looking around. "Are you all right?"

"Somebody broke in," Tara said. "But I don't think anything's been stolen. Do you know what they were after?"

He glanced at her with an expression of studied innocence. "How would I know?"

"They went through everything. I think they even read the ledgers, but they left them."

"They wouldn't find anything there," he said, looking pleased.

He was playing it so casually that she began to get an uneasy feeling that maybe there were documents he kept hidden somewhere else. Maybe that's what the intruders had been after.

"Listen," he said, "me and the boys are going to have a little council of war. No need for you to be here."

The boys—that meant Bowers, Yeah Mow, Mort.

"Jeff, is there anything wrong?" Tara asked.

"Now what could be wrong?" he countered.

But from then on an armed man hovered outside his office, day and night. New locks were fitted to the door and, for the first time, there was a safe in the office.

"Merely precautions," he explained. "You'd be surprised how many rogues are in town."

"Jeff, what are you afraid of?"

"Nothing, nothing. I just don't like people poking their nose into our affairs."

"*Your* affairs," she reminded him firmly.

Little could surprise Tara about Smith, or so she thought. Then, a few days later, a hand-painted sign appeared on his door. OFFICE OF THE COMMANDING OFFICER, it read.

He made his next entrance in the uniform of a U.S. Army officer and snapped to attention when he saw Tara. "Captain Jefferson Smith, ma'am, commanding officer, Company A."

"Company what?" she asked. "Jeff, what are you playing at?"

"Company A, First Regiment, National Guard of Alaska."

"I don't believe it!"

"We're at war, woman," he replied, loftily. "I'm raising a volunteer outfit, Skagway's own National Guard company."

"You mean you're raising your own private army," she said.

"Damn it, Tara, you can be the most aggravating female," he shouted. He took a sheet of paper from his desk and thrust it at her. "Private army indeed," he growled.

The paper had an officially printed letterhead embossed with the legend: OFFICE OF THE SECRETARY OF WAR, WASHINGTON, D.C. It read:

Dear Captain Smith,

The President joins me in commending your patriotic spirit in forming your militia unit. You and your volunteer forces and the enthusiasm with which you have rallied to the colours in this hour of your country's need is a tribute to the people of Alaska.

Your offer to put your unit at the disposal of the United States Army and to lead your men in an invasion of Spanish Cuba is greatly appreciated, but I can assure you that the forces we have available are adequate and there is no need for the War Department to require your services overseas.

Russell A. Alger, Secretary of War

"Well?" He stood beaming at her. "You still think I'm planning to start some cockeyed private war?"

She had to admit that it wasn't what she had expected.

Smith became totally committed to Company A. Recruiting posters went up in town overnight. He dictated to Tara a flamboyant order of the day, urging all "red-blooded Americans to follow the summons to arms in our country's hour of need". Near the Oyster Parlour a recruiting marquee was raised.

Along with many others Tara went to the recruiting rally at Jackson's music hall. Smith was on the platform, dressed in his uniform. He pointed dramatically at a crowd of roughnecks lounging in the front rows, and told them, "You are fine and brave men, and I'm sure you will follow me anywhere and at any time."

Everybody cheered. Then Mort and some other men went around the audience with collection boxes.

"What are you collecting for?" Tara asked.

"It's the welfare fund. For the company's orphans and widows."

"Yours must be the only unit in the world that collects for its widows and orphans before it's even got recruits."

"Absolutely," he agreed. "But you got to think ahead." He handed her a little wad of paper. "Here," he said. "Like you to sell some of those. Dollar a ticket."

"A benefit for the widows?" she inquired.

Smith nodded. "We want to sell fifteen hundred."

"What's the prize?"

"Seventy-five bucks," he said. "Not bad for a dollar, eh?"

"Who keeps the other one thousand four hundred and twenty-five dollars?" She handed the tickets back to him.

Smith shrugged. "Hell, I'm the CO of the outfit. I have to train my men. I have to get military supplies. Uniforms, rifles, sidearms. I'm having them shipped in. You don't want my soldier boys to

127

have wooden swords, do you?" He laughed.

Smith transformed Skagway. Huge banners declaring FREEDOM FOR CUBA and DOWN WITH TYRANNY spanned the streets. He even hired the Skagway Silver Temperance Band to give open-air concerts. However, of Smith's army itself the town did not see much outward evidence. He discouraged too many questions.

"Why be so mysterious?" Tara asked.

He smiled at her. "Skagway's going to see plenty of its militia when the time comes, I promise you."

All that was swept from her mind when, next day, Mort came into the office at the Oyster Parlour. "That German fellow is here."

"The photographer? Herr Hart?"

Mort nodded, unenthusiastic. "I'll tell him to go away. O.K.?"

But Tara was already rushing down the stairs, and there he was, his blue eyes lighting up behind his glasses when he saw her. He opened his arms to her and held her tightly.

"Oh, you don't know how good it is to see you, Ernst," she said.

He looked at her solemnly. "Tara, we must talk." He glanced around the bar. "Not here."

He seemed nervous, ill at ease. Tara led him upstairs to the office. "What's the matter, Ernst?" she asked, frowning. "Tell me, how did you track me down?"

"I heard you were with Smith."

She had a lot to explain, she knew that. "Ernst, I didn't find Daniel—" she began, but he cut her short.

"I know. Tara, Daniel is dead."

It seemed an infinity before the words assumed meaning. "No. He can't be." Tara's voice faltered. "How do you know?"

He reached for her hand. "He was murdered in Circle City. Somebody knifed him. He was found in a back alley."

"Oh my God." Tears were running down her face.

"Inspector Constantine identified him from this." Hart pulled out a handkerchief. In it was a gold wedding ring.

She took it, her fingers trembling. She could see the inscription inside the band. *Tara to Daniel.* It was his ring, the twin of the one she had worn.

"No," Tara moaned, her voice full of despair. She buried her face in her hands and was racked by sobs.

"I'm sorry," Hart whispered. "I think it must have happened very quickly, Tara. He had no pain, I'm sure."

"Did you see him . . . afterwards?"

He nodded. "Yes, I did see the body. He had been stabbed in the side. Just below the birthmark."

Tara spun around. "You said birthmark. . . ."

"Yes," he said. "That funny-shaped one, under his left arm. . . ."

"That's not Daniel," whispered Tara. "He had no birthmark." She leaned back and closed her eyes. "Thank God."

"But the Mounties are sure he must be Daniel."

"I tell you they're wrong," she snapped, almost savagely.

"Please, Tara, you must not delude yourself. The ring is proof—"

"What does a wedding ring prove?" Tara cried. "I haven't got mine have I? Maybe he sold it. Maybe it was stolen."

They sat in silence, and then Hart said, "I am sorry to have given you such a shock. If you're sure it is the wrong man, I wish we knew how he came to have the ring."

"We'll find out," Tara said confidently, "when I am reunited with Daniel. I'm running an advertisement for him in the paper. Someone is bound to answer."

Like a bad dream they wanted to forget, they didn't talk about it any more. Instead Hart eyed her admiringly. "Well, I must say you're looking very chic, Mrs. Kane. You might not have found Daniel, but it would appear you've struck gold."

She told him what had happened at Sheep Camp, but she didn't mention the baby or Jefferson Smith. Somehow she was reluctant to admit to Hart the role Smith was playing in her life.

"Ernst, I have a little cabin now. Come over on Sunday at noon. Have some home cooking."

He rose and blew her a kiss. "I'll count the hours."

The next day, when Smith turned up at the Oyster Parlour, he glowered at Tara. "What's that Sir Galahad with the tripod hanging around for?" he rasped.

129

"Ernst is passing through Skagway, so he looked me up."

"Yes, I heard. I don't want him in my place, you got that?"

"Anything else?" she asked coldly.

Their eyes locked, and he got up and left the room without a word. But he came back after an hour. She ignored him, her pen scratching in the ledger she was balancing.

"Tara," he said at last. "Sorry I bit your head off."

He walked around the office like a man making up his mind about something. Then he faced her. "Let's take a day off and go somewhere. You and me and, the kid. We'll have a picnic, out in the country. All day Sunday."

Inwardly she groaned. "Sunday?"

"What's wrong with Sunday?"

"Ernst is coming to have a meal. He won't be here long and—"

"Oh, I see. Herr Hart. A little tryst with Sir Galahad."

She stood up, flushed. "What's it to you anyway?" she cried. "I don't have to ask your permission, do I?"

"You're wasting your time with a gump like that," Smith said. "You can do better, honey."

"He's a *friend*," she yelled at him. "You don't even know what that means . . . and don't call me honey."

"O.K.," he said mildly. "We'll have our picnic some other time. You enjoy yourself with Hart."

"I will," said Tara, and without another word walked out, past the gunman on the landing and down the stairs.

WHEN Ernst arrived on Sunday he handed Tara a bottle of wine. Then he noticed the Indian girl, holding little John in her arms. "I didn't know you shared this place," he remarked, puzzled.

Tara took a deep breath. "Lydia works for me, and the baby is mine. By adoption, so to speak," she added hastily.

"Why didn't you tell me?" His tone was reproachful.

"Ernst, there is a great deal I haven't told you."

"Well," he said, "you'd better start."

He listened intently while she told him about the avalanche, and how she brought the baby into the world amid all that death and horror. When she finished she looked at him questioningly.

130

"You are not angry with me?"

"Why should I be? No, I admire you. Taking in that child, keeping him alive, looking after him. Now I understand."

"Understand what?"

He looked away as he replied. "Why you are with Smith."

"Ernst. I am not with Smith. I work for him. I needed a job, and he gave me one. I earn my wages."

"Tara," he said gravely. "You must get away from him. He is a bad man. There are rumours. . . ."

"I'm not interested in gossip," she retorted.

"No, you must listen," Hart said urgently. "He is raising an army, shipping in weapons, ammunition. He plans a *putsch*, a revolt. When he has enough men and guns he will take over the town, the railroad, seize the Chilkoot, the White Pass."

"That's crazy!" she cried.

"I beg you, Tara, you must leave here. Before it's too late."

"Ernst, I don't believe any of—"

But he cut her short. "I will protect you from him," he burst out. "I will look after you and the baby. Your worries are over. You need not have anything to do with the man ever again."

Tara said nothing. He was speaking rapidly. He grabbed her hand. "I will arrange everything. One day, God willing, we will marry, and we will be so happy, my dearest, together always."

Tara looked at him, unbelieving. Hart raised her hand to his lips and kissed it. "And the little baby, of course, he will be my son too. Thank God, *Liebchen*, I can save you from Smith."

"No." Tara pulled her hand away. "I don't want to live with you. I am married, and if I wasn't, I wouldn't marry you."

She softened when she saw his wounded expression. "Oh, I don't mean to sound unkind, Ernst. But this . . . this is absurd."

"So," he said, and there was bitterness in his voice, "you prefer that hoodlum to me. You like Smith better."

She stared at him amazed. "Jeff has been a friend to me, don't you understand that? I know what he is. I know what people say. But to me he has been generous, kind. I'm grateful to him. I like him." Tara stopped. It was the first time she had ever admitted it, even to herself.

"He is a *Schuft*, a scoundrel."

"You're jealous," she said gently.

To Tara's horror he fell on his knees in front of her and clung to her dress. "I love you," Hart whimpered. "You're the only woman I have ever met who's meant anything to me. Please, please say yes."

"Ernst," she said, "for heaven's sake, pull yourself together. I like you, but I don't love you. Please get up, I beg of you."

At that moment the cabin door opened. Tara saw Jefferson Smith standing on the threshold, a bunch of flowers and a bottle of champagne in his arms.

"My, my, what a touching scene."

"What do you want?" Tara demanded.

Smith's voice brought Hart to his senses. He got up, brushing specks of dust from his trousers in an effort to cover his embarrassment.

"Have I arrived at an inopportune moment, my dear?" Smith asked, solicitously. He sniffed the aroma from the stove. "Smells good. Yes, I think I'd like some lunch. How kind of you."

"Jeff, I don't recall inviting you," she began.

"I'm sure you meant to," he said blandly. "I'll open the bubbly. A drink to our hostess, Mr. Hart?"

"Tara." Hart cut Smith dead. "I'm not staying for lunch."

"Oh, for heaven's sake, there's plenty of food for everybody. Please stay, Ernst." She hastily laid an extra place at the table.

"How's my godson?" Smith asked.

"Godson? I thought Tara had adopted him," Hart said coldly.

"We both did." Smith smiled. "Sort of a joint stake."

The two men did not speak to one another while Tara served the soup. Smith then turned to Hart.

"I hope I wasn't interrupting anything by bursting in on you folks," he said casually.

Hart looked at him viciously. "I have asked her to marry me," he said.

Smith poured the champagne. "Have you?" he murmured mildly. "You want to marry her, protect her? You couldn't look after a lame cat. She goes on the trail with you, and gets back alone, half out of her mind, two-thirds dead, and on a murder charge. I'll never forgive you for that."

"I . . . I couldn't stop her," Hart said in a low voice. "She went off on her own. What could I do?"

"If I'd been in your boots, nothing in the world could have stopped me staying with her. No, you were too busy taking your pretty pictures. You're not worth a woman like that."

Smith pushed back his chair and turned to Tara. "I'm sorry about all this. I had no idea he was going to ask you to—"

He stopped, staring at the wedding ring, on the middle finger of her left hand.

She followed his look and nodded. "Yes, Jeff. It's Daniel's. Ernst brought it to me from Circle City. They found it on a dead man, but it wasn't Daniel."

"What happened to him, then?"

"I don't know. But one thing's for sure, Jeff," she said gently. "I'm not marrying anybody. I'm married already."

He gave a wry little smile. "I hope I'll see you tomorrow." He stood up and left the cabin without saying a word to Hart.

"I'm going now," Hart said, putting on his coat.

"Yes," said Tara quietly. "I think that's best."

"I don't think we should see one another again." His voice faltered. "Take care, dear Tara. I will always love you, and I only hope and pray you have made the right choice."

"There is no choice, Ernst. There's only one man I love."

Hart nodded. "Yes, Mr. Smith."

"Of course not!"

Hart shrugged. "You know, my dear, I think you are hoodwinking yourself. I believe you have fallen in love with that man."

"You're wrong," she snapped, but although her voice was firm she could not meet his gaze.

Hart inclined his head. "Goodbye," he said. "I am sailing back to San Francisco. I have over a thousand pictures of the gold rush, and my work is finished. Any other reason I have had for staying is over. It is all finished."

"Goodbye, Ernst. Thank you for everything," she whispered as she watched him walk away.

CHAPTER FOURTEEN

Tara's mood was buoyant as she rode back along the trail to Dyea. She had travelled this route with Bishop Beauchamp, unwittingly smuggling Soapy Smith's liquor by way of the spurious Reverend Bowers. Then the countryside had been white and freezing. Now, with the coming of summer, it was warm and ablaze with flowers. Goldenrod, daisies, poppies jostled with a myriad of ferns. The sun would not set until after ten o'clock; even then, there would only be twilight.

Dyea had changed too. There was more of it. She left her horse in the stables next to the blacksmith, and started to walk along the street. Since there was still no response to her advertisement she intended to try herself to find someone who might know something about Daniel. Ever since Hart had left she had been torn with doubt. Was she, as he had said, falling in love with Jeff Smith? She had to prove to herself that Daniel was still alive and that she loved him more than anyone.

She had a meal in an eating house, and just as she was paying her bill, the door opened. A U.S. Army officer with the silver bar of a lieutenant and the insignia of the infantry stood looking around. As soon as he saw Tara he came towards her and saluted.

"Colonel Bradshaw's compliments, ma'am. The colonel wonders if you could spare him a few minutes."

"What is it about?" Tara asked.

"I'm sure the colonel will tell you himself, ma'am. If you'll follow me." She had the uneasy feeling that it was not so much an invitation as an order.

At army headquarters Tara was ushered into the colonel's office. "Mrs. Kane, sir," announced the lieutenant, and Tara found herself facing two men. The colonel, a grey-haired man with sharp eyes, rose from behind his desk. The other man, who had also risen, was a civilian, in a city suit, with gold-rimmed glasses.

"I appreciate your coming here, Mrs. Kane," said the colonel without warmth. "I'm Colonel Bradshaw, and this gentleman is Mr. Wilkins, from the War Department in Washington."

He sat down again and cleared his throat. "Mrs. Kane, there is a reason for our presence in Dyea. The government has moved in the army because of certain eventualities."

"Let's put it this way, ma'am," interrupted Wilkins. "You are an . . . an associate of Mr. Smith. In Skagway."

"I know Mr. Smith," she said curtly. "But I'm here on a private matter. If you must know, I'm trying to locate my husband."

"We're interested in Mr. Smith, in his activities, and the people around him," Wilkins said flatly.

"Mr. Smith's activities are of very little concern to me," declared Tara. Certain things were coming back to her that Hart had said about Smith's militia and arms shipments.

"Well, Mrs. Kane, whatever you're doing here, you can give Mr. Smith a message." The colonel's voice was icy. "Tell him the government has moved a battalion of infantry into Dyea. Their orders are to keep the peace and to uphold law and order."

He opened the door for Tara. "Good day, ma'am."

She let herself into her hotel room to find a man waiting for her. "Forgive the intrusion, Mrs. Kane." He handed her a card. "I'm Edward Cahill, newspaper correspondent from Seattle."

"Please go," Tara said, opening the door.

"I think you'd better listen," he said. His authoritative tone made her close the door again.

"What do you want?" she asked, sitting down.

"You've got yourself in bad company, Mrs. Kane. I am a reporter, but I also work for the U.S. Government. That's why I'm interested in Jefferson Smith. Just as the military gentlemen are," he added with a smile. "We've sort of checked on things and we believe that maybe you don't really know what's going on."

She sat silently. She knew he was going to ask her to betray Smith, and she knew what her answer had to be.

"You must help us, Mrs. Kane," he went on. "We suspect Smith is planning to take over Skagway by force of arms. We think he wants to seize the railroad, the passes, maybe take over Alaska. Pretend he's claiming it for the United States. It's a disputed border anyway, and you can guess what that would do. Maybe war between us and the Canadians."

135

"That's rubbish. All he wants to see is Alaska as a state of the Union," intervened Tara.

"He wants to control the gold that's coming out of the Klondike," said Cahill brutally. "He wants to control the whole place and take his cut out of every ounce of gold that's found."

"How could he?" Tara asked.

"What do you think he's raising his phony National Guard for? It's nothing but a private gang, tough, hard mercenaries, dressed up in army uniforms to fool everybody. He's shipping in arms, Mrs. Kane, maybe Maxim guns, even light field guns. We suspect he's got an arsenal somewhere in Skagway. A warehouse maybe. We're trying to find out. We've got an agent working in Skagway."

"This agent of yours, did he break into Smith's office at the Oyster Parlour?" she asked.

He said nothing.

"Mr. Cahill," Tara said slowly. "I don't have any part in all this. I'm terrified of what you say he's doing. But you must also know this. He's been a good friend to me, and I can't repay him by . . ."

Cahill looked at her gravely. "All right," he said very quietly. "I believe you. Only, this is insurrection. Don't put your neck in a noose."

He went to the door. "Be careful, Mrs. Kane. Skagway is going to be a mighty dangerous place."

TARA could almost smell the tension when she returned to Skagway. Men were standing around in clusters, grim-faced, and the usually crowded streets were strangely quiet. The atmosphere of unease was even more evident outside the Oyster Parlour. A cordon of Smith's men were cradling shotguns and scrutinizing strangers.

Inside, Mort gave her a nod. "Welcome back, Mrs. Kane," he grunted without warmth.

She looked at the empty tables, and the bouncers sitting near the door, one of them with a Winchester across his knees. "What's happened?" she asked.

"Well." Mort contemplated Tara. "There's been a shooting."

It wasn't all that unusual. Guns were part of the scene all over,

Dawson, Fortymile, Skagway. Even a periodic shoot-out was not unknown. But this was different. Whatever had happened, people were angry and resentful. Something was simmering.

"Who was it?" Tara inquired.

He shrugged. "Some greenhorn. Better ask the boss."

Slowly Tara got the story out of Smith. "Yeah Mow got trigger-happy," he said. "Fellow called Glen Ashbury. Been hanging around the place." He shrugged. "It'll pass over. Folks are pretty worked up at the moment, but they'll soon forget."

The shooting had taken place in broad daylight. In front of dozens of passers-by Yeah Mow had shot down an unarmed man.

"Do you know anything about Ashbury?" she asked nervously.

"I couldn't care less." But she could see he was worried.

He snapped his fingers suddenly. "Maybe I'll fix a trial. We'll get Yeah Mow acquitted, and then everybody will calm down."

He waited for her reaction, but all she said was, "I've seen enough of your trials, Jeff."

Killing Ashbury was a big mistake. Tara saw a slogan white-washed on a wall: HANG SOAPY. People kept away from the Oyster Parlour. Three days later Smith told Tara that there had been an inquest. "Verdict's self-defence," he announced. "Yeah Mow got cleared. Six witnesses testified they saw Ashbury draw a gun first."

"But he wasn't armed, you said so yourself."

"I wasn't there, honey. These guys saw it."

There was a celebration that night in the Oyster Parlour, with Yeah Mow as guest of honour. The six witnesses drank with him. They were all men whose faces were known in the establishment.

The town did not forget the Ashbury shooting. At a time when Skagway promised to be the most important landing stage for the gold fields, thanks to the rail link with Lake Bennett, Smith's regime was threatening everything. The traders, the railroad, the backbone of the community knew that if news of Soapy Smith's hold over Skagway reached Seattle and San Francisco, it could put an end to the town's prosperity.

All the more reason, Jefferson Smith thought, for his making the forthcoming Fourth of July the most dazzling event in the history of the Klondike. "It's going to be the fanciest Independence Day

Alaska has ever seen," he announced to Tara. There would be a huge carnival, military bands, and a parade. "*That's* when we unveil the militia, and I'll invite every important citizen—the railroad people, the bankers, even the territory's governor."

Tara was writing out the invitations at the desk when she came across some papers she hadn't noticed before—bills of lading and cargo manifests that Smith had forgotten to lock away in his drawer. She picked one up and found he was importing "kitchen equipment" to the amount of five thousands dollars, and "garden gear" to the tune of four thousand dollars. What use did he have for gardening gear and that much kitchen equipment? She knew what she was looking at. Consignments of arms. Evidence that the government agent had sought in the office break-in.

Tara had been keeping her ears open too. Several times she had heard mention of the warehouse. When she asked Smith about it he had said something about storing his liquor there. There was only one way to find out if Cahill had been right about there being an arsenal.

The warehouse stood by itself at the side of a disused timber-mill. Tara dismounted from her horse and concealed herself behind a tree. Suddenly she froze. A man with a rifle came around the corner of the warehouse, like a sentry on patrol. In the distance she saw a mule train approach, accompanied by two armed horsemen. Each mule was weighed down by heavy crates.

Tara watched as the sentry unlocked the door of the warehouse and the men carried the heavy crates inside. Then she stepped out from behind the tree, and crept over to the big shed. The door was ajar, and she could hear voices. She peered through the gap and caught her breath as she saw row after row of rifles, boxes of ammunition, Maxim guns on tripods, and six machine guns.

"You shouldn't be here, Mrs. Kane," Yeah Mow said. She spun around. She hadn't heard him come up behind her. "Does the boss know you're here?" He was pointing a pistol at her.

"Of course," she lied.

"O.K.," he said. "You and me are going to say hello to him."

They rode back to town in silence. Yeah Mow spoke only once. "You're a pretty lucky lady. Usually, when people go snooping around that place, we shoot first and ask questions afterwards."

"Like the way you killed Glen Ashbury?" Tara asked.

"Guys don't break into the boss's office and get away with it."

Then she knew they had killed the U.S. Government agent.

YEAH MOW shoved Tara into a store room of the Oyster Parlour. "Get Mr. Smith right away," blustered Tara. "He's going to be mighty sore at you."

Yeah Mow smiled coldly. "You'll see him all right." He shut the door, and she heard the key turning in the padlock. As time passed she felt more and more apprehensive.

Finally she heard a key turning again, and Smith came in. He walked slowly over to a crate and sat down on it. "What were you doing there?" His tone was quiet.

"Finding out the truth for myself."

"Why did you have to sneak off to the arsenal? Why didn't you tell me you wanted a look? And you found out exactly what I've been telling you. I've been shipping in arms for my little outfit."

"Some little outfit. There's enough arms to equip a small army. To kill thousands. You didn't start this whole business to fight in the Spanish War. You're planning rebellion."

Smith stared at her. He said nothing. He sat rigid.

"I'm waiting," she said. "Deny it. Please."

"Why should I?" asked Smith. "It's the truth."

"No. You can't be that cold-blooded." Her voice was controlled, her hands clenched. "Don't tell me you don't care about what will happen. The people you'll kill. The bloodshed." She leaned forward. "Jeff, the government knows what you're up to. They've got troops ready to move in. I've seen them. Ashbury was investigating you. He was a government agent."

He kept his composure. "Come on now, that's mighty emotive talk. Nobody's moving in troops. All they need is a little persuasion—like a good front-row view of Skagway's finest flower—and they'll get that on the Fourth." He laughed. "There ain't going to be no shooting, unless somebody else starts it."

"They will, Jeff. That's why troops are in Dyea. You know what they'll do the moment you take over. Thank God I won't be there."

139

"What's that?"

"I'm pulling out, Jeff," she said very quietly. "I'll be in San Francisco when they hang you. I've had enough."

For the first time he looked worried. "You can't," he said. "I won't let you. Never." He took her in his arms and stroked her hair. Before she knew how it happened he was kissing her on the lips, first gently, then more passionately, and Tara did not resist. She closed her eyes and luxuriated in his embrace, her body yielding to him, her arms folding around him.

Then, slowly, he released her. They stood looking at one another, the atmosphere between them charged. He was imbued with a magnetism she had never felt in him. It left her breathless.

"You're so important to me, Tara," he said softly.

"If that's true, Jeff," she said, gazing into his unwavering eyes, "give up your crazy scheme. Promise me you'll never use your men against this town, the territory, anyone."

He looked into the distance, then turned back to her. "O.K., I'll think about things, I promise you. But stay until the Fourth. More than anything I want you there. You'll be the hostess, the first lady. If you do that . . . well, maybe I can do it all your way. He took her hand and kissed it. "Well?" he said. "Is it a deal?"

She nodded. "Yes," she said slowly. "I think it is."

CHAPTER FIFTEEN

Long before the big parade was due to begin, red, white, and blue bunting waved from rooftops and flagpoles, and Skagway's streets were filled with people in their Sunday best. Prospectors shot off pistols and rifles, and steamships in the harbour sounded their sirens.

Tara could hear the sounds of revelry as she dabbed perfume behind her ears. She was dressed in a new frock, her auburn hair swept up, her green eyes bright with excitement and happiness.

She dressed John in a little suit Lydia had made for him and wrapped him in a big embroidered shawl. "My John." Tara smiled proudly, balancing the curly-haired baby on her knee. "I need you as much as you need me. Together we can face the world and cope with anything. As soon as I can I'm taking you home, and there you'll have a proper life. I want to be a good mother."

Though she had not found Dan, in her own way she had struck it rich in the Yukon. She had John.

When Smith came for them he was wearing his army uniform, complete with sword. For a moment he stood and admired Tara openly. "I'm a very lucky man. I've not only got the honour of escorting a beautiful woman, I've also got the company of an extremely stylish young man." He stroked the baby's cheek.

"If you're both ready the carriage awaits," he announced formally, leading her to the door. Outside stood an open four-wheeler drawn by two magnificent horses, complete with driver.

They set off through the streets of Skagway, Tara holding the baby and Smith bolt upright beside her, waving his hand, performing to perfection his role of military commander, civic leader, and would-be statesman. Thousands of onlookers stared in amazement. Such elegance was new to the town.

The carriage stopped in front of a dais dominated by a giant Stars and Stripes. A loud roar rang out as Smith stood acknowledging the town's welcome. Then a brass band began playing "Dixie".

Smith had been born in the South. "My signature tune," he grinned crookedly, as he helped Tara out of the carriage. He led her to one of the three chairs that had been placed on the platform, another one of which was occupied by a bearded man in a frock coat. He rose as they approached.

"Governor," Smith said, "may I present Mrs. Kane."

The governor bowed, and Tara held out her hand to the man Smith wanted to kick out of the territory. He was an outsider, an ex-missionary appointed by the government in faraway Washington. "As you know, my dear," purred Smith, "Governor Brady is doing us the honour of taking the salute."

"I must say, Captain Smith, you're doing the town proud," rumbled Brady. "Looks like there's going to be a fine show."

"You haven't seen anything yet, Governor." Smith seated Tara on the chair next to Brady and winked at her. He then sprinted down the steps of the dais, disappearing out of sight.

The little brass band played Sousa marches, and soon Tara could hear from a distance the sound of hundreds of pairs of marching feet. The parade was approaching. Tara craned her neck and saw a man carrying Old Glory. He was followed by Jefferson Smith, mounted on a white charger, his sword drawn, a heroic figure riding in front of his army.

Drummers beat a blood-stirring tattoo, and the First Regiment, National Guard of Alaska tramped down the street, marching in very creditable military style considering its ranks included Smith's bouncers, barmen, and croupiers, who had been pressed into the ranks alongside genuine volunteers.

Brady was on his feet, his hand on his heart, taking the salute. "Magnificent. A wonderful body of men. A credit to Alaska."

If only you knew, Tara thought. Smith had promised Skagway the greatest show it had ever seen, and he kept his word. Three Scots pipers headed a series of wagons converted into floats, depicting Skagway's gold mining, the railroad, shipping, banking. Then came a wagon loaded with dance hostesses blowing kisses. Across the wagon was a big poster which read. JEFF SMITH FOR GOVERNOR. STATEHOOD FOR ALASKA.

Brady swallowed at that but managed a sickly smile as cheers went up from the crowd. Then, while the tail end of the parade was still passing, Smith appeared beside Tara on the dais. He sat down and whispered to her. "Well, how did that look?"

"The best parade a kid could wish to see," Tara whispered back. "But I don't think the governor was amused by that sign."

The procession had finally passed but the crowd still stood, packed. Smith moved to the front of the platform and raised his right hand for silence.

"Fellow citizens of Skagway," he began. "This great nation is at war, and we Skagway folk are going to play our part in licking the tyrants of Havana. We're doing our duty, but we believe also that we deserve a square deal. The people of Alaska call on the Republicans in Congress to keep their faith with us and give us our own elected congressmen."

The crowd stamped their feet, and guns fired into the air.

"Now we don't want anything but our just dues," cried Smith.

"What's Washington done for us? Made some lousy laws, taxed us, but what else? For years we've been the orphan. Hell, until the railroad we only had one wagon road running for two miles. That's going to change. This great territory, Alaska, is going to be right up there." He pointed to the Stars and Stripes fluttering in the breeze. "It's going to be one of those states.

"We need men in Washington who will speak for us," Smith continued. "Men of vision. Men who believe in Alaska and its future. Let's send those men to Washington. The future belongs to us."

He sat down and the crowd threw their hats into the air and cheered. Tara felt certain that he had meant every word he'd said.

"Great speech, Captain Smith," Brady broke in uneasily. "The party needs men like you."

"You think so, Governor?" Smith drawled. "Maybe we ought to talk about it sometime."

The noise and excitement became too much for young John. He began crying, and Tara decided it was time to take him home. She excused herself to Brady, who looked unhappy and dour. He stood alone, whereas Smith was surrounded by well-wishers, congratulating him on his patriotism. What short memories people had, she thought. Then she saw a scowling stranger go over to the governor and say something. A complacent smile spread over Brady's face, and he walked off with the man, his arm around his shoulder.

Tara forced her way through to Smith's side. "Jeff," she said, "I'm going back to get changed for the ball."

"I'll send Bowers with the carriage for you." She started to move off but Smith caught her hand. "And thank you, Tara. You don't know how much you've helped me."

Smith's Independence Day Ball was the nearest thing to a society event Skagway had ever seen. The Princess Hotel was ablaze with light, and when the carriage drew up outside Tara could hear orchestral strains drifting out of large French windows.

Bowers held her hand as they mounted the steps to the entrance hall. Tara was well aware of the glances people gave her, and she smiled brilliantly as she swept into the hallway. Let them stare, she said to herself. I'm going to enjoy every minute of this.

143

Bowers led the way to the enormous ballroom, where hundreds of candles reflected in the crystal pendants of a dozen chandeliers. Already guests were milling around drinking champagne. Tara was so enchanted she only became aware of Smith's presence as he gently removed her shawl and ran his eyes admiringly over her black taffeta gown. "My dear Tara," he said, kissing her hand. "You look stunning." He beckoned to a hovering waiter bearing a silver salver with glasses of champagne.

Smith raised his glass. "To the loveliest woman in the world and the belle of my ball," he toasted, and they both drank.

"Come," he went on, handing their glasses to Bowers. "It's time for us to start the dancing." He held out his arm and led her onto the floor. The other guests parted to let them through. The orchestra broke into a lively Strauss waltz and Tara allowed herself to be swept around the floor. Gradually other couples joined in so that the floor became a mass of whirling colour.

"How does it feel," he asked as he turned her this way and that, "to be the centre of attention, to have every man in the room desire you and every woman envy you?"

"That's nonsense, Jeff," Tara said, but she was pleased.

When the waltz stopped he led her to the buffet heaped with platters of poached salmon in aspic, cold poultry and meat, salads, trays of cheeses, and an exotic collection of desserts. They returned to their table, their plates piled high.

As Smith was about to sit down a man approached. Tara recognized him immediately. He was middle-aged, his face weather-beaten, his eyes crafty. She had seen him that very afternoon when he had buttonholed the governor after the parade.

"Must have cost you a pretty penny or two," the man remarked coldly, nodding at the dance floor, "but it won't buy us."

"I don't recall inviting you, Reid," observed Smith coolly. He turned to Tara. "My dear, my apologies. This gentleman is Frank Reid. He likes to think of himself as the city engineer."

Reid nodded to Tara curtly.

"Don't see your friends around," Smith drawled. He turned to Tara. "You wouldn't know them, my dear, but they keep themselves busy."

144

"They wouldn't come near one of your functions." Reid bent closer. "I just wanted to warn you, Smith. You're finished. You're not going to shoot people down again, I promise you. The decent people of this town have had enough."

"I think I have too. Right now you're boring me." Smith's eyes were hard, cold diamonds. "If you want to talk business, you know where to find me."

"All right, Smith. I've said my piece so you know what to expect. My respects, ma'am." He nodded at Tara and walked off.

Tara sighed in relief. "What an awful man."

"The dregs," Smith said. "I found that out a long while ago. We used to be partners."

Tara was amazed. "What happened?" she asked.

Smith shrugged. "Let's just say he and I no longer get on."

For some time they ate in silence, Smith deep in thought. Reid's appearance had brought Tara down to earth. Had all the magic been a dream, she wondered. The veneer of Skagway's attempt to emulate fashionable society was wearing thin. Everyone was getting louder and brasher. Elegant dancing was being replaced by thumping feet. Many guests sat slumped, glassy-eyed.

"Come," Smith said, getting up. "There's something I want to show you." Together they walked out, past the potted plants and intoxicated guests, and mounted the red-carpeted staircase. Smith took Tara's hand as he led her down a corridor. He opened a door and Tara found herself in a plush sitting room, lit only by candles. There was a large sofa upholstered in red velvet, and the walls were covered with the same fabric.

"Now take your shoes off and relax," he ordered, going over to a bar. She sat down, her posture the epitome of propriety.

"Try this for size," he invited, returning with two balloon brandy glasses. Suddenly there was an explosion of light outside the window, followed by the sound of people cheering. "It's the fireworks," Smith said.

Down in the street Smith's militia were handing out sparklers, while overhead Roman candles, rockets, catherine wheels zoomed and rained a web of shooting colour in the twilight.

"Oh, they're beautiful," sighed Tara as she watched a thousand

145

stars exploding in the sky. "They remind me of the northern lights. Did I ever tell you how they saved me? Like a sign from heaven to guide me back to Dawson." They watched the firework display for some time, until the noise of people yelling and laughing made them close the window.

Smith pulled the heavy drapes and Tara returned to the sofa and kicked off her shoes. She looked very attractive, the sheer blackness of her gown setting off the whiteness of her shoulders and the dark fieriness of her hair. She sipped the brandy.

"What was it that you wanted me to see, Jeff?" she asked.

"It's a little gift I've got for you." He came over and sat on the sofa. "It's something that's yours by right, Tara." He took her hand and dropped her wedding ring into her palm.

She gazed at the inscription: *Daniel to Tara.*

"Put it on," Smith said. "Next to the other one."

She looked at him, her expression a mixture of confusion and happiness. Then, slowly, she slipped the ring onto the fourth finger of her left hand. "Thank you, Jeff, so very much."

He had given her only what was hers, but it was the greatest gesture he could have made. She was flooded with affection for him. He was her friend, he'd proved himself to be so.

"Maybe you should ask why?" Smith suggested quietly. "I'd say a fellow who loves a woman is crazy to give her another man's wedding ring."

She glanced up at him sharply and was about to speak, but he put a finger gently on her lips.

"No, let me say it. I want to put my cards on the table, the whole darn pack. I started figuring why was I holding on to that little band of gold. To kid myself that there wasn't anybody else? One thing a good gambler mustn't do, he mustn't kid himself. I was acting like somebody scared of a ghost." He touched the ring. "*That* ghost. Because your husband is a ghost, Tara. Daniel's dead."

"Don't ever say that," whispered Tara. "He's not. . . ."

"He's dead," Smith repeated insistently. "You can't live with a ghost. You can't sleep with a dream. He's dead, and you've got to come to terms with that fact." He drew her to him, and she laid her head on his shoulder. "Tara," he said, stroking her hair. "I want you to marry me. I love you. I know you love me too."

"Even if Daniel is dead," she sobbed. "Even then I wouldn't marry you. I don't love you Jeff." There was a fleeting look of pain in his eyes. "I'm sorry, but you made me say it."

"I think you're lying, Tara. If you didn't love me, you couldn't have looked so happy, so beautiful, so in love this evening."

"Jeff, I don't . . ." But she couldn't meet his eyes. "Not yet anyway," she added, lowering her head.

"Because you won't let yourself, Tara. You want to run away from me because you're scared of the truth. Daniel's just a convenient excuse. Not facing the reality of his death means you're safe, because he's there to fall back on, even though he's only a memory. You know that you and I fit. We belong. Let's join forces and build a future. For one another—for John."

"Jeff, I'm taking John back to San Francisco. You know I've made up my mind. Nothing will ever change that decision."

"I'm not trying to alter that decision, Tara," Smith reasoned. "I want to come back to Frisco with you and John. We'll get married here first, and then we'll go back, the three of us, together."

"But what about Skagway? Alaska? Statehood?"

"They don't matter, Tara. Only we do."

"You'd give up everything?" she asked incredulously.

"That's how much I love you. Without you there is no future. If you say no, I'll stay here and run this territory. I'll own it. But if you agree to marry me, it'll be different. I'd feel a complete man because I respect you, I listen to you. With you I think right, I act right, I do right."

He pulled her closer. "This is crazy. The way a man usually shows a woman that he wants her is to kiss her, not sit talking . . ." He studied her. "You look so beautiful, Tara." And she did. Her face was tear-stained, her hair awry, but her eyes betrayed her passion for him, and there was nothing she could do to hide it.

Then he kissed her and she clung to him. They lingered together, not speaking for a long while. Slowly he removed the pins from her hair. One by one each auburn curl cascaded to her shoulders. She gazed into his clear, grey eyes, and they told her that he was going

147

to make love to her, and she knew she wanted him to. She put her arms around him and leaned back against the sofa.

Smith loved her, and he proved it by the way he made love to her. For both of them it was a fulfilment. They sought one another's mouths, their lips pressing together, his hands on her body, hers stroking his.

After the passion had faded they lay in one another's arms. "Tara," he whispered, "I love you so very much."

She looked up at him and smiled. "I think I love you too, Jeff," she replied softly.

Later they walked back to the cabin in silence, Smith holding Tara close to him all the way. Outside the door he stopped. "Tara," said Smith, taking her hands, "don't tell me what you've decided now. Take a few days to think over my proposal."

He bent down and kissed her lightly on the lips. "And always remember, my dear, no matter what your answer is, I'll understand. There'll be no recriminations, no arguments. I just pray, oh how I pray, that you'll say yes."

Then he walked off, Tara watching him go, a part of her wanting to run after him. But she remained where she was and, true to character, Smith never once looked back.

CHAPTER SIXTEEN

Tara knew that she loved Smith. She also knew what she owed to him. He had humiliated her in the past, but without him she would never have survived. And she had learned the most important thing from him. If the Mounties had taught her the practicalities of survival, from Smith she had picked up self-confidence. He had given her a belief in herself.

Yet she could not marry him. What would happen if, one day, Daniel did return? If she were married to Smith that would make her a bigamist. That was unthinkable. She and John would have to leave for San Francisco very soon. It was the only course.

As she made her way along Broadway she rehearsed how she would tell Smith. She was just about to open the door of the Oyster

Parlour when Mort, Bowers, and the deadly Yeah Mow rushed out, nearly sending her flying. They were all wearing guns.

"Sorry," apologized Bowers, steadying Tara. "We got trouble at the docks. Reid's men. Reid called out the boss." He ran off with the others.

A terrible fear swept through her as she started half walking, half running towards the waterfront. Ahead of her she saw a rapidly growing crowd gathering by a warehouse. She pushed through the throng. Some of Smith's gang stood blocking the sidewalk, their hands hovering near their guns. Beyond them were two men. Jefferson Smith and Frank Reid stood confronting each other.

Tara squeezed her way to the front and stopped dead in her tracks, heart racing. All around everyone was silent. Smith was holding a Winchester rifle, the barrel pointing at Reid, his finger lightly resting on the trigger. Reid stood a few feet away. He wore a gun belt and the butt of his pistol was outside the flap of his jacket. His fingers twitched near the gun butt.

"Jeff! Don't!" Tara cried out. Smith didn't even look round. His eyes remained fixed on Reid.

Reid took a step towards Smith. "It's the end of the road, Soapy," he shouted. "We've had enough of you and your men. I know what you've got planned for this town. You and your rat pack got twelve hours to get out of the territory."

Smith laughed. Reid spat at Smith's feet.

"You got a lot of nerve all of a sudden, Frank," goaded Smith. "Found your guts at last?"

The rifle was absolutely steady. Reid and Smith were only a foot or two apart, their eyes locked. Then, quite deliberately, Reid grabbed the barrel of Smith's rifle with his left hand, and tried to force it down. In his right hand he held his six-gun.

"You fool, don't make me kill you," warned Smith, ignoring the gun inches from his chest.

Horror-stricken, Tara saw Reid's finger tighten on his trigger. Then the hammer clicked, the chamber spun, but there was no shot. The bullet was a dud.

Smith's eyes did not blink. He jerked up the barrel of his rifle and fired. Reid rocked. He still held the six-gun, and pulled the

149

trigger once more, before he collapsed. Glass tinkled as the bullet shattered a windowpane behind Smith.

Smith stood looking down at Reid. His face was expressionless. He was about to turn when a voice called out, "Smith!"

From the crowd, his back to Tara, stepped a man.

"What do you want, mister?" Smith cried, facing him.

"You. . . ." the man said in a low voice.

He wore a gun belt, and his right hand hovered over the holster. Smith nodded. "That figures."

Out of the corner of her eye Tara saw Mort move forward, but Smith waved him back. "Anybody interferes, and they're dead," called out Smith. "This is between me and him. . . ."

The gunman went for his .45 just as Smith raised his Winchester again.

But the gunman fired first.

Smith staggered but managed to pull his trigger. The gunman reared like a stricken creature, then fell, face downward.

Smith dropped the Winchester and slowly sank to his knees. The gunman's bullet had gone through his chest.

Tara screamed and ran forward. She dashed to where Smith lay, a few feet from Reid. Nobody bothered about the dead gunman.

"Jeff! Jeff!" she sobbed as she knelt beside him. Smith groaned, his eyes shut. There was blood everywhere.

Tara felt herself roughly pushed aside and Bowers and Mort bent over Smith. Then they picked him up and carried him through the murmuring crowd. As they walked, his head lolled and his arms hung limply. Above the blackness of his waistcoat a red stain was growing.

Tara caught up with them and grabbed Smith's freezing hand. "You've got to live," she muttered. "You've got to live. . . ." She never let go of his hand during that terrible journey through the strangely still streets to the Oyster Parlour. All the way they were escorted by Yeah Mow and others from Smith's militia. They surrounded the grim procession, their guns drawn, eyes raking the gaping bystanders, daring them to interfere.

Somebody had already summoned a doctor, and by the time they arrived he was standing by the bar with his little black bag.

150

Gently Mort and Bowers carried Smith upstairs and put him on the couch in his office.

The doctor bent over him. "He's alive," he announced, "but he hasn't got long."

"Can't you get the bullet out?" Bowers asked.

"No point," replied the doctor. "Nothing I can do. He's shot to hell."

He left, and somebody covered Smith with a blanket. Then they all stood around, uncertain, gazing down at Smith as if they expected him to take charge again and issue orders.

Tara gradually became aware of a droning noise like a swarm of angry bees closing in. There was the sound of crashing glass downstairs. Almost immediately the door flew open and the bartender burst in. "We got to get out," he yelled. "There's a mob down there. The whole town's going wild. They've heard the boss is dead. They're grabbing guns and looking for us."

Yeah Mow checked the magazine of his gun. "Come on," said Mort. "Let's go."

They all ran out, leaving Tara and Bowers alone with Smith. Tara knelt down beside Smith, searching his drawn, white face for some flicker of life.

"Here," Bowers said, pouring her a brandy. "You need this."

Tara shook her head, then Smith spoke, "Hell, Tara, never turn down a good brandy." His eyes were glazed but open, looking at her. His voice was hardly audible, but he managed to smile.

From the street they could hear the crowd. It was an ugly sound, just like it had been in Dawson when the lynching party arrived outside Mrs. Miles's house.

"Charley," Smith muttered to Bowers. "Just leave us."

Bowers hesitated. "I'll be around," he said and went out.

Smith smiled at Tara. "You know what I want to know. You don't have to tell me if you don't want to. But it would be nice if you could." His face contorted as a spasm of pain shot through him, but he gritted his teeth.

"I love you, Jeff," choked Tara, the tears rolling down her cheeks. It was the truth.

"You'll marry me?" he whispered.

151

"Of course."

He sighed. There was a look of great relief on his face. "Well, Mrs. Smith, aren't you going to kiss the bridegroom?"

He was so weak he could not hold her, but his mouth sought hers urgently. She closed her eyes and pressed her lips to his.

"I never wanted anything more in the world than you," he murmured. "Tara, hold my hand."

Then she knew he was losing the feeling in his limbs. She had been grasping his hand tightly, and yet he hadn't even known.

"Tara, you're so very beautiful," he whispered. "I love you . . . I want to . . ." he tried once more. "See you . . . only you. . . ."

His face was still turned towards her, but his eyes could no longer see. Jefferson Smith was dead.

She bent down and held him to her for a long while. Then she kissed his cold, lifeless lips. "Goodbye, my dear true friend," she whispered. Gently she closed his unseeing eyes.

The door opened quietly, and Bowers walked in. For a moment he stood silent, looking down at Smith's body. "Guess he was right," he said at last. "He always said they'd never hang him."

He coughed. "We'll have to get out of here. Those worthy citizens will string us all up if they get the chance. You too."

"Me?" she asked, dazed.

"You were his woman." He looked at Smith's body. "He made me promise that if anything ever happened to him, I'd make sure that you were O.K. Now that's the last thing I can do for him."

Tara said nothing, she felt numb. Bowers insisted on escorting her home, taking her out through a back exit. Downstairs all the windows of the Oyster Parlour had been smashed. In the middle of Broadway the very people who had so willingly joined in Smith's Independence Day celebrations were now burning his effigy.

Bowers guided Tara through back streets and alleys to the cabin.

Gangs of Reid's followers were brandishing a hastily published edition of the Skagway *Intelligencer*. Reid was still alive but dying. The dead gunman's identity was a mystery.

That night bloodthirsty, rampaging bands of citizens gathered for the kill. Smith's men fled for their lives, hiding in the woods and hills around Skagway, followed by murderous posses. Towards midnight the Oyster Parlour was set on fire. In the cabin Tara watched the glow in the sky, silhouetting the town's skyline.

Then she heard the sound of horses outside, and the creak of a wagon, followed by a hurried knocking on the door.

She opened it cautiously and saw Bowers standing there. "You and the kid got to get away," he said. "They're going to burn you out." He picked up John from his basket, put him in her arms, and pushed her out the door. "Quick," he ordered, and helped her into the wagon. Then he climbed on and took the reins.

Tara shivered, clutching the baby to her. Then she noticed a coffin on the floor of the cart. She knew without asking that lying in that wooden box was Jefferson Smith.

"We'll take him to the graveyard," Bowers said. "Couple of the boys will be there." He looked at her sharply. "We owe it to the boss. . . . After that we'll get you and the kid away."

The wagon bumped along a path skirting the town. They had been rumbling along for some twenty minutes when Bowers reined in the horses and pointed into the darkness. They were overlooking the sprawl of Skagway, and she could see her cabin. Suddenly a glow appeared, and the cabin flared up.

Without a word Bowers moved the wagon onward again.

Skagway's graveyard was at the start of the trail northward. Bowers helped Tara off the wagon. He nodded to two men who were leaning on shovels. They walked around to the back of the wagon and began dragging off the coffin.

Bowers guided Tara to the hole that already yawned in the muddy ground. The two men carried the casket to the grave and lowered it into the hole. Then they started shovelling in the earth.

"It's been good knowing you, boss," Bowers murmured. Then he threw in Smith's dice and a deck of cards. "Keep a game going for me. The boys send their best, but you know how it is. Too many necktie parties going on, so they asked me to say it for 'em."

He stopped and glanced at Tara. She was staring into the grave, the tears drying on her face. She wasn't crying just for the man who had loved her, she was crying for the child she had lost, for the man she hadn't found, for all of them.

"Can you say a prayer for him?" Tara whispered. "Please."

Bowers shook his head. "Don't want to offend you, but the boss would die_laughing. Me saying a prayer for him? No. You just think one."

She held the baby close as she looked, for the last time, on Smith's resting place. Then she turned and climbed back in the wagon. Bowers got in and picked up the reins. Slowly they moved off. And, at least, in true Smith style, Tara never once looked back.

"I've got you a ticket for a berth tomorrow. On the *Columbia*," Bowers told her as they jogged along. "She sails for Frisco on the tide. The sooner you and the boy are out of this, the better."

Tara didn't say anything. Of course this was the only way. She gazed at the distant mountains, the rolling forests, and at that moment they looked beautiful. The memory of the hardships, the misery, the cruelty of the territory melted away because this country had given her so much more. She had John. She had regained her self-respect. She had found love again. And perhaps, one day, Daniel would come back and they would be together.

Bowers took them to a shack among some fir trees. "You'll be O.K. here until the ship leaves," he assured her. "I'll get you aboard the boat, never worry."

She knew he was risking his life to stay and protect her. There would be little justice in Skagway for Smith's right-hand man.

He seemed to read her mind. "Don't fret," he said. "The man who gets the better of Charley Bowers hasn't been born yet. God willing," he added in mock piety.

After he had gone the tears came again. A couple of times the timbers of the log shack creaked. She raised her tear-stained face to the door as if she expected to see Smith standing there, smiling at her nonchalantly, puffing his constant cheroot, slowly walking over, taking her in his arms. But it was only the wind.

When Bowers came for her in the morning he had changed his appearance; to the eyes of the townsfolk he was a dude to his toecaps. He brought a big shawl to cover Tara's head.

"If anyone stops us, you're my lady wife," he said. "Mr. and Mrs. Jenkinson, and their little boy. I work for the railway company."

The journey through Skagway passed without incident. The town had calmed down after its orgy of violence. Bowers pulled

154

up at the quay. The *Columbia* already had steam up. "You'd better get on," said Bowers gruffly, handing her the ticket.

"Charley . . . " began Tara, but the words died on her lips.

"This is for you, too. From Jeff." He pulled out a sealed envelope and gave it to her. Then he turned and rapidly walked away, like a man not trusting himself to say anything.

Holding John tightly in her arms and clutching the envelope, Tara slowly walked up the gangway. The *Columbia* was a smart, well-appointed ship. Tara found, to her surprise, that Bowers had booked her a first-class passage. She was shown to a tidy cabin. Already a cot had been set up for the baby.

She went back on deck, John in her arms. A young boy was selling the Skagway *Intelligencer* and Tara bought a copy, her final souvenir of the Klondike. As each of the ship's lines was taken in, another link with Alaska was broken and her heart seemed to ache a little more. The engines grew louder, and around her passengers waved to the well-wishers on the dockside. Bowers had disappeared.

"Goodbye Alaska," Tara whispered as the ship gently eased away from its mooring. She stayed on the deck for a long time, watching as the *Columbia* steamed away.

When finally the *Columbia* passed the northernmost tip of British Columbia, she remembered the letter Bowers had handed her. She went below to her cabin and sat down, with John on her lap. Slowly she opened the envelope. There was a note:

My dearest Tara,
    You won't get this unless I've finally thrown in my cards. I hope that will never be, because there's so much I want to do with you. So you'll never read this, if I'm lucky. I love you. Jeff

There was something else in the envelope. She held in her hand a banker's draft payable to Mrs. Tara Kane for the sum of one hundred thousand dollars in gold, signed, with a flourish, Jefferson Randolph Smith.

For a long time Tara stared at the cheque, her hand shaking. Then she put John's tiny hands on it. "It's yours, my love. With love from your godfather."

AFTER SHE HAD put John down, Tara sat on her bunk and opened the newspaper. The front page was dominated by a photograph of Reid, lying dead. Under it was an article:

SMITH'S KILLER NAMED. GUNMAN WAS ON RAILROAD PAYROLL
The man who shot down Jefferson Smith was a newly hired railroad employee. According to company officials he was a down-on-his-luck gold miner whose prospecting fortunes had failed. He had been hired only twenty-four hours before to ride shotgun on high value consignments. But Sir Thomas Tancrede, railroad boss, told the *Intelligencer* that the man at the time of the shoot-out "was not on company business. While we are not unhappy that the community is rid of Mr. Soapy Smith and his ilk, we did not hire a gunman to kill him." Asked why the killer should have taken on Mr. Smith, Sir Thomas Tancrede said he had no idea "but there must be a lot of people who had their own reasons for wanting to see Smith dead." The gunman, after firing the fatal shot, died immediately from Smith's bullet. He never spoke but the railroad has named him as Daniel Kane, 27, of San Francisco.

"It can't be true," Tara sobbed. She could not believe that she had seen Daniel kill Smith without knowing. That she had been less than ten feet away from him and not recognized him. That she had gone off with Smith and left her own husband lying in the street alone, abandoned. And that while Daniel lay dying, she had agreed to become another man's wife. . . .

Stunned and desolate, Tara wrapped herself in her cloak and went up on deck. She stared across the black sea. Before her stretched a rippling starry carpet, the silvery moon undulating in a liquid abyss. It was beautiful, hypnotic, calling.

And it reminded Tara of another natural phenomena—the Aurora Borealis. That had been a sign from heaven in the frozen wilderness. This was also a promise.

"Dear God," she sobbed, looking up at the sky. "You have taken so much from me, but you've given me the greatest gift of all. I have John, a future to live for. Who knows what lies ahead but, with your help, I'll get through." Always one day at a time.

George Markstein

George Markstein was out of breath when he arrived for our lunch scarcely five minutes late. "I'm so sorry to have kept you waiting," he apologized. "The flat where I work has been burgled. Only a few books and papers have been taken, but it's all very extraordinary."

As I ordered him a large drink, he enlarged on his recent losses. "The papers were to do with a book I'm writing about the strange circumstances of Goering's death and the rise of neo-Nazism. The robbers even stole an Iron Cross that a friend had given me. Who could possibly want such things so badly?"

George has always been curious about people, their reactions and motives. He was a crime reporter and later one of the pioneers of independent television, devising two top-rating series, *The Prisoner* and *Special Branch*. He scripted *Robbery* and *The Odessa File* for the cinema, and his first novel, *The Cooler*, was an immediate best seller.

I asked him about *Tara Kane*. "The idea came to me about five years ago," he recalled. "I discovered in a New York secondhand bookshop some vivid photographs of the Klondike gold rush taken by a German, Eric Hegg. Here was an amazing world, peopled with fascinating characters. Slowly the idea for the novel began to take shape."

A year or so later, in Hollywood, George unearthed—among other useful finds—a gold prospector's manual loaded with advice on everything from clothing to medicines. More and more outsize historical characters clamoured to join the book's cast—Major Constantine, the Reverend Bowers, Soapy Smith and his girlfriend Cad Wilson—and more and more dramatic real events jostled for a place in the plot.

But George needed a heroine. "Tara," he told me, "is quite simply my ideal woman. She is positive, full of ingenuity, and couldn't care less what people think of her."

I asked him if he had ever met his ideal woman. "Yes," he said, in his half amused, half enigmatic fashion. "I have always been very lucky in life. I have met my Tara."

NDB

ELEPHANT BILL

a condensation of the book by

J. H. Williams

Illustrated by Cecil Vieweg
Published by Hart-Davis, MacGibbon

The Elephants' Graveyard—myth or reality?

This is only one of the many fascinating mysteries of elephant behaviour that Colonel Williams unravels in this unique book. For many years he lived with elephants in the vast teak forests of Burma. He writes of the great animals with vividness, impressive knowledge and warm affection. And through his words there emerges a memorable picture of Burma and its jungle people.

This book was first published in Condensed Books twenty-five years ago. Since then it has become a classic among animal stories and we offer it proudly, to mark our Silver Anniversary.

"Colonel Williams has devoted more than twenty years of his life to elephants, and ended by writing a book of which, I venture to think, those thoughtful animals would themselves approve. . . . There is interest on every page, extreme excitement on some, and throughout an affectionate pleasure in doing justice to his elephant friends." —*Arthur Ransome*

CHAPTER 1

I have always got on well with animals. I like them and, with one or two notable exceptions, they always seem to like me. When I was a boy in Cornwall my first animal friend was a donkey. He had free range over the moors, but I always knew where to find him. During the World War of 1914–18, I was in the Camel Corps, and then, later on, transport officer in charge of a lot of mules. These experiences taught me much about animals, for both camels and mules are temperamental beasts, and mules have also a remarkable sense of humour, so that in dealing with them one gets plenty of exercise for one's own. That was valuable. My life has been spent east of Suez in places where if you lose your sense of humour you had much better take the first boat home.

Like millions of other fellows, when the war was over I began to think about finding myself a job. A friend told me that he knew a chap who did something with elephants in Burma. This sounded as though it would be what I wanted.

My friend wrote to the fellow, introducing me as a candidate for elephant management, and I wrote to the head of the Bombay Burma Trading Corporation—the company concerned. It was 1920 before I got back to England, but my letter led to an interview and before the year was out I was in Burma.

MY FIRST VIVID memories of Burma are not of the pagodas and rice fields and all I had read about, but of my first "jungle salt", Willie, the man under whom I was to begin my training.

I met him at his camp on the banks of the Upper Chindwin River, Upper Burma. He was, in his own words, down with fever, but he was sitting at a table, about mid-day, outside his tent, drinking a whisky and soda and smoking a Burma cheroot.

His welcome was icy, and I immediately guessed that he jealously resented anyone sharing his jungle life. About four o'clock in the afternoon I asked for a cup of tea—and was laughed at for not drinking whisky and soda. I vowed, privately, that I would see him under the table later on. About five o'clock seven elephants arrived in camp and were paraded in line for inspection. Willie did not speak to me as he walked off to inspect them. However, I followed him, uninvited. Judging by appearances, there was one worn-out animal which looked as though it might be the mother of the other six. Each animal was closely inspected and Willie entered some remark about each in a book. This took up about half an hour, during which he did not address a single word to me. I was careful not to ask any questions, as I saw that I should only be called a damned fool for my pains. However, when the inspection was over, Willie turned to me, saying: "Those four on the right are yours, and God help you if you can't look after them."

For all I knew, I was supposed to take them to bed with me. The next evening, when Willie told me to inspect my own four and to see that their gear was on their backs comfortably—as though I could tell!—I followed a lifelong rule when in doubt: I trusted to luck.

After the inspection that first night, as my tent had been pitched near his, I joined Willie at his camp table. On it were two bottles of Black Label—one of his and one of mine.

After half an hour or so Willie thawed sufficiently to ask me, "Are you safe with a shotgun?"—not "Do you shoot?" as is more usual.

Silence reigned after my answer. Willie emptied and refilled his glass several times. At last he opened up and, passing his empty bottle to me, remarked, "I drink a bottle a night and it does me no harm. There are two vices in this country. Woman is one and the other the bottle. Choose which you like, but you must not mix them. Anything to do with the jungle, elephants and your work you can only learn by experience. No one but a Burman can teach you and you'll draw your pay for ten years before you earn it.

Tomorrow I'll give you some maps and the day after you must push off for three months on your own. You can do what you damned well like—including suicide if you're lonely—but I won't have you back until you can speak some Burmese."

After this speech he walked off to his bed without even saying "Good night".

He was just like the jungle—as unyielding and unfriendly as a tree seems when one is lonely. But a few years later he had become a great friend of mine. He accepted me slowly, as the forests did.

AFTER FOUR AND A HALF YEARS' service in the army I believed I was past the age of adventures; but leaving on my first jungle trip, two days later, certainly gave me a thrill. With four elephants carrying my kit, a cook, two bearers and two messengers, I was on my own again. My life in charge of elephants had begun.

I had been on the march less than two days when the ancient female elephant known as Ma Oh (Old Lady) was discovered dead an hour before I was due to move camp. Willie had, I now know, somewhat unscrupulously palmed her off on me—and his terrible words, "God help you if you can't look after them," now ran in my ears. Seeing her enormous carcase lying in the jungle—just as she had died in her sleep—was a terrible sight, and it was awful that she had died within a few days of my being made responsible for her. How on earth, I wondered, should I get out of this mess? Willie's reception of me, the dead elephant, and his threat ringing in my ears combined to fill my cup with bitterness. "At the worst," I thought, "I can only lose my job. I'm damned if I'll buy them a new one!" It was a bad business but as I had no one to help me out I had to help myself, and I decided that the best thing I could do was to hold a post-mortem.

The "Old Lady" was scarcely cold before I was literally inside her, with her arching ribs sheltering me from the sun. I learned a good deal about elephant construction from her. Her carcase proved to be a cave full of strange treasures such as the heart, the gizzard and the lungs. The only snag was that I could not find any kidneys, and I was almost tempted to conclude that she must have died for lack of them. However, when I came to write out a report that evening I decided that "no kidneys" might not be an acceptable cause of death—so in desperation I left it at "found dead" and did not even mention my Jonah's journey.

Ma Oh's load was easily divided among the remaining three animals, and on I went. My instructions were to march to a certain village in the Myittha Valley, where I was to meet a head Burman named U Tha Yauk. I was on foot with my messengers and the two bearers, and we had outdistanced the elephants by several miles by taking a short cut up the bed of the creek. U Tha Yauk had come some way out of the village to meet me, and was squatting on a rock beside the creek up which we were travelling.

I greeted him with my three words of Burmese and laughed because I could say no more, and he laughed back; we marched on in single file until we came to a clearing around which there were about ten bamboo huts, all standing on bamboo stilts and thatched with grass. A Burmese girl dressed in her best, with a pretty little white coat, and a flower in her hair, came forward with a cane basket-work stool for me to sit on. Three men came up with green coconuts and, cutting them open at one end, poured the juice into a cup of hand-beaten copper and gave it to me with the reverent gestures of priests administering the sacrament. I drank off at least six cups of the cooling drink before I realized that a dozen people had gathered round to gaze at me.

Directly the elephants turned up, the crowd moved off to help unload them, and my cook was at once installed in his hut. My kit was soon piled up in one corner of my hut, which was divided by a bamboo matting wall into my bedroom on one side and my living room on the other.

In a quarter of an hour the room was furnished—with a ground-sheet covered with bright blue cotton dhurries on the floor, my camp bed, camp tables and camp chair. My bedding roll was undone and the mosquito net put in position. Meanwhile other Burmans were filling my tub in a bathroom at the back of the hut with tins of water from the brook. After dismissing the other helpers, my personal servant unlocked my basket packs and took out photographs to arrange on my dressing-table and put my revolver under my pillow. Then, when all was ready, he asked me to come in. As soon as I had looked round and sat down he took off my puttees and boots and disappeared. In the bathroom I found a Burmese boy, who poured two buckets of hot water into my tub and swirled it around, giving me a smile, as though to say: "Bath ready, sir."

I bathed, and by the time I went back into my hut I found the table was laid with a spotless white cloth, and that flannel trousers, socks and white shirt were spread out on my bed, but that my perfect valet had once more vanished.

My dinner was ready, and as I finished each course hands of unseen attendants passed up the meat and vegetables, the sweet and savoury, to my valet, who stood silently behind my chair as I ate. While I drank my coffee, he drew down the mosquito net and tucked it in and then gave a graceful bow saying, though I could not understand him: "By your leave I will now go."

Left alone, I was overcome by a great homesickness. The overpowering kindness of the Burmans was too much for me and I asked myself what I had done to deserve it. It never dawned on me that the Burmans wanted to show their sympathy with me in my loneliness and my ignorance of their language and all the difficulties that lay ahead.

CHAPTER 2

Next morning a new life began—my life as a pupil of U Tha Yauk. Fortunately, he was as eager to teach me as I was enthusiastic to learn. Every waking moment I had to study jungle lore and to observe the elephants and all their ways.

That morning I woke to the sound of elephant bells, and the camp was astir before I had dressed. While I was having my breakfast I could see that the camp was already full of elephants standing around unattended while the Burmans squatted in groups having their early morning meal. Each man had a steaming hot heap of rice, served on a wild banana leaf. Not a word was spoken while they ate, and as each man finished he rinsed his mouth and washed his hands from a coconut-shell cup of water. Then he walked off to his harnessed elephant, mounted in silence, and in silence the elephant and its rider vanished into the jungle to begin their day's work.

With the aid of a good map of the Indaung Forest Reserve, U Tha Yauk now made me understand I was to go on a tour with him from the valley, crossing five parallel creeks flowing from east to west into the Myittha River. On the sides of each of the watersheds he had a camp of elephants, ten camps altogether, each with an average of seven elephants, or seventy working animals all told. Judging from the map, the distance between the camps was six to seven miles, with hills three to four thousand feet high between.

At the first camp we reached I found about twenty Burmans, including a carpenter of sorts, erecting a set of jungle buildings. It was explained to me that this camp was to be my headquarters during the coming monsoon months. I soon realized that the elephant was the backbone of the Burmese teak industry.

The history of the Bombay Burma Corporation went back to the time of King Theebaw, when a senior member of the firm, who visited Burma, appreciated the great possibilities of the teak trade and was able to obtain a lease of certain forest areas. Sawmills were established at the ports, a system of rafting teak logs down the creeks and rivers was organized, and elephants were bought on a large scale.

Teak is one of the world's best hardwoods, partly because of the silica it contains. In Burma, it grows best at heights between two thousand and three thousand feet, in steep, precipitous country. The trees often stand ten or twelve to the acre, but usually only the largest tree is selected, and the remaining trees are left for the next cycle of felling, probably twenty-five years later. The tree chosen is killed by ringing the bark at the base, and the dead tree is left standing for three years before it is felled, by which time the timber is seasoned and has become light enough to float. As teak grows best in country inaccessible to tractors and machinery, elephant power is essential for hauling and pushing the logs from the stump to the nearest stream that will be capable of floating them during the flood-waters of the monsoon months.

In the early days, the Bombay Burma Corporation bought some

166

of its elephants from Siam, some from India, but the majority were obtained by capturing wild elephants in Burma and breaking them in. This process is known as "kheddaring".

When the Bombay Burma Corporation had built up considerable herds of elephants, it realized that elephant calves born in captivity could be broken in and trained more easily than captured wild elephants.

Finally when the Corporation's herds had reached a strength of nearly two thousand animals it was found that births balanced the deaths and that new supplies of elephants were required only on rare occasions. The kheddaring of wild elephants, on any extensive scale, thus came to an end.

The health, management and handling of the elephants in this enormous organization impressed me as the factor on which everything else depended. The routine work of elephant management in camp consisted in checking up gear-making, getting to know the oozies, or elephant riders, inspecting elephants and dressing any galls caused by gear rubbing, wounds caused by bamboo splinters in the feet, and other common injuries.

For my early training in all these tasks I am indebted to U Tha Yauk. After our first trip we spent several days in camp. I mixed with everyone, for ever asking questions and being given answers packed with information I had to remember. One day, going back to my hut for lunch, I first watched a most fascinating sight.

About a hundred yards below my hut was a large pool in the brook. Two elephants, each with her rider sitting behind her head, entered the pool, and, without any word of command that I could hear, they lay down in the water. The riders tucked up their lungyi skirts so that they were transformed into loincloths, slipped off their mounts into the water and began to scrub their respective elephants from head to tail with a soap which lathered freely. Then they washed it off the elephants, splashing water over them with their hands. The soap they used turned out to be the soapy bark of a tree. Soon I was standing on the bank of the pool and from there I watched five elephants being washed in the same way. Two of them were cows with young calves which rolled over and over and played in the water like young children. There were also two large

167

males, with gleaming white tusks which were scrubbed with handfuls of silver sand.

After they had all been washed and dried off, the elephants were paraded for inspection—all drawn up in line abreast, each rider dressed in his best. U Tha Yauk advanced with military precision and, after bowing instead of saluting, handed me a set of books, all ragged and torn. On the cover of each was an elephant's name.

I looked at one book and called out the name of the elephant; and the rider, hearing me, rode it up to me at a fast, bold stride. Both rider and elephant had a sort of natural magnificence. The oozie halted the animal just before me. He was a splendid beast with his head up, his skin newly scrubbed but already dry in the sun, a black skin with a faint tinge of blue showing through it which seemed to make it so alive. The white tusks, freshly polished, gleamed in the sunlight. The motionless rider appeared to be sitting on one leg while the other dangled behind the elephant's ear. On his face was an expression of intense pride—pride in his magnificent beast.

Suddenly, he gave an order and the elephant swung round to present his hindquarters, on which there was a brand, made with phosphorous paint when the animal was six years old.

I opened the book and read a number of entries, each with the date when he had been inspected during the last ten years. On the front page was the animal's history with his registered number and other details—such as that he had been born in Siam, bought when he was twenty years old, badly gored by a wild tusker, but had fully recovered after being off work for a year.

Thus I inspected each of the animals in turn and read their histories. As each inspection was finished the rider and elephant left the clearing and disappeared into the jungle.

When they had all gone I was taken round the harness racks— just a row of horizontal branches of trees on each of which hung the gear of one of the animals. All the harness except the heavy dragging chains was handmade by the riders. There were great cane basket panniers, woven breast straps of fibre, wooden breeching-blocks, padding from the bark of the banbrwe tree, ropes of every kind twisted from the bark of the shaw tree.

IN THOSE FIRST THREE MONTHS on my own I did most of the things worth doing in Burma. Tha Yauk helped me to achieve my ambition of shooting a wild bull elephant. My main reason for shooting him was not to secure the tusks, much as I coveted them, but to carry out a post-mortem to see what the organs of a really healthy elephant looked like, and to make another attempt to find the kidneys. This second post-mortem taught me a good deal about what had been wrong with Ma Oh. In fact, it showed me half a dozen reasons sufficient to explain her death.

After three months which passed all too soon I returned to Willie, having learned a great deal. When I arrived I got the greeting I expected: sarcastic remarks about my having let one of my elephants die in the first two days—no doubt by having overloaded her with all my blasted new kit.

I replied that I was surprised that she had lived as long as she had. Her liver was riddled with flukes and her heart was as big as a rugger ball.

"How do *you* know how big an elephant's heart ought to be?"

"I shot a wild tusker that Tha Yauk told me was forty years old, and I did a post-mortem on him to see how the organs of a healthy elephant compared with hers. His heart was only the size of a coconut."

Willie's whole attitude to me changed after I said this. What pleased him was that I had shot an elephant, not for its tusks, but in order to learn more about elephants. For Willie, like most men who live long in the jungle, hated big game to be shot. He felt far more sympathy with any creature which was part of his jungle than with any new arrival, armed with all his new kit.

That evening I became a companion with whom he could enjoy rational conversation instead of an interloper who had to be bullied and kept in his place. His great ambition had been to get someone who would take up the subject of elephant management seriously and it seemed to him that I might be the man he wanted.

Before I left him, two or three days later, he had advised me to take up elephants and to make them my chief concern and my life's work. I thus owe a great debt of gratitude to Willie.

The job of extracting teak and delivering it a thousand miles away has many branches, and up till that time none of the European assistants had specialized in trying to improve the management of elephants. Most of the details had been left to the Burman.

The average European assistant joining any of the large teak firms in Burma was put in charge of a forest area bigger than an English county. In it were scattered a total of about a hundred elephants, in groups of seven. By continually touring during all the seasons of the year, he might be able to visit every camp about once every six weeks. Under such conditions it would be a long time before he learnt to know his elephants even by name, still less by sight; and it would be a very long time indeed before he knew their individual temperaments and capacities for work.

I was more fortunate, as I was responsible for seventy elephants, all working in a fairly small area. I was thus often able to visit my camps twice a month and to spend a longer time in each of them.

What follows is largely the result of my having the luck to start in conditions that enabled me to get to know my elephants really well.

CHAPTER 3

It is impossible to understand much about tame elephants unless one knows a great deal about the habits of wild ones. The study of wild elephants usually entails shooting a few of them at some period, either deliberately for sport or ivory, or in self-defence. Most men who have shot elephants come afterwards to regret having done so—but "to hunt is to learn".

Wild elephants normally live in herds of thirty to fifty, and during the year cover great distances, chiefly in search of fodder. During the rainy monsoon months—from June to October—they graze on bamboo in the hilly forest country. After the monsoons are over they move into the lower foothills and the swamp valleys, feeding more on grass and less on bamboo.

The herds know their yearly cycle of grazing grounds, and in their annual passage wear well-defined tracks along the ridges of the hills. In places where they have to descend from a precipitous ridge down the side of a watershed they will move in Indian file, and by long use will wear the track into a succession of well-defined steps.

Wild elephants hate being disturbed on their feeding grounds but they do not usually stampede suddenly, like many other herds of big game. With an uncanny intelligence, they close up round one animal as though they were drilled, and their leader decides on the best line of retreat. He leads and they follow irresistibly, smashing through everything, like so many steam-rollers.

Most wild elephant calves are born between March and May. I believe that if the mother elephant is disturbed she will carry her calf during its first month, holding it wrapped in her trunk. I have seen a mother pick up her calf in this way.

For many years I could not understand the bellowing and trumpeting of wild elephants at night during the hot weather when most calves are born. The fuss is made by the herd in order to protect the mother and calf from intruders—in particular from tigers. The noise is terrifying. The herd will remain in the neighbourhood of the maternity ward for some weeks until the new arrival can keep up with the pace of a grazing herd. The ward may cover an area of a square mile and during the day the herd will graze all over it, surrounding the mother and her newly born calf, and closing their ranks round her at night. The places chosen are on low ground where a river has suddenly changed its course and taken a hair-pin bend. These spots are thus bounded on three sides by banks and river. The kind of jungle found in such places is always the same. They are flooded during the rains, but during the hot weather—the normal calving period—they are fairly dry with areas of dense kaing, or elephant grass, eight to twelve feet high, with an occasional wild cotton tree giving shade. They are eerie spots and to explore them is an adventure. Wild pigs breed in the same type of jungle and harbour their sounders of sucking pigs under huge heaps of leaves and grass which in size resemble ant-heaps four feet high.

It is common practice for a Burman oozie to ride his elephant quietly up to such a "pig's nest" of leaves and grass and, silently controlling the elephant by movements of his foot and leg, to instruct him to put one forefoot gently on the mound. Squeals and snorts usually follow from the old sow, and three or four sucking pigs join her in a stampede.

Once while an elephant did this I had the good luck to bag a right and left of sucking pig for the camp pot from an elephant's back. It was ridden by an oozie called Kya Sine, who knew every trick of the jungle and became my gun-boy until his death.

It is a peculiar thing that the elephant, which becomes so accustomed to man and has such confidence in him once it has been trained, should be so afraid of him in its wild state. Owing to this fear of man, they do surprisingly little damage to village crops, considering the vast numbers of wild elephant in Burma. They much prefer their own deep jungles and seldom leave them. The damage that they do has been greatly and most unfairly exaggerated. Solitary animals may, however, do great damage and become bold enough to drive off any human intruder. They do this almost as if it were a joke. Such animals, however, are eventually declared rogues and are killed.

Ordinary fences around crops are no good as a protection against elephants. The Burma Posts and Telegraphs know only too well that an elephant has merely to lean against a telegraph post in order to push it over, or to grip it with its trunk and give a heave to pull it up with ease. The only effective fence against elephants is what is called the "punge". This is often used as a trap, and it was a godsend during the Second World War to the XIVth Army, which often employed it instead of barbed wire. The punge fence, or trap, is made of a series of sharpened and lightly roasted, or smoked, bamboo stakes of varying lengths. One end of each is stuck into the ground at an angle of thirty degrees, with the point upwards and facing outwards. On the outside of the fence, concealed in the undergrowth, are very short stakes, protruding only three or four inches out of the ground, and behind these are stakes gradually increasing in length, the longest sticking out four or five feet. The depth of the fence may be as much as eight or ten yards.

I have seen wild boar stampeded down a track across which a punge fence had been erected. They were killed outright, skewered through the chest and out between the shoulder blades.

If an elephant charges a punge fence, a stake may easily pierce right through the foreleg. Once I had to extract such a stake, gripping the point with a pair of blacksmith's tongs and pulling it right through the leg. For, like a barbed fishhook, a piece of bamboo cannot be withdrawn by the way it has entered.

Pit-traps, which occur so frequently in books about elephant-hunting, are very uncommon in Burma. I think the Burmese elephant is too intelligent to fall into them. An effective and heinous trap which killed one of my own elephants was a spear, about the size of a light telegraph pole, heavily weighted and suspended in a tree over a game track. The release was by means of a trip-wire rope, and the spear came down with such force as to transfix the elephant, smashing his ribs and piercing his intestines. It must have taken at least a dozen men to erect this trap. I never traced the culprits. When I tackled the villagers on the subject, they would only say that the tree must have grown like that.

Wire ropes of all sizes have become common in the jungle, and the simple wire noose can be very dangerous and terrifies elephants, as the trunk is often caught. If an elephant's trunk is seriously injured it will die of starvation, since everything it eats has to be torn down or pulled up and handled by the trunk.

AFTER THE MONSOONS the full-grown male tuskers join the herd for courting and mating, which is very private. The bull prefers to remain on the outskirts of the herd and the female comes out to him. She gives the herd the slip in the evening and is back with them at dawn. Sometimes a rival tusker intervenes and a duel ensues. This is why elephant fights are always between two bulls. There is never a general dog-fight within the herd.

Elephant bulls fight head to head and seldom fight to the death without one trying to break away. The one that breaks away frequently receives a wound which proves mortal, for, in turning, he exposes the most vulnerable part of the body. The deadly blow is a thrust of one tusk between the hind legs into the loins and intestines, where the testicles are carried inside the body. It is a common wound to have to treat after a wild tusker has attacked a domesticated one.

Some males never grow tusks but these tuskless males are at no disadvantage in a fight. From the age of three all that the animal gains by not having to grow tusks goes into bodily strength, particularly in the girth and weight of the trunk. The trunk becomes so strong that it will smash off an opponent's solid ivory tusk as though it were the dry branch of a tree.

From the time that a male calf is three years old there is always interest among the oozies as to whether it is going to be a tusker with two tusks, or a tai (with one tusk either right or left), or a han (a tuskless male but with two small tushes such as females carry), or a hine, which has neither tusks nor tushes.

One of the most delightful myths about wild elephants is that the old tuskers and females eventually go off to die in a traditional graveyard. This belief has its origin in the fact that dead elephants, whether tuskers or females, are so seldom found.

I shall try to explain away the myth by describing what really happens. Take the case of a fine old bull that has stopped following the herd at about the age of seventy-five and has taken to a solitary existence. He has given up covering great distances in a seasonal feeding cycle and remains in the headwaters of a remote creek. His cheeks are sunken, his teeth worn out. Old age and debility slowly overtake him and his big, willing heart. During the monsoon months, fodder, chiefly bamboo, is easily gathered and he stays up in the hills. As the dry season approaches, fodder becomes scarcer and he moves slowly downhill to browse on the tall grass. Then, as the hot season comes on and there are forest fires, he is too tired and too old to go in search of the varied diet he needs and his digestion suffers. Fever sets in as the showers of April and May chill him, and he moves to water. Here, by the large pool above the gorge, there is always green fodder. He is perfectly happy, but the water slowly dries until there is only a trickle flowing from the large pool and he spends his time standing on a spit of sand, picking up the cool sand and mud with his trunk and spraying it over his hot, fevered body.

One sweltering hot evening in late May, he hears a mighty storm raging ten miles away in the hills, and he knows the rains have broken. Soon the trickle will become a raging torrent of broken brown water carrying trees and logs and debris in its onrush. Throwing his head back, with his trunk in his mouth as he takes his last drink, he grows giddy. He staggers and falls. He is down—never to rise again—and he dies without a struggle. The tired old heart just stops ticking.

Two porcupines get the news that night and in spite of the heavy rain attack one of his tusks, gnawing it as beavers gnaw wood. They have eaten only half through the second tusk when the roar of the first tearing spate of the rains drives them off.

A five-foot wall of water strikes the carcase—debris piles up while the water furiously undermines and outflanks this obstruction. At last the whole mass of carcase, stones and branches moves, floats, and then, swirling and turning over, goes into the gorge down a ten-foot waterfall and jams among the boulders below. Hundreds of tons of water drive onto it, logs and boulders bruise and smash up the body, shifting it further, and the savage water tears it apart. As the forest fires are God's spring-cleaning of the jungle, so the spates of the great rains provide burial for the dead.

By dawn the floods have subsided and the porcupines have to hunt for their second meal of tusk. Other jungle scavengers have their share. But the spate comes again the next night and in a week all traces of the old tusker have disappeared.

CHAPTER 4

I arrived in Burma just as a determined effort had been started to improve the management of elephants and their calves. In order to do this, it was first necessary to improve the conditions of the oozies, who must be considered as part and parcel of the Burmese timber-working elephant which they ride. These men are born with a knowledge of elephants. Their homes are in camps in the most remote parts of the jungle. They can sit an elephant from the age of six, and they grow up learning all the traditional knowledge, the myth and legend, the blended fact and fiction which is attached to this lovable animal. At the age of fourteen the average boy in an elephant camp is earning a wage. He starts life as a paijaik—that is, the man who hooks the chains to the logs—a ground assistant of the oozie.

It is a proud day in that boy's life when he is promoted to oozie and has an elephant in his own charge. There is no more lovely sight than to see a fourteen-year-old boy riding a newly trained calf elephant of six. The understanding between them is equalled only by that of a child with a puppy, but the Burmese boy is not so cruel to his elephant as most children are to puppies. The Burman oozie has a pretty hard life. In the first place, he has to catch his elephant every morning and bring it to camp. Catching his elephant involves tracking the animal a distance of about eight miles, starting at dawn through jungles infested with all types of big game. That in itself is a lonely job, and to do it successfully the oozie has to become one of the jungle beasts himself—as alert and as wary as they are.

He knows the shape, size and peculiarities of his own elephant's footprints with complete certainty. Once he has picked them up, he sets off following the trail. While he is doing so he notices many things: he finds the spot where the animal rested in the night, he observes its droppings, and can tell from them that his elephant has been eating too much bamboo and for that reason will probably have headed for a patch of kaing grass that grows on the banks of the creek over the watershed.

When he has gained the ridge he will halt and listen, perhaps for ten minutes, for the distinctive sound of his elephant's kalouk, or bell, which the oozie made himself. Elephant bells are made with two clappers, one on each side, hanging outside the bell, which is made from a hollowed-out lump of teak. No two bells ever have the same note and the sound of fifteen or more can only be compared to the music of a babbling brook.

As the oozie approaches his beast he begins to sing so as to let her know that he is coming. Then, instead of bursting through the kaing grass that stands nine feet high, he sits down on a boulder beside the creek and fills his homemade pipe and lights it. Between the puffs he keeps calling: "Lah! Lah! Lah! (Come on! Come on! Come on!)." But no sound comes from where his elephant is grazing, so he changes his words to "Digo lah! Digo lah!

177

(Come here! Come here!)." And he will sit and smoke and call for fifteen minutes without showing impatience. He gives her time to accept the grim fact that another day of hard work has begun for her. If he hurries her, she may rebel.

Presently the elephant emerges from the kaing grass, and, chatting away to her, he says: "Do you think I've nothing else to do but wait for you? You've been eating since noon yesterday."

Then his voice rings out with a firm order: "Hmit!"

Dropping first on her haunches, then reposing with all four legs extended, she allows him to approach her.

"Tah! (Stand up!)," he orders, and she does so, keeping her front legs close together. He then bends down and unfastens her fetter-chain and throws it over her withers. These hobbles are either chain or cane, and are put on fairly tight with little play between the legs. When the animal is hobbled it can either shuffle slowly on easy ground or progress by a series of hops. But in spite of this for short distances it can go as fast as a man can run. After unfastening the hobbles the oozie orders her to sit down, climbs onto her head and away they go.

When they reach camp the oozie has his first meal of the day, washes his elephant in the creek, and then harnesses her for work. Their job for the day is to climb a ridge two thousand feet above the camp and to drag a log from the stump to the creek.

When the oozie reaches the log with his elephant and his paijaik, he will trim it of knots so as to make it easier for dragging. He also cuts a hole in the thinner end of the log, through which the dragging chains are passed. He will then fasten the chains securely. After that there begins the wearisome task of dragging a log twenty-nine feet long and six or seven feet in girth—that is to say, over a hundred cubic feet of timber, or four tons dead weight. For a mile the path follows the top of the ridge. "Patience! patience! patience! Yoo! Yoo! Yoo! (Pull! pull! pull!)," calls the oozie. As the elephant takes the strain, she feels what power she must exert besides that of her enormous weight. The ground is ankle-deep in mud, and there are dozens of small obstructions which must be levelled out by the log's nose—sapling stumps, bamboos, rocks.

The elephant puts out her first effort and, bellowing like fury, pulls the log three times her own length and then stops. She rests then to take breath, and her trunk goes out sideways to snatch at a bamboo. It is her chewing gum as she works but it earns her a sarcastic comment from the oozie: "My mother, but you are for ever eating!" However, his patience is quite undisturbed. The elephant takes her time. "Yoo! Yoo! Yoo!" calls the oozie, but there is no response. "Yooo! Yooo! Yooo!" Then the elephant pulls again, but this time, as it is slightly downhill, she pulls the log six times her length before she halts. So it goes on until they reach the edge of a precipice—a four-hundred-foot drop. The elephant knows the exact margin of safety, and when the log is ten feet from the edge she refuses to haul it any closer.

The chains are unfastened, and the elephant is moved round behind the log. The oozie gives his orders by kicks and scratches with his bare feet behind the elephant's ears. So he coaxes her to bend down her massive head in order to get a leverage under the log with her trunk. Working like that, she moves it first four feet at one end, then rolls it from the middle, then pushes the other end until she has got it on to the very edge of the cliff, almost trembling on the balance. She will then torment her oozie by refusing to touch it again for ten minutes. Finally, when the oozie's patience is almost at an end, she puts one forefoot out as calmly as if she were tapping a football, and the log is away—gone. There is a crash in the jungle below, and then a prolonged series of crashes echoing through the jungle as the log tears down bamboos until it comes to rest four hundred feet lower down, leaving the elephant standing on the edge of the precipice above, with a supercilious expression on her face, as though she were saying: "Damned easy."

Half an hour later elephant and oozie have reached the log again, having gone round by a circuitous game-track to the foot of the precipice. Once down there, she has again to drag the log with the chains along a ledge. Dragging a log weighing four tons while negotiating a narrow ledge is a risky business, for the log might roll. But the elephant can judge what is safe to the inch—not to the foot—and she works with patience, patience, patience. Both oozie and elephant know that, should the log start to roll or slide over the edge, all the gear and harness can be got rid of in the twinkling of an eye. The elephant has only to whip round in her tracks, step inside her chain, and bend down her head for all the harness to peel off over her head as easily as a girl strips off a silk slip over her shoulders. For this reason it is very rare indeed for an elephant to be dragged over a precipice by a log suddenly taking charge.

After negotiating the ledge, there is an easy downhill drag for half a mile to the floating point on the side of the creek. By that time it is about three o'clock in the afternoon. The oozie unharnesses his elephant, puts on her fetters, slaps her on her backside and tells her that she must go off in search of food. For neither of them is their day's work really over. The elephant still has to find her fodder, not only to chew it but to break off, pull down, or pull up, every branch, tree, creeper or tuft of grass that she eats. The oozie has to repair his gear, trim logs or weave a new laibut, or breast-strap of bark. This bit of harness takes the full strain of the elephant's strength when dragging and has to be made accordingly.

Such is the oozie's day's work—and with it all he is a very happy man. His chief relaxation is gambling. He often literally loses the shirt off his back. I have seen one particular shirt worn by six different owners in a year.

Not only the oozie but also his wife and family need frequent medical attention, and they have no one to look to but the European assistant who lives nearest. Apart from all the diseases, accidents are constantly occurring in the jungle; the assistant has to be ready to take decisions which would make an ordinary medical man's hair stand on end. One may come into a new camp and find sick people down with beri-beri—two women with their breasts split like ripe tomatoes from the swelling characteristic of that disease—and one has to decide at once what to do. One has to be ready to tackle a girl with an afterbirth hæmorrhage or a man scalped by a bear. Malaria is more common than colds in the head in England. Dysentery and even cholera and smallpox epidemics are all liable to break out in the jungle. I am convinced that life in such conditions would be unbearable if it were not for the elephants, which exert a fascination over the Burmese, a fascination which Europeans soon begin to feel as well.

180

CHAPTER 5

During the war I was talking about elephants to two war correspondents, one American and the other Australian. The latter asked me: "Is it true that elephants are very shy about their actual love affair?" Before I could answer, the American chipped in with: "Of course they are; aren't you?" The mating of elephants is a private affair, and even the oozies of the tusker and the female concerned may not know that it has taken place. Often they know, but regard it as none of their business.

Europeans tell and even believe the most fantastic tales about the mating habits of elephants, but the love-making of elephants as I have seen it seems to me more simple and more lovely than any myth. It is beautiful because it is quite without the brutishness and the cruelty which one sees in the matings of so many animals.

Without there being any appearance of season, two animals become attracted by each other. The average female first mates between the ages of seventeen and twenty. She shows no sign of any particular season but apparently feels some natural urge. Days and even weeks of courtship may take place. Eventually the mating is consummated, and the act may be repeated three or four times during the twenty-four hours. For months the pair will keep together as they graze and their honeymoon will last all that time. After the day's work they will call each other and go off together into the jungle. My own belief is that this close relationship lasts until the female has been pregnant for ten months—that is, until she has become aware that she is pregnant.

The companionship of the male is then replaced by that of a female friend or "auntie". From that time onwards they are never apart and it becomes difficult to separate them. Indeed, it is cruel to do so. Their association is founded on mutual aid among animals, the instinctive knowledge that it takes two mothers to protect a calf elephant against tigers which, in spite of all precautions, still kill twenty-five per cent of all calves born.

Gestation lasts twenty-two months. After the calf has been born, the mother and the "auntie" always keep it between them as they

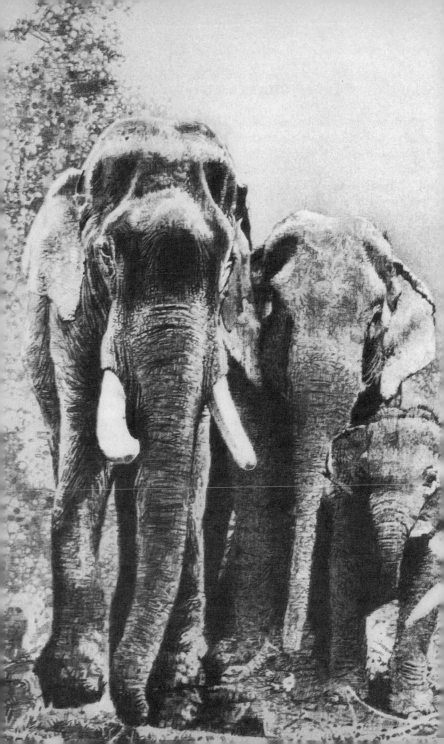

graze—all through the night—and, while it is very young, during daylight hours as well.

To kill the calf the tiger has to drive off both the mother and "auntie" by stampeding them. To do this he will first attack the mother, springing on her back and stampeding her; then he returns to attack "auntie", who defends the calf, knowing that in a few moments the mother will return. On many occasions I have had to dress the lacerated wounds of tiger claws on the backs of both a mother elephant and her friend.

A mother elephant in captivity has no suspicions that man will injure her calf. I have only once been attacked by one of the many mothers I have congratulated and that was an accident. I was patting a calf so young that it could not focus with its little piggy eyes, and it bumped hard against my bare knees and yelled out the cry for danger. As I jumped back, the lash of the mother's trunk missed me by inches.

A baby calf follows its mother at heel for three or four years, being suckled by the mother from the breasts between her forelegs. This position affords the calf perfect protection. At birth the calf's trunk is a useless membrane

growing rather to one side so as to allow the calf to suck more easily through the mouth. It does not become flexible and useful for three to four months.

At the age of five or, at most, six years, the calf has learned to gather its own fodder and gradually gives up suckling. Female elephants have an average of four calves in a life-time. Twins are not uncommon and two calves of different ages following their mother at heel is quite a usual sight. Larger families are not uncommon.

After weaning, young elephants go through an awkward stage, becoming a bit truculent owing to the desire for independence— much like human boys and girls.

At fifteen or sixteen they become very much like human flappers and young stalwarts. Young male elephants do a lot of flirting with the females from the ages of sixteen to twenty, sometimes being most enterprising. But the average animal does not show any signs of musth until the age of twenty. A male elephant will mate when he is not on musth, in fact he usually does. But when he is on musth all the savage lust and combative instincts of his huge body come out.

From the age of twenty to thirty-five musth is shown by a slight discharge of a strongly smelling fluid from the musth glands near the eye, directly above the line of the mouth. In a perfectly fit male it occurs annually during the hot months, which are the mating season. It may last about two weeks, during which time he is very temperamental.

From the age of thirty-five to forty-five the discharge increases and runs freely, eventually dribbling into his mouth, and the taste of it makes him much more ferocious. He is physically in his prime at that age, and unless he is securely chained to a large tree while on musth, he is a danger to his oozie and to other elephants. His brain goes wild, and nothing will satisfy him.

From forty-five to fifty musth gradually subsides. Tuskers that have killed as many as nine men between the ages of thirty-five and forty-five will become docile during musth in their later years. But no elephant on musth can be trusted unless he is over sixty.

Poo Ban was normally a friendly animal and would let me walk under his tusks, but he went on musth in the Taungdwin Forest area, killed his oozie and another man, then killed two female elephants and attacked all men on sight. Finally he entered villages, tore rice granaries open and became the terror of the valley. I offered a reward of three hundred rupees for his capture and decided to destroy him if he could not be captured.

He was marked down in a dense patch of bamboo jungle in Saiyawah (the Valley of Ten Villages), four marches away. With Kya Sine, my gun-boy, I set out, lightly loaded with two travelling elephants as pack.

The evening before I was to tackle Poo Ban I was testing my rifle with a half charge, with half the cordite removed and a soft-nosed bullet in the left barrel, keeping a normal hard-nosed cartridge in the right. I wanted to wound Poo Ban in one of his forefeet with the half charge and then recapture him, break his spirit and heal his wound. Kya Sine however begged me to let him go ahead and attempt to recapture him without shooting, so that he could earn the three hundred rupees. Unfortunately I gave in and before dawn he had gone on ahead. I arrived at three p.m. next-day to be met by men who said, "Kya Sine is dead." Poo Ban killed him during his attempt at recapture.

That night I bivouacked in an open place which had at one time been paddy-fields. It was a brilliant moonlight night and before I went to sleep I made my plans to recapture Poo Ban. I had no desire to avenge the death of Kya Sine—to whom I was devoted, and who had the greatest knowledge of jungle lore of any man I have ever known. The idea of revenge on an elephant would have been very distasteful to him.

I was asleep, lying in the open, when I was wakened by a clank! clank! clank! Luckily for me, a piece of chain had been left on Poo Ban's off forefoot. Two hundred yards away, in the open, a magnificent tusker was standing, head erect in challenge, defiant of the whole world. He was a perfect silhouette. I did not dare move an eyelid, and while I held my breath he moved on with a clank, clank, clank, which at last faded away like the far sound of the pipes over the hills.

At dawn I tried to put my plans into action. When he had been located, I took up my position, while twenty Burmans with four shotguns among them tried to drive him past me.

At last Poo Ban came out of the jungle with his head held high. He halted, and then made a bee-line across my front, travelling fast over the open ground.

Kneeling, I took the shot at his foot on which my plans depended. The bullet kicked up a puff of dust in front of his near forefoot as he put it down in his stride. I had missed!

Poo Ban halted and swung round to face me, or the bark of my rifle which he had heard. Then he took up the never-to-be-forgotten attitude of an elephant about to charge, with the trunk well tucked away in his mouth, like a wound-up watch spring. As he charged, it flashed through my mind that I had no time to reload. I depended on the hard-nosed bullet in the right barrel. I took a chest shot at twenty-five yards. His tusks drove nine inches into the ground, his head dropped. For a few seconds he balanced and then toppled over dead.

I dropped my rifle and was sick, vomiting with fear, excitement and regret. Poo Ban was dead, and I had failed to catch him alive. There was no court of inquiry. My report was accepted and I was given the tusks as a souvenir, a souvenir of a double failure that I bitterly regretted, and of the death of the finest and bravest Burman hunter I have known.

CHAPTER 6

There is undoubted cruelty in breaking the spirit and training wild elephants after they have been captured by kheddaring. The ideal age at which to capture a wild elephant is usually considered to be from fifteen to twenty, as it is then only a few years before it is sufficiently mature to do heavy work and to earn its original cost. But the spirit of a youngster of that age, whether male or female, takes a lot of breaking. It often takes a matter of weeks, while it is tethered to a tree with chains, and its continual struggling and fighting to break free cause the most shocking galling of the ankles and neck. Food is thrown to the animal, but insufficient and unsuitable food leads to great loss of condition. The wounds it receives are almost impossible to treat, and they become flyblown and ulcerated.

In the end the young animal becomes heartbroken and thin. Finally it realizes that it is in captivity for the rest of its days and, after the last heartbreaking struggle, will put up with a man sitting on its head.

But a calf born in captivity is far more easily trained. From the day it is born until it leaves its mother at five years old it is in contact with its mother's oozie. It flirts with him like a child, it pretends to chase him, then runs away again. But though so playful, it seldom trusts him much beyond accepting a tit-bit of fruit or a handful of rice from his hands.

In November of its fifth year the calf is weaned and from that moment becomes more independent. Five or six calves are trained at a time in one camp. An area of a hundred yards square is cleared, except for a few trees to give shade. In the middle a "crush", or triangular-shaped pen, is built of logs of about the height of the average five-year-old calf. The logs of which it is built are fastened with wooden pegs; no nails are used. The bark is stripped from the logs, which are rubbed smooth and smeared with grease—all precautions against galling the calf's hide. In camp, in addition to the calves with their mothers, is an elephant known as the koonkie (schoolmaster). This animal is usually a tuskless male between forty-five and fifty years of age, chosen for his docility and patience.

On the morning when the first calf is to be weaned, the mother and the calf are brought into the clearing and made familiar with the crush and its surroundings. Once the calf has been lured into the crush with a bit of fruit (or butted into it by the koonkie), the attendant Burmans quickly slip two stout bars in behind its hind-quarters. The mother is quite content to stand by watching these proceedings, and makes no attempt to charge the Burmans so long as she is loose, but she becomes terribly agitated if she is tied up and will make every effort to snap her chain.

The calf will usually struggle and kick for about two hours. Then it sulks and finally it will take a banana from the oozie out of sheer boredom and disgust.

187

Meanwhile, the calf's future rider has been attached to a pulley a few feet over its head. Two men on the ground, on either side of the crush, control this pulley and on a signal from the rider he is lowered slowly on to the calf's head.

"Damn you, get off!" screams the calf, bucking like a bronco. The would-be oozie has soon to be hauled up again, but no sooner has the calf quieted down and accepted another banana than the rider is lowered once more—and so on, until the poor little calf seems to say, "All right. Sit there if you must."

When it has finished the bananas it will buck again, but directly it starts eating, down comes the inevitable oozie.

So far so good. The poor calf is tired, but the Burmans, stripped of all but their tucked-up lungyis, are thoroughly enjoying the game, though they are dripping with sweat.

Suspended from another pulley above the centre of the calf's back is a heavy block of padded wood. This is also lowered onto its back and provokes more bucking bronco antics. A moment or two later the block is lifted, but directly the calf stands still, down it comes again. Once more there are determined struggles to get free, and so it goes on, and all the while the calf is being offered food and spoken to with kind and soothing words. Finally, in utter disgust the calf sits down with its front feet straight out, hoping that it will get rid of the pests.

A cheer goes up from the Burmans, a cheer which soon becomes a chant of "Tah (Get up)! Hmit (Sit down)!" As the weight is lifted, the calf gets up and all the Burmans chant "Tah!" As the weight comes down, and the calf sits, all of them chant "Hmit!" in chorus.

After a time the rider, still attached to the pulley, remains comfortably seated on its head. By evening, unless the calf is a really obstinate young devil, the rider can turn and, putting his hand on its back instead of the log of wood, order the calf to sit down by pressure and by saying, "Hmit".

Once that is possible, the calf is considered broken. Often it takes less than twelve hours with no cruelty whatsoever. Sometimes, however, in dealing with obstinate and truculent young tuskers, the game has to be kept up, by the light of bamboo torches, far into the night. Occasionally it may last even till the next morning. But however long it may take, the Burmans never give in and never give the calf any rest until their object is achieved. The great lesson is that man's will-power is stronger than its own and that man will always get his own way.

Before the calf is taken out of the crush on the following morning it is hobbled with well-greased buffalo-hide thongs, and it is then tied to a tree for twenty-four hours, being caressed and cajoled all the time by its future rider. He makes it sit down each time he approaches. He mounts on its head, remains there ten minutes, orders the calf to sit again and dismounts, and sometimes keeps it in the sitting position for five or ten minutes. Extraordinary patience is needed throughout. Once the Burman starts, he goes on until he gains his point. He never lets the calf win a victory, however temporary. Meanwhile the calf's mother has been taken away. It is common for her to call her calf for a couple of nights after their separation, but the tie between them has grown slender at that age and she does not really want it with her.

The calf is then taken for its first walk, attached to the koonkie by a buffalo-hide girdle. The koonkie thinks the whole thing a bore but he stands no nonsense. If the calf jibs, sits down or lags, he gives him one wrench that pulls him along. On occasion he will give him a real welt with his trunk.

It soon becomes a decorous walking-out and at a later stage the koonkie can manage two calves—one on each side of him.

I once had a camp with nineteen calves in training in it. They were a joy to watch. Each had a different temperament, and their innate differences of character were enshrined in lovely names. The trainer has the right to name calves, and long discussions go on among the assembled riders and the trainer before the calves are finally christened. Often some incident which occurs in the initial stages of training will suggest the name and I well remember one such instance. On the third night after the calf had been taken out of the crush and while it was tethered to a tree, some way from the riders' camp, it was attacked by a tiger, which sprang upon its back.

The calf threw the tiger off, and managed to keep it at bay for twenty minutes, until men from the camp arrived with bamboo torches. That calf became a hero, and the next day it was christened Kya M'Nine, which means "The tiger could not overcome him"—as lovely a name for an elephant as Black Beauty for a horse.

Sometimes there is humour in the name, such as Ma Pin Wa (Miss Fat Bottom). One young elephant of that name could scarcely have been called anything else. How she wobbled as she walked!

From the age of breaking, young elephants are kept under training until the finishing age of nineteen. For about two years they remain in the camp nursery, merely being caught daily and taught the simple words of command and the "aids" of the rider, as well as by foot control behind their ears.

The "aids" are simply movements of the rider's body by which he translates his wishes, almost instinctively, to his mount. Thus an intense stiffening of his limbs and leaning back will be at once understood as halt. A pressure on one side will be understood as turn to the left, on the other as turn to the right. Leaning forward and forcing downwards will mean stoop or kneel. A dragging up on the right side will be correctly interpreted as lift the right foot—on the other, as lift the left.

At about eight years old, young elephants carry their first pack and become "travellers", accompanying a European assistant when he tours the forest. They thus become accustomed to going over mountains and down streams, carrying light weights, such as camp cooking pots or a light roll of bedding.

During the early years the elephant never really earns its keep or does enough to pay the wages of its oozie but it is learning all the time. Up to the age of nineteen or twenty it will have cost about one thousand pounds, when the wages of the oozie, training costs and maintenance are added up. But thereafter the elephant has on the average a working life from its twentieth to its fifty-fifth year.

Each working year consists of nine months' work and three months' rest, necessary both to keep it in condition and on account of the seasonal changes. Each month consists of only eighteen working days and twelve rest days, animals working three days in succession and then resting two. Thus, during the nine months of the working year there are only one hundred and sixty-two working days. Each day averages about eight hours. Thus an elephant works one thousand three hundred hours a year. During this time an average animal delivers one hundred tons of timber from stump to a floating-point in a creek.

CHAPTER 7

By the time it is twenty-five years old, a well-trained elephant should understand twenty-four separate words of command, apart from the signals or "foot aids" of the rider. He ought also to be able to pick up five different things from the ground when asked. That is to say, he should pick up and pass up to his rider with his trunk a jungle dah (knife), a koon (axe), his fetter or hobble-chain, his tying-chain (for tethering him to a tree) and a stick. I have seen an intelligent elephant pick up not only a pipe that his rider had dropped but a large lighted cheroot.

He will tighten a chain attached to a log by giving it a sharp tug with his trunk, or loosen it with a shake, giving it the same motion with his trunk as that given by a human hand.

An elephant does not work mechanically. He never stops learning because he is always thinking. Not even a really good sheep dog can compare with an elephant in intelligence.

If he cannot reach with his trunk some part of his body that itches, he doesn't always rub it against a tree; he may pick up a long stick and give himself a good scratch with that instead.

If he pulls up some grass and it comes up by the roots with a lump of earth, he will smack it against his foot until all the earth is shaken off, or if water is handy he will wash it clean. And he will extract a pill (the size of an aspirin tablet) from a tamarind fruit the size of a cricket ball in which one has planted it, with an air of saying, "You can't kid me."

Many young elephants develop the naughty habit of plugging up the wooden bell they wear hung round their necks with good stodgy mud or clay so that the clappers cannot ring, in order to steal silently into banana groves at night. There they will have a whale of a time, quietly stuffing, eating not only the bunches of bananas but the leaves and indeed the whole tree as well, and they will do this just beside the hut occupied by the owner of the grove, without waking him or any of his family.

I have personally witnessed many remarkable instances of the quick intelligence of elephants, though I cannot claim that they equal the famous yarns which delight all of us, whether we are children or grown-ups—such as that of the circus elephant who saw a man who had befriended him sitting in a sixpenny seat and at once picked him up with his trunk and popped him into a three-and-sixpenny one!

But the following incidents seem to me to denote immediate brain reaction to a new situation rather than anything founded on repetitive training.

An uncertain-tempered tusker was being loaded with kit while in the standing position. On his back was his oozie, with another Burman in the pannier filling it with kit. Alongside on the flank, standing on the ground, was the paijaik attendant, armed with a spear which consisted of a five-foot cane, a brightly polished spearhead at one end and a spiked ferrule at the other. Another Burman was handing gear up to the Burman in the pannier, but got into difficulties with one package and called out to the paijaik to help him. The latter thrust the ferrule of the spear into the ground so that it stood planted upright with the spearhead in line with the elephant's eye. Then he lent a hand. The oozie, however, did not trust his beast, and said in a determined voice, "Pass me the spear." The tusker calmly put its trunk round the cane at the point of balance and carefully passed it up to his rider. But unthinkingly he passed it head-first. The rider yelled at his beast in Burmese, "Don't be a bloody fool—pass it right way round!" With perfect calm and a rather dandified movement, the elephant revolved the spear in mid-air and, still holding it by the point of balance, passed it to his oozie, this time ferrule first.

One of the most intelligent acts I ever saw an elephant perform occurred one evening when the Upper Taungdwin River was in heavy spate. I was listening for the boom and roar of timber coming from upstream. Directly below my camp the banks of the river were steep and rocky and twelve to fifteen feet high.

I was suddenly alarmed by hearing an elephant roaring as

though frightened and, looking down, I saw three or four men rushing up and down on the opposite bank in a state of great excitement. I ran down to the edge of the near bank and there saw Ma Shwe (Miss Gold) with her three-month-old calf, trapped in the fast-rising torrent. She herself was still in her depth, as the water was about six feet deep. But there was a life-and-death struggle going on. Her calf was screaming with terror and was afloat like a cork. Ma Shwe was as near to the far bank as she could get, holding her whole body against the raging torrent and keeping the calf pressed against her massive body. Every now and then the swirling water kept sweeping the calf away; then, with terrific strength, she would encircle it with her trunk and pull it upstream to rest against her body again.

There was a sudden rise in the water and the calf was washed clean over the mother's hindquarters. She turned to chase it, like an otter after a fish, but she had travelled about fifty yards downstream and crossed to my side of the river before she had caught it and got it back. For what seemed minutes she pinned the calf with her head and trunk against the bank. Then, with a really gigantic effort, she picked it up in her trunk and reared up until she was half standing on her hind legs so as to place it on a narrow shelf of rock five feet above the flood level.

Having accomplished this, she fell back into the raging torrent and she herself went away like a cork. She well knew that she would now have a fight to save her own life, as less than three hundred yards below where she had stowed her calf in safety there was a gorge. If she were carried down, it would be certain death. I knew as well as she did that there was one spot between her and the gorge where she could get up the bank, but it was on the other side from where she had put her calf. By that time my chief interest was in the calf. It stood tucked up, shivering and terrified, on a ledge just wide enough to hold its feet. Its little, fat, protruding belly was tightly pressed against the bank.

While I was peering over at it, wondering what I could do next, I heard the grandest sounds of a mother's love I can remember. Ma Shwe had crossed the river and got up the bank and was making her way back as fast as she could, calling the whole time—

a defiant roar, but to her calf it was music. The two little ears, like little maps of India, were cocked forward listening to the only sound that mattered, the call of its mother.

As darkness fell, a torrential rain was falling and the river still separated the mother and her calf. I decided that I could do nothing but wait and see what happened.

At dawn Ma Shwe and her calf were together—both on the far bank. The spate had subsided to a mere foot of dirty-coloured water. No one in the camp had seen Ma Shwe recover her calf but she must have lifted it down from the ledge in the same way as she had put it there.

Five years later, when the calf came to be named, the Burmans christened it Ma Yay Yee (Miss Laughing Water).

JUST BEFORE THE WAR, experiments in the use of local anæsthetics and even of general anæsthetics on elephants were carried out. No doubt these will be resumed one day. But up till the time of the reconquest of Burma, after the Japanese invasion, all elephant surgery was on old and somewhat primitive lines.

It needs confidence to walk under an elephant's jaw and tusks, armed with a heavy knife in one's left hand and a six-pound wooden club in the right hand, and then to tell him to hold up his head while you drive the knife up to the hilt into a huge abscess on his chest with one blow of the mallet.

One blow of the mallet is all you can get; if you try another you must look out for squalls. But if you do the job properly and make a quick and quiet getaway to his flank, he will let you go back ten minutes later to clean out the abscess and then syringe it with disinfectant.

Wounds caused by tigers, most often received by mother elephants protecting their calves, are exceptionally difficult to heal and often do not respond to modern antiseptics.

The Burman has cures for all the ills that may befall an elephant. Some are herbal, some are mystic spells and incantations, and some of them have had to be vetoed as being definitely harmful. But I have so far found no treatment for tiger wounds that comes up to the traditional Burmese method of plugging the wounds

194

with sugar. The Burman also used maggots to clean up gangrened wounds for centuries before the method was rediscovered in modern surgery.

It has been quite truly said that once an elephant goes down, due to exhaustion or severe colic, he has only a twenty-five per cent chance of getting onto his legs again unaided. Any method of keeping him on his legs improves a sick elephant's chances of survival. The Burman will do this by putting chili juice in his eye— a counter-irritant that must be agony. But it is effective and about doubles the animal's chances of recovery. No matter how far modern veterinary research goes, we shall always rely to a certain extent upon the Burman's knowledge.

I know without question that an elephant can be grateful for relief given to it from pain and sickness. For example, I remember Ma Kyaw (Miss Smooth, an expression often used to describe any Burmese girl with a strikingly good figure). She had fearful lacerations on the barrel of her back from tiger claws, and I treated her for them every day for three weeks. In the early stages she suffered great pain, but although she made a lot of fuss she always gave way and let me go on. When she was sufficiently healed I sent her back to camp under a reliable Burman with instructions that she was to be given light dressings of fly repellent on the wounds.

Two months later I was having a cup of tea in camp outside my tent while seven elephants were being washed in the creek near by, preparatory to my inspecting them. The last animal to come out of the creek was Ma Kyaw. As she passed me about fifty yards away, with her rider on foot, I called out, "How is Ma Kyaw's back?"

Her rider did not reply, as he had not caught what I said, but Ma Kyaw swung round, at right angles to the direction in which she was going, and came towards me.

She walked straight up to where I was sitting, dropped into the sitting position and leaned right over towards me so as to show me her back. Having patted her I told her to "Tah (get up)," and away she went, leaving me with the agreeable conviction that she had come to say thank you.

CHAPTER 8

Elephants are good swimmers and are extremely buoyant. When the oozie is going to cross a large river, such as the Irrawaddy, with his elephant, he fits a surcingle under its belly and over the withers, kneels on the animal's back and grips the rope in front of him, using a stick to signal his "aids".

For a time the elephant will swim along gaily with a rather lunging action. Then, all of a sudden, the oozie will snatch a deep breath as his mount goes down, like a submarine, into fifteen feet of water. The animal, for pure fun, will keep submerged almost to bursting point, trying to make his rider let go.

But the oozie knows that an elephant can only stay underwater for the same length of time as a man. So he holds on. The elephant, meanwhile, is doing a fairy-like dance on tiptoe along the bottom, while the poor old oozie is wondering if the animal will ever surface. Suddenly both reappear, blowing tremendously and taking great gasps of breath.

When elephants have to be moved long distances by water they are frequently taken on rafts, or barges, towed alongside a paddle-steamer. Getting elephants onto such flats needs endless patience. First one has to find a leader which the other beasts will follow, and then one has to camouflage the gangway with tall grasses or palms on either side of it to a height of twelve feet.

Once I had to ship two flat-loads of twenty elephants from a river station on the Irrawaddy. I was assisted by a very capable Anglo-Burman and we started work at dawn but had only got one flat loaded by noon. The irate old skipper of the paddle-steamer was due to leave at two p.m. By five p.m. we got the last elephant on board the second flat and the skipper's temper was as bad as mine. Just when I thought my job was finished and the skipper's had begun, he blew the steamer's siren—of all the damn fool things! And at the same time the enormous side paddles started to churn alongside the loaded flats full of elephants, on either side of the steamer.

The captain's shock was greater than mine, as sixteen elephants trumpeted and roared, drowning every other sound. I think he thought half of them had broken loose and were boarding his steamer after his blood, whereas sheer terror kept them in their places. He had to reckon with me, however.

We eventually got the animals settled down and under way and put in an hour's steaming before tying up for the night. Leaving my assistant to check on the chains, I made for the saloon to make it up with the skipper over a peg.

At midnight I was still yarning with the skipper when my assistant arrived to say that a young tusker had collapsed. His doing so had caused little commotion. As far as I could discover, he had fallen down dead-beat from fatigue. To get anywhere near him, one crawled through a forest of elephant legs.

After I had given him half a bottle of brandy without results, I decided there was nothing more I could do but let him lie and wait for the dawn. I had gone to my cabin when my assistant came back, looking very shy, to say that the Burman oozies wanted to put a temple candle for each year of the elephant's life round the prostrate body and might they try it?

The theory was that when all the candles were alight, but before they burned out, the animal would rise. My reply was, "Yes. Buy twenty-one blinking candles but don't set fire to the ship!"

That was the last I saw of him that night, but at dawn he came to my cabin to say, "It's worked, sir. The animal is up. But you were one year out in his age. We had to do it a second time and use twenty-two candles!"

He was so sincere that I did not like to say what I thought, which was that the elephant was a young animal which liked sleeping with the light on.

As regards sleep, elephants are rather like horses. They get most of it standing up and they will only go down when they think that, for a brief period at night, all the world is asleep. The time is never the same, but it is always at that eerie hour when even the insects stop their serenades. It never lasts longer than half an hour if the animal is fit, but while it lasts he sleeps very soundly. For an hour previously the elephant stands absolutely motionless without feeding. Then he seems satisfied that all is well, and down he goes in a slow, silent movement, as if overcome by some unseen jungle god. In bright moonlight it is a most beautiful but uncanny sight.

Elephants and ponies do not get on together. The elephants sometimes become so scared of ponies that a whole train of them will stampede at the sight of one, with the result that oozies are injured and gear is smashed. This feeling is exceeded only by their hatred and fear of dogs. In fact, a dog is one of the few animals at which an elephant will lash out with its trunk, and I have never known a dog and an elephant to make friends. This hatred cannot easily be explained. It is possible that elephants are afraid of dogs biting their trunks, or it might be an instinctive fear of rabies, which is the dread of everyone who keeps a dog in camp, Burman and European assistant alike.

Nevertheless, practically every European assistant keeps a dog. The elephants hate them and one is always losing one's dog, owing to leopard, tiger, bear and snakes. It is easy to ask why, under such conditions, do you keep a dog? But I know of no other existence where a dog is so necessary as a companion to share every moment of one's life and to drive away loneliness.

A dog usually sleeps in one's hut or tent, but even so it is a great worry. For only if it is fenced in behind chairs and boxes under one's camp bed can one feel reasonably sure that a leopard will not take it while one is asleep.

One assistant had his cocker spaniel snapped up by a leopard when it was sleeping chained up beside his bed in his bamboo hut. He did not wake until it was too late to do anything. The chain was broken and both had vanished. He was determined on revenge, so the next night he borrowed a dog from the elephant men and tied it up to his office box beside his bed. Then he put out his lamp and sat up in an upright chair in one corner of the room, prepared to wait all night if need be.

The familiar babble of chatting ceased in his servants' camp, the glow of the fires died down. At last the hour of stillness arrived, when all sounds seemed to cease. Then there was a sudden tension in the room and he could feel his heart pounding. The dog suddenly tore at his chain, pulling the heavy specie box to which it was tied across the bamboo floor.

The assistant raised his loaded shotgun, and switched on his torch, and on the bamboo steps in the doorway stood a leopard, blinded by the light. The assistant fired both barrels and it fell dead. In a moment the camp was stirring with lights and his servants were uttering exclamations of delight. One of them ripped up the white belly of the leopard and pulled out a black knot of the curly coat of his master's beloved spaniel.

This was too much for my friend, who turned away and ordered his people back to bed, telling them to take the terrified camp dog with them. He told me that he cried himself to sleep that night and that he thought it had done him good.

I met him at his next camp, and while we were talking after a day's work, an oozie and his wife approached. The man was holding a baby honey bear in his arms. It was about the size of a coffee pot. They squatted down side by side in front of us, she with her shoulders bare and her tamain tucked across her breasts. I asked the man where he had got the little creature, and he told me that the tree-fellers had killed its mother three weeks before.

"Would you like to have the baby, Thakin Galay?" the man asked my friend, for they had heard of the loss of his spaniel.

It was a charming expression of sympathy which they did not put into any other words.

"No," my friend and I both said together.

The little bear seemed to understand and began to make queer babyish squeals and fumble about—and, with a perfectly simple, natural movement the Burman passed it to his wife, who put it in her lap, untucking her tamain from across her breasts. Then she lifted up the little bear and put her nipple in its mouth.

When we had thanked them again for the offer of their pet, they rose, bowed and departed with the bear cub still at her breast. She had been feeding it three or four times a day, filled with all the Buddhists' pride that they were doing something of importance in their lives by preserving life and convinced that their action would put them on a higher plane in Nirvana.

There was nothing unusual in this. The jungle women will suckle baby fawns and any young creature which inspires them with pity. "It deserves pity," are words often on their lips, and their pity at once moves them to succour and keep alive the orphan. Thus they will adopt new-born tiger or leopard cubs, and bears, not hesitating to save the lives of the hated enemies of their menfolk which would become dangerous if they were reared. There is a wonderful gentleness in these jungle people.

The Burman has no sympathy, however, with any eccentric European who keeps a snake as a pet.

I have been told the story of one "jungle salt" in the Pyinmana Forest who did keep such a pet. She was a seventeen-foot python whom he called Eve. She had a silver collar and chain, and he took her on all his tours in a basket carried on one of his elephants.

Eve did little except sleep and eat at longish intervals. She lived in his hut or tent, finding warmth during the day between the blankets of his bed, and at night getting warmth from her master. But he kept her lying outside his bedclothes.

In the end familiarity bred contempt of danger. One cold night

when her master was asleep, Eve glided under the bedclothes, and lay beside him, seeking warmth. While he slept she gradually twined her coils around his body. The assistant woke to find his legs and hips in a vicelike embrace. The more he struggled, the tighter Eve drew her constricting coils. His yells for help brought his camp servants running to his bedside, but he was not released until Eve had been cut into several pieces.

The Burman who told me the story gave it a moral twist of his own by saying that women are safest on the other side of the blanket and that snakes are best dead.

Elephants are not usually frightened by natural phenomena without very good reason. They do not mind thunderstorms in the way that dogs do, and they remain calm in the face of forest fires. I have only once seen elephants really frightened by natural phenomena, and that was due to their realizing that they were in a gorge where water was rapidly rising in a spate.

Rain was coming down as though it would never cease. I had decided to take a short cut through the Kanti Gorge. I was travelling with eight young pack elephants, and it would save us a climb of two thousand feet from one watershed to another. After passing down the gorge, I meant to move up a side stream. My spirits were high, the oozies were singing, and our circus was travelling in Indian file down the hard, sandy bottom of the stream.

Both banks of the gorge were sheer rock, to a height of about thirty feet. The gorge was three miles long, and the stream was about ankle deep when we started down it. By the time we had gone a mile one could hear the unmistakable sound of a heavy thunderstorm breaking in the headwaters of the stream. The elephants showed their nervousness by half turning round. The bore of water eventually overtook us, and it was soon lapping under the bellies and round the flanks of the smaller calves.

By some instinct not shared by man, the elephants knew there was more water coming down. They began what would soon have become a stampede if they had not been hindered by the depth of the water and kept under partial restraint by their riders. It became a terrifying experience, as there was no possibility of turning back and no hope of getting up the sides. During the last mile all the elephants began bellowing; that, with the sound of the torrential rain and the raging water, made it seem a pretty grim situation.

I never knew a mile to seem longer. Bend after bend came in view, with never a sign of the mouth of the creek I knew, which would provide for our exodus from the black hole in which we floundered. Logs were floating past and, though I had no time to be amused then, I noticed how the elephants' hindquarters seemed to have a magnetic attraction for them. Just as a log was about to strike its hindquarters, the elephant would swing its rear end to one side, giving the log a glancing blow so that it cannoned off like a billiard ball from the cushion and passed on to the chap in front —and so on all down the line.

We were fortunate, really, as the smaller animals were just afloat when we went round the bend to go up the side creek. The water was up to my armpits, and I was holding my rifle in both hands above my head. The side creek came down in spate only half an hour after we had started up. If we had met the combined spates at the confluence, all our kit would have been lost.

The elephants scrambled up the first feasible bank after turning in off the main river, and at a general halt they seemed to look at me as if to say: "And you call yourself a jungle man!"

CHAPTER 9

Savage elephants are as rare as really wicked men, but those that are not savage sometimes give way to moments of bad temper. Their most tiresome and dangerous habit at such moments is to pick up a large stick or stone with the trunk and throw it with great force and accuracy at some onlooker. One has to be prepared to jump when this happens.

Of course, during the musth period all males are of uncertain temper. My interpretation of musth is that it is an instinctive desire in the male elephant to fight and kill before mating. The mere act of mating does not cool his passion. He would rather fight for his chosen mate before he won her, driving off and killing an intruder during the time that he is making love.

The great majority of cases in which oozies are killed by their elephants take place when their charges are on musth. For some unknown reason, the animal may then suddenly attack his rider, first striking him with tusk or trunk, then crushing him to death with a knee when he is on the ground.

Strange as it may sound, there is very little difficulty in finding a new rider for such an animal. Many riders take pride in riding an elephant known to be dangerous. Such men find life easy; they care nothing for anything or anyone. They are usually opium-eaters, but in spite of that they work well.

In addition to the rider, a dangerous animal has a really good type of spearman attached to it as an attendant, whose duty is to cover every movement of the rider when he is entirely at the mercy of the elephant—undoing his fetters, for example. Although the spearman carries a spear, the secret of his control is by the eye. He keeps his eye fixed on the elephant's. The two men are usually sufficient to control a savage elephant.

I have known one case of what seemed like remorse in an elephant. He was a tusker who killed his rider. But he guarded the body and would let nobody get near it for a whole week. He grazed all round it, and charged in mad fury at anyone who came near. When the body had quite decomposed he wandered away from it; ten days later he was recaptured without any difficulty and behaved quite normally. He was not on musth.

The wickedest elephant I ever knew was called Taw Sin Ma (Miss Wild Elephant). She was about twenty-five years old when I first knew her, and there was nothing in her recorded history which gave any explanation of why she should just loathe every European she saw. Even at inspection she had to be chained to a tree and when one was a hundred yards away she would begin to lunge and strain at her chains in order to attack.

I had a nasty experience with her, when she first attacked me and then chased me, following me by scent for four miles.

I met her by chance when I was walking from one camp to another. I came on her suddenly and she went for me at once. I raced off, not knowing for two miles whether I was on the right track back to the camp I had left. There would have been no hope for me if her hobbles had snapped or come undone, unless I had found refuge up a tree. As she was hobbled, my pace was a little faster than hers. She wore a brass danger bell around her neck (docile elephants wear wooden bells). Often it sounded from the bell as though she were nearly up to me.

I dropped a haversack, hoping she would halt and attack it, but I heard no check in the sound of her clanking bell. When I had climbed to the top of a ridge I halted for a few moments to locate her. Then on I plunged, trying to act on the law of the jungle that one must never hurry and always keep cool. Once one breaks that rule every thorny bush that grows reaches out a tentacle to impede one, to tear and scratch.

My relief was great when I met two men, busy with a crosscut saw on a fallen teak tree. But I had only to shout out the words: "Taw Sin Ma!" and they joined me in my flight without asking questions. They soon took the lead and, as I followed, I at least had the satisfaction of knowing I was on the right track to camp and safety.

One of them got into camp well ahead of me and gave the alarm on my account. When I got in I met a chattering group of elephant riders and their families, all of them doubled up with laughter or smacking their hands on their hips in mirth at the sight of me—all, that is, except Maung Po Net (Mr. Black as Night), who prepared to go out and meet his "pet".

There was no alternative but to join the Burmans in their joke—for I often wanted them to share in mine. So I joined in their laughter and their hip smacking.

Within an hour a rider came back with my haversack, quite undamaged and not even trodden on, and Po Net rode Taw Sin Ma back into camp. The expressions on both their faces seemed to indicate that the same incident might be repeated next day. It did not, as I at once issued twenty-five feet of chain for Taw Sin Ma to trail behind her whenever she was at large grazing.

Some riders teach their charges tricks that give a wrong impression of the animal's real disposition. Bo Gyi (Big Man), a young elephant, always charged his rider as soon as he appeared to catch him and bring him to camp. But at ten paces the animal would stop dead and sit down for his fetters to be undone, as gentle as a lamb. Any other rider would bolt.

The secret—that it was just a matter of standing one's ground—was only discovered after the rider who had taught him the trick had been killed by a bear. The elephant was at large for a month after his rider's death; nobody would face him. Finally a reward of three hundred rupees was offered for his recapture.

A young village lad turned up one day, saying he could capture him. Two days later he came into camp riding the animal and smiling gaily and was paid his three hundred rupees. Two of my own men had gone with the lad and had watched the whole procedure from a hiding-place near by. The secret had come from a young Burmese girl, a former sweetheart of the dead rider. The young lad was her new lover and no doubt boy and girl found the three hundred rupees a useful start in life.

Young calves, if they have not been properly trained, are apt to get savage if not well-handled afterwards. One particular calf named Soe Bone (Wicked Bone) delighted in chasing me whenever he got an opportunity. We decided he was not too old to learn his manners. "Shoot him in his toe nails with roasted rice," was the suggestion. So I emptied two cartridges and, after filling them with rice instead of shot, I wandered out of camp to find Soe Bone. He was in a sandy creek throwing wet sand over his body and was under a bank only three feet high.

"Hello, little chap!" I said, greeting him.

"Little chap to you," he seemed to reply, and charged.

I stood my ground and gave him a left and right in the forefeet so as to sting his toe nails. Did it stop him? I nearly lost my precious shotgun as I made my getaway. He was up that bank with his fetters on almost as quickly as I could turn to run. And did he love me next time he saw me?

We decided to put the little devil back into a crush and cane him. A substantial crush was made, and into it he was enticed and trapped. My head Burman came to fetch me, carrying in his hand a six-foot whippy cane. At least a dozen Burmans were there to witness the caning of this naughty schoolboy, as even Soe Bone's own rider had no use for his chasing game.

I was asked to give him the first twenty strokes. And what a behind it was to whip! I went to his head first and showed him the cane. He showed me the whites of his eyes as if to say: "Wait till I get out of here," but I changed his mind for him, and he squealed blue murder. Then everyone present, except his rider, was ordered to give him half a dozen, whereas his rider was permitted to stay behind and give him tit-bits after we had all gone.

I saw him next morning, being loaded with some light kit as we were moving camp, and he looked rather ashamed of himself. Suddenly he saw me, carrying a stick, and instead of pricking his ears as he did when he was going to chase me he gave one shrieking trumpet and bolted into the jungle.

One of the most remarkable incidents I ever had with savage elephants concerned a young Shan woman of about twenty. I was sitting in my hut near the camp one evening, very worried over a seriously injured spearman, Maung Chan Tha, who had been gored that afternoon by an elephant named Kyauk Sein (Jade-coloured Eyes). Maung Chan Tha had been trying to save the life of the rider, Maung Po Yin, who had been killed instantaneously by the elephant; the beast had then attacked the spearman. The animal had gone on musth and was at large in the neighbourhood.

I was discussing the case with my head Burman when suddenly, quite unannounced, a tall, fine-looking girl walked into my hut and I recognized her as the widow of the dead rider. She was not wailing or weeping, or carrying her youngest child, which is the custom on such occasions. She just stood erect and in a firm, unemotional voice said: "May I have a dismissal certificate from you for my husband, Maung Po Yin, who was killed today by Kyauk Sein?"

"Yes," I replied. "And your compensation, if you will wait till tomorrow, as I am busy arranging to get Maung Chan Tha to hospital." I added how grieved I was and, in sympathy, asked her if she had any children.

My head Burman answered, instead of her, that she had none, and then, addressing her as though he were most displeased with her for coming to see me in such an unceremonious way, said: "You can go now. I shall be coming back to camp soon."

She moved quietly out of the room, a tall and graceful figure.

207

When she was out of earshot I turned to my head Burman and asked, "Is that Po Yin's wife?"

"Yes," he replied. "She takes more opium than Po Yin did and that is the reason why she has no children."

I was very much surprised, as it was the first time I had ever heard of a Shan girl taking opium. Then my old Burman said in a quiet voice, "Give me ten ticals of opium tonight, and she will recapture Kyauk Sein tomorrow, because she has often caught him for Po Yin when he was in a heavy opium bout."

I gave him the opium he asked for, but I went to bed that night with a very disturbed conscience. To add to my troubles, Chan Tha died before dawn.

About ten o'clock, my old Burman came to me saying:

"Kyauk Sein is coming in with Ma Kyaw riding him."

I could scarcely believe my eyes: Kyauk Sein was passing through the camp with the Shan girl riding him, oblivious to everything, her eyes fixed straight in front of her. Her long black hair was hanging loose down her back and she wore her blue tamain girdled above her breasts, leaving her beautiful pale shoulders bare. I did not interfere and was soon informed that Kyauk Sein was securely tethered to a tree.

That evening Ma Kyaw was brought to me to receive the compensation due to her. She was dressed in her best, wearing a multi-coloured tamain, a little white coat, and a flower in her jet-black hair. She knelt and shikoed three times and then sat down in front of me. She kept her eyes lowered.

After paying her the compensation due to her for the loss of her husband, I gave her an extra bonus for recapturing Kyauk Sein. When I told her this, I could see a wisp of a smile at the corners of her mouth. I then wrote for her a certificate such as is customarily made out for all men killed in accidents. These certificates are for the benefit of the jungle nats (gods), who require them before admitting the spirit of the dead rider to their domains. The certificate ran, "I hereby give leave to Maung Po Yin, rider of Kyauk Sein, to go where he wishes, as he has been dismissed from my service," and I signed it.

When I had risen from my table and given the money and the

certificate into her hands, she wiped away two crocodile tears, got up and went quietly out into the dusk.

Next day, when I asked my old Burman about finding a new rider for Kyauk Sein, he told me: "Oh, that is all arranged. Maung Ngwe Gyaw is an opium-taker, too. He has 'taken on' (not married) Ma Kyaw, and they tell me that the biggest opium-taker of the lot is Kyauk Sein. Another ten ticals of opium would be useful."

I do not believe to this day that the girl took opium, but she was a resolute character and the elephant Kyauk Sein knew her well enough to take opium out of her hand. I think she completely stupefied the animal before she caught him.

The ways of the jungle are strange, but all is not savage, hard and cruel in it. For every savage elephant that attacks or kills his rider there are ninety-nine that are docile and friendly.

CHAPTER 10

I find it hard to realize now, after living for twenty-five years in the jungle with the most magnificent of all animals, that for the first three and a half years my eyes were blinded by the thrill of big-game shooting. I now feel that elephants are God's own and I would never shoot another. However, I can still live over again the thrill when I was young enough to take any opportunity that offered which gave me even chances of life or death.

I remember how for two whole months I spent day after day near the mouth of the Manipur River trying to get a solitary wild bull elephant—and every day was hard, and ended in disappointment. He was well known by the name of Shwe Kah, which my elephant riders had given him.

Shwe Kah had gored two of my tuskers badly and had continually worried my elephants. Many of my riders had seen him and they described the dimensions of his tusks outside the lip, by stretching both arms out horizontally to show their length and by encircling their legs above the knee with the outstretched thumbs and fore-fingers of both hands to indicate their girth.

I had numerous opportunities to bag other wild elephants at that time, but I was set on getting Shwe Kah. I saw him twice but not in a position for a shot. I then went on leave for a month, knowing I should be back in the same area during May, the best month in Burma for big game.

One night during my leave I met a very pleasant Sapper Major who told me he was more than keen to bag an elephant before he left Burma. I said, "I'm going back on the twenty-fifth for a tour of jungle camps, during which I hope to get in some big-game shooting myself. Can you get a month's leave?" He jumped at it. I explained that I would do all I could to put him onto the track of a decent wild tusker, but that Shwe Kah was to be mine only.

He joined me on the appointed date and we set off, poling up the Myittha River in a country dug-out. Shortly after we reached Sinywa (Wild Elephant Village), a Burman arrived to say there was an enormous wild tusker, believed to be Shwe Kah, not three hundred yards from their camp, a mile away.

Without any hesitation I was off. My companion candidly admitted that he was far too tired to leave camp. By three p.m., under a sweltering tropical sun, I had got near enough to this wild elephant to hear an occasional flap of his ear. There was no other sound, as he was browsing in elephant grass twelve feet high, through which I had ventured, following up his tracks. I knew that the river bank could not be far to my left. I stopped and took a quick swallow from a water-flask, as that was probably the last refresher I should get.

I was suddenly alarmed by realizing that my presence had been detected by the elephant, probably, as so often happens, by scent. There was a never-to-be-forgotten noise of the animal cracking the end of his trunk on the ground—it makes a sharp clear, metallic, ringing sound, owing to the trunk being hollow. Then there followed an awful silence. I had no alternative but to stand my ground. Both of us were left guessing, but the elephant broke first and made away from where I was standing, whereupon I made direct to where I imagined the river bank to be. Not many seconds passed before I heard a tremendous splashing, and through the tall grass I saw a magnificent tusker elephant crossing the river fifty yards below me, moving fast.

Without hesitation, I jumped down the eight-foot bank, landing in three feet of water but sinking into the mud to the tops of my boots. I was bogged. It was now or never. I decided on a heart shot, as he was moving quickly and I was unsteady.

Crack! He was quite seventy-five yards away when I fired. He stumbled a bit, recovered, and then swung round like a polo pony and came back, not twenty-five yards below me. He was wild with rage—so wild that he did not see me. I was stuck and had no hope of regaining the bank. As he climbed up where he had slid down before, I realized that he was mortally wounded and noticed that his tusks did not appear as big as those of Shwe Kah.

I gave him another heart shot and there was no mistake this time. He collapsed stone dead against the top of the bank. Before I had extricated myself from the mud, my gun-boy, who had remained behind in a tree on the bank, went off to inspect him and came rushing back to me yelling: "Amai (Oh, Mother)! Amai! You have shot a Kyan Zit."

I was far too excited and occupied to appreciate what he meant. It was about half-past four in the afternoon and sweltering hot. I well remember my feelings when I realized that I had not bagged Shwe Kah, as I could not now get a licence to shoot another wild elephant for a year. However, all my disappointment vanished as soon as I saw the head of the magnificent beast I had shot. For he was something very rare and was already causing great excitement among all the elephant riders who had come rushing along from their camp. "Kyan Zit! Kyan Zit! Kyan Zit!" was all they could repeat.

I could not have been more astonished if I had shot a unicorn. The words "Kyan Zit" describe a rare type of elephant tusk that has grown in rings or corrugations like the sections of a piece of sugar-cane. The Burmans speak of such an animal as such a rarity as to be almost mythical, a king of elephants to whom all other elephants do obeisance, in terror of his strength.

Long discussions followed among the riders standing round and admiring the rare tusks. A head man arrived from camp to supervise their removal. Then the women of the camp arrived with children and babies in arms, all to be shown Kyan Zit.

211

Up to this time I had not allowed any of them to touch him, as I knew that once they started on a dead elephant they combined the qualities of souvenir hunters and vultures after flesh.

I then heard someone yelling my name. It was my guest, who on hearing my two shots in camp had hopped off his camp bed and, without waiting to put on his shoes, had come along with two or three of the men from my camp.

"Lord, how magnificent!" was his only remark, as he opened up his camera and took several snapshots. Then we settled down to supervise the removal of the tusks.

The human vultures now started operations. Whole baskets of meat were carried off to camp to be dried in the sun. There was enough to last them many months. It was my Burman hunter's perquisite to have the coveted aphrodisiac snips, which consist of the triangular tip of the trunk and the big nerves out of the tusks, which are also a native medicine for eye troubles.

By the time we had removed the tusks and the forefoot it was almost dusk. More men and women from Sinywa Village had arrived to carry away meat.

That was my last elephant, and I never shot big game again.

Nevertheless, though I dislike it now, I have no regrets in regard to those early years. For it was those years that laid the foundations of a love and understanding of the jungle and the elephants in it. I shot four elephants, but on the other side of the account is all I have tried to do for hundreds of their fellows.

J. H. Williams

James Howard Williams was born in England in 1897. He joined the army at the age of seventeen and served during World War I in Mesopotamia and Afghanistan. This gave him a taste for the Far East and in the early 1920s he joined the Bombay Burma Corporation. He immediately became deeply interested in elephants and their welfare.

When the Japanese overran Burma in World War II, "Elephant Bill" was put in charge of a rescue operation to move women and children to safety in India. He marched his elephants 170 miles over the Manipur hills, taking his wife and small son in one of the groups. Returning to the hills with his elephants, he ran a refugee camp and helped many more people to escape to India. When he rejoined his family in 1942 he became Elephant Adviser to the XIVth Army in Calcutta. He saved 120 elephants from Japanese control and their contribution to the war effort included bridge-building and rescuing the wounded.

After the war Colonel Williams went back to England with his wife and children. Here, in complete contrast to tending elephants, he grew anemones and daffodils in a Cornish market garden.

During a trip to America, two reporters took him on the town, getting story after story out of this brilliant raconteur. In consequence an article about "Elephant Bill" appeared in the *New Yorker*. This was read by Rupert Hart-Davis, the British publisher, who immediately rang Williams, now back in Cornwall. The result was the enormously successful publication of *Elephant Bill*. It revolutionized Colonel Williams's life; he was an excellent public speaker and soon was much in demand for lecture tours. He wrote two more books: *Bandoola*, the story of a special elephant, and *The Spotted Deer*, about a trip he made to the Andaman Islands off the coast of India.

Colonel Williams died tragically during an emergency appendix operation in 1958, but he lives on in the entrancing stories of the animals he knew.

THE BRENDAN VOYAGE

An epic crossing of the Atlantic

A CONDENSATION OF THE BOOK BY

Tim Severin

Published by Hutchinson

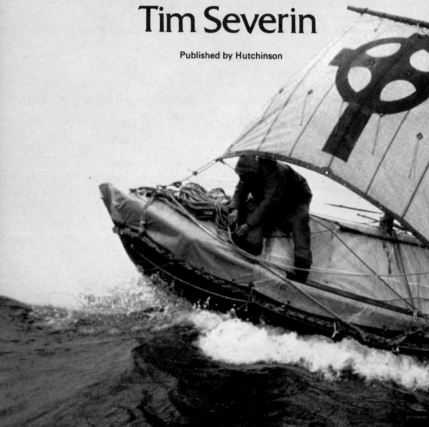

In the sixth century A.D. Saint Brendan and an intrepid band of monks set sail from Ireland in a leather boat, and after a perilous journey reached their "Promised Land" across the Atlantic. So says the mediaeval manuscript of the *Navigatio*—but is this account fact or legend? Did Brendan discover America, a thousand years before Columbus?

Tim Severin was determined to find out. After months of experimentation, he and his crew built a replica of Brendan's tiny boat and embarked on a breathtaking voyage. They were buffeted by gale-force winds, almost swamped by heavy seas, threatened by huge whales. At the last, trapped in deadly ice floes off Greenland, their quest suddenly turned into a struggle for life itself.

CHAPTER 1

The seventh wave is said to be the worst, the one that does the damage in the turmoil of an ocean gale. Modern oceanographers know this is just a superstition of the sea. But still, clinging to the helm of a small open boat in the heaving waters of a bad Atlantic storm, the temptation to count the waves is irresistible. The mind longs for anything that might impose a pattern on the jumble of destruction that unfolds each time the boat rises to the crest of a roller. A frightening grey vista stretches to the horizon: rank upon rank of massive breaking waves, each one capable of swamping, destroying, or capsizing. So always, at that brief moment before the boat drops into the next trough, the eye seeks to pick out the seventh waves, real or imaginary, the monsters that lift their heads in menace above their companions, before they, too, sink down to hide in ambush.

On that wind-torn evening in late May, 1976, it seemed to my tired mind that the wave pattern was changing to random groups of three. The leading wave of each group would come towards us, steeper and steeper by the moment, until it could no longer support its own mass. Its crest toppled forward, and then came sliding down the wave front in a self-generated avalanche of foam and released energy. When it struck, the boat shuddered and faltered. The helm twisted savagely in my hand, then went slack,

217

and we were picked up bodily and rushed forward in the grip of the white water. In that dangerous instant the gale clawed at us, striving to slew the boat sideways so that she would be parallel to the advancing wave crests. Should that happen, we were lost, for then the second great wave would sweep over the vulnerable length of the hull. Each wave, I feared, would be our last.

No one could tell us how to steer our boat through the gale, for no boat quite like her had been afloat for the past thousand years. She was long and slim, with tapering bow and stern curving gently upward. Her most extraordinary feature was that she was made of leather. Her hull was nothing more than forty-nine oxhides stitched together like a patchwork quilt and stretched over a wooden frame. It was this thin skin, only a quarter of an inch thick, flexing and shifting as the boat moved—just like the skin over a man's rib cage—that now stood between us and the fury of the Atlantic. I recalled the bleak warning of one of the world's leading authorities on leather before we started our voyage.

"Oxhide," he had explained in his precise university tone, "is very high in protein. It resembles a piece of steak, if you like. It will decompose in the same way."

"What happens when the leather is soaking wet in seawater?" I had asked.

"Ah well. That I'm not sure," he replied. "We've never been asked to test it."

In fact, if the leather hull was not strong enough, the thread holding it together would simply rip through the hides like the top of a cardboard package being torn along the perforated line. Then the oxhides would peel away like petals, and the wooden frame underneath would spring open and in a brief moment disintegrate. Privately, I doubted it would ever come to that. Much more likely was the possibility of our capsizing. Our boat had no keel to hold her steady. If one of the tumbling wave crests caught her wrong footed, she would be sent spinning upside down, her crew tipped into the water where there was no hope of rescue.

Why on earth, then, were my crew and I sailing such an improbable vessel in the face of a rising gale? Our strange craft was called *Brendan*, in honour of the great sixth-century Irish

218

missionary saint who, it was said, had sailed to America. This astonishing claim was based on authentic and well-researched Latin texts, dating back at least to A.D. 800, that told how the saint and a party of monks had sailed to a land far to the west in a boat made of oxhides. If the claim was true, then they would have reached America almost a thousand years before Columbus and four hundred years before the Vikings. Such a notion, sceptics declared, was harebrained. To cross the Atlantic in a boat made of animal skin was unthinkable. But the obvious way of checking the story was to build such a boat and then see if it would sail across the Atlantic. So there we were, my crew and I, out in the ocean.

THE GALE could not have caught us at a worse time. Our adventure had only just begun. *Brendan* was still untested, and only thirty miles to starboard, much too close for comfort, lay Saint Brendan's own country—the jagged Atlantic coast of Ireland. This same coast had destroyed at least twenty galleons of the Spanish Armada, and compared to a Spanish galleon, our *Brendan* was a seafaring nightmare. We could not sail upwind, and if the gale swung into the west, we would be driven as helplessly as a leaf down onto the iron-bound cliffs and half-submerged reefs. We had no choice but to run helter-skelter before the gale, driven along by a single square sail slung as low as we dared, while *Brendan* tobogganed down the waves.

I looked at my crew and wondered if they appreciated the situation. George Molony did. He was one of the best sailors I knew; we had sailed many miles together on small boats. For that reason he now held the job of sailing master on *Brendan*, responsible for getting the very best performance from the boat under sail. Rolf Hansen, too, knew the risks. He was from Norway and normally spent his summers exploring his country's coastline in a massive sailing boat, built at the end of the last century. But Peter Mullett, the cameraman of our team, worried me. He had sailed alone from England to Greece in his own boat, so he was no stranger to the sea. But now he was feeling the pain from damaged muscles he had strained two days previously when we were rowing *Brendan*.

Arthur Magan, the youngest member of the crew, was totally oblivious to any danger, for the very good reason that he was laid low by seasickness. *Brendan* had a most peculiar sea motion, more like a life-raft than a conventional vessel. She heaved and swayed, then bobbed, swayed, and heaved while Arthur curled up in misery, his eyes screwed tightly shut. Every now and again a burst of spray swept over him, running down his face and dripping off his oilskins. Only when his turn came to go on watch did Arthur take an interest in his surroundings. Then, with a visible effort of self-discipline, he hauled himself into a sitting position, clipped on his lifeline, and dragged himself to the helm. Secretly I applauded his willpower, but it was obvious that only three men from a total crew of five were fit to handle *Brendan* if the gale picked up.

It was almost impossible to get any rest between watches. *Brendan* was essentially an open boat. Just behind the stubby mainmast was a low tentlike structure with barely room for three men to lie down. Here we also had to find space for spare clothes, cameras, and sleeping bags, and all the navigation equipment. Besides, whenever a wave broke over the stern, it dropped a thick dollop of water right into the shelter. Farther forward, by the short foremast, there was another small tent, not much larger than a good-sized kennel. Here two crew members were expected to sleep, but here the leaks were even worse.

When my turn at the helm was over, I crawled into my berth in the main shelter, wedged myself into position, and lay there worrying. Under the thwarts my feet and head were touching the bulkheads, and I could feel them shifting as the boat rose and fell with the waves—shifting *in opposite directions*. The boat was like a whale, and I was lying inside its ribs like Jonah and feeling the boat change her shape to meet the pressures of the sea. All around I could hear creaks and groans. The sides of the boat pumped gently in and out as though the *Brendan* were breathing.

"Help! Help! We're sailing backwards!" George roared. A wave crest had caught *Brendan* and without warning spun her back to front. Peter and I bolted out of the cabin. Lightly dressed, we were quickly soaked to the skin, but we had to bring the headsail under control. We swarmed forward to where it was pinned against the mast by the force of the gale, and with brute strength wrestled it around again. With a soggy thud the sail bellied out, and began to pull *Brendan* out of trouble. Very slowly the boat wheeled away downwind, and for two aching wavelengths we watched and waited as the vulnerable side of our leather craft was exposed to the rollers. But they swept under us without doing any harm, and we went careening onward.

Night came, a foul, black night complete with driving rain that reduced visibility to a few yards. I crawled into my sleeping bag and closed my eyes, feeling utterly limp.

"Where the hell did that come from!" Peter's cry woke me instantly. I tumbled out of the shelter and found Peter heaving desperately on the tiller. Less than a hundred yards away, with all her lights blazing, was a large fishing trawler bearing straight down on us. Her bows were sending up huge bursts of spray as she slammed down on the waves, and she was rolling wickedly. It was impossible that she could have seen us in the murk.

"Light a white flare!" I yelled at Peter. "Light a flare!"

But it was already too late. Peter tried to turn *Brendan* away, but the wind had locked us on what seemed to be a collision course. The trawler's streaming black hull slid past us so close that we could make out the welding on the steel hull plates. The lights from her portholes swept over us as we looked up, aghast.

The water boiled white around us from the trawler's screws, and then she was gone, swallowed up in the raging gale. *That* was a risk Saint Brendan never had to face, I thought to myself.

By dawn the wind rose to its worst, just short of storm force, tearing the tops off the waves. *Brendan* was rushing madly farther and farther out to sea. We trailed a heavy loop of rope from the stern to act as a brake and, we hoped, to smooth the worst of the wave crests. The inside of the main shelter was a shambles of camera lenses, pilot books and sodden clothing. There, Peter had finally taken refuge. He had strained his arm more during the near mishap with the trawler, and he was obviously shaken.

The new day brought an improvement in the weather. The gale began to ease, and by degrees our spirits rose. The Primus stove was lighted. Hot coffee followed an anonymous stew of macaroni

221

and vegetables, and *Brendan*'s crew began to take a more intelligent interest in their surroundings. George made the happy discovery that it was much easier to steer the boat if the helmsman stood facing out over the stern and watching the waves.

After the worst of the gale seabirds promptly reappeared. An occasional puffin scurried busily past, his stubby wings jerking frantically up and down and his clown's face with the great coloured beak making him look for all the world like a child's wind-up toy. A number of yellow-headed gannets, the largest seabirds in this part of the world, patrolled majestically for food, cruising steadily on their six-foot wingspan before plummeting down on their prey or swooping to indulge in slick acrobatics in the up-currents that lifted briefly from the faces of the big waves. Their nonchalance made the rough water seem less threatening, as did the seagulls, which landed on the water and bobbed among the waves with an air of unconcern.

So, too, it occurred to me, *Brendan* might defeat the sea. Perhaps this was one of the secrets Saint Brendan had known. We still had nearly three thousand miles of sailing through some of the trickiest waters in the world, but I felt a quiet satisfaction that we had survived our first gale of the voyage and advanced a few more steps towards our goal.

CHAPTER 2

The idea of the Brendan Voyage was born at the kitchen table in the house in the southwest of Ireland where my wife and I spend our holidays. "There's something odd about the Saint Brendan text," Dorothy remarked one evening.

Her casual comment immediately caught my attention. "What do you mean by 'odd'?" I asked her.

"It doesn't have the same feel as much of the other literature written at about the same time. For instance, it is the story of a saint, so one would normally expect to find a long list of miracles performed by him. But Saint Brendan doesn't perform any miracles. His only special skill is that he has extraordinary wisdom."

"What else?"

"Well, the story has a remarkable amount of practical detail, far more than most early mediaeval texts. It tells you about the geography of the places Brendan visits. It carefully describes the progress of the voyage, the times and distances, and so forth. It seems to me that the text is not so much a legend as a tale which is embroidering a firsthand experience."

My wife's critical judgment was worth listening to. She had a wide knowledge of mediaeval texts. In fact, we had first met in the library at Harvard University, where we were both doing research: she for her doctoral thesis and I on the history of exploration.

"Saint Brendan has certainly puzzled the historians of exploration," I commented. "No one seems to be able to make up his mind whether the saint's voyage was fantasy or fact."

"Well, I don't see why Saint Brendan couldn't have got there," said my wife firmly.

"No, neither do I. After all, you and I know that it's possible to cover enormous distances in small vessels. We've done it ourselves. Perhaps it's time someone tried to find out whether Saint Brendan's Atlantic voyage was feasible or not. But a fair test would mean using the boats and materials of that time."

The house in which we were sitting was not so far from where Saint Brendan had been born and lived, preached, and been laid to rest. In that evocative atmosphere it seemed entirely logical to research and to build a replica of his vessel, and to see if his story could have been true.

Of course there would be an immense amount of preliminary work to do. First, I had to satisfy myself that the scholarship behind the project was sound. I was determined at all costs not to let the voyage become a mere survival test. I was under no illusions: the passage would involve physical risk. To warrant such risk, the endeavour had to produce worthwhile results.

For several months I carefully dredged up all the data I could find about Saint Brendan, about early voyages across the Atlantic, and about the key text itself, the *Navigatio Sancti Brendani Abbatis*, "The Voyage of St. Brendan the Abbot", more usually known as the *Navigatio*. The saint's background gave me useful clues. He was one of Ireland's most important holy men, one who had a profound influence on the Celtic Church. Most probably he was born near the lakes of Killarney in County Kerry about A.D. 489. He studied under the famous teacher Saint Enda, and in due course rose to become an abbot. At that time the Irish church was organized almost exclusively into monasteries scattered around the country, and Brendan was responsible for the foundation of several of these, including Clonfert in County Galway. There he was buried some time between A.D. 570 and 583.

What struck me most was Saint Brendan's proven reputation as a traveller. Again and again I found references to journeys made by him. He sailed to the Hebrides off Scotland to hold an important conference with Saint Columba, founder of the great monastery on Iona. It was said that Brendan also travelled to Wales. Other less well-documented reports spoke of his going to Brittany, to the Orkney and Shetland Islands, and even as far afield as the Faeroe Islands. Obviously Saint Brendan had spent a great deal of his time travelling around the northwestern perimeter of Europe in small vessels. In short, he was a sailor's saint; he was known, in fact, as Brendan the Navigator.

But it was the *Navigatio* that sealed his reputation. This was the Latin text which my wife and I had both read as students and remembered as something out of the ordinary. It described how Saint Brendan had been visited by another Irish priest who described to him a beautiful land, far in the west over the ocean, where the word of God ruled supreme. The priest advised Brendan to see this place for himself, and so Brendan built a boat specially for the voyage, its hull a framework of wood on which he stretched oxhides. Then he loaded ample stores, spare hides and fat to dress them, and set sail with seventeen monks to find this Promised Land.

For seven years they wandered from one island to another, had many adventures, and finally managed to explore the fringe of the Promised Land before setting sail once again for Ireland. Some of their adventures were obviously fabulous. For instance, they were said to have landed on the back of a whale, mistaking it for an island. When they lighted a fire to cook a meal, the heat woke the whale and the monks just managed to scramble back into their boat before the whale swam off, the fire still burning on his back like a beacon. Other episodes seemed equally unlikely: the *Navigatio* described how Brendan and his crew came upon a huge pillar of crystal floating in the sea; later they were chased by a fire-breathing sea monster; at one island they were pelted with hot rocks. So it went. The *Navigatio*, some scholars said, was a splendid collection of seafaring yarns.

But several eminent authorities disagreed. The episodes bore a striking resemblance to geographical facts. The floating pillar of crystal could have been an iceberg. Perhaps the sea monster was a pugnacious whale, or a walrus. The burning rocks might have been molten slag thrown up by an eruption in Iceland.

I pulled out modern atlases and sea charts, and tried to match up these theories with the practical realities of the North Atlantic. The way Saint Brendan's itinerary fitted the various Atlantic islands was certainly startling. A single similarity—for example, the volcanoes of Iceland as the basis for the story of the hot rocks—could have been explained as a coincidence. But it would have required a whole string of coincidences to explain the complete run of other similarities—from the Islands of Sheep which Brendan visited early on in his journey and which sounded very like the Faeroe Islands, right through to the thick white cloud he encountered just off the Promised Land, which might have been the notorious fog zone off the Grand Banks of Newfoundland. As a practical sailor, I knew that it was awkward to sail by a direct route from Ireland to North America. This track is contrary to the prevailing winds, which blow from the southwest and west. Saint Brendan would have been forced to go around the westerly wind belt, either to north or south, battling his way from island to island and working his way by stages.

Excitedly I consulted the navigation charts of the North Atlantic. The logical route leaped off the page. Using the prevailing southwest winds, one could sail north from Ireland and up to the Hebrides, off the coast of Scotland. Then north again, slanting across the westerly winds to the Faeroes. From there lay a tricky passage to Iceland, but after that the currents were all favourable, helping the boat across from Iceland to southern Greenland, and then sweeping down to the coast of Newfoundland, Labrador, or beyond. On the map this route looked very roundabout, but that was an illusion of map projection. It was very nearly the shortest way between northern Europe and North America; above all, it was the Stepping Stone Route taken by early aviators in short-range aircraft, also by the Vikings, and . . . earlier still perhaps by the Irish.

It dawned on me that the Brendan Voyage was going to be a detective story. I had the clues before me in the text of the *Navigatio*. One by one they might lead towards a solution. I would have to inspect the places along the Stepping Stone Route that might conform to the places recorded in the *Navigatio*.

ONE MARCH DAY I found myself walking down a steep track to the spot from which Saint Brendan was said to have set out for the Promised Land. I was deeply affected by my surroundings. This was Saint Brendan's own country, the Dingle Peninsula of County Kerry and Ireland's farthest reach out into the Atlantic. It is a place where the sweep of green hills and moorlands ends in the blue-grey ocean, where the air is so clear one almost has a sense of vertigo as the land seems to tilt towards the horizon. Here Saint Brendan's name—spelled, in the older version, "Brandon" —is still commemorated in almost every natural feature.

Brandon Creek, for example, lies on the north side of the peninsula, a cleft in the line of massive cliffs that guard the coast. To reach it, one crosses bog country, marked by clumps of brown peat stacked for drying and by occasional tiny fields rimmed with walls of loose rock. It is a place of few inhabitants, though where the narrow road finally runs out on the lip of the creek I found two houses. One could have been cut from a picture postcard. Its rough stone walls were beautifully whitewashed; there were flowers in tubs, and the neat thatched roof was held down against the ferocious winter gales by a lacework of cords, their ends weighted with smooth oval rocks gathered from the sea, every rock as neatly whited as a pearl in a necklace.

It was an unforgettable day, brilliant sunshine alternating with the stinging showers so typical of west Irish weather; so clear were the aquamarine waters of Brandon Creek that they would not have looked out of place in a tropical island. Gazing away from the mouth of the creek to the northwest, I thought, out there lies North America. If this is where tradition says Saint Brendan started his voyage, this is where my boat will start too.

I began walking down the track leading past the thatched cottage. At that instant, with a thrill of excitement, I saw them. Drawn up on the side of the road were four strange black shapes—boats turned upside down. They were the traditional canvas-covered curraghs, boats found nowhere else in the world. Relics of the Stone Age, they are believed to be among the last surviving descendants of one of the oldest types of boat in the world—the skin boat. Here, in Brandon Creek, I first laid eyes on the heirs to the craft which Saint Brendan was said to have sailed.

Crouching down, I peered underneath one of them to see how it was made. Inside was an elegantly beautiful cagework of thin laths, frail-looking but in fact capable of withstanding great compression. Stretched over this frame was a tight skin of canvas, tarred on both sides to make it waterproof. Tucked under the curragh was a set of oars of a pattern I had never seen before. About nine feet long, they were so slender that they had no blade whatever, and they were fitted with curious triangular blocks of wood, pierced with a hole that matched a pivot pin when rowing. I judged the curraghs too small for anything more than inshore skiffs, yet to my eye they seemed perfect, delicately engineered and gracefully curved. A rain shower had slicked their hulls so that the four glistening black shapes looked as sleek as porpoises rolling through the sea.

I yearned to go for a ride in one. A cheerful woman at the thatched cottage said I was likely to find a number of curragh men in the bar in the village of Dunquin, as the weather was too rough to take the curraghs out fishing. There, the barman pointed out three men sitting in a corner. I went over to them.

Not one could have been under fifty-five. They were uniformly dressed in baggy tweed jackets and battered trousers. All had gaunt, knobby hands, large and reddened raw faces with strong noses and heavyset bones.

"I am interested in going for a spin in a curragh," I said. "I wonder if any of you could take me out."

"No," said one, "it's too dangerous today. We'd all be killed. Maybe tomorrow."

"What if I paid you three pounds each just for a quick spin?"

"Ah now! That would be different!"

So off we went. A fourth crew member—a younger man with a bright yellow flower stuck jauntily in his hatband—was recruited just before we started down a steep path to a landing place where a dozen curraghs lay upside down on their stages near the water.

To carry the boat to the water's edge, the crew crouched underneath it, pressed their shoulders against the thwarts, and straightened their backs. The curragh shot smartly into the air like a strange black beetle heaving itself up onto four pairs of legs, which then marched off to the slipway. With a swift movement the boat was lowered to the ground and tipped right side up; with the next wave she was swirled afloat as casually as a toy.

One by one we jumped in, taking care not to put a foot through the thin canvas. The oarsmen settled in their places; one good strong heave and the curragh shot forward into the waves. In a moment we were out in the sound and curvetting like a horse over the waves. Balance was critical; if the boat stayed level, she flew over the waves and scarcely a drop of water came aboard. I bombarded the crew with questions. How many curraghs were still used in the Dingle? About a hundred. What were they used for? Servicing lobster pots and setting salmon nets. Would they stand a rough sea? Yes, if they were handled right. What happens in a capsize? The boat stays wrong side up, and you drown.

"Can you carry heavy loads all right?" I asked.

"Why, yes. In spring we take cattle out and leave them to graze on the islands," came one answer, and someone else added a comment in Gaelic which made the others laugh.

"What did he say?" I asked.

228

"He said the cows are less trouble. They don't ask so many questions."

When we were ready to return, I asked the crew to perform a small but important experiment—to row the boat on a figure-eight course. I wanted to learn how the curragh rode the seas at different angles. Up to that moment the oarsmen had been keeping the boat heading directly into the waves or directly away from them. The crew muttered and shook their heads, but I insisted. Eventually they agreed, and off we went rather gingerly. Everything turned out splendidly. The curragh skimmed through the troughs and crests, then turned handsomely as the waves curled under her. My crew beamed with pleasure, and so did I. Now I knew for certain that the curraghs were not just inshore skiffs. They handled like true sea boats. The voyage was one step closer.

Back ashore, I paid off my curragh men, who were evidently delighted with such easy money, and asked them who could tell me more about their craft. They were unanimous: John Goodwin of Maharees; no one else knew as much or built them so well.

SO IT WAS that I met the seventy-eight-year-old curragh builder, whose advice was to underpin a major part of my boatbuilding. He had spent his lifetime accumulating information about curraghs because he loved them. Building them had been his father's trade and his grandfather's before him. John still used the tools he had inherited; a few hand drills and wood chisels, a knife and a hammer, and a small selection of wooden battens marked like yardsticks were all he needed to produce the sophisticated and elegant boats for which he was famous.

Just as important for me, John loved talking about curraghs. Hour after hour he plied me with stories. Proudly he showed me a photograph of himself and his three brothers sitting bolt upright in a racing curragh in which they had won the championship of Kerry. As we walked together past a row of upturned curraghs, he would stop and point out minute differences between one and another. When I showed him a faded photograph taken in the 1930s of a curragh frame, he immediately identified the man who had made it. Another time I asked him about the days when curraghs were sailed as well as rowed. After a moment's thought he began rummaging around in the rafters of the tarred shack where he built his boats, and pulled down an old sail. It was a museum piece, and he let me measure and copy it, while he spent another half hour telling me how to rig and sail a curragh to best advantage. It was advice that was to prove vital.

One story in particular stayed in my mind. On a wintry day earlier this century, John said, a steamer had been driven into a local bay by a terrible storm. The vessel was in real danger, but she managed to get down an anchor to hold her temporarily. Her master sent up distress rockets to call out the lifeboat from shore before the anchor broke. But the storm was so fierce that the lifeboat had to turn back after suffering damage. Then two local curragh men launched their frail craft into the raging sea and with great daring rowed out to the steamer. One man leaped aboard and persuaded the steamer's master to hoist anchor. Then he piloted the vessel through the shoals and reefs to safety.

I asked John if he would build a curragh for me, and show me how it was done. With him I spent a hot afternoon tarring and stretching the canvas hide into position, and in the end I had a small two-man craft of my own, built to the traditional pattern. When I collected the boat from him, I asked John, "Do you think a big curragh could get all the way to America?"

He grinned at me. "Well, now," he finally replied. "The boat will do, just as long as the crew's good enough."

To my wife's chagrin, I stole the linings from the dining-room curtains to make a sail for my little curragh and spent all of Christmas Day stitching it by hand. Then I sailed up and down the estuary outside our house to see how the boat behaved. It was bitterly uncomfortable, but the effort was worth it. By the end of the Christmas holidays, I knew that although she wobbled alarmingly and refused to sail upwind, she and her ancestors had been designed to carry a mast and sails.

IT WAS ABOUT this time that I became aware of a curious phenomenon which I could only call Brendan Luck. My encounter with John Goodwin was one example. As another, I discovered that a definitive study of Irish curraghs had been written by James Hornell, the naval historian, tracing the boats back to Saint Brendan's day and beyond into the writings of Julius Caesar and other classical authors who had recorded the skin-covered vessels of the natives of Britain.

But perhaps the most bizarre stroke of good fortune occurred when I was trying to work out how Saint Brendan might have rigged his ocean-going curragh. It seemed to me that such a long, slim boat must have carried two masts, but in all my research I had never seen a picture of an early mediaeval boat equipped with more than one—not even Viking ships. Then one day I was in the cellar of the London Library, working on quite another subject. By chance I happened to walk through a little-used section, and as I passed the stacks a book caught my eye. It was mis-shelved, having been put in back to front. Casually I pulled it out to turn it the right way around, and my eye fell upon the title. It was long and scholarly, in German, and roughly translated as "A Record of Ship Illustrations from the Earlier Times to the Middle Ages". I flipped the book open. From the page where it fell open, one illustration jumped up at me. It was a drawing of a two-masted ship, and it was undoubtedly mediaeval! To my astonishment I read that the picture was of Saint Brendan's ship stranded on the whale's back! There were some five thousand illustrations in the book, and only this one showed a twin-masted boat.

An important name kept cropping up in the libraries: John Waterer. He had written the majority of books and articles on the historic uses of leather. I got in touch with him and found myself invited to the vaults of Saddlers' Hall, the headquarters of one of the ancient guilds in the heart of London. John Waterer turned out to be as deep-dyed an enthusiast as John Goodwin. An energetic gnome of a man with twinkling eyes and huge ears, he darted about his vault full of leather saddles and bridles, leather tapestries and book bindings, even leather mugs and jugs; his agility belied his eighty-three years.

Waterer could not have been more helpful. Patiently he told me about the different ways of turning animal skin into leather by tanning and by other treatments. He explained why one leather differed from another according to the treatment or according to its source—whether it came from ox or calf, goat or sheep, or even such exotic animals as moose and buffalo. He had begun work in the leather trade as a luggage-maker. Like John Goodwin, he had been gripped by the fascination of his work and had probed deeper and deeper into its history. Now he was the acknowledged authority in the field.

A fortnight later I attended a meeting he arranged at the British Leather Institute. Brendan Luck was still with me, and I found myself explaining my ideas about Saint Brendan to three men whose expertise could help to turn my dream into reality. Dr. Robert Sykes was head of the Research Association of the British Leather Manufacturers and had an international reputation. He was precise, sensible, and at first a bit sceptical. Next to him sat Carl Postles, tanyard manager for W. & J. Richardson in Derby, a family business that had been making saddlery and other fine leather goods since the seventeenth century. Finally there was burly Harold Birkin, whom I was to get to know and admire very much over the next few months. Harold lived, talked, and doubtless breathed the business of making leather for special purposes. From a small tannery in Chesterfield, he sent a variety of exotic leathers to customers all over the world. His leather was used deep in coal mines for air pumps or out on the snowfields of Antarctica for dog-team harnesses.

"Saint Brendan is said to have built his boat from leather tanned in oak bark," I told these experts. "Do you think this was right, and would it have survived an ocean crossing?"

"Oak-bark-tanned leather is certainly authentic," Dr. Sykes replied. "The normal way of tanning leather in western Europe right up to this century was some form of vegetable tannage, usually oak bark if it was available, and taking as long as twelve months to tan fully. Oak-bark leather is very rare nowadays. In fact, I only know two, perhaps three, tanneries who still make it. There's one in particular down in Cornwall."

"What about dressing the leather?" asked Harold. "It sounds to me as if dressing the hull is going to be just as important as the leather itself."

"The *Navigatio* merely says the monks rubbed the skins with a grease or fat before they launched their boat," I told him.

Turning to Dr. Sykes he asked, "What sort of fats would they have had, Bob?"

"Tallow, or sheep's fat, beeswax, perhaps cod oil, and for waterproofing"—and here Dr. Sykes paused—"possibly the grease from sheep's wool. It's virtually raw lanolin and has been known since Pliny's time; people have used it for waterproofing shoes right up to recent times."

We finally agreed that Carl and Harold would send to Dr. Sykes samples of all the suitable sorts of leather. Dr. Sykes would then test these samples at his laboratories: soaking them in seawater, rolling and drying, flexing and stretching them, measuring and weighing them, to see what happened.

So began a delightful period of work. The British leather-makers took the Brendan project to heart, and what splendid people they turned out to be. It is a close-knit industry in which everyone seems to know everyone else in friendly rivalry, but all shared an appreciation of leather. I visited tanneries, saddle-makers, and luggage-makers. At the Richardson's tannery in Derby I noticed on several windowsills small scraps of leather floating in jam jars. "What on earth are those?" I asked Carl Postles.

"Oh, the tannery workmen have heard about your crazy Saint Brendan idea, and everyone has been testing pieces of leather to see whether they float."

"And do they?" I asked.

"Not for longer than four days." He grinned. "You're going to need a life-raft."

Then one afternoon, after ten weeks of tests at the laboratories, I had a momentous telephone call from Dr. Sykes.

"I think we've identified your hull leather," he said. "You were right. Oak-bark leather is the best."

"How do you know?"

"We've done every test we can manage in the time available, including a test of how much water penetrates the leather."

"What happened?" I asked.

"After dressing with grease and extensive testing, all the other

233

leathers began to fail. Many became waterlogged, rather like wet dishcloths. But the oak-bark samples scarcely changed at all. In the end the oak-bark leather was actually two or three times more resistant to water than any other sample. If you still want to make that leather boat, then you should use oak-bark leather."

With a glow of triumph I put down the telephone. Once again the simple factual accuracy of the *Navigatio* had been demonstrated, this time to the satisfaction of a skilled scientist.

THERE REMAINED the problem of where to get the oak-bark leather, and here I had another stroke of luck. At a leather fair in London I met Bill Croggon of Josiah Croggon and Son Ltd., the oak-bark tanners from Cornwall. I was warned that the Croggons were a very conservative firm. "They've been making oak-bark leather in the same manner and in the same place for nearly three centuries," I was told. "It's up to you to persuade them to let you have some."

When I explained to Bill Croggon what I wanted, he looked thoughtful. "I'll have to talk it over with my brother," he said. "It takes a very long time to make oak-bark leather—nearly a year. When would you want it?"

"Well, I'd planned to set sail on Saint Brendan's Day, May sixteenth," I said.

"What a coincidence! That's my wife's birthday!" Somehow I knew then that the Croggons would be helping the Brendan project.

So it turned out. I went down to the little Cornish town of Grampound and met the family—grandmother, sons, and grandsons—helpful, hospitable, and soon as excited about the Brendan voyage as I was. They took me around the tannery. I was astonished to see one workman actually scraping the hair from an oxhide by hand, using a double-handed scraper and looking exactly like a woodcut illustration of a leatherworker printed four hundred years ago. We went up to the tanning pits, row upon row of tanks dug into the ground and filled with a rich liquid made of ground-up oak bark and water, which looked like thick beer with a creamy froth and smelled sickly sweet. In this "oak-bark liquor" lay the oxhides, slowly absorbing the tannin in the mixture, which formed a tight bond with the skin fibres and turned a perishable oxhide into some of the finest leather known. "It's a technique that can't have changed much since Saint Brendan's day," commented John Croggon. "Of course you'll have to have the best hides. You're trusting your life to them."

The Croggon brothers and their men examined each hide minutely for flaws, for barbed-wire scratches, for the holes left by warble flies, for cuts made by a careless skinning knife. It must have taken days of backbreaking work, and without ever a word to me. In the end, the Croggons provided fifty-seven of the finest oak-bark-tanned oxhides I could have wanted. When a professional saddle-maker saw them, he gave a low whistle of appreciation. "I've never seen leather like it," he said. "I've been told about it, but never expected to see so much in one place."

From the Croggons' tannery the hides went up to Harold Birkin to be greased. Tests at the research laboratories had revealed that wool grease was in fact the best dressing, and I telephoned a wool mill in Yorkshire. "I wonder if you could supply me with some wool grease."

"Yes, of course. How much grease do you want?"

"About three quarters of a ton, please."

There was a stunned silence.

The only trouble with the combination of wool grease and leather was the appalling smell. Even the workers in Harold Birkin's tannery—and tanneries are notoriously pungent places—complained that they could smell the stuff from half a mile away.

Under Harold's close attention each evil-smelling oxhide was folded in half and suspended in a tub of hot wool grease. Then it was put flat on the ground and more molten grease was poured on it. Another hide was placed on top and the process was repeated for all fifty-seven oxhides until there was a huge, sticky, multi-layered sandwich of leather gently absorbing the vital grease.

I STILL LACKED an indispensable expert: someone who could produce a proper set of technical drawings from which to build the boat. He would have to be a historian as well as a qualified

235

naval architect. I asked the Royal Institute of Navigation and was promptly given one name: Colin Mudie.

Colin Mudie had sailed across the Atlantic with Patrick Ellam in the tiny yacht *Sopranino* in the 1950s. He also had a reputation as an unorthodox designer. Nothing daunted him. Arctic explorers took their sledges to him to have them made into convertible boats; he designed power craft for high-speed racing, even a submersible yacht. Yet he had also designed production boats that were built by the thousands.

When I went to his home, I anticipated a bluff, bearded sea dog. Instead I was greeted by a small, fragile-looking man with a darting manner, a huge mane of long hair, and the most piercing blue-grey eyes I have ever seen. For all the world he looked like a hungry and alert owl, blinking as he invited me into his study.

In two hours I found out exactly why Colin Mudie was so highly regarded. He sat at his desk listening intently to my thesis and absentmindedly sketching on a pad. From the point of his pen flowed little ships and shapes, oars, and masts, details of waterlines and carpentry. When I finished, he merely looked up at me and said, "There's nothing impossible either about a leather boat or the voyage you want to make. I can do a design study for you, and then, if you want to go ahead, I'll follow it with drawings for a boatyard to work from. But what neither I nor anyone else can give you is the knowledge of how to handle this boat at sea. That knowledge has been long lost. It is up to you to rediscover it."

For eight weeks Colin worked with all the data about Irish leather boats I had gleaned. Twice he telephoned me. Once it was to tell me he thought he'd found a reason for the Dingle curragh's characteristic double gunwale. It was, he suggested, a throwback to the days when the leather hull was pulled over the gunwale like a skin over a drum. This would require a basic frame of great strength, especially in compression, and the double gunwale is an ideal construction. On the second call Colin confirmed my hunch that the original leather curraghs had carried two masts. His calculations showed that the traditional mast position was exactly right for a foremast. It was reasonable to suppose that in the old days there had been a mainmast to balance it.

In the end the drawings were ready, four large sheets covered with lines and figures in Colin's neat hand. With them under my arm and fifty-seven slippery, greasy oxhides pungent with wool grease, I set out for Ireland.

It was time to start building the boat.

CHAPTER 3

Not long before, I had been worrying whether I could find shipwrights to do the job. I need not have fretted. Only in Ireland was it possible to stroll into a boatyard, spread out a drawing, and casually ask, "I wonder if you could help build this for me? It's a sixth-century design, and I'll be covering the hull with oxhides myself, but I want an expert to build the wooden frame."

The manager's eyebrows rose a quarter of an inch. He took two slow puffs on his pipe and then murmured, "That shouldn't be any trouble. I'll check with our head shipwright if he's got space."

This was no run-of-the-mill boatyard. The Crosshaven yard in County Cork was where the Irish lifeboats were sent for overhaul; where Sir Francis Chichester built his record-breaking *Gypsy Moth V*; and where I heard it stated that they preferred never to build two boats to the same design because this was "too dull". Crosshaven was a boatyard in the old style: no fibreglass, scarcely any steel, but masses of timber and a cheerful confidence in their ability to build anything meant to float. Above all, they didn't mind my bringing smelly oxhides onto the premises, to be followed shortly afterwards by a medley of saddlers, leatherworkers, students, amateur helpers, and a mascot dog.

Pat Lake was the head shipwright. To my delight he himself elected to build the frame for the boat, working in the evenings in his spare time and helped by a pair of picked assistants. "Pat," I asked him, "can you do it in such a way that the frame is held together temporarily? Once you have shaped the main structure,

I will then replace your fastenings with authentic mediaeval ones."

"What were those fastenings made of?" he asked.

"Leather thong, most probably. Metal was too valuable to be used. Besides, I think if we lash the frame together like a wicker basket, this ought to make the hull more flexible."

"What sort of timber do you want me to use?"

"Oak for the double gunwales, and ash for the frames and the longitudinal stringers. We know these types of wood were growing in Ireland in Saint Brendan's day."

"We've got some oak here in the yard that has been seasoned for eight or ten years and is as hard as iron. But I wouldn't be happy about using ash. If it keeps getting wet in seawater and then drying out, it begins to rot. Before long you'd be able to poke your finger through it."

"I'm sure that ash is the right timber," I replied. "No other wood available in mediaeval Ireland was supple enough to follow the sharp curves of the hull frames."

"Right, then. But it's going to be difficult to find ash in the long, straight lengths we'll be wanting."

Here was an unexpected snag. I had to have trunks of ash thirty feet long and straight in the grain. But I had forgotten Brendan Luck. I was given the name of a consultant expert in the timber trade, and I went to see him at his office. I took a deep breath and began my usual explanation: "This may sound strange to you, but I want to build a mediaeval boat made of . . . ."

The timber expert held up his hand to stop me. "Some years ago a man called Heyerdahl came in to us for advice about balsa wood," he said. "I believe we found some for him. Just tell me what timber you want, and we'll see if we can help."

Through his contacts I found myself in County Longford in the very heart of Ireland, at a timberyard run by a family called Glennon. Had it not been for the strong Irish accents, I could have imagined myself with the leather-making Croggons in Cornwall. Each was a case of a small family business specializing in a traditional material. Once again a family brought to the Brendan project a huge enthusiasm that no money could have bought.

Paddy Glennon took me on a tour of their timberyard. He was

238

like an art connoisseur showing a visitor around his gallery. Here was the trunk of a four-hundred-year-old oak tree that had been handpicked to make a keel for a new wooden trawler. "Aren't you sorry to cut down such splendid trees?" I inquired.

"Oh, no. You see this black mark here near the root? That's rot. The tree has entered its old age. In time it would have rotted right through and been destroyed."

"Do you think you could possibly find me some really large ash trees?"

"As it happens," said Paddy, "we are felling some timber on one of the great estates near here, and there's some beautiful ash."

Once again the experts guided me into a fascinating subject—fine timber. "Heart of oak, bark of ash" was one of Paddy Glennon's mottoes. He advised me to use the heartwood from the oak tree for the gunwales, but it was the fine white wood from the outer trunk of the ash that was the strongest. Best of all, Paddy advised, was the wood from a mountain tree "which has to scrabble for its living" and grows light and strong. When it came time to select suitable ash for the mast and oars, Paddy himself took me across the countryside, hunting from tree to tree until we found just the one he sought—tall and straight, about eighty years old, in its prime. "I'll see to it personally that the mast timber is taken from the north-facing side, where the white wood is best. You'll find no ash stronger for your purpose."

I mentioned to him Pat Lake's worries about using ash in a boat. "The old fellows here used to soak their wooden tools in oil or grease, and this kept them in good condition," Paddy said. "How does that sound to you?" Another piece of the jigsaw puzzle clicked into place. The grease from the leather would unavoidably rub off onto the wood as the boat flexed in the sea. The logic was inescapable: here were two materials—leather and ash—which were normally vulnerable to seawater, but the same treatment with the same basic material—grease—rendered them suitable for a mediaeval boat.

Paddy Glennon invited me to meet his wife and have supper in their home. During the meal he asked all about the Brendan project and cross-examined me about the reasons behind it. And

239

when I was about to leave the table, he suddenly said, "You are not to expect a bill from Glennons."

I was overwhelmed. This was a most generous gift indeed. I started to thank him, but he went on: "My family has made a good living out of Irish-grown timber. We've always dealt with native-grown hardwoods when most other firms were importing their timber. If you're going to build an Irish boat out of Irish timber, I want it to be made of Glennons' timber. It'll help to pay back some of what the native timber has given to us. But"—and here he grinned—"there's always a 'but'. If your early Christian boat gets across the Atlantic, I want you to bring back just a small piece of our timber so that we can keep it in the office."

A week later a lorry delivered a load of superb white ash to the Crosshaven Boatyard, and Pat Lake and his shipwrights set to work. They used exactly the same methods John Goodwin followed up in the Dingle. The two gunwales were made from flint-hard oak joined with wooden pins. These were placed one above the other in a sandwich and shaped to the characteristic banana curve of the Dingle curragh. Next, the double gunwales were turned upside down so the boat could be built from the bottom upward.

One by one the light, curved transverse strips of bone-white ash were carefully put into position until they looked like a line of hoops. By pulling and pushing, Pat Lake got exactly the profile he wanted. Then he began to attach the stringers, the long, slim ash strips running fore and aft which completed the latticelike frame. He lightly tapped in a single wire nail at each intersection, until the basketwork was the shape of Colin Mudie's drawings.

Now it was up to me. I had been busily experimenting with the leather thongs to lash the frame together. Dr. Sykes at the leather research laboratories had advised that the best leather for this job was made by tawing, a process using alum, which had been known since Roman days. Carl Postles at the Derby tannery had sent over two big bales of thongs, and I began a few practice tests with them by tying together wood laths and hanging them in seawater. I quickly found that it was vital to soak the thongs, stretch them, and then tie the lashings while the leather was still wet otherwise the thongs did not grip. Unfortunately, tying knots

240

in slippery wet thongs is like trying to join two snakes: the thongs simply slide apart. One hilarious Sunday morning, testing a new type of knot, I tied the thong to a ring bolt in the floor of my garage and began heaving away with all my might. Suddenly the thong slipped, and I went hurtling backwards out of the open door and landed on the pavement flat on my back, waving a wet thong in the air. I found myself in the path of the village congregation on its way back from church. "That's what education does for you," someone muttered.

In the end I found a knot that seemed to hold effectively; in a curious way it looked much like the braided patterns found in Irish manuscript illustrations. George Molony came from England to help with the long job of lashing the frame together.

· George had always been my first choice for crew. Twenty-six years old, he had served in the army and later gone to the Middle

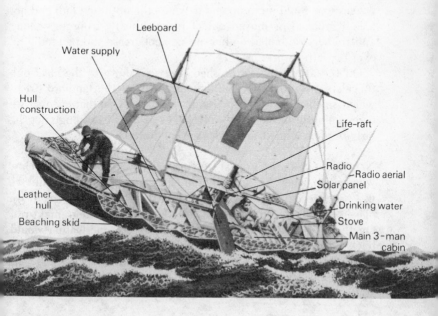

East to train soldiers for an oil-rich sheik. He had answered my advertisement for someone to help sail a small yacht in the Mediterranean, and had come cruising with my wife and me. Six foot tall and rangy, George was a consummate sailor, able to get more out of a boat by tirelessly resetting sails and adjusting the helm than anyone I had sailed with. Above all, he was reliable.

Now, crouched together inside the upturned boat frame, we started the laborious task of lashing it. Each wire nail had to be pulled out and discarded. In its place a leather thong was wrapped around the wood, tightened, and knotted, and then the free end was led on to the next thong, and so on and so on. It was backbreakingly slow work, poking fingers through the gaps in the frame, groping for a slippery strip of leather, and heaving the knots tight until our muscles cracked. Some days we were helped by friends from the village. By the time we had finished, we had hand-lashed sixteen hundred joints and used nearly two miles of leather thong. But it was worth it. The wooden skeleton of the boat was now gripped in a fine net of leather so strong that a dozen men could jump up and down on the upturned hull and not a lath groaned or moved out of place. Finally, to protect thong and timber, we boiled up buckets of wool grease and painted it all over the latticework.

On the afternoon we finished, we went down to the local pub to celebrate and were promptly pursued by the landlord's dog, which smelled the wool grease on our clothes. So that evening we ceremoniously burned our workclothes in the first, though not the last, sacrifice to mediaeval working conditions.

NOW CAME the most crucial step in the whole reconstruction. How were we to cover the wooden hull with the hides? What should we use for thread? How should we stitch the hides together? If we placed our stitches too close, the leather between them might rip. On the other hand, if we stitched too widely, the leather would buckle and water would pour in through the gaps.

The Irish National Museum in Dublin had a superb collection of early Christian artifacts, which I spent hours examining. The craftsmen from Saint Brendan's day used metal and wood and leather so cunningly that their work stood comparison with the very best modern examples. I realized that in conforming with mediaeval practices we would not be limiting our techniques; rather, we would be hard pressed to rise to their level of skill.

A master saddler came across from England with his best apprentice to advise George and me on possible leatherworking techniques for the boat. To try to mould the hides, we warmed them, soaked them in water, and beat them with great hammers. We tried every technique I had seen in the museum, and we tested the traditional methods of the master saddle-maker, methods with splendid-sounding names like backstitching, two-hand stitching, blind stitching, and the furriers' stitch. Occasionally the results were disastrous. We dipped one hide in water that was too warm, and the leather cracked and split like a neglected shoe. George and I looked at one another, wondering what would happen if we made a similar mistake but failed to spot it before we put out into the Atlantic. At last we worked out a technique that seemed simple and effective. We overlapped the oxhides by a margin of one to two inches and then stitched a strong double line of thread along the joint. It took care and patience, but the workmanship was at least within our capabilities, and the joints showed a crude strength. Then it was time for the master saddler to go back to the firm who had kindly loaned him to us.

I knew that without constant advice and supervision from an expert George and I and any amateur helpers were likely to make a shambles of the work. But where could I possibly find one? From the very beginning of the project I had been visiting saddle-makers in London, Birmingham, and all over Ireland as well. Everywhere I was told politely but firmly that every good saddler, and there were probably less than a hundred still at work in the entire British Isles, was needed at his bench. My only compensation for my trouble was that I earned a firsthand impression of fine leatherwork. I met the deft craftsmen who still handled tools that had not changed for centuries: awls and punches, pincers and scribers, crimpers, edge-shavers, and half-moon knives. The saddlers' benches smelled richly of leather and beeswax polish; and the saddlers bent over their work in their leather aprons, endlessly stitching away with their huge, strong hands and powerful shoulders developed by years of pulling the double-handed stitch taut with a snap that still made good hand-sewn leather far stronger than any machine could stitch it.

Finally, one saddler told me of an Irish harness-maker who had vanished from the world of leatherworking. John O'Connell had worked on harnesses for the royal stables. "Always laughing was John O'Connell," the saddler told me, "and if you find him, you can't miss him. He's about the same around the middle as he is tall. Built like a barrel. And a great one for the girls. He married a girl from Ireland, and I believe he decided to go back home. I've never heard from him again. Find John O'Connell, and you'll have found one of the best harness-makers in Ireland."

One day after we had begun building our boat at Crosshaven, I went to Cork to interview a retired saddle-maker. Unfortunately, he had long since lost his skills, but I stayed to chat with him about the business. "Did you by any chance know of someone by the name of John O'Connell?"

There was a pause while he thought back. "Yes, I knew John. He was very good. Some time ago I was looking for someone to help me and I wrote to him, but he wasn't interested."

I was agog with excitement. "Do you remember his address?"

"Let me think." Another agonizing pause. "It was in Summerstown Road, here on the edge of Cork City."

Scarcely believing my luck, I stayed a few minutes longer and then hurried out to my car. Summerstown Road was easy to find, and I banged on the door of the first house, trusting to the fact that in Ireland everyone knew everyone living in the same street.

Without a second's hesitation the woman who answered my knock replied to my question, "John O'Connell's at number seventeen."

I dashed across the road and rang the bell there. The door was opened by a small keg of a man with the weatherbeaten complexion of an outdoor worker, and massive hands and shoulders. He looked at me inquiringly.

"You're John O'Connell . . . the harness-maker?" I asked.

He looked stunned. "That's right. How did you find me?"

244

John had failed to find harness work in Cork, and had taken a job as a construction worker. He lived not fifteen miles from the boatyard where we were working. I asked him if he had still kept his leatherworking tools.

"My wife complains that I never throw anything away," he said with a chuckle. "Just wait a minute while I go upstairs and fetch them down."

He came back with a battered leather Gladstone bag and pulled it open. "I inherited most of them from my father. He was a horse-collar maker. I was apprenticed to him and served my full term before I went to England."

John O'Connell agreed to join us at the Crosshaven Boatyard. Horse collars were the branch of traditional leatherwork closest to our work for the boat. Step by step John began to train George and me and all the volunteers I recruited. He taught us to roll our own thread, turning a single strand of flax into a thick fourteen-strand cord. Clad in leather aprons we looped and twisted the flax, rubbing it with lumps of black wax mixed with wool grease and beeswax, and rolling it on our thighs. At first we got into terrible tangles. John O'Connell merely grinned and started each man over again. Gradually we picked up the knack, but we never equalled John himself. His hands moved in a blur, and he never needed to watch the threads spinning and twisting.

Next, John turned to the stitching of the leather. He started us on the plain backstitch. He demonstrated how to pierce half-inch-thick leather straight and true with a quick stab of the saddle-maker's awl and to follow through with the blunt needle, its tip touching the point of the awl as it was withdrawn. A second's delay and the leather would close around the hole. At the start we almost abandoned hope at ever being able to copy his methods. In four days of work we averaged a paltry six inches of stitching per day, and we had at least two miles to go.

We began with the easier work, piecing together the oxhides that would cover the central segment of the hull, joining them as if stitching together a quilt. Neighbours and friends came from my village to help us, and we learned that it was the knack that mattered in driving a good stitch, not brute strength. Our best recruit was a mere slip of a girl who left a neat, firm line of stitches that joined the hides as if they had been welded.

Once we had mastered the backstitch, John O'Connell took us on to the faster but more complicated two-hand stitch, using two needles to carry two separate threads down the line of awl holes, working from both sides of the leather. Normally a harness-maker would have done the two-hand stitch by himself, but our oxhides were so big that we had to work in pairs. One stitcher stood on the outside and opened a hole with a stab of the awl; his partner, curled up beneath the upturned boat, poked the needle out towards the pinprick of light. Back came a second needle; then the partners gathered up the slack of the two threads in their fists and, grunting, tugged the stitch home together. The technique took patience, dexterity, and a sense of rhythm if it was to be done right. And if it was done wrong, John O'Connell was merciless. "Rip it! Rip it!" he would say, and out would come his razor-sharp saddler's knife and one slash would sever an entire day's painstaking labour.

Gradually the work crept forward, two oxhides in place, four . . . six, and then suddenly we were working on the second tier of hides. John was satisfied with the quality of the work, but we were falling behind schedule. I had to find more stitchers. A technical college in London offered a course in saddlery; perhaps I could get a class of students to come over to help. I telephoned the instructor and offered to pay his students' fares to Ireland.

He sounded doubtful. "What would they learn?" he asked.

"I've got John O'Connell looking after the work," I pleaded.

"What! John O'Connell, the harness-maker?" Now he sounded impressed. "Well then, you've got the best man. I'll give the students permission to join you for a week."

So nine of them came across to Ireland, tumbling one morning from a battered van at the Crosshaven Boatyard. To the amazement of the shipwrights, they brought with them their transistor radios, sleeping bags, and a strange assortment of old clothes ranging from moleskin overcoats to long woollen scarves and striped sports shirts. They chattered and joked . . . and they worked superbly. At its peak the boat had no less than nine students, eight volunteers, George's sister Ellen, George, myself, and John working on it; and if you peered underneath, there was our mascot: George's dog, Biscuit, who sat all day under the upturned hull, licking the faces of the "inside" stitchers and begging sandwiches at lunchtime. In the evenings we drove back, completely worn out, to the village, where kindly neighbours had cooked up vast pots of stew and left them on my doorstep.

The students enjoyed themselves so much that they stayed two extra days, and by the time they roared off cheerily in their dented van, we had only to fit and cover the bow and stern sections. We anticipated extra wear and tear in these areas, and so we doubled the thickness of the leather. On the bow, where the boat might run onto a rock or sharp flotsam, we made it four layers thick—more than an inch of solid leather. Only John O'Connell had the strength for this work. From his Gladstone bag he produced a pair of great, heavy half-moon needles; as I watched him drive them through the leather with his prodigious strength, I thanked our luck that we had found such a man.

Finally the leathering was done. We had used forty-nine hides to cover the frame. Several hides had been damaged in our first attempt to sew them, but we still had an ample supply of extra material if the boat needed repairs during the forthcoming trials or the voyage itself. George and I crawled for the last time under the upturned boat, and with rope cut from oxhide we pulled down the hanging edge of the skin and fastened it inward to the lower gunwale. Pat Lake, the shipwright, and Murph, his second-in-command, climbed onto the upturned hull to fit on a shallow skid of oak to protect the leather when we should manhandle our mediaeval boat up onto a beach. From the finest Glennon ash we fashioned masts and oars.

At last she was ready.

EAMMON CASEY, Bishop of Kerry, blessed our new boat. On January 24 he arrived in full regalia at the beach where the boat lay, the flags on her rigging snapping and crackling in a sharp wind. On the peak of the mainmast flew the flag of Ireland, and on the foremast our own pennant, the twin-tailed "Brendan banner", consisting of a ringed Irish cross in red on a white background. A bottle of Irish whiskey seemed more appropriate than French champagne to christen the first ocean-going leather boat to be launched in Ireland for perhaps forty generations.

A sizeable crowd had gathered to witness the ceremony. As cine cameras were focused, the inevitable Doubting Thomas bustled among the spectators, offering to take bets: "Five to one she doesn't float; five to one she sinks within the hour."

"You're on for fifty pounds," called one of my friends, but by the time he got out his money, the little bookmaker had vanished.

Bishop Casey was magnificent. Isolated from the wind inside his purple and lace, he spoke the traditional prayers over the new boat. He blessed her mission, her crew, and the crowd, and read a poem in Irish that he had composed for the occasion.

Then came the moment. My daughter, Ida, stepped forward with the scissors and in a small, clear voice announced, "I name this boat *Brendan*," and cut the ribbon. A cloud of atomised Irish whiskey swept over the crowd as the bottle shattered against *Brendan* and she began to slide down towards the water. With scarcely a ripple she floated lightly off her cradle; her crew of shipwrights heaved at their oars; and *Brendan* pulled away, floating high with her bunting rippling and the crowd applauding.

It was much too stormy and cold to risk *Brendan* at sea, so we trundled her up on a timber lorry to the shallow lakes of the river Shannon for trials. We stepped the masts, hung the steering paddle, and pushed off to see what happened under sail. It was an idyllic morning. The hull canted slightly as a gentle breeze filled *Brendan's* two square sails, and the long, slim boat glided over the peaty brown Shannon water. The broad river curved past deep green meadows. Swans took off before our bows, paddling with their feet and undulating their long necks to gain speed and height as they left behind the powerful rushing sound of their wings. Clouds of ducks rose from the winter-brown reeds and a cart-horse came galloping down to stare at the strange, silent gliding craft. The whole scene—the square white sails moving silently over the brown reeds—had an unreal air.

As we glided into Lough Corry, scarcely more than a widening in the river, a puff of wind struck us, and suddenly everything became alive. The boat heeled more steeply; the water began to surge against the steering oar. A rope jerked adrift from its cleat, and suddenly there was chaos. Each sail needed four ropes to control it, and each rope developed a life of its own. The heavy crossyard swung over, the sail slapped against the mast, and we found ourselves grabbing at unidentified ropes and hauling in hopefully, trying to discover which rope would quell the riot. As *Brendan* shot forward, the crew clung on, ropes burning their hands. The far bank loomed up and I leaned hard on the steering oar; *Brendan* began to turn, but it was too late. With a splintering of dry stalks we went hurtling spectacularly into the reed beds.

A dozen times a day we crashed into the reeds, which served as handy buffers, but gradually we got to know *Brendan*'s limitations. With four oarsmen she was too unwieldy to row against the wind, because her bows were blown downwind and we hadn't the strength to get her back on course. More worrisome was the fact that when left to her own devices, *Brendan* lay broadside to the wind at a dangerously exposed angle. We learned that *Brendan* refused to go against the wind like an ordinary yacht. She pointed her bows bravely enough to the wind, but lacking a keel she slid sideways across the water like a tea tray. On the other hand, she was far more stable than we had anticipated, and running with the wind astern she went famously, twisting and turning at a touch of the great steering paddle.

This was how *Brendan* would be at sea, an exhilarating one-way ride with the wind on the stern. A pair of ash shovel handles extended the breadth of our main crossyard so we could carry more sail; and after a day on which it snowed, we rigged the two tent structures that would give us shelter on the voyage. And always we watched the leather hull for signs of leaks. At first the water did trickle in, perhaps ten gallons a day, but then the trickles gradually slowed to half that rate and we found it scarcely necessary to bail *Brendan* unless it rained.

When we were sufficiently confident, we took our boat back down to the coast. Once again we found it was impossible to row against the wind, and we spent one dreary, uncomfortable night bottled up in a bay. We tried capsizing her and found she floated like an upturned whale; she was virtually impossible to turn right way up. We placed plastic buoyancy blocks inside her so that we could do so. When she was totally swamped, we learned that five of us using buckets could bail her dry inside ten minutes.

In Saint Brendan's *Navigatio* it had been written that the monks

> got iron tools and constructed a light boat ribbed with wood and with a wooden frame, as is usual in those parts. They covered it with oxhides tanned with bark of oak and smeared all the joints of the hides on the outside with fat. Into the boat they carried hides for making two other boats, supplies for forty days, fat for preparing hides to cover the boat, and other things needed for human life . . . and requirements for steering a boat. Then Saint Brendan ordered his brothers in the name of the Father, Son, and Holy Spirit to enter the boat.

In the twentieth century it had taken nearly three years of work and research to reach the same point. Now, like the original monks, it was time to put to sea to look for our way to the Promised Land.

CHAPTER 4

Yellow and brown, *Brendan* lay at the head of Brandon Creek on Saint Brendan's feast day, May 16, 1976, the day I had scheduled for our departure. Bright yellow tarpaulins had been stretched over bow and stern to make her easier to locate if a search-and-rescue mission had to be mounted to save her, as some Cassandras prophesied. "They'll need a miracle if they hope to cross the Atlantic in that," one spectator said, "more than Saint Brendan ever did!"

But we weren't going anywhere that particular day. A full gale was raging.

There had been a hectic, last-minute flurry. In theory, at least, we had a stowage plan to help us find room aboard *Brendan* for enough stores, water, and equipment for five men. How much easier it had been, I thought to myself, for Saint Brendan and his monks. They would simply have put to sea with spare leather and fat; their everyday woollen clothes, especially the hooded habits; leather flasks of water; wooden dippers for bailers; dried meats, cereals, and roots for food; and—most important—a sublime faith that God would take care of them.

But now for *Brendan*'s crew to set out wearing mediaeval clothing or eating a mediaeval diet would teach us nothing new. It would only make our modern task more difficult and uncomfortable. We were embarking not to prove ourselves, but to prove the boat.

We had a radio powered by a pair of twelve-volt car batteries rechargeable by two solar panels lashed to the cabin cover. We had various still and cine cameras. The rest of our equipment was relatively basic: a life-raft and a box of distress flares, jerry cans of water and paraffin, a small radio direction finder, a sextant and navigation tables, and a bundle of charts. Most of our drinking water was stored in soft rubber tubes—the modern equivalent of the monks' leather flasks—tucked under the slatted floor of the boat where they would also serve as ballast. Our food was packed in plastic bags, each containing sufficient food for five for one day. There were tins of meat and fish and baked beans; packets of dried soups and vegetables; dried fruit and bars of chocolate; and an apparently endless supply of Scots oatmeal cake, which I hoped would prove a substitute for bread.

Brendan's monks had probably cooked on a peat or wood fire kept burning in a fire tray or in a cauldron, which could also be carried ashore. And, of course, they were accustomed to eating cold food. On the other hand, I had placed great value on the morale-boosting effect of regular hot meals, and so had arranged for a Primus stove to be built into a cook box the size of a foot-locker. Its hinged lid and two side flaps served as a windshield; and the entire stove hung on gimbals. The cook box could be used in almost any weather.

There was one surprising item on the slipway in Brandon Creek.

By the boat lay a soggy heap of sheepskins, smelling strongly. Polar explorers had found sheepskins excellent insulation when sleeping on the ice and as they were a typical material from Saint Brendan's day, I thought it worth trying them as sleeping mats.

For our clothing I had selected modern sailing suits. Each member of the crew was colour-coded so that our garments did not get muddled. George wore orange; I had yellow; and as befitted our most Irish crew member, Arthur Magan had chosen green. We nicknamed Arthur "Boots", because he arrived wearing a pair of size twelves that would have done credit to an oversized cowboy. In fact, nearly everything about Arthur came in the larger sizes. He was burly and stood over six feet, with a shock of yellow hair that stuck out at all angles. His crumpled untidiness suggested a friendly young bear just emerged from hibernation. At twenty-three he was the youngest member of the crew—but also the strongest. When anything was jammed or when a mast needed lifting, we called on Boots. When he heard about *Brendan*, he had written me a letter which was a model of brevity:

Dear Tim,

I am writing to offer myself as a possible crew member. Mrs. Molony gave me your address. I was at school with George's brother.

I have been sailing since I was large enough to go near a boat. I have also spent several winter months recently fishing in trawlers in Icelandic waters.

I realise nothing can be gained by writing letters to each other. I am available at any time to come down and see you if you are interested.

Yours gratefully,
Arthur Magan

So I had invited him to come to Cork, and two days later he clumped into the boatyard in his size twelves, glanced briefly around the boat, mumbled his name, took off a patched and mended tweed jacket, and began working alongside us.

Like his letter, Boots's sentences were brief. Bit by bit I learned that his family lived near Dublin, that he had spent much of his childhood near the Dingle, and could "sail a boat a bit". Later I would also discover that he was a magnet for the girls. Young ladies could not resist the challenge of trying to feed him, tidy him up, and generally take care of him. At landfall after landfall on the voyage he would be returned to *Brendan* by his latest girl friend, despair mingling with sadness in her expression, as before her very eyes he began to dissolve into his usual chaotic state the moment he stepped aboard. And as likely as not we would later discover that he had left some of his clothing behind, and these would be sent ahead to our next port of call.

Arthur himself took such matters in his stride. He never offered any information unasked. One morning before we left his father read in the newspaper that a certain Boots Magan was going on the *Brendan* voyage. "Do you know anyone called Boots?" he asked over the breakfast table.

"Yes. Me," was his son's brief reply.

That rainy morning in Brandon Creek, Peter Mullett, *Brendan*'s photographer, was dressed in a bright red sailing suit that made him look more like a cardinal than the London sparrow he was. Peter had been a successful magazine photographer before he became exasperated with city life, threw up his job, and moved to the west of Ireland with Jill, his glamorous ex-model wife, and his son, Joey. There he bought a plot of land, built a small cottage with his own hands, and settled down to live as simply as possible. When he heard about *Brendan*, he arrived at the boatyard with a large suitcase. "Have you brought your cameras with you?" I asked. "Yes," he replied, and opened the case. On one side a professional's array of camera bodies, lenses, and sundry equipment lay neatly cradled in foam padding. But what caught my eye was the opposite half, a comprehensive and well-used carpentry kit. *Brendan*, I thought to myself, was not getting just a photographer, but, equally valuable, a man who could mend her wooden frame en route.

Rolf Hansen in his Norwegian blue sailing suit was the fifth and last to join the crew. He had come from Norway to volunteer, and was an old-boat fanatic whose hobby was collecting the reminiscences of retired fishermen in remote Norwegian coastal villages.

Short, barrel-chested, bespectacled, Rolf was second only to Boots in physical strength. Like the Irishman he was a man of few words, partly because he spoke only a smattering of English but also because he regarded seafaring as a serious business. When someone ventured to ask him if he was married, Rolf answered very seriously, "I am married to the sea."

I wondered how well the five of us would get along together. *Brendan* would have to be sailed properly if she were to survive, and there was little margin for error. A single mistake—a rope jammed around a cleat during a squall or a sail suddenly blown hard against the mast—would capsize her, with disastrous results. More important, we were about to venture into sub-Arctic waters where few modern yachts cared to go. This was not to be a sun-drenched cruise in bathing suits; we would have to be muffled in heavy clothing for weeks on end. Royal Navy survival experts had drilled us in safety procedures. According to them, if anyone fell overboard incorrectly dressed, he would be dead in five minutes.

FORTUNATELY, the bad weather on Saint Brendan's day had not discouraged our friends. Many came to the Dingle Peninsula to see us off and held a farewell party at the nearby hotel with a conviviality that only the Irish could manage.

"Why do you want to go on this voyage?" a reporter asked each crew member in turn.

"Because I enjoy sailing and want to learn how to handle this type of boat," George answered.

"It's a challenge," said Peter.

"Because I love the sea," Rolf replied.

"For the crack. For the fun of it," grunted Arthur, taking a long pull at his pint of stout.

"What do your wives think of your going off into the Atlantic like this?"

"You can't stop Peter from doing what he wants to do," Jill Mullett said. "Besides, it's time he had another project to occupy his interest."

Judith, George's wife, agreed. "I think George ought to do what he wants to do."

My wife managed to pass off the question. "Tim's always doing this sort of project," she told the journalist with a smile, "and after all, I'm a mediaevalist, and so I approve of anything that is good for mediaeval studies."

Then came the inevitable question. "Aren't you worried?" The three wives looked at one another. "No," they replied firmly.

MAY 17 dawned fine, with high clouds chasing across the sky and thunderheads lurking on the horizon. The swell left by the gale was heaving into the creek, and I went up to one of the two cottages at the top of the road to consult Tom Leahy, who lived there and kept a curragh in the creek.

"Would you say that we could sail today?"

He looked at me steadily. "Wait till the tide turns," he advised. "You should have a few hours to get clear. And I wouldn't leave it any longer. I don't like the look of the weather and if the wind swings round to the northwest, it'll bring a heavy sea into the creek. You'll be trapped there, and the surge could break your boat to pieces."

"All right, Tom. Will you be escorting us out?"

"Of course, and the prayers of my family and me will go with you," he said.

It was Tom's curragh that I had first examined so many months ago. He was the last man regularly working one out of Brandon Creek. I thought it fitting that he should see us on our way.

All that morning the local people began to filter down to the creek: farmers with their families clinging to muddy tractors, holidaymakers in cars, students on foot and on bicycles. A pair of local policemen were there to control the crowd, but they were far more interested in peering into *Brendan* with the other sightseers. A small group of priests settled themselves comfortably on a wall, and called out their blessings. Down on the quay an old woman pushed forward from the crowd and thrust a small bottle of holy water into my hand. "God bless you all, and bring you safe to America," she said. I tucked the bottle of holy water safely inside the double gunwale in exactly the same place where every Dingle curragh, however small, still carries one. John O'Connell was looking worried and tense. So, too, were the wives and families. "Look after our son," said Arthur's father to me. It was high time we were gone.

"Come on!" I called to the crowd. "Give us a hand to push her off the slip." There was a confused blur of faces, of hands and shoulders pushing at the brown leather hull, and with a soft slithering groan *Brendan* floated off the slipway.

"Goodbye, Daddy." I heard Ida's small voice clearly across the water. Fortunately, she and Joey Mullett were having such a good time together that they regarded the departure as a game.

"Time to put up the flags," I called to George, and he hoisted them to the mainmast in the order of the countries we intended to visit: the tricolour of Ireland, then the Union flag for Northern Ireland, Saint Andrew's Cross for Scotland, the flag of the Faeroes, the flag of Iceland, the Danish flag for Greenland, the Canadian Maple Leaf, and finally the Stars and Stripes. At the peak, on its own, flew the twin-tailed Brendan Banner.

There was so much to do at the last minute there was no time to be nervous. All of us wanted to be on our way out to sea.

As if on cue, the wind died away almost completely. I took the helm while George and the others settled themselves to the oars. "Give way, together!" I called, and *Brendan* turned and began to roll out of Brandon Creek into the Atlantic. Deep-laden and sluggish, we began to push against the swells heaving into the entrance. "This is like rowing a supertanker with a ball-point pen," grunted George, glancing along the slim blade of his oar. On either side of us skittered a curragh. Tom Leahy was in one. Each boasted a tiny Irish tricolour jauntily tied to its prow.

The crowd waved and shouted good wishes; and then, as we cleared the mouth of the creek and passed the cliffs rising on each side, I turned back and saw a sight that etched itself indelibly into my mind: two hundred or more people were scrambling and scurrying to the headland for a final view. The sight had a dreamlike quality, for the sun was in the far west and the flat light picked up the silhouettes of the people along the crest of the hill like a frieze. From the farthest tip of the cliff they could see us growing smaller and smaller and disappearing into the ocean. So

Brendan's frame was made of native Irish ash. Timber for the masts and oars was handpicked from the tough north-facing sides of the trees. Heartwood of oak was used for gunwales.

John O'Connell, who once made harness for the royal stables, stitches together two of the forty-nine oxhides used to cover *Brendan*'s frame.

The 1600 joints in the boat's framework were each lashed together by hand. Nearly two miles of leather thong were needed.

i

Kerry fishermen look down on *Brendan* as she rests in Brandon Creek—by tradition the departure point of the saint.

A blustery January wind whips *Brendan*'s flags and pennants on launch day at Crosshaven Boatyard.

Brendan on her 4500-mile odyssey tc the New World.

Tim Severin, off watch, reads by lantern light.

George Molony at the helm
in rough seas.

Edan Kenneil. He rarely
wore anything on his feet, even
on the coldest days.

"Boots" Magan and the
skipper. Boots was the
youngest member of the crew.

Trondur Patursson practices with his harpoon. Off the Labrador
pack ice he scored a direct hit on a pilot whale.

Brendan sets sail from Iceland and her snow-streaked mountains.

(Overleaf) *Brendan* approaches her "Promised Land".

many people had helped us, I thought, so many had shown confidence in us, that we could not let them down.

As soon as we were well clear of the entrance and there was no longer any risk of the tide setting us down on the nearest headland, I ordered our sails to be raised. The wind was fair, the Celtic crosses on *Brendan's* sails filled out, and soon we began to gather speed. We pulled aboard the unwieldy oars, and *Brendan* began to settle down on her course. The two escorting curraghs turned back and soon were no more than specks, dropping out of sight in the troughs of the waves. We were finally on our way.

CHAPTER 5

Beneath us *Brendan* rose and sank on each wave crest. Very slightly the hull bent and straightened to the changing pressures of the seas, and the masts creaked against the thwarts in sympathy. Aft, at the steering position, the massive four-inch shaft of the steering paddle nuzzled gently against the crosspiece of an H-shaped frame that held it in place. Every now and again the shaft dropped back into the crotch with a dull thump felt along the length of the hull. But apart from this sound, the boat was remarkably quiet. The leather skin seemed to muffle the usual slap of wavelets against the hull, and the thong-tied frame damped the tremors customary in a stiff-hulled sailing boat. The result was a curiously disembodied feeling, a sense of being a part of the sea's motion, moulded to the waves.

This sensation was enhanced by the way *Brendan* lay low in the water. The surface of the sea came within sixteen inches of her gunwale, so that even a modest wave loomed over her. But as each wave advanced, *Brendan* canted her hull slowly and deliberately, and the wave slid underneath harmlessly. The up-and-down movement was disconcerting. First Arthur, then Peter began to turn slightly green. It was no good advising them to breathe fresh

257

air, for the whole boat was virtually open to the winds. The only remedy was to try to distract oneself by tackling the various tasks that had to be done. There were ropes to coil and stow, halyards and sheets to be rearranged so they did not tangle one another. We stored our food bags to make the best use of space, lashed down the water cans, arranged the oars neatly along the centre of the boat, and made sure the anchor was ready at hand.

There was very little conversation. Each man was thinking of the days and weeks that lay ahead. None of us, I fancy, cared to think too much about our main purpose in the voyage. That was a luxury reserved for the future, a mental excursion to indulge in during the long periods of tedium which characterize any small-boat trip. For the moment it was enough that the sails were filling and pulling *Brendan* along over the grey Atlantic.

We split the four-hour watches into two-hour shifts, with two men on duty in each. With only five men on board this meant that each person had to do four hours, followed by only six hours of rest. *Brendan* always needed a helmsman in charge and this placed a great strain on us all. Luckily, we soon discovered that the second man on duty could stay on standby, out of the wind and rain, provided he was ready for an emergency.

That first night we slept only fitfully, except Rolf, who crawled into his sleeping bag and dropped off, content to be back at sea. Meanwhile, *Brendan* plodded steadily northward. It was a very black night, with increasing cloud and several heavy rain showers. Puddles of water collected in the waist of the boat; rain dripped down the helmsman's arms; rain saturated the sheepskins we had left on the rowing thwarts, so that they squeezed like a sponge when we sat on them. More worrying, the sails absorbed so much water that they doubled in weight.

At dawn George pointed to the mainmast. "I don't like the way the mast's bending under the weight of the sail, Tim," he said.

"The ash ought to be strong enough," I replied. "That timber should almost bend like a fishing rod before it goes."

"Yes, but look what it's doing where it rests in the mast block." His foot rested on a block of oak in the bottom of the boat. "Look, as it rocks, the mast is going to chafe away the side pieces.

Then it will come adrift. We could lose it overboard in a squall."

I agreed we had to reduce the pressure of the wet sails. We lowered them a couple of feet and fastened leather thongs to their lower edges so they did not swing so much to the roll of the boat. Still both masts swayed and bent alarmingly.

By now it was breakfast time, and we rigged up the stove. We had agreed that each man should cook one meal, turn and turn about. I cooked the breakfast. But after each of the others had a turn, they elected me to do all the cooking.

Unavoidably our first few meals were flavoured with wool grease. We found it everywhere—on the thwarts, the ropes, the stove; and of course it crept onto our knives and forks, canteens and cups. Only *Brendan's* liquor store avoided the curse. It seemed that our well wishers were determined to send us off in an alcoholic stupor. There were bottles of whiskey and Irish stout, Norwegian aquavit for Rolf, and even some ferocious-looking brew called The Black Death, presented by a friendly Icelander. But pride of place went to our two-gallon keg of superb malt whiskey, specially made for *Brendan* by the Irish Distillers. As soon as we had settled down and cleared the boat, we broached this keg, lifted our tin mugs and toasted "Saint Brendan and the voyage!"

During the first full day's sailing, *Brendan* moved stolidly northward. Astern the peak of Mount Brandon sank lower and lower on the horizon. We passed the Shannon estuary, the last safe haven for about forty miles. Navigating *Brendan* along this lee shore was really only a matter of identifying each port of refuge in case a gale blew us down on the coast. I had hoped that *Brendan* on her first run could sail clear of the great finger of Slyne Head, which points west into the Atlantic; it was to be the first turning point of our coastal passage, but the wind gradually moved into the west, and for every ten miles *Brendan* sailed forward, she lost a mile slipping sideways. She plodded forward with so little fuss that the second night she ran down a bird sleeping on the water. The bow actually tipped the poor creature upside down in the water. There was much flapping, and an irate-looking gannet eventually surfaced in our wake, grumbling with vexation before it flew off to less disturbed waters.

The dawn light was shrouded by mist that reduced visibility to less than a mile. Then a group of isolated reefs loomed up ahead, with the swell breaking in a wide ring around them. They were the Skird Rocks, well inside Slyne Head. *Brendan* could not possibly get around the headland until we had a fair wind, so I changed course, and *Brendan* bore away to find shelter in the Aran Islands. I was not downcast. In thirty-six hours we had come over a hundred miles, and what better landfall than the islands where Saint Brendan came to discuss his idea for a voyage to the Promised Land with his mentor, Saint Enda?

As the mist broke up before the morning sun, the islands appeared. *Brendan* came sailing in past their northwest tip, and we saw first the lighthouse, then the land itself with its green patchwork of fields. George was steering to take best advantage of the wind, and we hugged the coast as closely as we dared. We could just distinguish the figure of a man in a field. What would he think, I wondered, if he looked out to sea and saw a sight which harked back a thousand years—an ocean-going curragh coming in from the Atlantic, a small black curve against the glittering surface of the ocean, and the distinctive squares of mediaeval sails? We glimpsed a small black speck bobbing about in the waves. "I think that's a curragh," I called to George, and he altered course to investigate. The two men in the boat were hauling lobster pots, but the moment they noticed us they bent to their sculls and sent their curragh racing towards us. They rowed in perfect unison to within five yards, neatly spun their boat, and kept pace with *Brendan*, gazing at us. One of them had a fiery red bush of curly hair and a splendid beard to match. "Are you the crowd for America?" he called out. "Welcome to the islands. Would you like some crab?"

"Yes, please!"

A hail of crabs flew in an arc to the *Brendan*, and Rolf scrambled to seize them before they scuttled into the bilges. "Thank you very much," I called. "Where's the best place to land?"

"Go into the bay. You'll be safe enough there. Just follow the line of our lobster pots, and turn in when you no longer see the lighthouse behind you."

Brendan dropped anchor in a wide bay. We had landed on Inish-more, largest of the three main Aran Islands. From the anchorage the ground sloped up to the crest of the hill where the island ended abruptly, steep cliffs falling sheer into deep water. It was as if the island had been tilted on one edge for our inspection, and from sea level we could admire the pattern of hundreds upon hundreds of tiny fields whose loose stone walls divided up the land like a honeycomb. The effect is all the more striking because the grey walls are not broken by gates. Instead the farmers pull down a section of the wall when they want to drive in cattle, and then build up the stones behind them.

That afternoon, after an enormous lunch of crab boiled in a bucket of seawater, we all went ashore and walked up towards the far crest. The sky had cleared, and in the tiny fields the turf was sprinkled with thousands of buttercups, violets, gentians, and other spring flowers. We found a narrow track between the walls, followed it, and finally came out onto open land. Across the hill-side the bones of the island lay exposed, enormous slabs of lime-stone that rain and wind had pock-marked and slashed with scars along the fault lines. Here the stone walls were more tumbled down, until suddenly the eye picked out a pattern, and we saw that we were walking through the concentric rings of stone ramparts that encircled the hilltop. The track had turned into an ancient roadway which led straight to the last and most important rampart sitting upon the hill crest like a drum. In its side blazed the bright eye of a single entrance, the light pouring through it.

This was the gateway to the fort of Dun Aengus, one of the most spectacular sites of prehistoric Europe. Climbing through, we came out onto the cleared space inside the rampart. Where the back wall should have been was only empty sky, for we had come to the very lip of the cliffs at the island's far edge. Inching cautiously forward, we looked straight down the cliffs, past the backs of the seabirds wheeling far below us, to the surface of the ocean two hundred feet below.

Dun Aengus is one of several massive stone fortresses on the Aran Islands, built by Irish clans in the first centuries of the Christian era, before Saint Enda settled his monks in modest stone

261

cells down by the seashore and began the monastic school that was to become one of the most famous in all Ireland. The forts represented another strand to Saint Brendan's quest for the western land, for among the ancient Celtic beliefs had been the idea of a land towards the sunset peopled by departed souls and strange creatures. When Christianity was introduced to Ireland, this old idea was given Christian garb. It became a land promised by God to men of great virtue, a reward on earth.

The Christian monks were well equipped to fit this notion of the distant land into a more accurate geographical frame. They understood that the world was round, "like a well-formed apple", for Irish monks gathered an incredible store of scholarship from all over western Europe. During the troubled fifth and sixth centuries many scholars came to Ireland from the upheavals of the Continent, bringing with them manuscripts and the knowledge of the classical authors; Ireland became the grand repository for this intellectual treasure. In due course the Irish monks set out to carry their knowledge back to the mainland. They founded schools, advised kings and even emperors and established monasteries from Lombardy to Austria. They and their pupils were regarded as Europe's wandering intelligentsia.

It was this vitality that produced Saint Brendan's *Navigatio*. Like the heroes of old, Brendan was the hero who set out to find the Promised Land and experienced many adventures on the way. There is even a theory that the *Navigatio* isn't a Christian work at all, but merely a Christian gloss on an old and imaginary Celtic tale. Investigation of that idea had taken me to the residence of the president of Ireland, Cearbhall O Dalaigh,* whose wife is an expert on the early Irish language.

Over tea Mairin O Dalaigh and I talked about the Brendan project until there was a knock at the door and the president himself came darting in. A great supporter of the Gaeltacht, the Irish-speaking area of the west, he was most enthusiastic for the

*Cearbhall O Dalaigh, president of the Republic of Ireland from December 1974 until his resignation in October 1976, died on March 21, 1978.—THE EDITORS

Brendan project. He dashed to his bookshelves. "Have you seen this? Or this one?" he asked, pulling down one volume after another in rapid succession. Soon the floor, sofa, and chairs were covered with opened books. He whisked me off to another wing of the building where the walls were hung with his art collection. We stopped in front of a small painting of a curragh nestling in the cleft of some rocks. "Found that years ago," said the president. "I've always liked it very much indeed. Where do you think it was done—in Donegal, or in the Aran Islands, perhaps?"

The memory of President O Dalaigh's bubbling enthusiasm came back to me during *Brendan*'s stay in the Aran Islands. Everyone on Inishmore associated themselves with the project. *Brendan* was *their* boat. The curragh men came back twice more to present us with more crabs and lobsters. The local wives took it in turns to bake us fresh scones. A bush telegraph was also signalling our passage along the Irish-speaking coast, and later I discovered that schoolchildren had been stationed all along to look out for *Brendan*.

TWO DAYS OF bad weather held us in the Aran Islands, and then the wind eased and we headed for the mainland coast of County Mayo. We hoisted both our flax sails, and soon discovered that it was too much. The mainmast again bent alarmingly, and *Brendan* leaned over so far that I thought we would scoop water aboard. The mainsail eased away, *Brendan* came level, the mast straightened, and we ploughed briskly across the channel towards a line of small islands that extended from the shore. At the right moment the sails came tumbling down; *Brendan* rounded the outer reef, and we rowed our way into shelter and dropped anchor.

Brendan had picked our spot for us. Not half a mile away lay a small uninhabited island which in the sixth century had been the home of Saint MacDara. We landed and visited the simple grey stone chapel, one of the oldest in Ireland. Half-sunk in the turf stood a low stone cross, just like the crosses on *Brendan*'s sails, but no more than two feet high.

St. MacDara's Island made it easier to appreciate another strand woven into the *Navigatio*. Many of the early Irish monks had felt an overwhelming urge to seek solitude on the islands off the west coast, where they could contemplate and pray, like the ascetic Desert Fathers of the Middle East who had retreated into the deserts to serve God.

Full-fledged monasteries grew up on some of these islands. Saint Brendan visited one which the *Navigatio* called Saint Ailbe's Island. The *Navigatio* does not give enough geographical details to pinpoint it accurately. However, traces of Irish religious settlements have also been found in several islands off the west coast of Ireland as well as in the Hebrides, the Orkneys and the Shetlands—all on the Stepping Stone Route towards North America.

The early Christian church on St. MacDara's Island was the last one the modern *Brendan* was to visit in Ireland. Next morning we awoke to a fresh breeze from the south and, despite gale warnings on the radio, we weighed anchor and seized our chance to take the leather boat slanting away on a course which cleared Slyne Head. For a few hours we made glorious progress, spinning along at more than five knots. We could not check our speed properly, for the log was malfunctioning.

But then the weather deteriorated. In the low clouds we lost sight of the lighthouse on Slyne Head. Rain showers began sweeping regularly across us, and it grew colder. By evening we were in the grip of our first gale, and driving faster and faster out to sea. We dragged ropes behind us to slow ourselves down, and took turns bailing the water that swirled in the bilges. At the time we had prearranged, I switched on the radio transmitter and tried to get through to the coast station at Valentia, but I could hear nothing except static. To avoid tangling our trailing warps, George hauled in the log. Now *Brendan* was not only cut off, but we could not guess how far the storm was driving us out into the Atlantic.

For twenty-four hours we ran before the gale. We swallowed some hot sweet soup to keep up our strength, and privately I calculated how much drinking water we had on board. Our headlong flight into the open ocean was completely unplanned, and we had no reserves.

264

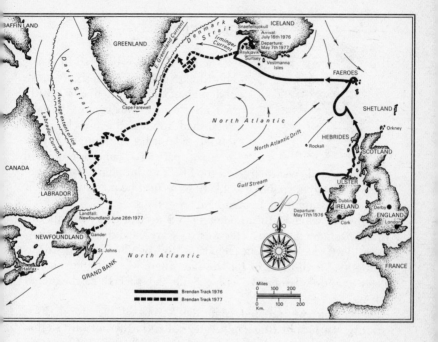

After, according to my calculations, *Brendan* had been driven about a hundred miles off the coast, the wind eased and swung into the west, blowing our boat back towards land and safety. On the afternoon of the second day we were able to cook a hot meal and tidy up some of the mess created in the cabin by breaking waves and sodden clothing. As my fingers thawed, I made notes in my diary about the lessons we had learned: in future, we should never set out to sea without a full water supply; every man needed extra socks and gloves to keep out the chill; our plastic food packs were unreliable; far too many of our stores were now a soggy mess. We were so worn out that during the third night we were glad when the wind died away to a calm. After half an hour's rowing, which seemed to get us nowhere, we curled up and rested, letting *Brendan* drift slowly down towards the northwest corner of Ireland on the tide and swell.

CHAPTER 6

For two days we sheltered in Bally-hoorisky, Northern Ireland, to make and mend, and to catch our breath. When we were rowing against the gale, Peter had strained the muscles down the left side of his chest, and was now in great pain. By radio I requested assistance, and eventually we got him to a hospital. The doctors warned that the trouble was likely to recur if he put any strain on the muscles, and then it could be more serious.

This was a blow. In an emergency I needed every member of *Brendan*'s crew fit; and Peter was sensitive enough to admit that, once hurt, he would be reluctant to commit himself whole-heartedly for the rest of the voyage. There was really no choice: Peter withdrew from the crew. Sadly he packed his bags and left us.

Meanwhile we profited from the lessons of the storm. First priority was to shift *Brendan*'s water ballast farther forward so that her bow dipped down and gripped the sea better and her stern rose more quickly to the following waves. Then Rolf set about making some sense of the hugger-mugger in the cooking and eating area. With odd scraps of wood and string he ingeniously rigged up a food locker and a couple of shelves to keep our everyday supplies of tea, coffee, and sugar out of harm's way. He had to use string in place of nails or screws because *Brendan*'s hull flexed so much that any rigid fastening would have snapped.

On the afternoon of May 30 *Brendan* hung motionless in the tide, waiting for a wind. But this time there was a completely different feeling on board. The remaining crewmen were rested and fit, and the vessel had shown us convincingly that, given half a chance, she would carry us safely through high seas and heavy weather. The result was a marked upsurge of confidence, both in ourselves and in the boat.

As soon as the wind picked up next morning to a good stiff

breeze, George was all for testing *Brendan*'s new paces, now that we had shifted ballast. Under his expert eye the slanting sails began to draw her briskly across the wind. She was still skidding on the surface of the sea, so we could not claim to be sailing against the wind, but we were certainly making excellent progress; instead of running downwind away from the waves, we were sailing parallel to them and riding easily across their crests. All that day we managed to keep this course, ignoring the occasional wave which toppled and broke aboard as *Brendan* hurried northwest towards Scotland. It was a new sensation to be at the steering paddle watching the water sliding briskly past the massive ash blade and feeling the boat responding to any fine adjustment on the helm. At last, I felt, *Brendan* was *sailing*. She was a little cumbersome, it was true, but she handled like a real boat.

We made our landfall at the island of Iona on the second morning. Iona had been the jewel of the Irish overseas mission. Here in A.D. 563 Saint Columba had landed by curragh after sailing across from Ireland. According to legend, he ordered his monks to bury the curragh lest he be tempted to return to his homeland. Under the saint's unswerving leadership Irish monks proceeded to establish one of the most important Celtic monasteries in the whole of Europe. Iona became the springboard for the Christian conversion of Scotland and northern England. On the mainland and throughout the islands, Columba and his successors established daughter houses in Iona's image. But then came the Vikings, who attacked Iona in 795, again in 802, and again in 806. Under this constant harassment the monks moved back to Ireland.

Today there is once again an abbey upon Iona, the home of an ecumenical brotherhood of some one hundred and thirty Anglicans, Baptists, and Catholics called the Iona Community, and bound together by a common commitment to Christian prayer and action in the world. It carries its mission overseas and into the industrial towns of Britain. Each year as many members as possible return to Iona for a week's retreat and to repledge their commitment. Very kindly, the warden of the community gave *Brendan*'s crew lunch in the abbey's refectory.

Iona also gave us a new crew member. I was accosted on the beach by a fantastic figure.

"Are you the skipper of that strange-looking boat?" he began excitedly. "I'm told you're looking for a crew member."

"Yes," I answered cautiously, looking the man over. He was a big, rather gaunt fellow, with a lock of long hair which kept escaping from under his army beret, falling over his eyes, and being brushed back with a nervous gesture. His face was dominated by a great beak of a nose, and he was waving his very long arms so that he looked like some sort of strange, flapping, predatory seabird. His broad shoulders were encased in a shabby navy sweater far too long for him—it reached to the knees of his frayed jeans, which were embroidered with boats, flowers, and animals. He was without shoes, socks, or boots, and he was apparently oblivious to the fact that he was standing in icy-cold water. I was impressed.

"I'm the captain of that blue yacht out there," the apparition hastened to say, with a grand sweep of an arm towards a battered sailing trawler anchored in the bay. "We do charters through the Hebrides. But my two brothers can take over for the summer. I'd like to join your crew, if you'll have me." Then, as an afterthought, he asked, "By the way, where are you going?"

Thus, in a scramble of ragbag enthusiasm, arrived Edan Kenneil, soon to develop into *Brendan's* jester and resident live wire. With his constant high spirits Edan was a welcome addition. He was one of nature's leap-before-you-look characters whose bravado carried him head over heels through life from one scrape to the next. He could sail and steer, he didn't mind cold or damp, and—to my delight—he was willing to share the cooking. Indeed, his only major vice was an insatiable appetite. He would eat virtually anything and everything, and we soon learned that any leftovers on our plates would be speared by his darting fork. His constant hunger and his enormous flailing arms soon earned him the nickname "Gannet", in honour of his airborne cousin whose gluttony was legendary.

Edan needed two days to settle his affairs before joining us, and we agreed to meet at the nearby island of Tiree. When we left

Iona, the great bells of the abbey began to ring out a farewell for us, and the warden stood at the water's edge waving goodbye until we rounded the headland. We sailed under a sky that seemed to press lower and lower upon us, until we were swallowed up into drizzle and murk and ploughed forward in a world of our own.

The sea was about to teach us a lesson in mediaeval navigation. Anxiously I kept glancing at the log ticking off the miles we had covered. Visibility was less than a hundred yards. I glanced at the chart and calculated for the twentieth time the distance between Iona and Tiree. I didn't trust the log, but already it was showing that we had covered the whole distance between the two islands. The pilot book warned me that we were approaching a coast foul with off-lying rocks; and the radio forecast yet another storm.

Suddenly Arthur gave a shout: "Land! Land! Dead ahead!" Through the murk a line appeared, a barely visible distinction between sea and shore. The wind was blowing us straight ashore.

"Helm up!" cried George, and Rolf scrambled forward to re-adjust the sails so we could alter course. Arthur dropped a leeboard on a retaining chain into the water to try to reduce our leeway. *Brendan*'s nose swung northward, but the line of the land followed with her. We were still running towards the shore.

"Can you bring her up any more into the wind, George?" I asked.

"Not without stalling her."

Rolf swung out the lead line. "Four fathoms!" he called out to me. Blinded by the fog and in the grip of the tide, I had let *Brendan* run into a bay on the southeast edge of Tiree. There was no port ahead, only rocks which might puncture our leather hull.

"Rolf! Boots!" I shouted. "Get to the oar benches! One on each side to give her direction! George, if we're lucky, we can scrape her out of the north side of the bay, but it will mean going inside the outer reefs. Keep her as hard on the wind as you can. I'll go forward as lookout." I scrambled forward and began calling instructions back to George as we picked our way between the rocks, partly sailing and partly rowing. The combinations of wind and swell and leeway, of the tide and the backwash, were infinite, and it would be disastrous if we blundered.

"Hold her steady! Steady as she goes!" I called to George, as we slid past the first rock peaks.

"Starboard! Starboard! Rolf, pull away as hard as you can!" And *Brendan* rounded another clump of reefs. A startled-looking seal plummeted off a rock as we went scurrying by. Fronds of seaweed less than a yard beneath the water showed where the reef lay. No keel boat would have dared go that way, but *Brendan* drew less than one foot of water, and I blessed the fact. This is how the curragh men manage to manoeuvre among the rocky shores of Ireland. We were nearing the end of the gauntlet. There was one last group of rocks ahead of us, with waves sucking and swirling majestically around their kelp-covered sides.

"Starboard some more, George!"

"No good!" he called back. "We can't come any closer to the wind." Rolf heaved frantically at his oar—eight, nine, ten quick strokes—but it was not enough. *Brendan* started to swing broadside to the rock and drift down on it; in less than a minute we would strike.

"We'll have to risk going inside, through that kelp," I shouted. "Hard to port, and Boots, give her all you've got."

Brendan began turning. The wind filled her sails, and she surged forward straight at the dark line of kelp. How deep did the reef lie here? Picking up speed, we charged at the gap. The seaweed plucked at *Brendan*'s leather skin with a soft, brushing sound, and our boat wriggled gracefully over into safe water without a scratch. Boots and Rolf dropped their oars and slumped exhausted. I climbed down and joined George at the helm.

"That was a close shave," I muttered to him, "and another lesson. I mustn't let *Brendan* get caught in a bay ever again, or we are likely to lose her."

Tiree was another of the Hebridean islands where the Irish monks had established themselves. They were obviously a cantankerous lot, because stories of their short tempers are found throughout the islands. On the beach of Tiree, it was said, Saint Columba slipped and fell when he trod on a fish lying in the shallows; he condemned the fish to have both eyes on the same side of its head to avoid such an accident in future.

Edan joined us in Tiree as promised and, as we were getting ready to leave harbour, he picked up an oar and took a couple of practice strokes at the water. I had spent three years at Oxford as a coxswain in rowing eights, and I knew an oarsman when I saw one. "Hey, you've rowed before?" I called out to Edan.

"Yes. I was captain of the Eton boat when we won the World Schoolboy Championships in Switzerland."

Only Edan, I thought to myself, would have forgotten to mention this qualification before.

From Tiree we picked our way northward, through a magnificent sunset, into the channel between the Outer Hebrides and the mainland of Scotland. This was a superb sailing ground, sheltered from the Atlantic by the island chain. Here we could sail in comparative peace and learn more about our strange vessel.

I was worried about the strength of the stitches that held the oxhides of *Brendan*'s skin together. The flax thread seemed very soft—I could dent it with my fingernail. But the stitches didn't seem dangerously weak. When we were building *Brendan*, the manufacturer had sent samples of his thread, together with snippets of *Brendan*'s oak-bark-tanned leather, to be tested at laboratories. As expected, the flax thread proved actually stronger when wet than when dry and more resistant to rot after it had been stitched into the leather, for the tannin from the leather had migrated into the thread and in effect had tanned the flax as well. As I scratched at *Brendan*'s wet hide, I quietly hoped this phenomenon would endure.

Our next port of call was Loch Maddy, on the Hebridean island of North Uist. On the day we left, we enjoyed excellent sailing weather—a fine strong wind blowing clear up the channel and raising very little seaway. "Well, George," I said, "here's our chance to see just how fast *Brendan* goes."

He grinned. "Not worried about breaking the mast?"

"No. It's our last chance before the open Atlantic to try her out."

"Splendid. We'll put up every scrap of canvas we've got— including the lower bonnets and both side panels. We'll rig a backstay to hold the mast, just in case."

Edan gave a great whoop of joy. "Now we'll see her go," he

said, and he and Rolf began lacing on the extra canvas. The enlarged sails began to drive *Brendan* forward. Smoothly she gathered speed, the water curling back along her leather sides.

"Haul up the leeboards," George ordered. With less drag and no keel to hold her back, *Brendan* fairly tore along. I glanced at the log indicator. We were travelling at six or seven knots, going like an express train. The three-inch shaft of the steering paddle was bending noticeably under the pressure of the water rushing past.

A swell was entering the channel between the islands, and when we hit it, the effect was like riding a roller coaster. *Brendan* began to toboggan, running down the wave fronts at eight or ten knots. From time to time she actually began to surf, racing forward on top of a wave. Then the log would spin up to its maximum of twelve knots, and the needle stuck there, hard against the end stop. The ride was exhilarating and breathtaking. Here was a boat from the Dark Ages sailing as fast as many modern yachts. The flax and leather rigging thrummed; the massive H-frame of the steering oar clanked and flexed. After two hours of this headlong progress, I reluctantly gave the order to reduce sail, for fear we might tear the boat apart or run her under.

We had shown ourselves just what an ocean-going curragh could do under ideal conditions, and our reward was a perfect ending for the dash up the channel. The wind held us all the way to Stornoway. We rounded the lighthouse in style, dropped the headsail, and glided past the island ferryboat, its rail lined with waving passengers and crew. A figure beckoned us from the wharf, and we curled towards him. A word of command and the mainsail came quietly down. Arthur took two solid strokes on his oar, the tiller came over, and *Brendan* dropped neatly into her berth as though we had been sailing leather boats all our lives.

"Ye've disappointed us," said a glum-looking figure on the wharf. "The boys in the lifeboat crew were hoping to have a bit of exercise pulling you in. Still," he added, looking down at our strange craft with doleful Scots pessimism, "you'll probably keep 'em busy enough when you try to sail for Faeroes. I canna say I would want to sail with you."

CHAPTER 7

Two hundred miles of open water, exposed to the full sweep of the Atlantic winds, lie between Stornoway and the Faeroes. Midway between Scotland and Iceland, the cluster of eighteen main islands which form the Faeroes rise abruptly from the sea, the crest of a submarine ridge. One of the remotest places in Europe, the Faeroes are in every way the offspring of the sea. The islanders depend upon the sea for their livelihood; at the age when most children are learning to ride bicycles, they already know how to handle the little boats in which they pass from island to island; and their daily lives are dominated by Atlantic weather patterns that obscure the islands in thick wet clouds for most of the year and bring rain two days out of three. Both for Saint Brendan and for our latter-day *Brendan*, the Faeroes were a key point. If the *Navigatio* did in fact describe the Stepping Stone Route to America as the Irish monks had used it, then the Faeroes were the first logical long-distance staging post in the chain.

The *Navigatio* told how Saint Brendan and his monks had sighted a remote island. Exploring it, they found large streams full of fish and great flocks of splendid large white sheep. On Good Friday an islander appeared, bringing a basket of fresh bread. Later he revictualled their boat and gave the travellers sailing directions for the next part of their voyage. In answer to Saint Brendan's questions he explained that the sheep grew so large because they were not milked but left alone in their pastures; the natural environment was so gentle that they could be left to graze day and night.

Several scholars have pointed out how closely this description of the Isle of Sheep fits the Faeroes. The influence of the Gulf Stream produces comparatively mild winters, and the climate and pasture are indeed suitable for sheep raising. In fact, the Faeroes' very name seems to be taken from the Norse words

Faer-Eyjaer, meaning "Sheep Islands". Probably the Vikings picked up the name from the previous inhabitants. Possibly the islander who aided Saint Brendan was another of the wandering clerics of the Irish church; there is strong independent evidence that Irish monks settled in the Faeroes at an early date.

The possible identity of the Isle of Sheep with the Faeroes occupied my thoughts in Stornoway as we prepared *Brendan* for our first long-distance sea crossing. Though two hundred miles on the charts looked easy enough, it could turn out to be at least twice that distance if the winds were against us, forcing *Brendan* to follow a zigzag course. In the old days the Hebridean fishermen called the Faeroes "the Faraways". A single bad gale spewed from the prevailing westerlies could skittle *Brendan* past the Faeroes entirely and on towards Norway. Stornoway's professional fishermen did not help matters as they peered down at *Brendan*, lying in their harbour, and muttered dolefully among themselves. The Doubting Thomas of our arrival kept reappearing with sea-wise questions which always ended in the same refrain: "I wouldna want to sail with you."

Once, from behind me, Arthur's Irish accent turned Scots for a moment and uttered a mocking warning: "We're all doomed! Aye, we're doomed for sure!"

But Stornoway's returning trawler fleet gave us a cheerful farewell, tooting their sirens as *Brendan* sailed out and turned her bows northward. By the morning of June 17 we were well clear of the Butt of Lewis, the outer tip of the Hebrides.

Once again we were only four on board, as Rolf had had to return home to Norway from Stornoway for urgent personal reasons. I asked George to draw up a new watch schedule because he, of all of us, put so much effort into his work that no one could begrudge his choice. Watchkeeping was the vital framework of our daily existence. Each man exercised strict self-discipline, and made sure he showed up for his watch at exactly the right time. To do less would have been unfair, and could have become precisely the sort of irritant that finally erupts into a quarrel.

Each of us knew that we were living close together under very raw conditions. We were like men locked in a cell measuring thirty-six feet by eight feet—of which less than a quarter was actually sheltered and livable. Potentially the scope for argument and animosity was almost limitless, and minor irritations could be blown up into a cause for hatred. All of us knew the risks and adopted the traditional attitude aboard a small boat: live and let live. By and large we kept ourselves to ourselves and behaved accordingly. We might discuss modifications to the boat as a group, or make individual suggestions on technical matters, but the final decisions in all matters affecting the voyage were left to the skipper. There was no doubt that when we sailed out into the Atlantic, *Brendan* was an efficient and well-integrated boat.

Our daily lives were surprisingly easy. Under most conditions the helmsman's main job was to keep a lookout for changes in the weather, especially for a shift of the wind, and to make sure *Brendan* stayed on her set course. But no great accuracy was required at the helm. As the navigator I simply worked out the general direction in which we should sail, and the helmsman lashed the crossbar of the tiller with a leather thong so that *Brendan* stayed within twenty degrees of the right direction. With so much leeway and the rapid wind shifts it was a wasted effort to be any more accurate. *Brendan* held her course well. Far better, I had decided, to let her sail herself, and to adopt a mediaeval frame of mind, patient and unhurried. A week or two added or subtracted to our passage was of no significance, and the benefits of our leisurely outlook were noticeable.

So we lived a relaxed existence. Edan and I divided up the cooking; Arthur and George usually did the dishes. As for sanitary facilities, one could either hang outboard at the stern or, in rougher seas, use a bucket wedged securely amidships.

George made regular inspections of all the sailing gear, especially of the ropes and halyards, which were subject to considerable wear. We were always digging out our sewing kits to mend tears or to whip the ends of frayed ropes. The flax ropes stretched slack when dry and shrank into iron rods when wet. We found the best technique was to set them up as taut as possible when dry, and then keep them doused with water. Arthur's job was to keep the coils of rope neatly stowed and ready for action, and with so much rope on board it kept him busy. In between times he spent hours meticulously maintaining the cameras which were recording *Brendan*'s life. Arthur had taken over the photography when Peter had to leave us, and our youngest crew member was developing into a first-class cameraman.

Cine photography and radio - communications, along with navigation, fell within my province. Once every twenty-four hours I switched on the little radio set to give a shore station our position, which was relayed in turn to the intelligence unit of Lloyd's of London, who were kindly keeping our families informed. Occasionally, however, we failed to establish any contact—hardly surprising, as even in a mild seaway the swell overtopped our antenna. Navigation was simplicity itself. After leaving Stornoway I relied on sun sights taken with a sextant and crosschecked on radio bearings. But I was content if we merely raised landfalls roughly where we expected them along the Stepping Stone Route.

Edan, true to character, provided the light entertainment on board. We all knew when he woke up in the morning by the cries of "Food! Breakfast! How about breakfast?" which came echoing down the boat from his cubbyhole near the foremast. A few minutes later Gannet himself would come clambering into view, eagerly poking his nose into the food locker. His clothes were never the same two days running. One day he wore his beret; another, a knitted cap; once, a knotted handkerchief. His oilskin jacket might be replaced by an old sweater, or a furry diver's undersuit, which made him look like an enormous baby in a snowsuit. Once he showed up in a tweed sports jacket and tartan trousers, and was greeted with shouts of delight. Another time he arrived in oriental garb: a flimsy Indian cotton shirt, embroidered, its tail flapping in the breeze like a Calcutta clerk's. He must have been freezing cold, for—as usual—his feet were bare. Quite where Edan concealed this extraordinary wardrobe, in the tiny space of his sleeping berth, no one could fathom. Yet he still managed to dig out packet after packet of cigars, which he smoked jauntily all the while; and he sipped at the cache of duty-free whiskey he had laid in at Stornoway. His manic ways and bubbling spirits enlivened even the dreariest intervals.

Arthur and Gannet were both avid bird watchers, and the farther north we sailed the more varied the birdlife became. Our reference book of birds was in constant demand. Halfway to the Faeroes we had recorded fifteen different species, and we spent hours watching the behaviour of the gulls and terns which constantly tended us, shrieking and twittering. Our most elegant companions were the fulmars, the premier acrobats of these waters, who glided in endless loops and circles around us hour after hour, riding close to the waves on stiff wings, their fat, fluffy bodies like huge moths.

A pair of Arctic terns took up their station on our mast, fluttering nervously and cheeping anxiously to one another as the other seabirds came near them. Occasionally they would break formation to search for fish in our wake, and once we witnessed a terrific air battle when our two small terns drove away a hulking skua which came marauding in our direction. Gallantly the two smaller birds hurled themselves into the attack and drove off the intruder with much shrieking; when they returned to the mast, we could distinctly hear their chirrups of pride. But their victory was brief. Scarcely ten minutes later a pair of skuas arrived, and this time there was no contest. The two terns fled for their lives, turning at wave-crest level as the powerful skuas struck at them.

For two days *Brendan* made steady progress northward. Gale warnings continued, but the wind held fair and my calculations put us halfway to the Faeroes. Daily, George or I inspected the leather skin, poking our fingers through the wooden frame to see whether there was any deterioration. By now the leather was completely saturated, and an inch or two of seawater constantly swirled along the bilge. But the leather seemed to be holding up well, except for two patches near the H-frame. By sighting along the gunwale I could detect that *Brendan*'s curved stern had begun to droop, flattening the profile and wrinkling the skin. The oxhides in this area were no longer stretched tight over the frame but bagged and corrugated like an elephant's posterior. Prodding a finger against the skin, one could easily pump it in and out like a soft balloon, but this did not seem to affect the material. Our mediaeval leather was holding up remarkably well, and I suspected

277

that the increasing cold was a help, hardening the protective layer of wool grease. Here again, I suspected, we were learning why the Irish chose to sail to their promised land by a northern route: in the warmer waters of a southern voyage the protective grease might have washed away, and the leather begun to rot.

But our daily inspections revealed that the sea had been taking its toll of *Brendan*'s wooden framework. The steering handle was held in position by a cross rope fastened to the opposite gunwale. The strain on this rope was so great that the gunwale, of seasoned oak an inch and a half thick, was literally being torn apart. George lost no time in shifting the rope to another strong point and doubling the lashings which held the steering frame together. Later I crawled forward to inspect the mainmast and found that the main thwart had been bent upwards in a curve, probably by the same forces which were causing the stern to droop.

Thoughtfully I crawled back and considered our position. *Brendan* was changing her shape. I did not believe it was yet dangerous, but it was very evident that we were utterly dependent on the strength of our basic materials. It occurred to me that what a sixth-century boatbuilder might have lacked in his knowledge of naval architecture he gained in the quality of the materials he used, materials which he had selected critically and then prepared with the utmost care. We were learning this lesson in a host of small ways. Item by item our modern equipment was collapsing. Our shiny new metal tools, for example, had virtually rusted away, despite a protective coat of oil; after a month aboard *Brendan* a tempered saw blade simply snapped like a carrot. Of our modern materials, only the best stainless steel, the solid plastic, and the synthetic ropes were standing up to the conditions. When a modern item broke, we tended to replace it with a homemade substitute devised from ancient materials— wood, leather, or flax—that we could sew and shape to suit the occasion. The product usually looked cumbersome and rough, but it survived and we could repair it ourselves. When metal snapped, or plastic ripped, the only choice without a workshop on board was to jettison the broken item.

It all added up to the realization that the sailors of Saint

Brendan's day were in fact better equipped materially—as well as mentally—than is usually acknowledged. Even their clothing was admirably suited to the conditions. As the weather turned colder, we replaced our clothes of artificial fibre with old-fashioned woollen ones, reeking of natural oil. We may have looked and smelled unlovely, but our sweaters, thigh-length sea-boot socks, and cowl-like woollen helmets were not materially different from the garments available in Saint Brendan's day.

JUNE 19 AND 20 brought us only a moderate advance. The wind headed us for a time, and *Brendan* actually lost ground, ending up thirty miles farther away from the Faeroes. There was nothing to be done, and we accepted the situation with our newly minted mediaeval philosophy. Eventually the wind died away completely, and we simply waited to see what Providence would bring.

Then, "Trawler in sight! Coming down from the north." When the trawler was close enough to read the name—*Lord Jellicoe*—I switched on our portable VHF set.

"*Lord Jellicoe*. Curragh *Brendan* calling. Come in, please."

Silence. Only the hiss of the loudspeaker. I tried repeating the call. Again silence. Then suddenly a startled voice crackled back: "*Lord Jellicoe*. Who's that?"

"Curragh *Brendan*. We're off your starboard side, about half a mile away. Can you give me a position check, please?"

"Wait a minute." *Lord Jellicoe* ploughed on, while presumably her navigator was roused to work out the unexpected request. Just as she was disappearing over the horizon, she signalled the information I wanted. Later that same evening we heard the flat Yorkshire accents of her skipper calling up a coast station.

"Humber Radio, maybe you can tell us something. We passed a strange vessel some time back this afternoon, and I'm told that it's carrying a crew of mad Irish monks. Is that right?"

We never heard Humber Radio's reply, because *Brendan*'s crewmen were doubled up with laughter.

June 21, the longest day of the year, made us realize that we were now in high latitudes. Even at one o'clock in the morning I could still read the logbook by reflected light in the sky. For the rest of the sailing season we had no need for navigation lights which was just as well, for I was a miser with our precious batter power. That evening we made the final contact with the friendl coast operator at Malin Head radio station; in his Irish brogu he wished us luck for the Faeroes. As if in response the wind changed to the south, and *Brendan* began to advance again in th right direction. All the next day they continued light. In a heav shower we collected several inches of fresh water in a tarpaulin a an experiment. In an emergency, I calculated, we could just abou survive in that damp climate on rainwater.

June 23 answered the question of how the early Irish monk would have located the Faeroes in the vastness of the Atlantic. was an ordinary summer's day for those regions, with occasion sunshine and a great deal of cloud. *Brendan* was still more tha fifty miles away from the islands, yet we picked them out wit ease from the columns of cloud building up over them, thousand of feet into the air, changing shape every few minutes in powerfu up-draughts, the sign of an abrupt change in the weather.

We had a lowering sunset—a red sky with the purple shadow of the islands in the distance, beautiful but ominous. We wer now close enough to be able to identify the individual islands i the group, and I carefully consulted our charts and pilot book Our best course was to aim straight for the centre of the Faeroe run through one of the narrow channels between them, and the try to duck into shelter on the lee side. But there was one snag On every tide the Atlantic sluices through the Faeroes in a immense rush of water, sometimes so strong and swift—eight t nine knots is not exceptional—that even large ships must tak care. Caught in these tide rips a leather sailing boat would b helpless.

I checked the compass bearings and marked *Brendan*'s positio on the chart, just before the storm line swept down on us fror the south, a bank of rain which in minutes cut visibility fror twenty miles to three.

"Everybody in safety harnesses, please," I ordered, and w buckled on the belts and clipped lifelines to the boat. "Ganne you handle the headsail sheets; Boots, take the mainsail, and loo

280

after the leeboards. George, you're the best helmsman on board; you take over the steering. I'll handle the pilotage."

Brendan groped her way in the general direction of the Faeroes. After an hour we had a brief glimpse of the islands as the sea-level cloud lifted. At once I saw that I would have to abandon my original plan. The main tide was running in a circular motion around the island, and had picked up *Brendan* and was carrying her clockwise around the group. We would be lucky to get into land at all, without being swept past the Faeroes to the west. Mykines, the most westerly island, was closest to us, but its landing place could be approached only in calm weather. But Vagar, the next island, had a fjord that offered good shelter; it seemed worth a try.

By now the wind had risen to half a gale and *Brendan* was driving blindly through the rain with the tide under her closing the gap at a terrific pace.

"Keep as close to the wind as you can," I asked George. I guessed we must have entered the area of eddies and tidal backcurrents. We needed every inch of headway if we were not to be slammed sideways into the sheer cliffs of Mykines. The wind was blowing so hard that although *Brendan* was pointing east she was going almost north, sliding sideways across the waves.

"Cliffs!" bellowed Edan. There, half a mile away, was a leaping band of white water.

"My God! Look at that!" Arthur breathed. It was indeed a remarkable sight. The cloud was so low that we saw only down a narrow tunnel, about six feet high, between the cloud base and the grey ocean. At that same moment *Brendan* entered a back eddy running against her, so that her forward movement suddenly slowed to a crawl. Yet the gale kept her sliding sideways, ever sideways, towards the cliffs. It was like slipping down a tunnel in a nightmare. There was no escape. All of us fell silent. We knew it was a race between our snail's-pace advance and our sideways lurch towards the cliffs. Hardly breathing, we watched the grey cliffs inch closer and closer.

"I think we'll do it," I said hopefully to George. "I can see the end of the island."

"I hope the mast doesn't go," he muttered. "That really would be curtains."

The mainmast was curved more than we had ever seen it, drawn down by the intense pressure of the gale on the mainsail, which still carried its bottom bonnet and one side bonnet.

"We'll have to leave the bonnets up," George said. "We need all the driving power we can get to pull free of the tide."

"Keep an eye on the mainmast where it passes the thwart," I shouted forward to Boots. "If it begins to splinter, cut the bonnets free with your knife."

A few moments later our world suddenly seemed to stand still. The normal motion of the boat and the waves stopped, as though we had gone into suspension. Through some quirk of the tide race in the gale the waves, instead of moving horizontally, simply rose up and down as if marking time. At the same moment the cloud base rose another thirty or forty feet, and we saw thousands upon thousands of seabirds—gulls, guillemots, razorbills, fulmars, gannets, puffins, skuas, and terns—pouring out from the cliffs of Mykines. They came in squadrons, wheeling and turning, swooping and dipping towards the queer, lumpy, contorted sea. Driven by primaeval experience, they had emerged to fish at a time when they knew the combination of wind and tide would bring the shoals of fish close to the surface of the water.

Brendan was at last clawing past the trap where Mykines reached out its heel of cliff towards us. In the space of ten yards we suddenly broke free from the counter eddy and plunged into the main tidal stream running into Mykines Sound, two miles wide, which separates Mykines from Vagar. *Brendan* shot forward into the gap. On each side of us the fjordlike cliffs rose up seven or eight hundred feet, funnelling the wind into a full gale. *Brendan* fled into the sound, the needle of our log swinging smoothly up to six knots, to eight, to ten, to the end stop at twelve knots, where it stayed. The mass of water sluicing through the narrow channel was being accelerated by the gale to six or seven knots, so that *Brendan* must have been making close to twenty knots. She was breaking all speed records for skin boats!

With every gust she leaned over, gunwale almost in the water.

The sea swirled by. Heaving on the tiller, George struggled to keep her running straight. If *Brendan* broached, we would be rolled over.

"Ease the sheets! Spill the wind!" he called to Arthur and Edan. "We have to slow her down." But the moment we slackened the ropes they began to snap and crack like bullwhips, and I was afraid that they would crush someone's hand or finger.

Abruptly there came a loud report like a rifle shot, quite distinct above the shriek of the wind. "What was that?" I yelled.

"Masthead stay snapped," George yelled back.

"There's no time to fix it," I replied. "Just keep going. We'll have to risk the mast and keep running on. We daren't lose speed."

Brendan careered forward, right in the grip of the tide race now and fairly flying through the gap. There was no way we could enter harbour on Vagar. George weaved her slightly from side to side, trying to spill the wind from the bulging sails. But it was not enough. A fierce gust struck, and there was an abrupt ripping noise as the lower bonnet tore free of the mainsail.

"Drop the mainsail!" I yelled, and it came sliding down. Arthur pounced on it and wrestled the flapping canvas, spread-eagled across it.

The sail had done its work before bursting. It had driven us almost the length of the Sound, and we could see the open Atlantic once again at the far end.

"I'm glad the sail went then," I commented to George. "A little earlier and we would have been in real trouble."

Even when the tide spat us out of the Sound, *Brendan* was still at the mercy of a full southerly gale, so I decided to try to lie in the lee of the Faeroes, riding to a sea anchor under a scrap of riding sail. There, in comparative peace, we hung for an hour, brewed a cup of tea, and relaxed from the excitement.

"Sorry about that, lads," I said. "It looks as though we've lost our chance to land in Faeroes."

George put down his tea mug and peered towards the horizon. "The rain's lifting, and the wind seems to have come round a bit. I think if we go now, we might just have a chance of getting into one of the other islands. But we'll have to act quickly."

We lost no time. Up went the sail, and *Brendan* slanted off towards the high cliffs of the principal island, Streymoy. We failed by half a mile to gain the entrance to Sakshovn, the only shelter facing us on Streymoy, and *Brendan* was swept inexorably towards the north tip of the island. George steered *Brendan* until she was no more than fifty feet from the cliff wall, sliding past in hair-raising style, but out of the main blast of the wind. As we came to the tip of the island, he put the helm hard over to make a ninety-degree turn to starboard; astonishingly, we plunged into the grip of another tide eddy running directly against us.

Once more it was an uncanny sensation. *Brendan* was carrying full sail, main and headsail, and they were billowing out, straining on the masts. The rigging was taut; a bow wave curled back impressively; the log showed that our speed through the water was six knots. Yet we were not moving an inch! The tide race was cancelling out our progress. There was nothing we could do. For fully an hour *Brendan* poised there, fifty feet from the cliff face, as if suspended in the air by a magician. Then the tide changed, the rip slackened, and *Brendan* sailed serenely forward.

Soon afterwards we spotted a small Faeroese fishing trawler putting out from one of the channels between the islands. It altered course and towed *Brendan* into nearby Tjornuvik, where a cluster of gaily painted houses set into an embayment in the cliffs looked like a child's set of building toys. Arthur and Edan paddled ashore in the rubber dinghy to stretch their legs on land. Meanwhile, a Faeroese asked me about our landfall.

"We came through Mykines Sound," I told him.

He looked startled. "In this gale?"

"Yes, the wind was behind us, and it was a thrilling ride."

He was astounded. "It's some of the most dangerous waters of our islands," he said. "You were lucky. If the wind had turned against you, then I think your boat would have been destroyed."

THE FAEROESE were fascinated by *Brendan*. The village children put out in their little boats to gaze at her; and when the next day *Brendan* was towed up narrow Sundini Sound to the capital at Thorshavn, entire families came out of their houses to watch her progress. Each turn of the channel brought more hills into view, one behind the other, every slope clothed only in moorland and rock, for native trees do not grow in these windswept islands. Many streams came gushing down the green slope high above the Sound. This is a breathtakingly beautiful land.

Thorshavn's quayside was thronged with onlookers, and immediately we were deluged with questions, not about the voyage itself but about *Brendan*. Every question revealed how strong was the seafaring tradition of the islanders. How was the hull fastened together? What were *Brendan*'s draught and her displacement? Did the side-mounted rudder work well in a following sea? It was more like being cross-examined by a board of shipwrights than by ordinary townsfolk. Old men wearing traditional red stocking hats with the top turned smartly over one ear hopped nimbly aboard and prodded the leather, clucking with appreciation. The local radio station asked me to give an account of how *Brendan* was constructed and how she behaved at sea.

And, of course, the Faeroese were marvellously hospitable. Boots and Gannet were swept into an embrace of comfortable hospitality. When the two began to show a strange enthusiasm for doing the *Brendan*'s breakfast dishes, George and I were suspicious. So we followed them one morning when they went ashore with the bucket of dirty dishes, and tracked them down to the seamen's hotel. Sure enough, we found the pair of them sitting at the kitchen table consuming a second—and free—breakfast while an admiring squad of Faeroese girls was doing all the work for them.

One morning I came back from a shopping trip to find a very striking couple waiting for me. The girl had beautiful features, large brown eyes, and a sallow skin—unusual among the Faeroese, who are very blond. That gave her a gipsy look, which was enhanced by her long black hair and a voluminous skirt. Her companion could have stepped straight from an illustration in Grimm's fairy tales. He was a powerful, thickset figure, sitting motionless on *Brendan*'s gunwale. He was wearing very strong boots, rough corduroy trousers, and a homemade brown sweater. He had the large, powerful hands of an artisan, and a most

285

splendid growth of hair worthy of Neptune himself, so luxuriant that it formed a solid mass extending from his chest to an arc a good three inches out from his scalp. From a serious face framed in the midst of this wild tangle, a pair of calm brown eyes gazed steadily at me. "Hello," I said. "Can I help you?"

The Neptune said nothing, but gazed at me for a full five seconds before calmly looking towards the girl. She spoke for him: "On the radio interview yesterday you said that you had room for one more person on your crew, and you would like someone from the Faeroe Islands. This man would like to join you."

Good Lord, I thought to myself, even a Viking raiding party would have thought twice before taking on this fellow.

"Yes, that's right, but I'm looking for someone who's very experienced in a boat, if possible a person who can help take photographs."

"This man is better than that," she said proudly. "He's an artist, and a very good one. Also, he has sailed his own boat to the Mediterranean and has been a fisherman on Faeroe boats off Greenland. He is a serious man."

I can see that, I thought to myself, stealing a surreptitious glance at the heavily bearded figure. He had still not moved a muscle. "Perhaps he could show me some of his work?" I inquired tactfully.

Neptune muttered something to his girl friend.

"His name is Trondur Patursson, and he is shy to speak English," she said. "But he invites you to his home tomorrow."

"We'll be delighted to come."

Next day they reappeared in a small, battered car. *Brendan*'s crew squeezed in, and we rattled off across the spine of Streymoy. Eventually we came to a narrow road which snaked down to a tiny hamlet on the water's edge dominated by, of all things, a Viking house, a massive overgrown log cabin built of huge and ancient timbers stained dark brown. Its windows and wooden doors were picked out in red, and on the roof was a carpet of turf like a slab of mountain pasture. It was unquestionably Norse and completely authentic.

"This is Trondur's family home," the girl said.

I looked at the house, then past it to a neatly whitewashed church on the edge of the little harbour. In a field to one side, the roofless carcass of an even grander church rose out of the meadow; its architecture appeared to be late mediaeval.

"What is the name of the village?" I asked.

"Kirkjubo," she replied. "Sometimes it is called Brandarsvik."

So there we were—my silent volunteer was from St. Brendan's Creek. Though no tangible remains of Irish occupation have yet been found, every Faeroese learns in school that the Irish priests were the first people to settle in their remote islands.

The Paturssons were among the longest-established families in the Faeroes. Their log house was almost a national monument by Faeroese standards, the oldest continuously occupied house in the islands. The Paturssons had lived there for eighteen generations; and before that it had been owned by the local bishop.

The Paturssons themselves were as traditional and interesting as their house. Squads of children rushed in and out; Grandmother presided, an elegant and stately lady who deferred only to Potl, Trondur's twin brother, older by quarter of an hour, who was now the head of the family. It was Potl who greeted us cheerfully, dressed in his farming clothes. Half an hour later he reappeared in traditional Faeroese regalia: silver-buckled black pumps, dark-blue knee socks with scarlet tabs, blue broadcloth knee breeches, and an embroidered waistcoat and short jacket embellished with a triple row of silver buttons. Totally unself-conscious in this splendid eighteenth-century attire, he stalked ahead of us to the little church, rang the bell to summon the congregation from the hamlet, and led them in response to the prayers of the austere, white-ruffed Lutheran pastor. Meanwhile, above us, the ribbed wooden roof of the church creaked in the gale like a ship working in a sea.

Afterwards *Brendan*'s crew was treated to a memorable meal in the old Faeroese style. There was leg of mutton, killed and then dried slowly in the wind so that it had the consistency and colour of Parma ham and a distinctly rank flavour. There were boiled fulmar's eggs, which Trondur and Potl collected from the cliff faces in a perilous exercise that involved dangling from a rope's end over a two-hundred-foot drop. There was even dried whale meat and a rubbery slab of pure whale blubber with its black rind that reminded one exactly of high-grade tyre rubber. Everything was Patursson-prepared; the Paturssons had even helped drive the whale ashore and harpooned it to death.

"My word, look at all that," breathed Edan. Soon he was gobbling away as fast as he could, with the others trying to keep up with him. I saw Trondur's eyes twinkle as without a word he carved a sliver off the slab of whale blubber and offered it to Edan, who was in full swing, devouring like a vacuum cleaner. Heedlessly he took the blubber in one bite.

"Ugh!" His jaws abruptly froze, and his eyes widened in horror. "Ugh! It's like rubber soaked in cod oil," he blurted out.

"Go on, Gannet. It's rude to spit it out," said George. Edan screwed up his face, took a mighty swallow, and for the first time on the voyage looked green about the gills; he put down his knife and fork while the rest of us nearly choked with laughter.

After the meal we went up to the farm where Trondur lived, and saw some of his sketches. Borgne, his beautiful interpreter—and fiancée—was wholeheartedly in favour of Trondur's going with us. It would give him new material for his drawing and sculpture, she said. And like a true seaman, all Trondur had to do was pack his kit bag and he would be ready.

Trondur's joining the crew of *Brendan* was one of the best moves of the entire voyage. From the moment he came aboard, his command of English improved daily. He helped us prepare *Brendan* for the next challenge—the long crossing to Iceland in the face of westerly winds. He and Edan improved the forward tent to make it more watertight; farther aft, George and Arthur replaced the ash legs of the steering frame with heavy balks of oak, three inches thick, lashed into position with leather thongs. Despite Edan's protests, we loaded Trondur's favourite sailing diet aboard: dried fish, dried whale meat, and yet more chunks of whale blubber. Most of it was hung from the rigging, and it gave off a truly mediaeval smell, strong enough to be noticed above all *Brendan*'s other odours. And so, draped with our new larder, we were ready for the next phase in our adventure.

CHAPTER 8

The Patursson family made a brave little group as they stood on the quay-side at Brandarsvik and waved and waved goodbye to *Brendan*. Their figures grew smaller and smaller, and the magnificent vista of the Faeroese coastline opened up on each side, sheer cliffs falling directly into the sea. The sun was setting, and its rays silhouetted the western islands, here and there striking a patch of colour from the rocky flanks of the hill. On July 3 we cleared the Faeroes and set course for Iceland.

Trondur at once proved his worth: he taught us how to fish properly. As a five-year-old boy he had learned the skills of generations of Faeroese fishermen. Certainly there was a trick to success in these depths of water. Trondur produced a massive lump of lead, perhaps five pounds in weight, and a very long line. His lures were three simple hooks with brightly coloured rags on them. Soon *Brendan* was wearing yet another decoration—a dripping row of fresh-caught fish hanging like washing on the line, and we were trying out every variation of cod—boiled cod, fried cod, cod in batter, cod stew, cod with rice or potato or parsley sauce, even a tasty cod spaghetti.

On the second day a fine southeast wind sprang up, and we made excellent progress, fifty miles in a gentle sea, so that we had time to doze and chat and relax. A fog came down at eight in the evening. It was full daylight and we could enjoy the spectacle of the millions of pearly droplets which formed on every surface, most of all on Trondur's magnificent head of hair as he sat on the stern, sketching in his note pad.

Edan came up with one of his schemes—to launch messages in bottles. For one thing it gave him an excuse to empty the last few inches of our current bottle of whiskey, and for another it gave him a chance to try out his prose. George reached over the side and retrieved one of Edan's bottles as it bobbed lazily past.

Aboard leather boat *Brendan*, west of Faeroes.

Dear Reader

I am so glad you have picked up this message, which was thrown into the sea between Faeroes and Iceland. Please let me know where and when you found the bottle.

Then followed Edan's signature and address.

"Just think of it," said Edan. "Some delightful girl, strolling along the beach in her bikini, sees this bottle resting on the sand, picks it up and reads my message. I'm sure she will write. That'll show you."

"I have my doubts about the bikini," I said. "With the prevailing southwesterlies it's much more likely that your bottles will finish up near North Cape on the Arctic Circle."

"Ten to one the only blonde who'll write back to you will be a lonely Norwegian fisherman," said Arthur, "six foot tall, over two hundred pounds, and smelling like a sardine factory."

Whoosh! Just at that moment there was a massive sigh, like a huge gasbag emptying, followed by a gentle, rippling sound. "*Hval!*" cried Trondur with delight, as we all leaped to our feet. *Whoosh!* There it was again, and this time we saw the cause of it, a great, sleek black island of wet skin which came to the surface not twenty yards aft of *Brendan* and wallowed there gently for a moment with the water running off it. "Good, big *hval*," said Trondur admiringly, as the rest of us gaped. The whale was something like sixty feet long and perhaps eight or ten times *Brendan*'s weight. Suddenly one realized how puny our little low-slung boat must seem to this huge animal. But we had no feeling of danger, only a fascination for this huge creature who had deliberately emerged from the depths right beside us.

"He's come to take a close look at us," said George in a hushed voice.

"Hope he doesn't come too close," muttered Edan. "One nudge from that fellow and we'll all be swimming."

"No," I said, "he's probably interested in *Brendan* sitting motionless on top of the water. We probably look enough like a whale to make him curious."

The whale heaved and sighed beside us, gently and deliberately. Then it sank down, and the next time it surfaced it was a quarter of a mile away, swimming quietly and without hurry to the north.

I thought back to the visit I had paid in the previous autumn to the whale research unit of the Natural History Museum in London. I had promised to try counting all the whales we saw. "We really know surprisingly little about the habits of whales on a worldwide basis," said the scientist in charge.

"Do you think we're likely to get close enough to identify a particular species?"

"I don't really know. But"—and here he paused—"the minke whale is commonly described as curious and he may come up to take a really close look at you, while the fin whale sometimes rubs himself up against small boats."

Just what *Brendan* needs, I thought, an itchy whale having a scratch on the leather hull, to say nothing of tipping her over.

Scarcely two hours after seeing our first visitor, which was probably a large fin whale, Edan suddenly let out a cry. "Hey, look at that! There are dolphins under the boat! No, they're whales, and there's a solid mass of them right under us!" As he called, the distinctive black fin and the boot-shiny back of a small whale broke out of the water scarcely three or four feet away. Looking down we could see an extraordinary pattern of large, moving shadows, a living escort of sea creatures not more than six feet beneath the hull. There were scores of them, and we could pick out two dolphins that seemed to be travelling in company with them, almost as scouts. Then the whales began to surface around *Brendan*, filling the air with a constant hissing and sighing of their breath as they came to the surface some ten or fifteen at a time, followed by others in a strange marine ballet. They were pilot whales, one of the smaller species, though almost as long as *Brendan*.

Later the same day, as I watched another very large whale swim deliberately towards the boat pushing a massive bow wave of water in front of it, I began to wonder about the story of Saint Brendan and the whale. Superficially, of course, it was preposterous to think that someone actually could land on the

291

back of a sleeping whale, mistaking it for an island. Yet there was no doubt now that a leather boat held some sort of attraction for whales. Up to Saint Brendan's time these huge animals would never have seen a boat or met humans, but remained secure in their own great size and gentle manner. The Irish priests would have been in the same position as explorers who enter virgin jungle and meet animals totally ignorant of man, animals unafraid and curious about the stranger. When one connects this fact with the far greater whale population in earlier centuries, with the curiosity of whales as we in *Brendan* encountered it, and with the fin whale's known habit of rubbing against boats, it was scarcely surprising that the Irish priests came back amazed, bearing tales of their boat's touching huge monsters. Seen in this perspective, the whale stories increased rather than diminished the realism of the *Navigatio*.

But not all the sea monsters in Saint Brendan's narrative had been so friendly. His boat was chased by a great animal spouting fire from its nostrils and pushing a great wave ahead of it. Just as this monster seemed about to devour the boat, another appeared and a tremendous battle ensued; the newcomer killed the first, and the monks later found its body washed up on a beach. They cut it up and ate some of the flesh.

On July 7 I felt that this episode, too, had found a possible explanation. Trondur, who had an almost uncanny instinct for detecting the presence of a whale, was sitting quietly sketching. Suddenly he raised his head and looked northward. He seemed tense, which was unusual for him.

"*Spaekhugger*," he said flatly. We looked puzzled. "*Spaekhugger*," he repeated. "In Faeroes, we not like this whale. It is not so big, but has big—" and here, at a loss for the right word, he pointed at his teeth. He drew an outline of the whale with charcoal strokes on his sketchbook.

One glance was enough. He had drawn the characteristic shape and piebald blotches of the grampus, or killer whale. I was not altogether surprised. From the start of the project I had heard more jokes about the killer whale than I cared to remember. It is carnivorous and—quite simply—there was a risk that one would mistake *Brendan*'s leather skin for a potential meal. Packs of hungry killer whales often attack and demolish larger whales. Would they now mistake *Brendan* for a dead or wounded whale?

Trondur pointed. A pack of six killer whales was strung out in the classic hunting pattern, swimming abreast with perhaps one or two hundred yards between each animal, so that they covered a front of about three-quarters of a mile. No wonder the Spanish fishermen call them *lobo del mar*, "the wolf of the sea"; they hunted with the same deadly efficient organization.

The pack swept south, sinking down, then reappearing almost in unison with heavy, wheezing breaths. The third time they surfaced they were close enough for us to determine that there were five smaller animals and a sixth, much bigger one—the bull. According to sea lore, the rest of the pack takes its direction from the bull, who is more experienced and acts as a director of the hunt. On its present course, I saw, this pack was going to pass well astern of *Brendan*.

Then the bull sensed our presence, and his fin turned majestically. We gazed, fascinated by this display of unhurried power. *Hiss! Ripple!* His great bulk surfaced again on a direct course for *Brendan*, and sank down. *Puff!* A mist of spray and steam leaped a few feet into the air as he came up for breath again, this time no more than fifty yards away. We could see now just how massive he was; a fully grown killer whale perhaps five or six feet shorter than *Brendan*, with three or four times her displacement. Alone of all whales, he looked totally sinister. The thin, cruel fin, a good six feet tall, came slicing up every time he surfaced.

The final time the bull rose beside *Brendan*, the fin was just twenty yards away, standing above the water as tall as any of us. We heard the full hiss of the creature's nostrils and could actually smell the stale air it expelled. Then the great back dipped, there was a flash of black-and-white flanks, and the killer slid right under the boat, all eight or ten tons of him, curious, intelligent, and completely in control. I saw George clip his safety line to the steering frame. We held our breath, absolutely silent, for what seemed like an age.

293

Whoosh! The great black fin came sliding up out of the water on the opposite side of *Brendan*, the great lungs emptied, and the killer whale began turning ponderously back towards his pack. We, too, let out our breath. We had been inspected and found wanting, and we were extremely glad.

We witnessed some evidence of the killer whale's ferocity four days later: a school of pilot whales suddenly surfaced around us. Some were darting in one direction, others turning back the way they had come, plunging out of sight without taking breath. A few even leaped clear of the water. "I think *spaekhugger* are chasing them," said Trondur. I again thought back to the *Navigatio*'s description of the battle of the sea monsters. Had the Irish priests been worried by a large whale? And at the last moment had this whale been the victim of a killer's attack? The details seemed quite in agreement with the mediaeval description: the bow wave sent forward by a large approaching whale and the mist spouting from the killer whale. What other "sea monster" was there which, when killed, would float away to a beach and become food for the monks? Once again the mundane facts, stripped of their fanciful telling, emerged and made a sensible story.

On July 8 we finally received our weather luck. The wind picked up from the east, and *Brendan* began to reel off the sea miles. The wind was exactly what we wanted. The thought that a gale from the southwest might drive *Brendan* sideways towards the long and dangerous coast of Iceland was enough to make me lay a course that headed almost due west, leaving a safety margin of seventy miles between *Brendan* and that inhospitable shore. Running before the wind from the east, we covered seventy miles on the first day, and on the second one hundred and sixteen. Not bad progress, even for a modern cruising yacht, and we were by no means pushing *Brendan* to her limits.

Then the wind freshened into half a gale, and the seas began to tumble in cold grey ranks fifteen feet high. We lowered the mainsail five feet and took down the headsail altogether. *Brendan* began to labour. Her frame squeaked and grunted; the rope holding the steering oar in place began to emit the most alarming high-pitched creaks as it was stretched.

294

Sooner or later, we knew, some of our gear would begin to fail. The first item to break was one of the splendid new oak posts of the steering oar's H-frame, which we had installed in the Faeroes. Hastily we trebled the leather thongs that held it in place, and though we carried on, we had learned the lesson: oak could not withstand the strain; it was too stiff and resisted the motion of the boat instead of flexing with it. Next the leather strap that held the crossyard to the mast gave way; the constant seesaw motion of the yard wore through its stitching. So we broke out needle, leather awl, and flax thread and made repairs at sea to keep *Brendan* running briskly on her course.

Inside the main cabin the constant dash of spray over the roof was beginning to tell. An ominous damp stain expanded a little farther each day, inching nearer the vulnerable radio set. The easterly gale was now blowing us so fast that there was a risk we would be blown clear past Iceland if we did not claw up to the north. But the new course laid the starboard side bare to the rollers, and the spray steadily trespassed into our living area. I became accustomed to find my "privileged" skipper's berth wet at each end.

Fortunately we were now completely accustomed to our surroundings, and our morale was remarkably high. Each of us was reacting to the conditions in his own way. Arthur had decided that the best place to be in foul weather was warmly curled up in his sleeping bag. But if he curled up, George could not lie down properly, so there was much friendly banter between them as George kept count of how many hours each day Arthur could pretend to be asleep, surfacing only for meals and his turn on watch. As for Edan, the heavy weather did not take the edge off his appetite, though he complained that his cigars were getting soggy in the spray. He still liked to take a tot of whiskey in the evening, but the rest of us had long given up the desire for a drink or even a smoke.

Trondur remained absolutely unruffled. On the first windswept evening he taught us another useful trick. From his pocket he pulled a pair of shapeless oiled wool mittens and, to our astonishment, leaned over the side and dunked them into the water. Then he squeezed them out and put them on half-sodden. "It's better," he said. "Not so cold later." He was quite right; the gloves acted like wet-suit gloves and reduced the wind's chill.

Food became the number-one topic. To save money I had bought a supply of very cheap powdered coffee, and this now proved to be a false economy. After a while not one of us could face the revolting brew any longer. We rediscovered the delights of childhood drinks—hot malted milk, chocolate, or meat extract. Our main courses, corned beef or tongue, were very popular, and there seldom seemed to be quite enough to satisfy all our appetites, so that Skipper's Special—a mush of apricots, jam, and crushed biscuits—was a popular event.

By July 11 the easterly winds had abated from gale strength, but were still pushing the boat westward so effectively that I was worried we would miss Iceland altogether. We struggled to get north, setting and resetting the sails to their best effect and adjusting and re-adjusting the leeboards. Still *Brendan* slipped sideways to the west, past southwest Iceland. Never again would I doubt the theory that many seaborne discoveries have been made by accident; if a vessel was as responsive to the weather as *Brendan*, it was very easy to find yourself five or six hundred miles off target after a week of storms.

Then, quite abruptly, the east wind dropped, and we could catch our breath. We knew we were not very far from land because we saw puffins flying past the boat, and these birds seldom range very far from their nesting grounds. Once more Trondur had a new trick to show us. "*Crrk!*" he called with a low, throaty sound as a puffin went whizzing past, looking curiously at *Brendan* but keeping a safe distance. Again, "*Crrk!*" The bird wheeled in a tight arc and came back. "*Crrk!*" The bird was being drawn by the noise, closer and closer, until Trondur could keep it patrolling back and forth, puzzled by the strange sound. Seeing our interest, Trondur pointed at the usual pair of terns hovering high above *Brendan*. "Now this bird will come," he told us, and taking a white rag he tied it to the end of the boat hook and waved it in the air. Sure enough, the terns swooped closer for a look. Trondur waved the lure again. Down farther came the terns, until finally he permitted one of them to land briefly on the sail.

"Pity they're so small," said Edan. "There's scarcely a bite of flesh on them."

"Not so good," said Trondur.

"What about those birds?" Edan looked hungrily back at a noisy flock of fulmars which had settled on the calm waters astern. "Some fresh food would be nice after all that dehydrated muck. I can taste the preservatives hours after every meal."

Trondur reached for a slab of whale blubber, cut off a little chunk, strung it on the hook of his fishing line, and removed the lead weight. When he gently dropped the line overboard, the blubber floated down towards the fulmars, which immediately paddled towards it. One bird took an experimental peck, found the blubber good, and began to feed upon it. Immediately the flock began to fight over the morsel. One particularly gluttonous bird took up the whole lump in his beak and flapped off across the water. His gluttony was his undoing. The fishing line tautened; the weight of the bird's own rush set the hook firmly into its beak; there was a startled squawk, and Trondur was rapidly reeling in his threshing victim. Soon there were five birds on *Brendan*'s thwart.

I boiled the gulls slowly, prodding them with a knife. They were tough, but after two hours they seemed to be ready, and I added some dark sauce and a few lumps of dried whale meat to make a gravy, and served them. There was a split second of doubt before Edan took a bite. "Delicious," he announced. Seagull à la *Brendan*, it seemed, was a three-star success. Only the bones were left, picked clean. It was yet another example of how, a thousand years before, the Irish monks could have survived the long passages without vast quantities of supplies.

It took us nearly six days to creep back closer to the Iceland coast, gently coaxing *Brendan* through winds that perversely blew from the north and east. We began to see Icelandic fishing boats, a welcome relief, since we had sighted only two vessels in the entire crossing from the Faeroes.

One day an Icelandic Coast Guard Service plane roared overhead, not fifty feet above our mast, and our radio crackled into life. "Hello, *Brendan*. Is all well on board? The newspapers report *Brendan* is leaking. Can we give any help?"

"No, thanks," I replied. "The only leak must be among the journalists. If you ever want a leather aeroplane, we'll build it for you."

Mile by mile we crept closer to Iceland's coast. One afternoon when we were becalmed, George enlivened the day by boldly plunging overboard wearing one of our immersion suits. He bobbed gaily around the boat for half an hour, looking like a bright-red tailor's dummy with his feet sticking up in the air. As we were in latitude 62°N, the water was quite cold, yet when he climbed back on board, George was only just beginning to feel chilled. We did not know it then, but those bright-red immersion suits were to play a vital role in our struggle for survival off the Greenland pack ice.

Finally we had a sight of distant land, the magnificent peak of Snaefellsjökull, the great volcanic cone which rises more than forty-seven hundred feet over the western bay of Iceland. The white mountain top, permanently capped with ice and snow, was the beacon for our arrival. Snaefellsjökull, too, gave us the wind we wanted. On July 17 *Brendan* began to slant more purposefully towards Reykjavik, and we made a sweepstake on our time of arrival. Our excitement mounted as *Brendan* passed the outer harbour buoy. Trondur, of course, had guessed the time most accurately and won the sweepstake. The Reykjavik pilot boat came chugging out and I looked back over my shoulder. As if to symbolize the pressure of life on land, with all its problems, its people, and its responsibilities, a large cruise liner was bearing down on us, thirty thousand tons or so of tightly scheduled commerce and investment, hurrying to enter the harbour.

"I'll heave to so the liner can get past," I shouted to the pilot, as he closed us. "I'm afraid we're not very manoeuvrable."

"Oh no," he called back. "That ship can wait. We have come out to guide *Brendan* to a berth waiting specially for you. But there is a strong wind inside and I think we should tow you."

"No, thank you," I called back. "We would like to give it a try ourselves. Perhaps you could stand by with a towline just in case."

298

I handed the tiller to George, and he excelled himself. *Brendan* glided delicately between the pierheads, so close that her cross-yard almost brushed the legs of the spectators on the seawall. She turned through an S-bend and Edan hauled down our sails. Trondur and Arthur stepped quietly ashore with the mooring lines, as unconcerned as if they were stepping off the pavement.

CHAPTER 9

One day, said the *Navigatio*, Saint Brendan and his crew found themselves being blown by a southerly wind towards an island which was very rough, rocky and full of slag, without trees or grass, full of smith's forges.

Brendan said to his brothers: "This island worries me. I do not want even to get near it. But the wind is driving us straight towards it."

As they were sailing alongside it, a stone's throw away, they heard the sound of bellows blowing like thunder, and the thud of hammers on iron and anvil. . . . Behold, one of the inhabitants of this island came out of doors as if to do some task. He was very shaggy and full of fire and darkness. When he caught sight of the servants of Christ passing close to the island, he went back into his forge. Then he came down to the shore carrying in his hand a tongs with a burning lump of slag of great size and heat. Immediately he hurled the lump at the servants of Christ, but it flew more than two hundred yards above them. The sea where it fell began to boil as if a volcano was burning, and smoke rose from the sea as from a fiery furnace.

And when the man of God had got about a mile away all the people of the island came running down to the beach, carrying lumps of their own. Some began throwing their lumps after the servants of God. It looked as if the whole island was on fire like a huge furnace, and the sea boiled as a cauldron of meat boils when it

299

is thoroughly heated up. . . . Then the holy father comforted his monks, saying "Oh soldiers of Christ, be strong in true faith and in spiritual weapons because we are in the confines of hell. Be vigilant and be brave."

Most scholars agree that the *Navigatio* was probably describing the eruption of an island volcano, complete with its shattering bombardment of glowing lava, ash bombs hurling from the crater, the thud and rumble of subterranean explosions, and the heavy roar of the eruption itself. But was the author of the *Navigatio* merely repeating the description of a volcano which he had picked up from classical writers? Or did Irish monks actually witness a live volcano in action? The volcanoes of Iceland lie exactly on the Stepping Stone Route to North America and could produce exactly the scene described in the *Navigatio*.

In November 1963 a new volcano abruptly reared up out of the ocean near Iceland to form a new island, which was called Surtsey. Everything I had read about that eruption—the thirty-thousand-foot column of steam, the flying bombs hurtling eighty-five hundred feet up and splashing back into the sea, the muffled explosions as the sea invaded the underwater vents, the emergence of the newborn island—echoed the volcanic description of the *Navigatio*.

At Reykjavik's university I called on Sigurdur Thorarinsson, one of Iceland's leading volcanologists. "I remember thinking how accurate was the old Saint Brendan text when I first landed on the new island by rubber boat," Thorarinsson said. "It was not long after the island appeared above water, and the vents were still throwing out ash bombs. As far as I know, there is no similar description by a classical author of a volcano formed by submarine eruption."

The *Navigatio* is not the only document to state that Irish monks were sailing to Iceland in the seafaring era of the early Irish church. Independent evidence for these early Irish visits comes from the Norsemen. The *Landnamabok*, or "Book of Settlements," written in Iceland in the twelfth century, describes how the Norsemen first reached the island and found already living there "the men whom the Northmen called Papar; they were Christian men, and it is held that they must have come over the sea from the west, for there were found left by them books, bells and croziers. . . ."

By a happy coincidence the Icelandic scholar who has done the most recent study on the Papars was the president of Iceland himself, Dr. Kristjan Eldjarn. He was one of the first people to greet us at the quayside in Reykjavik when *Brendan* docked.

"We are allowed to believe that the Irish hermits were here," he told me, "but we still have not found any item definitely associated with them. The *Book of Icelanders* is still thought to be a very reliable historical source; and the place-names tell their own story, like Papos, the island of Papey, and Papafjord, and others whose precise location we do not know. We can still believe that they were named after the Irish hermits who lived here."

"The Papar names you mention," I agreed, "all lie in the south-east of Iceland facing across to Faeroes—exactly where I would expect to make landfall sailing the shortest route to Iceland."

President Eldjarn looked wistful. "We have just begun to search for Irish remains in Iceland, and there is much ground to cover. Iceland and Ireland were certainly very close throughout the early Middle Ages."

PERHAPS IT WAS this traditional Irish-Icelandic link that explained the warmth of the welcome which the Icelanders gave *Brendan* and her crew. Offers of help and hospitality poured in. The small boatyard of Baranaust, near Reykjavik's main harbour, offered to help haul *Brendan* out for inspection, and I promptly accepted. *Brendan* had been afloat for eight weeks, far longer than most people had thought a skin boat could survive without at least a new coat of grease on the leather.

Brendan's hull was a reassuring sight. There were only one or two slight gashes near the bow, where she had obviously struck sharp edges of flotsam. We examined every inch of the stitching, but not a thread was out of place. The boat was as sound and as tight as the day we had set out from Brandon Creek. Only her shape had changed. Near the stern two deep wrinkles ran diagonally across the oxhides where the stern had begun to droop, allowing the leather skin to slacken. And on the starboard side, where she had lain on the beach at Iona, the soft sand had pressed in the leather between her wooden skeleton ribs so that it looked almost corrugated. But what really encouraged us was the way the wool grease was still sticking. Those critics who said that a leather boat had to be beached and regreased every week were wrong. *Brendan* still bore a protective layer which now had a greenish tinge of algae and a crust of barnacles. We cleaned it carefully with wooden scrapers, and checked the leather underneath. It was perfect. The following day a gleeful troupe of small Icelandic boys had the time of their lives painting a fresh layer of hot wool grease over *Brendan*'s hull, getting themselves thoroughly sticky in the process. Luckily we had kept the original ash legs for the steering frame, and so were able to replace the oak which had cracked.

The director of Iceland's telecommunications centre also came down to offer help. "We could improve your radio system," he told me. "I suggest installing crystals for aircraft radio frequencies. Once you are out of range of Reykjavik there's only one coastal station, in South Greenland, before you get to Canada."

"But isn't it against regulations for a boat to use the aircraft frequencies?" I murmured.

He grinned. "Perhaps, but most likely you'll be speaking to Icelandic aircraft or to us at Reykjavik, and we won't object."

To our great good fortune the commanding officer of the Icelandic Coast Guard was the courteous and urbane Petur Sigurdsson, a man passionately interested in the sea and its history, and in the boats used by the Irish monks. *Brendan* was given a berth in the coast guard base; we were provided with a better anchor, extra warps, a spare car battery for the radio, and an oil bag to spread oil on the water in a storm. When I took the bag back to *Brendan*, Trondur nodded approvingly. "This is good," he announced. "Oil from fish is needed, but best is whale oil." Twenty-four hours later he turned up with a jerry can of oil scrounged from the whaling station outside town. Transferred to the oil bag, it was to assist *Brendan* when she was struggling against the Greenland storms.

When I visited the coast guard headquarters to thank Petur, I found myself looking at the big glass operations screen on which they marked the movements of their patrol ships. Still visible was the dotted line that signified our approach to Iceland. At each noon position an artistic hand had drawn a tiny sketch of *Brendan* and, where we met heavy weather, huge waves were shown looming menacingly over our little boat. "When you were coming into Iceland, we were keeping an eye on you," said Petur quietly. "Just in case we were needed." I felt very grateful.

Within a week we were ready to set out for Greenland. But for three weeks the wind blew strongly out of the southwest, precisely the direction in which we wanted to go. To assuage our impatience as we waited, Petur arranged for George and me to go on the Coast Guard Ice Patrol plane off Greenland.

As we droned westward at a few hundred feet, I peered down. Days of southwesterly winds had whipped up long, rolling seas which left white foam streaks all the way to the horizon. Along the path that *Brendan* would have to sail there were no ferries, no freighters, not even a fishing boat to be seen. Instead, about one hundred miles off the Greenland coast, we came to a great ledge of pack ice extending out from the land and continuing northward towards the Pole. From the air the ice looked clean and inviting compared to the foul mood of the ocean. But where the two met I could see how the great floes dipped and swirled, their shiny white surfaces suddenly changing to a hostile blue-green as the waves washed over them. Most certainly this was no place for a mediaeval leather boat to venture.

When we landed back at Reykjavik, I made up my mind. There was far too much pack ice even to think of landing in Greenland. It would be wiser to wait and continue our journey the following spring, the season of easterly winds. I consoled myself that this was what the Irish monks had done, advancing from one island to the next, season by season. Saint Brendan himself, according the the *Navigatio*, had taken seven seasons to reach the land in the west.

Petur Sirgurdsson looked relieved. "I'm sure you're right. *Brendan* has done well to get here, but now the sailing season is too late. Let the coast guard look after the boat for you during the winter. You can continue your voyage in the spring."

I assembled the crew aboard *Brendan*, feeling depressed and worrying whether the project would hold together. I explained the situation to them. "Of course I would like to invite each one of you to be aboard *Brendan* again next year. I think we all agree that *Brendan* has shown she can make it to the New World." George, Arthur, Trondur, Edan—each replied promptly that he would be back.

WE ALL RETURNED to our homes. In the spring it turned out that Edan's charter business needed his attention, so while he could come to Iceland to help us get *Brendan* ready, he decided he could not sail with us.

In May we returned to Reykjavik and went immediately to the coast guard hangar to inspect *Brendan*. She lay just as we had left her. We did not even need to regrease her hull before we lowered her straight into the water and began loading.

There were one or two changes after our previous summer's experience. We loaded one hundred and sixty gallons of water, nearly twice as much as before, because I planned to attempt the voyage to North America in a single long run. We included two small VHF radios to increase our chances of talking directly to commercial airliners overhead. We altered our food to follow a more mediaeval diet. We loaded smoked sausage, smoked beef, salt pork, a large supply of hazelnuts, oat cereal, and a fine cheddar cheese. These were the foods the Irish monks would have eaten, and I decided to take them too, not for authenticity but simply because they were the best food for the journey. Oat cereal was what Trondur called "good work food". It would not matter if the smoked and salted meats were swamped by a wave or soaked by rain; they would survive and taste just as good. In fact, our mediaeval diet was to prove a major success.

The 1976 season had demonstrated so clearly the advantages of woollen clothing that we each brought extra woollen socks; woollen hats, mittens, trousers, and scarves. Our friendly boatyard presented each of us with a superb woollen Icelandic sweater, and

Trondur collected a mysterious-looking package from the airport. "Faeroes gives clothes, too," he announced. "This is what Faeroe fishermen wear." He pulled out five sets of splendid grey woollen underwear, twice as thick and warm as anything I'd ever seen.

It is simplicity itself to re-rig a mediaeval boat. We merely propped the masts in their steps, lashed down the oars, attached the steering paddle by its leather strap, and *Brendan* was ready to begin the second and major stage of her odyssey. At a few minutes past five on the evening of May 7 a light wind wafted us gently to the west. We opened a bottle from our fresh supply of Irish whiskey and filled our mugs, and I proposed a toast: "Fair winds!" "Fair winds!" the others replied. We knew that the most difficult and potentially dangerous stage of the voyage lay ahead.

CHAPTER 10

The weather treated us almost too kindly for the first week. We had no more than light airs and calms, and *Brendan* drifted slowly westward. At Trondur's suggestion we adopted the watchkeeping system favoured by Faeroese fishermen: two watches— working four hours on and four hours off around the clock. Trondur would pair off with Arthur, and George with me. Each watch would decide its own arrangements. When the weather was fine, one man steered the boat while his partner could rest, or read, or cook a light snack. When the weather grew worse, the two watchkeepers would take the helm turn and turn about, just as they saw fit. When it was very rough, we were to learn, twenty minutes at the helm made a man completely numb. At noon we prepared the main hot meal of the day, which all four of us ate together. And this season we shared the chore of cooking, which was a far better arrangement.

In some ways it felt as if we had never interrupted our voyage. A school of minke whale surfaced and blew around us. A young minke about thirty feet long, consumed with curiosity, spent fifteen minutes cruising up and down each side of the boat, some twenty yards away, puffing and snorting and rolling under us. Two mornings later a large colony of seals popped up to inspect *Brendan*, heads bobbing like sleek footballs all around us as they gazed curiously at the leather boat. Then, all at once, they sank beneath the water and vanished from view.

We had human visitors, too—a passing fisherman who presented us with lumpfish from his catch, which Trondur skinned and cooked up into a fish stew; and a party of hunters in a speedboat. They had been shooting guillemot, and they also gave us part of their catch, much to Trondur's delight. He plucked, boiled, then fried, and finally sauced the guillemot with sour cream to produce as fine a meal as any French chef. "One guillemot," he announced judiciously as he ladled out our helpings, "is same as two fulmar or three puffin, all good food."

Trondur was obviously back in his element. During the winter he had made a beautiful new harpoon. Hour after hour he lovingly honed the leaf-shaped head—identical in size and shape to Stone Age spearheads—to a bright, razor-sharp edge. The picture of Trondur sitting hunched over his harpoon seemed to symbolize nothing so much as age-old Man the Hunter.

Sometimes we could see, seven miles above our heads, the silver dots of airliners flying between Europe and America, drawing their vapour trails across the sky. How, I wondered, would their passengers react, comfortably seated in their chairs with their plastic headsets and plastic meal trays, if they knew that far below them four men in a leather boat were crawling at less than two miles an hour across that innocent-looking ocean, largely dependent for their survival upon skills and materials that had not changed in a thousand years?

AFTER FOUR DAYS *Brendan* had progressed so sluggishly that we could still see the snowcapped peak of Snaefellsjökull through the clear nothern air. This clarity must have helped early voyagers. Norse shipmasters would sail west from Snaefellsjökull until the mountain sank below the horizon, and soon afterwards, if the weather was clear, they would be able to distinguish ahead of them the first peaks of Greenland. Along this track the distance between Iceland and Greenland is about two hundred and fifty miles, and the mountains at each end make perfect landmarks. On a fast passage the navigator might not be out of sight of land for more than a day or two.

The phenomenon known as the Arctic Mirage may have helped them still further. When a stable mass of clear air rests on a much colder surface, the optical properties of the air change the light and like a giant lens it can bend so that objects actually far beyond the normal horizon now appear much closer at hand. It is possible that Irish and Norse mariners venturing out from Iceland, or driven westward by gales, saw light reflected from Greenland's glaciers well beyond the normally visible limits of the horizon and suspected that land lay in that direction.

Our weather continued very mild. The sun shone brilliantly through the clear air and sank down in magnificent sunsets. Only the cutting edge of the wind reminded us that we were less than one hundred miles from the polar pack ice. Before emerging on watch it was wise to struggle first into cotton underwear, then a suit of woollen underclothes, then the heavy Faeroese underwear, two pairs of socks, trousers and shirt, two sweaters, and finally oilskins. Each of us produced his own choice of clothing, but Trondur outshone us all when he appeared in a magnificent furry Chinese beaver hat, its earflaps waving so that it was difficult to tell where the beaver fur left off and Trondur's luxuriant tangle of hair and beard began.

For safety's sake I tried to report *Brendan*'s position once each day to the shore radio stations, which passed the information on to the coast guard. Whenever the sky was clear, therefore, I took sextant readings. To set our course there was only one golden rule: keep sailing west, always west.

Friday the thirteenth of May proved to be our best day's progress to date. A breeze of force three or four out of the east pushed *Brendan* along for sixty miles. Now the weather, after a spectacular display of the Northern Lights, began to flex its muscles and behave more as if we were in the Far North. The wind swung to the southwest and built up ominous black thunder-clouds ahead. *Brendan* stopped in her tracks and began to shy sideways, northward, under an overcast sky and a steady drizzle.

Saint Brendan's day, May 16, was the last day of "normal" weather—thick overcast with occasional rain showers just short of turning into sleet. It was a stark contrast to our saint's day the previous year, when, nearly thirty degrees warmer, we had waited in Brandon Creek for our departure from Kerry. Now, in 1977, in the middle of the Greenland Sea, but more relaxed and experienced, we toasted the saint in Irish whiskey. "Ouch!" grunted Boots when he dipped his cup into the water for the washing up. "I'd say we'll see ice at any time."

"Cold, is it?" I asked.

"Freezing," he declared. "I wouldn't fancy my chances falling into that."

All day long the rain continued to come down, and despite the improvement in our living shelter, the water seeped in. Just before midnight the Icelandic coast guard's patrol ship *Thor* loomed out of the mist behind us. On Petur Sigurdsson's instructions she had come all the way to check our aircraft VHF radio, which was not giving a proper signal, and how *Thor* had managed to locate us in that gloom and swell we never learned. After an hour in which we tested the VHF set between the two vessels, *Thor* slid away into the darkness. She had come well off her normal patrol route, and I knew that henceforth *Brendan* had passed out from under the coast guard umbrella unless there was a dire emergency. Ahead of us lay only the bleak coast of Greenland, whose only permanent inhabitants in those latitudes were a tiny band of meteorologists at the small weather station of Tingmiarmuit. During the last few years the worsening ice had driven away even the Eskimos who had hunted along that inhospitable coast.

As if to underline my sense of foreboding, the barometer began to fall rapidly. George and I made ready. We dug out a tarpaulin and stretched it as tightly as possible over the waist of the boat. Two oars acted as a ridgepole and left a tunnel underneath the tarpaulin just big enough for a man to crawl into if he had to work the bilge pumps. The Irish monks carried leather tents and spare sheets of leather aboard their curraghs and presumably rigged themselves a similar shelter to throw off the breaking seas. Otherwise a severe gale would have sunk their boats.

Brendan, heavily laden for the long passage direct to North America, rode so low that as the wind and waves increased she heeled over and began to scoop water aboard. Bilge pumping became a regular chore, and when the watches changed Arthur and George climbed forward to reduce sail. We ate a hot stew of sausage, and waited for whatever the gale might bring.

The wind was too strong for *Brendan* to do anything but run away from it, and we were being driven farther north than I had planned. Ninety miles ahead, off the east coast of Greenland, lay the pack ice, which ran north and then curved east, sweeping back towards Iceland, so that we were being pushed into a great embayment of ice.

Our next radio contact was encouraging. My call was answered by the coast station at Prins Christianssund on the southern tip of Greenland. So *Brendan* was now, in radio terms, at the halfway point between Iceland and Greenland. The weather also gave us a brief respite, and we could prepare another hot meal. But soon the wind turned against us once more and picked up strength. For three days now we'd been struggling in circles. The huge swells came as great marching hills of water, heaped up higher than *Brendan*'s mainmast by the wind blowing counter to the main ocean current. If I was talking to George at the helm, it was disconcerting to see a great wall of water loom up behind and above his head, which would suddenly begin to lift against the backdrop as *Brendan* rose to the swell. Abruptly the skyline would appear, and all at once I could see the broad unfriendly vista of Atlantic rollers stretching all the way to Greenland before *Brendan* sank into the next trough and the grey-blue water closed in about us once again.

At 6:20 a.m. on May 20 we picked up a faint signal from Prins Christianssund which gave the weather forecast I had been dreading: a southwest gale of force nine (about 45 mph), precisely from the direction in which we were headed. Sure enough, within an hour we were struggling to lash down the mainsail. We left

309

only the tiny headsail up to draw us downwind and give the helmsman a chance to jockey the boat among the ever larger seas. We had left one precaution until almost too late; the heavy leeboard should have been taken in, for now the weight of water jammed it solidly against the hull. Each time the boat heeled to the pressure of the wind, the leading edge of the board dipped into the sea and, like a ploughshare, carved a great slice of water from the ocean and thrust it over the gunwale and into the bilges. In ten minutes we could feel *Brendan* growing more sluggish.

Clearing the leeboard was typical of the workaday chores aboard. Lurching and clumsy in our heavy clothing, George and I manhandled the unwieldy board into the boat. We knew that a single mis-step could send either of us sliding overboard, with no chance of survival in those chill waters. Next we tugged the tarpaulin into place to shoot off the breaking seas that leaped the gunwale. Ten minutes of pumping, and the water level in the bilge was down to a safer margin. Then it was time to pay out the main warps in loops from the stern to slow *Brendan* down. I was fearful that she would somersault if she went too fast down the face of a wave. Finally we poured whale oil into our oil bag, and dangled the bag from a short stern line. The streak of oil in our wake partly quenched the worst of the wave crests directly behind us, but it was all the helmsman could do to keep *Brendan* running directly downwind of the slick. Each wave swung the little boat out of control. In the next five hours of flight we squandered every mile of hard-earned progress from the previous day. And no end of the gale was in sight.

Arthur was off watch, asleep in the main shelter, when the first drenching took place. George was at the helm; I was crouched under the forward tarpaulin steadily pumping out water. As if in slow motion, I felt *Brendan* begin to tip forward, bows down. The boat seemed to hang there at a weird angle. Curious, I thought to myself, she usually levels off more quickly than this. Then George bellowed, "Pump! Pump as fast as you can!" and I heard the heavy onrush of water down the length of the boat. *Brendan* squirmed like a gaffed salmon and began to level off. Water bubbled and gushed up between the floorboards beneath me.

Frantically I redoubled the speed of pumping, and heard the *thump*, *thump*, *thump* as George briskly operated the pump near the helmsman. Trondur emerged from his shelter and crawled to the starboard midships pump. When the water level was under control, I climbed back and peered into the shelter. "A big wave broke over the stern," George explained. "It pushed in the rear flap of the shelter and poured in."

"Did it drown the radios?" I asked anxiously. I dabbed carefully at them with a dry cloth, then tentatively flicked on the power. To my relief they came to life. "I think I'd better put extra plastic bags around them in case we get pooped by another wave."

It was lucky I did so. When the watches changed. George and I crawled inside and lay down in our sleeping bags. We were half asleep when another solid sheet of water cascaded into the cabin. "Pump her! Quick, pump her! She's heavy!" somebody shouted. Frantically, George clawed out of his sleeping bag and raced out of the shelter, wearing only his underwear. In the same movement he scooped up his immersion suit. He zipped himself into it and swarmed forward to get to the bilge pumps. At the helm, Arthur was desperately wrestling with the steering paddle, trying to keep *Brendan* straight to the waves. Trondur, his oilskins glistening, was getting ready to bail with a saucepan.

Quickly I jotted our last estimated position, tore the leaf from the message pad, and stuffed it in my pocket. If *Brendan* filled and sank, our only chance was to broadcast a Mayday with an accurate position. Then I, too, clambered into my immersion suit and went forward to help pump. This was a full emergency.

Pump! Pump! Pump! We heaved back and forth at the pump handles, sending feeble little squirts of water back into the ocean. *Brendan* lay almost stopped dead and sluggish, while the water inside her swirled ominously back and forth. She was so low in the sea that even the smaller waves lapped over the gunwale and added more water to the bilges. It was a race against the distinctive rhythm of the sea. As I heaved frantically at the pump handle, I wondered if there was another wave waiting to break and fill her. Would she stay afloat? And what a godforsaken place for this emergency to happen—halfway between Iceland and

311

Greenland. What was it the experts had said? Survival time in this near-freezing water was five minutes or less.

The full strength of the Atlantic was showing itself. Whipped up by the gale racing all the way from Greenland, the waters were thrashing in wild frenzy. Here and there cross waves slid across the main wave direction and collided, bursting upward as though cannon shells were exploding.

Pump! Pump! Pump! It took forty-five minutes of nonstop work with *Brendan*'s pumps and Trondur's saucepan to reduce the water in the boat to a safer level. Then we could assess the damage. Structurally *Brendan* seemed as tight as ever. The steering frame was still in place, and the seams of stitching had held. It was easy to see where the wave had struck, at the unprotected flank of the boat, through the open gap beside the steering paddle. The metal cook box had taken the full brunt— one side was stove in and completely twisted.

Inside the cabin, everything at floor level was awash: sleeping bags, sheepskins, clothing. Only the radios and equipment perched above had been saved, together with the contents of our personal kit bags, which, thank heavens, had remained waterproof. Our spare clothes, at least, were dry.

George was shivering with cold and pulled on proper clothing at last. "I hope your theory is right," he muttered, "that body heat will dry out our sleeping bags." I concentrated on mopping up the puddles on the floor. After half an hour's work it was obvious we would have to be content with the glistening wet interior. Exhausted, George and I crawled back into our sleeping bags, trying to ignore the fact that we were drenched to the skin and that they lay clammy upon us. For nearly thirty-six hours we'd been working with scarcely any sleep.

Boom! Again a heavy wave came toppling over the stern, smashed aside the shelter door, and poured in, slopping over my face as I lay with my head towards the stern. In a split second the situation had returned to exactly where it had been before. Once again it was back to the pumps for an hour, hoping silently that another wave would not add to the damage while *Brendan* was vulnerable. Then back to the chore of mopping up.

I put out a radio call to try to report our position in case of disaster, but no one was listening. We were many miles off any shipping lanes, and with the radio's tuning unit drenched with water and waves overtopping the aerial I thought it was very doubtful that we were putting out a readable signal.

"We've got to do something about these big waves," I said. "We're exhausting ourselves pumping and working the boat."

But how? We needed some way of closing the large gap between the cabin and the helmsman's position, something extremely strong yet something we could erect at a moment's notice in the teeth of a gale.

Then I had it. Leather! Under the cabin floor lay a spare oxhide and several slightly smaller leather sheets intended as patches. Now they could be used to plug a far more dangerous hole in our defenses. Why hadn't I thought of them before?

I prised the leather sheets from beneath the cabin's deck boards. "Get a fistful of thongs," I told George. "I want to lace the hides together." He crawled forward. The leather sheets were stiff and unwieldy in the cold. So much the better, I thought; they'll be like armour plate.

Quickly I pointed out to Trondur what needed to be done. Immediately he grasped the principle and gave a quick grin of approval. Then he was off, knife in hand, scrambling up onto *Brendan's* unprotected stern. With one hand he held onto his treacherous perch, and with the other he worked on the leather sheets we passed up to him. Every now and then the roar of an oncoming breaker warned him to drop his work and hold on with both hands while *Brendan* bucked and shuddered. Meanwhile, Arthur, at the helm, kept *Brendan* as steady as he could, and George balancing on the port gunwale, pinned down each sheet of leather to prevent its being swept away by the gale. With the full power of his strong sculptor's hand, Trondur drove his knife point again and again through the quarter-inch-thick leather, twisted and sawed, and carved out neat hole after neat hole like a machine. It was an impressive display of strength. Then George fed the leather thongs through the holes and laced on the overlapping plates.

In less than fifteen minutes the job was done. A leather apron covered the larger part of *Brendan*'s open stern, leaving just enough room for the helmsman to stand upright, his torso projecting up through the apron.

Boom! Another breaker crashed over the stern, but this time it caromed off safely and poured harmlessly back into the Atlantic. The battle that night was won. Only a fraction as much water was now entering the bilges, and it was easily pumped out.

But poking up through his hole in the leather plating, the helmsman had a hard and bitter time of it. Facing aft and steering to ride the waves, he was battered achingly in the ribs by the sharp edge of the leather; meanwhile, the wind scoured his face and from time to time a breaker would flail his chest. Each man stayed only fifteen minutes at the helm before he had to be replaced, his hands and face numb in the biting cold.

But it was worth it. Even if we were losing the distance we had made, we had survived the encounter with our first major Greenland gale. We had made Brendan seaworthy with our own ingenuity and skills, using the same basic materials available to Saint Brendan and his sea-going Irish monks. It was cause for genuine satisfaction.

CHAPTER 11

By eight o'clock next morning the gale had eased enough for us to begin sorting out the jumbled mess in the cockpit. I could not raise contact with any shore station on the main radio, but that evening our signal was picked up by an Icelandic Airlines flight, whose pilot promptly relayed our position. That, at least, was one worry out of the way; the last thing I wanted was for our friends in the Icelandic Coast Guard to start searching for us on a false alarm.

Whether the mediaeval Irish seafarers had to endure such bleak conditions is doubtful. Most historians of climate agree that

314

between the fifth and eighth centuries the weather of the North Atlantic was often warmer than it is today, and storms less frequent. That may explain why the *Navigatio* had so little to say about bad weather. In general, Saint Brendan's curragh seems to have been troubled as much by calms as by gale-force winds. But there was one occasion when the weather took them by surprise: After their narrow escape from the hostile sea monster who attacked them, the travellers beached their curragh on an island. They were stranded there for three months by heavy rain and hailstorms. Some have suggested that this unseasonal bad weather indicates that the monks had landed in South Greenland, where the weather can be notoriously foul even in summer.

A more intriguing clue to the possibility that the Irish navigators landed in Greenland is to be found in the writings of its Norse discoverers, who reported coming across human habitations of stone, "both in the eastern and western parts of the country, and fragments of skin boats and stone implements". The only habitations other than tents known to have been used by the Greenland Eskimos were subterranean burrows; sometimes these burrows were roofed with skins, but they would certainly not be described as habitations of stone. The Irish monks, on the other hand, built stone cells all over the west coast of Ireland and in the Hebrides. As for the skin boats the Norsemen found, these were not likely to have been Eskimo kayaks, because the skin cover of a kayak will disintegrate if it is not regreased and looked after very carefully. By contrast, the oak-bark-tanned leather of the Irish curraghs could last for a very long time indeed.

Our modern weather luck, as we now struggled towards Greenland's coast, was causing me real anxiety. We were being pushed much farther north than I had anticipated. To clear the eighty-mile-wide shelf of pack ice striking out from South Greenland, *Brendan* needed to head southwest. So I decided to take a gamble; we would steer close to the ice, where the local wind often blows parallel to the edge, and where *Brendan* might find the wind she wanted so desperately. But the danger was obvious; if we were caught by an easterly gale, *Brendan* would be driven headlong into the pack ice.

I did not have to explain the risk to *Brendan*'s crew. They watched the pencil line on the chart, which showed us daily inching nearer the Greenland coast. Each man kept his own counsel, but it was clear that all appreciated the importance of every slight variation in the wind direction.

Foul weather continued to afflict us all the next week. When the air temperature hovered within a few degrees of freezing and the wind got up, the chill factor was harsh enough to restrict us to our damp sleeping bags as much as possible. Yet we remained remarkably cheerful, provided only that *Brendan* was making progress in the right direction. It was when she was stopped or was being driven back by headwinds that life became wearisome.

Each man reacted in his own way. As sailing master, George must have felt the most frustration, for with the wind against him—or no wind at all—there was little he could do to help us reach North America. Yet he never lost his meticulous sense of care for *Brendan*. He checked and rechecked the ropes for wear and re-adjusted lashings. With his army training he always left his sleeping bag neatly rolled, his gear carefully wrapped and stacked and out of harm's way. And one could set a clock by his well-regulated watchkeeping routine.

Arthur was the complete reverse—a rumpled, chaotic, easygoing shambles. Arthur's sleeping bag, when he was not in it, was usually serving as a squashed-up cushion. His stock of sweaters and scarves ran loose and turned up in strange places. It was a standing joke that Arthur never remembered a hat. Invariably he would lurch out of the shelter to begin his watch and a minute later pop his head back in with a plaintive, "I say, could you pass my cap, please? I'm not sure where it is, but it should be somewhere." Arthur always had the bad luck. If a sneak wave broke over the gunwale at mealtime, it was Arthur who was sitting in the wrong place so that he received the cold seawater down his neck or in his cup. When it began to rain heavily, it always seemed to do so just as Arthur started his watch. But with unwavering good nature he remained unruffled by his mishaps.

Trondur had spent so much time at sea in boats that he had developed his own brand of patience.

316

"When do you think the wind will change?" I would ask him.

Trondur would look at the sky, at the sea, and pause. "I say nothing," he would announce calmly, "sometime north wind." And when the weather was really atrocious, with driving rain, poor visibility, and an unpleasant, lumpy sea that had *Brendan* staggering, he would say, "Is not so bad. It can be worse than this in winter," and go about his work with such calm assurance that he raised the morale of all. Trondur always found something to keep himself busy. If he was not fishing for fulmar, he was sketching shipboard scenes or working over his drawings. The inside of his berth under the bow tarpaulin was a veritable artist's shelter. He had rigged up a fishnet hammock to hold his paper and pens, ink bottles, and pencils. Drawings and half-finished studies were hung up to dry.

On the whole, there was little idle conversation among the crew. Knowing there was much empty time ahead, we tended to dole out our thoughts and our comments little by little. But by and large each kept his opinions to himself, and in an old-fashioned way concentrated on running the boat. By unspoken agreement it seemed the best way of enduring our ordeal.

Sailing aboard *Brendan*, we were finding, was becoming a very personal experience despite the fact that it was also a shared adventure. The helmsman was often the only man to see the distant single spout of a whale, the sudden jump of a dolphin, or a changing pattern in the sky. Watchkeeping in a gale was perhaps the most personal experience of all, because then the helmsman was acutely aware that the lives of the other three depended on his skill. Every big wave brought a challenge which only he could judge and meet. Each wave successfully surmounted was a minor victory, only to be forgotten in the face of the next onrushing one.

Some moments, by contrast, were seared in the memory of the man concerned. On May 23 I was alone at the tiller, steering through yet another maelstrom as cliff after cliff of water rose up behind the boat. Almost casually I happened to glance over my shoulder to port and there, unannounced by the usual crashing white mane of foam, was a single maverick wave. It was not particularly high, a mere ten feet or so, but it was moving purposefully across the other waves, and now it reared nearly vertical along *Brendan*'s length. "Hang on!" I yelled at the top of my voice, and grabbed at the H-frame.

Brendan began to tip away from the face of the new wave. She leaned over and over until, on the lee side, I found myself looking almost straight down at the water and still hanging on to the upright of the H-frame. My God, I thought, she's going to capsize! She can't possibly hold this angle. Instead, *Brendan* began to slide sideways down the face of the wave.

The next instant the wave enfolded her in a great mass of water which poured across her like a deep, steady river. Seawater swept across the leather apron and plucked at my chest. Looking forward, I could see that *Brendan* was totally submerged. Only the mast could be seen, projecting from the water like a submarine's periscope. And like a submarine emerging, *Brendan* struggled up from the sea. The air trapped under the tarpaulin and in the shelter simply pulled her up; the water swirled off quietly, and she sailed on as if nothing had happened. The only casualty was my peace of mind. From my vantage point at the helm I knew exactly how close we had been to capsizing. When the watches changed again, I mentioned the rogue wave to Arthur. "Yes," he said. "Everything inside the cabin went an underwater green." And there, by tacit agreement, we left the subject. Such episodes seemed best left without discussion.

ONLY SEVENTY or eighty miles from the edge of the Greenland pack ice, we were at last rewarded with a break in the weather. On the morning of May 25 a much-needed calm succeeded the high winds. The calculated risk of running close to the ice edge paid off as in the afternoon the wind began to blow steadily from the northeast, and *Brendan* started to move parallel to the ice, heading towards Cape Farewell. For four days the wind stayed near gale force, but now it blew always out of the north or northeast, and *Brendan* fairly scampered along, helped by the East Greenland current, which pushed her an extra twenty or twenty-five miles a day. In the twenty-four hours of May 26 *Brendan* put one hundred and fifteen miles on the log, equalling her best day's run of the previous season. We were gradually using up our stores and water; that meant *Brendan* was nearly a third of a ton lighter, and she rode more easily.

Living conditions grew more basic every day. The contents of the cabin had been stripped down to essentials—there remained only our sleeping bags, a kit bag of clothes for each person, the radios, the sextant, a bag of books, and the cameras—nothing else. We were growing accustomed to living with permanently wet hair, wet shirt sleeves where the water oozed past the cuffs of our oilskins, wet socks, and wet sweaters. Fortunately no one suffered any illness; there were not even any cuts or sprains. The only problem was that Trondur's hands puffed up with fat red swelling on knuckles and fingers. He only shrugged and said it was a normal affliction for fishermen who handled nets and lines in cold water.

On May 29 *Brendan* at last cleared the tip of the ice ledge extending south from Cape Farewell, and we breathed more easily. We were now crossing the wide approaches to Davis Strait, which divides Greenland from North Labrador. Here, to our frustration, we came into an area of calms, light airs, and pea-soup fogs.

Tedium became our new enemy. Once or twice we glimpsed enough sun to make it worthwhile hanging the sleeping bags in the rigging and trying to dry out our clothes. To pass the time, there was a shipboard craze for fancy ropework, and *Brendan*'s rigging sprouted complicated knots and splices and intricate lashings. To add to the boredom, there was an increasing sense of remoteness brought about by the constant fog that limited our horizon, sometimes to no more than fifty yards. The only consolation was that in these desolate waters there was very little chance of being run down by a ship.

The voice of Prins Christianssund Radio grew fainter and fainter until finally it vanished entirely. We still could not make contact with the Canadian stations ahead of us. Above, we heard jetliners reporting their positions to air-traffic control, but they did not reply to *Brendan*'s calls and we seemed very alone.

On June 11 we picked up a Canadian Coast Guard advisory

signal giving *Brendan*'s description and announcing that as nothing had been heard from us for sixty hours, any vessels hearing our signals were to report to the coast guard. Frustratingly, we could not reply to the message ourselves because of heavy atmospheric interference. But on the following day a sudden improvement in conditions allowed both the Canadian and Greenland radio stations to pick up our position report. The Canadians advised us that the main pack ice was retreating steadily northward, and from the chart it looked as if *Brendan* would be clear of the Labrador ice. Only a week earlier the 8273-ton ferryboat *Carson*, built as an icebreaker, had hit ice on her first run of the season up to Goose Bay, about two hundred miles east of us, and sunk. Military helicopters had rescued her passengers from the ice floes without loss of life, but her sinking was a grim warning.

On June 13 we finally got a favourable wind, and *Brendan* ran up the miles all that afternoon and the following night. During the evening watch George mentioned that he was disappointed. "It seems a pity to have come all this way and never to have seen any ice," he said, "I don't expect I'll ever be up here again." Next morning at dawn he was making himself a cup of coffee when he called out in delight. "Hey! Ice! I do believe it's ice." There, floating by like some strange Chinese carnival dragon, was a queerly contorted chunk of ice, bobbing gently like a child's toy. We all lined up to watch. *Brendan* was beginning to slide past humps and bits of loose ice. They were extraordinarily beautiful, lurching and dipping. Occasionally pieces would split away, and then the whole chunk would revolve as its balance changed, spinning over to reveal some entirely new profile. All the while the constant surge and wash of the swell on the ice came to our ears as a low, muted roar.

Trondur beamed with pleasure. "Good," he said. "Now we see more birds and more whales. Near ice is good fishing."

I pointed away to the east. "Trondur, what is that white line over on the horizon? It looks like iceblink. Do you think there is pack ice in that direction?"

"Yes," he said. "There is much ice."

I was puzzled. According to the latest information, there should not be any ice in that direction. "I expect it's a big isolated raft of ice broken from the main part," I said confidently. "I expect we've come between the land and some stray drifting ice."

I was wrong. Unwittingly, I altered course to starboard to pass inside the ice "raft" and sailed down towards the iceblink. As we came closer, the ice edge became more definite. It was an awesome sight, made up of brilliant white floes jammed together. The large floes, made of ice from several years of freezing and from broken chunks of bergs, stood above the general level in strange sculptured shapes, some soft and round like melted butter, others grotesque and jagged. Smaller ice debris drifted along the main edge and into *Brendan*'s path. We wove our course between the floes, innocently admiring their shapes. One small floe was banana-shaped and was promptly dubbed the ice curragh.

Treacherously the wind began to shift into the northwest, and try as we might we could not prevent *Brendan* from sidling closer to the ice edge. The sun clouded over from time to time, and the pretty shapes looked less enticing. "The swell is really grinding the ice," George commented. "Look at that big, dark floe over there." He was pointing out a block of ice the size of a two-storey house. Each time the swell moved it, this chunk rose up ponderously, tilted, and then came smashing down on its dark underbelly so that the water gushed from the undercut edge. "It wouldn't be very pleasant if *Brendan* got driven under the edge of that one," I commented.

Steadily we glided past the ice edge, keeping it to port. Arthur was taking photographs, George was steering, and Trondur sat on the shelter roof gazing at the marvellous vista. In the distance we could distinguish the massive shapes of true bergs locked in the depths of the ice field. "I don't think we're going to clear the tail of the ice raft," said George in a worried tone. "What if we're just running ourselves into an ice bay? I can't see how we would get out without being crushed."

I glanced inquiringly at Trondur. "*Brendan* must find a hole in the ice," he said. "There is safe." Pulling out his pencil, he sketched what he meant—*Brendan* should try to find an open

321

patch within the body of the pack ice and lie there as if in a lagoon. But the ice edge was unbroken; there was no haven. Just at that moment George exclaimed, "A ship!"

She looked like a fishing boat. "I'm afraid she won't see us," I said. "White sails against white ice."

Suddenly George had a brain wave. "The signal mirror!" he exclaimed, and quickly dug out the little metal mirror.

Blink! Blink! Blink! We took it in turns to focus the sunlight on the distant ship. Blink! Blink! "She's turning! She's seen us!"

A quarter of an hour later the boat was almost within hailing distance. George peered through the binoculars. "Her name is *Svanur*, and hey! Trondur, I do believe she's a Faeroese boat." Trondur beamed with anticipation. He cupped his hands and bellowed a string of Faeroese across the water. His shout was greeted with a mass of waving arms from the boat's crewmen, who were lining the rail.

"One thing is sure," I said. "When they hear Faeroese coming from *Brendan*, they'll know it can only be Trondur Patursson."

In fact, the Faeroese fishing boat knew all about *Brendan*, not only from our visit the previous year, but also via the mysterious network of sea gossip which links the fishing boats and small freighters that ply the far North Atlantic. The voyage of the leather boat was a topic of conversation in the ports of Greenland and Iceland; and *Svanur* had just come down from Greenland, loaded with a cargo of shrimp for Gloucester, Massachusetts. Nevertheless, had it not been for the bright flash of the signal mirror, she would never have spotted *Brendan*.

Trondur pumped up our little rubber dinghy and paddled across to *Svanur*. After ten minutes he came back. "The captain says there is very heavy ice all ahead of *Brendan*. *Svanur* has been steaming six hours and could not find a way through it." If a well-built fishing boat designed for those waters was backing off the ice, then it was wise for *Brendan* to do the same. Trondur continued, "*Svanur*'s captain said if you want, he will pull *Brendan* around the corner of the ice where we can pick up the wind again."

"Please tell him that I accept his offer."

Trondur paddled back with a towline, and soon *Svanur* was plucking us out of danger. More Brendan Luck, I reflected. Doubtless we would have been able to work ourselves clear of the ice once the wind had changed, but in future I would be more wary. The pack could move faster than the ice patrol could keep track of it; next time, I promised myself, I would keep *Brendan* to seaward of it. I did not know how soon that promise would be broken.

I took only three hours for *Svanur* to pull *Brendan* out of her predicament. Trondur, who had stayed aboard *Svanur* for the tow, came back with a bag of frozen bread, a sack of potatoes, a supply of milk, and a great box of frozen shrimp.

"That's a splendid haul," I grunted, taking the box from Trondur's hands.

"Yes," he replied, "*Svanur*'s captain lives not so far from us, on the island of Hestor." Only the wandering Faeroese fishermen, I thought, could make so light of a chance meeting off the pack ice.

We were still busily stowing this welcome supplement to our rations when George exclaimed, "Good Lord—it's another ship!" Sure enough, rolling down from the north was the US Navy supply vessel *Mirfak*. "This place is like Piccadilly Circus," I said. "Two ships in a day. Everyone has to come around this corner en route to or from the Arctic."

Mirfak stopped about two hundred yards from *Brendan*. "What ship are you?" she asked by radio.

"*Brendan* out of Reykjavik and bound for North America."

There was a long pause. "Can I have that again?" came a puzzled voice.

"*Brendan*, out of Reykjavik and bound for North America. Our boat is an archeological experiment. She's made of leather, and testing whether Irish monks could have reached America before the Vikings."

"I had better take this down in writing," said *Mirfak*'s radio operator. "Where did you sail from?"

"Reykjavik. We've had pretty good weather this side of Greenland, but we took a battering between Iceland and Greenland."

"I should say so. Things can be pretty bad in this steel tub. I can't imagine what it's like in your little boat. Can we give you any help?"

"Some fresh vegetables and meat would be very welcome if you can spare any. We ran out of fresh food a little while back."

"That's easy."

I turned to George. "Your turn in the dinghy."

Ten minutes later he pulled back to *Brendan*, the dinghy low in the water. "I had to stop them," he puffed. "They gave me so much food it would have swamped the dinghy." Piled around his legs were sacks of oranges, apples, yet more milk, tins of coffee, slabs of meat. It was an incredibly generous haul.

"Look at that lot," said Arthur. "Marvellous. We ought to set up a corner shop here and trade with passing vessels. We'd never starve."

I made one more request. "Could you give us a position check, please?"

"Yes," came the reply, "we're getting a read-out from the satellite now."

That was a nice touch, I thought to myself—a sixth-century leather boat receiving her position from a twentieth-century navigation satellite. Then *Mirfak* was gone.

CHAPTER 12

We were now some sixteen hundred miles along our route from Iceland. Across the ice field lay Labrador, only two hundred miles away. The Canadian Coast Guard radio stations now arranged a special listening watch for us and on the afternoon of June 15 a small plane flew over the boat for five minutes and took pictures. By radio the plane warned us that large areas of pack ice lay to our south and west, but there was little to be done. *Brendan* was still becalmed.

At quarter past three the next morning, however, I was awakened by the sound of water sliding past the leather hull. That's odd, I thought to myself, *Brendan* is not heeling to the wind. I heard Trondur and George speaking softly, and became aware of some sort of commotion. Then I heard them moving back down the boat.

"What's up?" I asked.

"Oh, Trondur just lost a pilot whale he had harpooned," George replied casually.

Trondur had been on watch by himself when a large school of pilot whales surfaced around *Brendan*, splashing and puffing. Without bothering to wake up anyone, he clambered forward to his cabin, unshipped his harpoon, and scrambled up onto the very bows of the boat where he could get a clear throw. Awakened by the clambering, George got up, too, and emerged just as Trondur saw his chance—a pilot whale of the right size swimming near the boat.

Chunk! From a kneeling position on the bow Trondur tossed his harpoon three or four yards to starboard and made a clean hit. Immediately the animal dived. There was a tremendous flurry among its closely packed companion whales; the water churned as they thrashed in panic. The shaft of the harpoon snapped under the press of bodies, and then all the other whales were gone, leaving the stricken animal to its fate.

Fascinated, George watched as Trondur began to play the whale like a fisherman with a salmon on the end of a line. At first the thirty-foot harpoon line was pulled taut. Trondur had tied the free end to the foremast, and the harpooned whale began towing *Brendan* briskly along. If the whale had been any larger, this could have been dangerous, but Trondur had selected a whale about fifteen feet long, small enough to handle from *Brendan*. As his quarry grew tired, he began to haul in on the line, and the animal darted back and forth underneath the bows, trying to rid itself of the imbedded harpoon. Flashes of foam and phosphorescence rolled off its body and fins as it fought to escape. Inexorably, Trondur continued to haul in, but at the crucial moment, when the whale was right alongside the boat, the head of the harpoon pulled free. A second later the animal was gone.

"Harpoon too far back in whale," said Trondur, shaking his head sadly. "More forward and it would have been good."

I wondered to myself what on earth we would have done with a fifteen-foot pilot whale on *Brendan*. But Trondur the Hunter had done remarkably well to harpoon the animal in the dark. "Never mind," I said. "You picked a good whale. It was towing us in the right direction at a good two to three knots."

Our adventures and misadventures all seemed to be happening in the dark. On June 18 the barometer began to fall rapidly; so did the temperature. George and I took over the watch on a foul black night. Our only consolation was that *Brendan* was thrusting briskly through the murk, sailing at a good pace. Suddenly, about 3:00 a.m., there was a high-pitched, crackling sound, rather like stiff calico tearing.

"What on earth was that?" I exclaimed.

"I don't know," George replied. "I thought the sound came from the hull. Still, there's nothing we can do about it in the dark," and he settled back down on the thwart.

Crack! . . . *Crack!* . . . *Crack!* Something weird was happening. A strange snapping noise, this time much louder, was indeed coming from the hull. George was peering down into the darkness, trying to see a few yards.

"It's ice!" he suddenly shouted. "We're running into ice!" *Brendan* was hitting lumps of ice at speed, and they were swirling and bumping along her flanks so hard that they rattled and crackled along the oxhide skin.

"Drop the sails!" I yelled. "If we collide with heavy ice at this speed, we'll knock her to pieces. Our only chance is to stop and wait for daylight."

George moved into action, and I went forward to help him secure the sodden canvas. As we worked frantically, we felt under our feet *Brendan*'s hull shuddering softly against unseen obstacles. We hurried back to the helm and took out the two most powerful torches we had. Their beams penetrated only fifty yards through the spray and sleet, but they revealed a sight which brought the adrenalin racing. In place of the well-defined ice edge

326

we had seen a few days ago, there was now a nightmare jumble of ice monsters of every size and description, with channels of clear water opening and closing between them as the floes moved with the wind. I realized that the same northwest gale which had been spinning *Brendan* so happily on her way had swept over the main ice sheet and burst it open, spraying ice right into *Brendan*'s path like shrapnel.

This type of sea ice, known as Very Open Pack, would have presented no problems to a large ship, whose powerful engines would have been able to shoulder her forward. But how much of a battering would our leather hull withstand, I wondered, and what would happen if a couple of ice floes bumped together and *Brendan* were caught in the middle? Would she burst open like an overripe banana? And just how much sailing room was there among the floes which lay ahead? The devil of our situation was that there was no way to plan a strategy. For about an hour George and I tried to keep the boat out of trouble. Without her sails, *Brendan* was still moving through the pack ice at one or two knots, driven by the pressure of the wind on the masts and hull. But sail-less, *Brendan* was at her worst—slow to manoeuvre and able to turn only through a very small arc. If too much helm was applied, she merely drifted sideways, out of control.

"There's a big floe dead ahead," George warned. "Try to get round to port." I pulled the tiller over as far as it would go, but it was not enough.

"Get the foresail up!" I shouted. "We've got to have more steerage way." George clipped on his lifeline and crawled forward along the gunwale. Reaching the foremast, he heaved on the halyard to raise the sail. It jammed. A loose thong had caught in the collar that slid up and down the mast. With a shudder from the top of her mast to the skid under her, *Brendan* ran her bow into the great lump of sea ice. It was like hitting a lump of concrete. *Thump!* We struck again. *Thump!* Once more. Then slowly, ungracefully, *Brendan* began to pivot on her bow, wheeling away from the ice floe. It was like a car crash filmed in slow motion. *Thump!* The boat shivered again. We had a feeling of total helplessness. Only the wind could bring her clear. *Thump!*

This time the shock was not so fierce. *Brendan* was shifting. A scrape, and she was clear.

"Is she taking water?" George called back anxiously.

I glanced down at the floorboards. "No, not as far as I can see back here," I replied. "Try to clear the headsail. This is getting tricky."

Scarcely had I spoken than out of the dark just downwind of us loomed a massive floe, twice the size of *Brendan*, rolling and wallowing like an enormous log, one end pointing like a battering ram straight at us. George leaped up the foremast to try to clear the jammed sail.

"Hang on tight!" I bellowed at him as the swell gathered up *Brendan*. *Crack! Thump!* The impact flung George backwards from the mast. He's going to fall between *Brendan* and the floe, I thought, horrified. He'll be crushed. But George was still clutching the jammed halyard, and it brought him up short. For a heart-stopping moment he dangled backwards over the gap like a puppet on a string. Next, as the swell passed beneath us, *Brendan* swung over a wave-cut ledge projecting from the floe. The ledge rose under us, caught *Brendan* with a grating sound, and began to lift up and tip her. We're going to be flipped over like a fried egg, I thought, as *Brendan* heeled and heeled. Then, with another grating sound of leather on ice, our boat slid sideways off the ice and dropped back into the water.

Crash! The next collision was broadside, halfway down the boat's length. *Brendan* jostled forward another six feet, and it was obvious that the next blow would strike the steering paddle and snap its shaft. That would be the final problem; to be adrift in the pack ice with our steering gear smashed. Now the great floe was level with me where I stood at the tiller bar. The face of the floe stood taller than I, and in the light cast by my torch the ice gleamed and glowed deep within itself with an unearthly mixture of frost white, crystal, and emerald. From the waterline a fierce blue-white reflected up through the sea from the underwater ice ledge.

Here comes the last blow, I thought. I felt a wave lift the leather hull, saw the ice swing heavily towards me and—feeling slightly foolish—could think of nothing else to do but lean out with one arm, brace against the steering frame, put my hand on the ice floe and push with all my strength. To my astonishment, *Brendan* responded. The stern wagged away and forward from the ice wall, and instead of a full-blooded sideswipe we received a glancing blow that sent a shiver down the hull but left the steering paddle intact. One wave later the great floe was rolling and grumbling in our wake. It had been a very close call.

Trondur and Arthur were soon up and dressed in sweaters and oilskins, ready to help. I should have called them earlier, but their off-watch rest had seemed too precious. Now their assistance was needed, because I planned to try to get *Brendan* through the ice by increasing our speed. We might blunder into the consolidated pack ice and wreck the boat, but it was a risk we had to take. It was better than gyrating into loose floes and being broken up. "Boots! Trondur! Go forward by the foremast. We'll raise and lower the foresail as we need it, and trim the sail to port or starboard depending on the position of the bigger ice floes. George, could you act as lookout?"

As George called out the position of each floe, I called instructions to Boots and Trondur. "Up foresail!" "Down!" We slipped past a white shape of ice, ghostly in the dark. "Up foresail! Sheet to starboard!" and I hauled the tiller bar over so that *Brendan* slid past the next floe. It was a crazy icy toboggan run in the dark with a minimum of control, no way of stopping, no knowing what lay fifty yards ahead. Arthur and Trondur, standing one by each gunwale, had opened a gap in the tarpaulin, and the upper halves of their bodies poked out like the crew of an open-cockpit aeroplane from World War I. But the hoods of their oilskin jackets made them look more like monks in cowls, and the impression was heightened by the red-ringed cross on the foresail, which raised and lowered and bellied out with a thundering clap above their heads. Beyond them the eerie white shapes of the ice floes loomed out of the blackness of the night.

After three hours of this surrealist scene, dawn lightened the horizon. We were surrounded by pack ice. Off to one side was a huge, picture-postcard iceberg, a sleek monster with virgin white flanks sloping spectacularly to the ocean. But the berg was at least a mile away.

Our real troubles lay close around us, in the contorted shapes of the floes which had ambushed us in the night. Now there was enough light so we could avoid them. Surely the way ahead must be clear, I thought to myself. *Brendan* had shown her worth yet again. Her leather skin and hand-lashed frame had survived a battering. No more could be expected of her.

"Is there any water in her yet?" George asked again.

"No," I replied. "She came through like a warrior."

But my hopes were soon dashed. Ahead we began to discover mile upon mile of ice, floe after floe, oscillating and edging southward under the combined effects of the gale and the current. *Brendan* could neither hold her position nor retreat. Her only course was forward and sideways, hoping to move faster than the pack ice until eventually we outran it and emerged somewhere beyond its leading edge.

All that day we laboured on, trying to work our way diagonally across the pack and find its limits. *Brendan*'s ability to manoeuvre was so limited that virtually every floe had to be skirted on its leeward side. This meant sailing directly at the floe, putting over the helm at the last moment, and skidding around its lee. Our advance was a cross between dodg'em cars at a fairground and a country square dance, except that our dancing partners were curtseying leviathans of ice.

The strain on the crew was terrific. We tried to revert to our normal watchkeeping system but time after time every man had to be called into action—hauling and re-adjusting the sheets to alter the slant of our course, and, when the worst befell, leaning out to poke and prod with boat hooks to fend off the ice.

There was no time for proper meals. At noon Trondur cooked up a hot mush which we spooned down between emergencies, and there was just enough time for coffee later in the day.

Bump, slither, swing sideways, charge at the gap, don't think about the quarter-inch of leather between yourself and icy sea. Hour after hour the ordeal continued until by dusk, with the wind still blowing half a gale, the ice appeared to be thinning out.

And this time we really did seem to be nearing the edge of the pack.

Then the Brendan Luck finally ran out.

Two large floes swung together, closing a gap *Brendan* had already entered. The boat gave a peculiar shudder as the floes pinched her, a vaguely uncomfortable sensation soon forgotten in the problem of extricating her from the jaws of the vice. Luckily the two floes eased apart enough for *Brendan* to slip free, but five minutes later I heard water lapping next to the cooker and glanced down. Seawater was swirling over the floorboards. *Brendan* had been holed.

THERE WAS NO TIME to attend directly to the leak. The first priority was still to get clear of the pack ice while there was enough daylight to see a path. "One man on the bilge pump, one

TRONDUR PATURSSON

at the helm; one forward controlling the headsails; and the fourth at rest," I ordered, and for two more hours we worked *Brendan* clear of the pack until there was enough open water to run a fairly easy course and set the mainsail, double reefed. The man at the headsail could at last be spared, and after twenty-four hours of sustained effort we could revert to our normal two-man watch-keeping system.

"We can't tackle the leak tonight," I said, "but it's vital to learn more about it. I want each watch to work the bilge pump at regular intervals and record the number of strokes and the time it takes to empty the bilge. Then at least we will know if the leak is getting worse. If we've torn the stitching somewhere, more stitches may open."

"Ah well," said Arthur cheerily, "that's what the right arm is for—pumping. It's our watch, Trondur. I'd better get to work." And he crawled forward to the bilge pump.

Pump. Pump. Pump. It took thirty-five minutes of nonstop pumping to empty the bilge, and just fifteen minutes later the water level was as high as ever and threatening to get worse. Pump. Pump, Pump.

"How many strokes to empty her?" I asked.

"Two thousand," Arthur grunted as he collapsed, exhausted. That was within our physical limit, I calculated, but only temporarily; one man could steer while his partner pumped and kept *Brendan* afloat. But this system would work only while our strength lasted. If we ran into bad weather, and waves began once again to break into the boat, we could no longer keep emptying *Brendan* fast enough. The nearest land, two hundred miles away, was the thinly inhabited coast of Labrador, from which little help could be expected.

"We've got six hours before daylight," I said. "There's nothing for it but to husband our strength until dawn and then tackle the leak. It's best if one man in each watch keeps pumping continuously, turn and turn about. If we can keep the bilge empty, *Brendan* will ride lighter and take fewer waves on board."

That night was the most physically tiring of the entire voyage. It was difficult to rest or sleep properly. On watch one man stood for half an hour at the helm, then went forward to take over the pump; there was scarcely time to nod to one's partner as he struggled wearily back towards the helm. There, peering through the murk, one tried to decide whether the white flashes ahead were the manes of breaking waves or the telltale sign of a growler in *Brendan*'s path.

As soon as the first watch ended, I called the Canadian Coast Guard radio station at St. Anthony in Newfoundland and reported our situation and estimated position. "We are not in immediate danger. But could you please investigate the possibility of air-dropping to us a small motor pump, with fuel, in case we cannot contain the leak? I will call again at 14.15 hours GMT to report progress. If no contact is made at 14.15 hours or 16.15 hours, we may have activated an emergency locator transmitter on 121.5 and 243 megacycles. Over."

"Roger, Roger," replied the calm voice of the radio operator at St. Anthony. Later I learned that the Canadian Coast Guard responded unstintingly to our request for standby help. An aircraft was readied at Halifax, and the operations room at St. John's calculated that an icebreaker could reach us from Goose Bay in twenty-one hours. "But to be honest," said an officer who was on duty that night, "after the loss of the *Carson*, which sank in the same ice not many days before, we rated your chances of getting out as nil. How could a leather boat survive when a steel icebreaker went down?"

Partially relieved by the thought that if worst came to worst, we could call for help, I sat hunched in my sleeping bag and tried to concentrate. *Brendan* was leaking at a rate of over two thousand pump strokes an hour. This represented a sizeable leak, and obviously we had to track it down without delay at first light. And what then? I could not imagine how we would ever stitch on a patch underwater. The more I thought about our straits, the gloomier I felt. It seemed so futile if *Brendan* were to sink so close to the end of her mission. She had already proved to her crew that an early mediaeval Irish skin boat could sail across the Atlantic. But how could other people be expected to believe that if *Brendan* sank two hundred miles off Canada?

The situation did not become any more cheerful during that night. Driving rain reduced visibility to a few yards. All of us were desperately tired. The constant strain of bilge pumping battered mind and muscle. Squirm down the tunnel under the tarpaulin to reach the handle of the bilge pump. Grasp the handle with the right hand, lie on one's left side on top of the thwart, and pump four hundred to five hundred strokes. By then the muscles of the right arm and shoulder would be screaming for relief. So, reverse position laboriously, lie on the other ribs, and pump for as long as possible with the left arm. Then begin pumping all over again, until at last came the welcome sucking sound of the intake pipe, and you could begin the laborious return journey to the helm, arriving just in time to find that the water level had risen to exactly the same place as when you had started. Now it was the turn of your watch companion to empty the bilge.

The steady rhythm of the pump, the dark, wet tunnel, and the aching tiredness combined to produce a sense of detachment from one's surroundings. The feeling was heightened by the incongruously pretty little flashes of phosphorescence which slid overboard with every second or third wave crest, and dripped brilliantly down inside the boat's leather skin. The motion of rocking back and forth relentlessly at the pump handle was matched visually by a strange phosphorescent glow in the translucent bilge pipes, like a ghostly heartbeat.

At 6:00 a.m. dawn came, and I looked at the crew. They were haggard with exhaustion, but no one had the slightest thought of giving up. "Well, here's the battle plan," I explained. "Each man has a cup of coffee and a bite to eat. Then Trondur and Boots work on both pumps amidships to get the water level as low as possible and keep it there. This will allow George and me to work down the length of the boat and check the bilge for leaks."

The others looked very tough and confident, and utterly unperturbed. We had just eight hours, I reminded myself, to find and repair the leak before I should be in touch with the Canadian Coast Guard. I wondered where we should commence our hunt. Then, quite unconnected, a thought occurred to me. Last night, while pumping in the dark, the flashes of phosphorescence over the gunwale had been repeated almost simultaneously *inside* the boat and in the bilge-pump tube. The phosphoresence must have travelled from outside the hull to inside by a direct link—the leak.

I traced the line of the bilge pipe to its intake amidships on the port side. At that point I hung headfirst over the gunwale. There, just on the waterline, was the most encouraging sight of the day—a dent in the leather hull about the size and shape of large grapefruit. With growing excitement I scrambled back inside the hull and began shifting the food packs stored there. I saw the cause of our trouble: under tremendous pressure from outside, the leather had buckled inward into the gap between two wooden rigs and opened a tear about four inches long. The force had been so great that it had literally split the oxhide. The skin had not been cut or gashed; despite a tensile strength of two tons per square inch, it had simply burst. Now, whenever *Brendan* wallowed, a great gush of seawater spurted through the tear. A combination of the curve of the hull, the wider gap between the ribs at that point, and the nipping between the two floes must have driven a knob or sharp corner of ice through *Brendan*'s hull. By the same token, however, we also had room to wield a needle between the ribs.

"Great news!" I called. "I found the leak. And it's in a place where we can mend it." Then I went round the boat, hanging over the gunwale to see if there was any more damage. In fact, apart from that single puncture, the leather was still in excellent condition.

George and Trondur came forward. "The patch had better go on from the outside," I told them, "where the water pressure will help squeeze it against the hull. First we'll make a pattern, then cut the patch and stitch it in place."

"We must cut away some wood," suggested Trondur, examining ash ribs.

"Yes, whatever's needed to get at the work properly."

"I'm going to put on an immersion suit," George announced. "This is going to be a cold job."

He was right. He hung down over the gunwale, his face a few inches above the water, and held the patch in position. From

335

inside Trondur poked an awl through the hull and the patch, followed by a nine-inch-long needle and flax thread. With a pair of pliers, George tugged and pulled, and eventually hauled the needle through. Then he took over the awl, stabbed from the outside of the hull and groped around until he could poke in the tip of the needle; Trondur gathered it up from inside.

It was a miserable chore. Each time the boat rolled on a wave, George was lucky if he went into the water only up to his elbows. With the heaviest waves his head went right under, and he emerged spluttering and gasping. Each large wave then went on to break against the hull and drenched Trondur. The sea temperature was about zero degrees centigrade. All this after nearly two days without proper rest. But inch by inch the stitching progressed, a pancake of wool grease and fibre having been stuffed between the hull and the patch to serve as a seal. Then the last row of stitches went in. This row was completely underwater, and George had to use the handle of a hammer to drive the needle through.

Finally, after three hours, it was done. The two men straightened up, shivering with cold, and each had a well-earned tot of whiskey in a mug of coffee. Even Trondur was so exhausted that he went off to curl up in his sleeping bag. After Arthur pumped the bilge dry, scarcely a trickle came in through the mend. I inspected the patch.

"It's almost as neat and tidy as if you had put it on in the Crosshaven Boatyard and not in the Labrador Sea," I said. "John O'Connell would be proud of you."

"Well," George replied with quiet understatement, "that's a job I would not like to have to do again."

That afternoon I reported our success to the coast guard radio station. Then, for the first and only time in the entire voyage, we let *Brendan* look after herself. We dropped all sail, lashed the helm, and all four of us retreated to our sleeping bags for a few hours. My last thought before dropping off was that we had been able to repair *Brendan* because she was made of leather. If her hull had been made of brittle fibreglass or metal, or perhaps even of wood, she might well have been crushed by the ice.

CHAPTER 13

Neatly patched and safely clear of the pack ice, *Brendan* began the last lap of her voyage towards Newfoundland. We had been at sea for six weeks in our tiny boat and were feeling worn. Anxiously scanning the horizon for signs of land, we began to see logs floating in the water, occasional patches of weed, and an increase in birdlife. But *Brendan* seemed to be dragging herself forward with deliberate sloth.

There was plenty of time to reflect that ours was not the first Irish leather boat to have reached the fringes of the Arctic sea ice. The *Navigatio* says:

"One day . . . there appeared a column in the sea which did not seem to be far away. And yet it took them three days to get near it. When the Man of God had come near, he looked for the top, but could see very little because it was so high. . . . Moreover it was surrounded by an open-meshed net. The openings were so large that the boat was able to pass through the gaps. They did not know what the net was made of. It was silver in colour, but it seemed to be harder than marble. The column itself was of clearest crystal."

Stripped of the storyteller's imagery, the incident is not difficult to interpret. Icebergs are visible from very far off because of their size and colour, and because in clear weather they stand up from the horizon. Apparently Saint Brendan's crew failed to realize that the iceberg itself would be moving along with the current, perhaps at one or two knots, and this would greatly extend the time it took them to catch up. They then seem to have run into the ring of broken ice which often surrounds a major iceberg recently released from the pack. Probably the outer floes were of opaque sea ice in contrast to the pure-white glacier ice of the main berg.

337

The *Navigatio* continues:

The Man of God said, "Push the boat through a gap, that we may inspect the wonders of our Creator."

When they had gone in and looked here and there, the sea appeared to them to be as clear as glass, so that they could see everything down below. . . .

They then sailed all day along one side of the column and through its shadow could still feel the heat of the sun. All the time the Man of God kept measuring the one side. Seven hundred yards was the measurement.

From the geographer's point of view the iceberg is very important to the *Navigatio*, because it emphasizes that the main events of the voyage took place along a northerly trans-Atlantic route, and not, as has been suggested, along the easier southern route using the trade winds to the West Indies.

LIGHT AIRS and calms off Newfoundland also meant fog and mists. *Brendan* was now in one of the foggiest areas of the North Atlantic, and once again the *Navigatio* bore out the facts. According to the text, Saint Brendan went back to the Island of Sheep after seven years of fruitless voyaging and took on board sufficient stores for forty days and—very important—a pilot. The pilot was the steward who lived on the Island of Sheep. After forty days the boat came into a thick fog which enveloped her.

"Do you know what this fog is?" asked the steward.

"What?" replied Saint Brendan.

"This fog," the steward replied, "encircles the island for which you have been searching for seven years."

Three days of mist and low cloud had hidden the sun from *Brendan*, too, when on June 23 we picked up a radio message that the Canadian Coast Guard vessel *John Cabot* was hoping to rendezvous with us that day. Our little boat was being swept south by the Labrador Current, and without an accurate sun sight

338

my dead reckoning of our position was thirty miles off. So *John Cabot* found us quite by chance.

Captain Les Eavis came over in a rubber dinghy to see what life was like aboard *Brendan*. He was an old sailing-ship man himself, and *Brendan*'s rig intrigued him. "Well, you didn't need any help," he concluded. "It's nice to see that such things can still be done. Just let me know if there's anything we can let you have."

Before she steamed off, *John Cabot* left us with more fresh food, extra paraffin, and five pairs of dry socks from her first mate's wardrobe. Her visit had finally broken our sense of isolation. The weather held mild, with light winds which were so fickle, switching to all points of the compass, that *Brendan* closed erratically with the coast of Newfoundland. The weather would bring us to land when and where it chose.

One bright afternoon a pair of dolphins put on a superb display of acrobatics, leaping for sheer joy in head-to-head double arcs as if they were entertainers in an aquarium. During the night of June 25 we were able to distinguish very faint pinpricks of shore lights to the south of us, and when a dull grey morning broke, we began to make out the indistinct line of land ahead. Our noses confirmed the sighting. Wafted across the water by a gentle offshore breeze came the definite smell of pine trees from the great forests of Newfoundland. At last, and gradually, we began to accept the fact that we were certain to make landfall. The radio began to chatter with messages from coast guard radio stations. Two helicopters loaded with photographers clattered out and circled around us. Suddenly a pair of small coast guard boats came skimming over the water towards us. "There's a small fishing port three miles or so up the coast called Musgrave Harbour," shouted the coxwain of one of them as he roared up. "We can tow you in there if you like."

"No, thank you. First we want to land by ourselves," I called back. I checked the chart once again. Downwind of *Brendan* lay the small island chain known as the Outer Wadhams, uninhabited except for lighthouse keepers. The islands were an ideal spot for a quiet landfall; the nearest was called Peckford.

"Trondur, stand by to drop over an anchor. Boots, pull out an oar and get ready. We're going to make our touchdown."

George went forward to lower and stow *Brendan*'s little foresail for the last time. Under mainsail alone she crept towards the rock-ribbed shore. "Let go the anchor!" There was a splash as Trondur dropped it overboard.

"George, can you take a line onto land?"

Brendan eased forward, not with style or speed, but in the same matter-of-fact manner that she had crossed three and a half thousand miles of sea. The red-ringed cross on her mainsail began to sag as I eased the halyard a few feet to slow the boat even more. Arthur made a couple of dips at the water with his blade to keep the boat straight, and quietly, after fifty days at sea, *Brendan* nosed onto the rocks. George leaped. His feet splashed and touched ground. I thought, We've made it!

Brendan touched the New World at 8:00 p.m. on June 26, 1977. She had demonstrated without a shadow of a doubt that the voyage could be done with mediaeval material and mediaeval technology. There was no longer any practical objection to the idea that Irish monks might have sailed their leather boats to North America before the Norsemen, and long before Columbus.

Tim Severin

He has shaved off his *Brendan*-grown beard, but otherwise Tim Severin looks today about as one would expect an open-boat skipper to look. At thirty-seven he is tall and wiry, with sharp green eyes that miss nothing: he is soft-spoken, but has a decisive manner and an air of being *organized*: to keep track of appointments he carries two logbooks, one in his pocket, a larger one in his briefcase.

His interest in the history of exploration began in the late 1950s at Oxford. During one summer vacation, on a motor-cycle, he followed the route of a famous early explorer from Venice to China; the result was his first book, *Tracking Marco Polo*. For his second, *Explorers of the Mississippi*, he started out by canoe down the river from its source at Lake Itasca in Minnesota; the canoe broke up in rough water around St. Paul, but Severin eventually made it to the Gulf in an aged power-boat.

To help finance the building of the *Brendan*, he sold almost everything he owned, including his sailing dinghy and car; the *Brendan*'s bare hull alone cost nearly five thousand pounds to put into the water, even though the lumber and the tanned ox-hides were donated. But his financial sacrifice may prove worthwhile: the book has aroused enormous interest, and is being published in every western European country.

Severin admits there were times aboard the *Brendan* when he was really afraid. He thinks especially of a strong gale between Iceland and Newfoundland. "A couple of huge waves broke over the stern," he recalls, "and we were in danger of being swamped."

All that is behind him now. These days he and his wife Dorothy and their six-year-old daughter Ida, live peacefully in a rented house in London—Dorothy teaches Spanish literature at the University of London—or in their cottage by the sea in County Cork.

A STRANGER IS WATCHING

a condensation of the book by

Mary Higgins Clark

Illustrated by Steven H. Stroud
Published by Collins

It is Monday morning.
The stranger is watching the beautiful
woman on the television screen.
She is the writer Sharon Martin,
debating the issue of capital
punishment on TV with magazine
editor Steve Peterson.
Peterson's wife was found strangled
two years ago.
The stranger reviews his plan.
He will kidnap Sharon, and Steve's young
son, Neil, witness to his mother's
murder, and hide them in a
dungeonlike room in the depths of
the world's busiest railway terminal—
Grand Central Station. A ransom
demand . . . a time bomb set . . . an execution,
Wednesday, 11:30 am.
It is a perfect plan. It cannot fail . . .
A spine-tingling story that grips the reader
right up to the nightmare ending.

1

He sat perfectly still in front of the television set in room 932 of the Biltmore Hotel. The alarm had gone off at six o'clock, but he was awake long before that. The wind, cold and forbidding, rattled the windowpanes and that had been enough to pull him out of the uneasy sleep.

The *Today* show came on, but he didn't turn up the sound. He didn't care about the news. He just wanted to see the interview.

Shifting in the stiff-backed chair, he crossed and uncrossed his legs. He'd already showered and shaved and put on the green plaid polyester suit he'd worn when he checked in last night. The realization that the day had come at last made his hand tremble and he'd nicked his lip when he shaved. It bled a little and the salty taste of blood in his mouth made him gag.

He hated blood.

Last night at the desk in the lobby he'd seen the clerk's eyes sliding over his clothes. He'd carried his coat under his arm because he knew it looked shabby. But the suit was new; he'd saved up for it. Still the clerk looked at him like he was dirt and asked if he had a reservation.

He'd never checked into a real hotel before, but knew how to do it. "Yes, I have a reservation." He'd said it coldly and for a minute the clerk looked uncertain; but when he didn't have a credit card and offered to pay cash in advance, the sneer was back. "I will check out Wednesday morning," he told the clerk.

The room cost a hundred and forty dollars for the three nights. That meant he only had fifty dollars left. But that would be plenty, and by Wednesday he'd have eighty-two thousand dollars.

Her face floated across his mind. He blinked to force it away. Because, as always, the eyes, like great lamps, were watching him.

A commercial was ending. Suddenly interested, he reached out and twisted the volume knob. The interview should be next.

The familiar face of Tom Brokaw, the *Today* anchorman, filled the screen. Unsmiling, his voice subdued, he began to speak. "The restoration of capital punishment has become the most emotional and divisive issue in this country since the Vietnamese War. In just fifty-two hours, at eleven thirty a.m. on March twenty-fourth, the sixth execution this year will take place when nineteen-year-old Ronald Thompson dies in the electric chair. My guests . . ."

The camera dollied back to include the two people seated with Tom Brokaw. The broad-shouldered man facing him was in his early thirties. His sandy hair was streaked with gray and somewhat disheveled. His eyes were winter blue.

The young woman beside the interviewer sat stiffly erect. Her hair, the color of warm honey, was pulled back in a soft chignon. Her hands were knotted into fists in her lap. She moistened her lips and pushed back a strand of hair from her forehead.

Tom Brokaw said, "On their previous appearance here six months ago, our guests made strong cases supporting their opposing views. Sharon Martin, syndicated columnist, is the author of the best-selling book *The Crime of Capital Punishment*. Steven Peterson, editor of *Events* magazine, is one of the most articulate voices in the media to urge restoration of capital punishment."

His tone became brisk. He turned to Steve. "Mr. Peterson. After witnessing the emotional public reaction to the recent executions, do you still believe that your position is justified?"

Steve leaned forward. "Absolutely," he said.

The interviewer turned to his other guest. "Sharon Martin?"

Sharon was achingly tired. In the last month she'd worked

twenty hours a day, contacting senators, judges, humanitarians; speaking at colleges, at clubs; urging everyone to write the governor and protest Ronald Thompson's execution. The response had been overwhelming. She had been sure Governor Greene would reconsider. She found herself groping for words.

"I think," she said, "I *believe* that our country has taken a giant step backwards into the Dark Ages." She held up the newspapers at her side. "Just look at this morning's headlines. They're bloodthirsty. This one. 'Doomed Killer Protests Innocence,' and this, 'Nineteen-Year-Old Dies Wednesday.' They're all like that—sensational, savage!" Her voice broke.

Steve glanced at her swiftly. They'd just been told that Governor Greene was calling a press conference to announce her refusal to grant Thompson a stay of execution. The news had devastated Sharon. They never should have come on this show today. The governor's decision made Sharon's actions pointless, and God knows Steve didn't want to be here. But he had to say something.

"I think every decent human being deplores the need for the death penalty," he said. "But remember it has been applied only after exhaustive consideration of extenuating circumstances. There is no *mandatory* death sentence."

Brokaw then asked, "Do you believe that the fact that Ronald Thompson committed the murder only days after his seventeenth birthday, making him barely eligible for adult punishment, should have been considered?"

"As you know," Steve said, "I will not comment specifically on the Thompson case. It would be entirely inappropriate."

"I understand your concern, Mr. Peterson, but you had taken your position on this issue several years before—" He paused, then continued. "Before Ronald Thompson murdered your wife."

Ronald Thompson murdered your wife. After two and a half years, Steve could still feel surprise and outrage that Nina's life had been snuffed out by the intruder who came into their home, by the hands that had twisted her scarf around her throat.

Trying to blot the image from his mind, he looked directly ahead. "Long before the tragedy in my own family, I concluded that if we were to preserve the sanctuary of our homes, the freedom to come and go without fear, we had to stop the perpetrators of violence. Unfortunately the only way to stop potential murderers seems to be to threaten them with the same harsh judgment they mete out to their victims. And since the resumption of executions two years ago, the number of murders has dropped dramatically in major cities across the country."

Sharon leaned forward. "Don't you realize that forty-five percent of murders are committed by people under twenty-five, many of whom have tragic family backgrounds and a history of instability?"

The viewer in the Biltmore's room 932 studied the woman thoughtfully. This was the writer Steve was getting serious about. She wasn't at all like his wife. She was taller and had a slender athletic body. His wife had been small and doll-like with jet-black hair that curled around her forehead and ears.

Sharon's eyes, green mixed with blue, reminded him of the ocean that day last summer. He'd heard that Jones Beach was a good place to meet girls, but it hadn't worked out. The one he'd started to fool with in the water had called, "Bob!" and a minute later this guy was beside him, asking what his problem was.

What was Steve saying? Oh, yes, something about feeling sorry for the *victims*, not their murderers.

"My sympathies are with them too," Sharon cried. "But don't you see that life imprisonment would be punishment enough for the Ronald Thompsons of this world?" She forgot the television cameras as, once again, she tried to convince Steve. "How can you—who are so compassionate—want to play God?"

It was an argument that began and ended the same way it had six months ago when they'd met on this program. Finally Tom Brokaw said, "Can we sum up by saying that you still believe, Mr. Peterson, that the sharp drop in murder justifies execution?"

"I believe in the moral right—the duty—of society to protect itself, and of the government to protect the sacred liberty of its citizens."

"Sharon Martin." Brokaw turned quickly to her. "Your view?"

"I believe that the death penalty is senseless and brutalizing. I believe that we can make our homes safe by punishing violent offenders with swift, sure sentences, by building the necessary correctional institutions. I believe that our reverence for *all* life is the final test of us as individuals and as a society." ·

Tom Brokaw said hurriedly, "Thank you both for being with us on *Today*. I'll be back after this message. . . ."

THE TELEVISION set in room 932 of the Biltmore was snapped off. For a long time the muscular, thick-chested man sat staring at the darkened screen. Once again he reviewed his plan, the plan that would begin with putting the pictures and the suitcase in the secret room in Grand Central Station. The next step would be bringing Steve Peterson's son, Neil, there tonight. But now he had to decide. Sharon Martin was going to be at Steve's house this evening minding Neil until Steve got home. He'd planned to eliminate her there. But should he? She was so beautiful. When she looked into the camera, it had seemed that she was looking at *him*—as though she wanted him to come for her. Maybe she loved him.

If she didn't, it would be easy to get rid of her. He'd leave her in the room in Grand Central with the child on Wednesday morning. Then at 11:30 when the bomb went off, she, too, would be blown to bits.

THEY LEFT the studio together. Sharon's tweed cape felt heavy on her shoulders. Her hands and feet were icy. She pulled on her gloves carefully over the antique moonstone ring Steve had given her for Christmas. As they stepped into the windblown morning, it was beginning to snow, thick, clinging flakes. "I'll get you a cab," Steve said.

"No. I'd rather walk. It will help clear my head. Oh, Steve, how can you be so positive, so relentless?"

"Don't let's start again, dear." Steve looked down at her. Sharon's paleness became accentuated as snow melted on her cheeks. "Can you go home and get some rest?" he asked.

"I have to turn in my column."

"Well, try to get a few hours' sleep. You'll get up to my place about quarter of six?"

"Steve, I'm not sure."

"I am. The Lufts are going out for their anniversary, and I want to be in my home tonight with you and Neil."

Ignoring the people scurrying into the Rockefeller Center buildings, Steve put his hands on Sharon's face and lifted it. He said gravely, "I love you, Sharon. We've got to talk about us."

"Steve, we don't think alike. We . . ."

Bending down, he kissed her unyielding lips. He stepped back and signaled a passing cab. When it pulled over, he held the door for her. "Can I count on you for tonight?" he asked.

She nodded silently. Steve shut the door and watched the cab turn down Fifth Avenue. Then he quickly walked west. He had stayed overnight at a hotel because of having to be at the studio at 6:30, and was anxious to call Neil before he left for school. Every time Steve was away from home, he worried. Neil still had nightmares, still woke up with suffocating attacks of asthma. Mrs. Lufts always called the doctor quickly, but even so . . .

The winter had been so cold. Maybe in the spring, when Neil could get out more, he'd build up a bit. He looked so pale.

Spring! Today it was spring. During the night winter had officially ended. You'd never guess it from the weather.

Steve realized that he and Sharon had been seeing each other exactly six months now. When he'd picked her up at her apartment that first evening, she'd suggested walking through Central Park to the Tavern on the Green. He warned her that it had become much cooler in the last few hours and reminded her it was the first day of fall.

"Wonderful," she said. "I was just getting bored with summer." For the first few blocks they'd been almost silent. He studied the way she walked, easily in stride with him, her slender frame accentuated by the tawny gold suit that matched the color of her hair. He remembered the sharp breeze and the deep blue of the autumn sky.

That evening had been so good. They'd lingered over dinner, talking. Her father was an engineer for an oil company. She and her two sisters were born abroad. Both sisters were married.

"How have you escaped?" They both knew what he was really asking: Is there anyone important in your life?

But there wasn't. She'd traveled almost constantly for her last newspaper before she started writing the column. She didn't know where the seven years since college had vanished.

They walked back to her apartment holding hands. She invited him up for a nightcap. While he made drinks, she touched a match to the kindling in the fireplace and they sat watching the flames.

Steve could still remember vividly the way the fire threw shadows on her classic profile, highlighted her beautiful smile. He'd ached to put his arms around her then, but simply kissed her lightly when he left. "Saturday, if you're not busy . . . ?"

"I'm not busy."

And on the drive home, he'd known that the restless, ceaseless heart hunger of the last two years might be ending. . . .

It was 8:15 when he turned into the building on the Avenue of the Americas. The corridors were deserted. He nodded to the security guard at the elevator, then went up to his thirty-sixth-floor office and dialed his home.

Mrs. Lufts answered. "Oh, Neil's fine. He's just eating his breakfast. Neil, it's your dad."

Neil got on. "Hi, Dad, when are you coming home?"

"By eight thirty sure. I have a five-o'clock meeting. The Lufts still want to go to the movies, don't they?"

"I guess so."

"Sharon will be there before six so they can leave."

"I know. You told me." Neil's voice was noncommittal.

"Well, have a good day, son. And dress warmly. It's getting pretty cold. See you tonight."

"Bye, Dad."

Steve frowned. It was hard to remember that before Nina's death Neil had been such a vibrant, happy-go-lucky kid. He wished that Neil and Sharon would get closer. Sharon was trying to break through Neil's reserve, but he just wouldn't give an inch.

Time. Everything took time. Sighing, Steve reached for the editorial he had been working on the night before.

2

THE occupant of room 932 left the Biltmore at 9.30 a.m. and headed east on Forty-second Street. The sharp, snow-filled wind was hurrying pedestrians along, making them tuck their necks into upturned collars. It was good weather for him, the kind when people didn't notice what other people were doing.

His first stop was a thrift shop on Second Avenue below Thirty-fourth Street. He walked the fourteen blocks. Walking was good exercise, and it was important to keep in shape.

At the thrift shop, he went over to the rack with the women's coats. Pushing through the shabby garments, he selected a dark gray tent-shaped wool one that looked long enough. He saw a tray of folded kerchiefs, and reached for the largest, a faded bluish rectangle. The sales clerk stuffed his purchases into a shopping bag.

The Army-Navy store was next. He bought a large canvas duffle bag. In a First Avenue Woolworth's, he bought three boxes of surgical tape, six rolls of wide bandage, and two large spools of twine. He took his purchases back to the Biltmore.

Slipping the deadlock on the room door, he placed the shopping bags on the bed. With infinite care he lifted an old black double-locked suitcase from the closet and laid it on the foot of the bed. Extracting a key from his wallet, he opened the suitcase. He made a thorough check of the contents: the pictures, the powder, the clock, the wires, the fuses, the hunting knife, the gun. . . . Satisfied, he closed the bag again.

Carrying the suitcase and a shopping bag, he left the room. This time he went to the lower lobby of the Biltmore and took the stairway which led to Grand Central Station. The early morning commuter rush was over, but people were still scurrying to and from trains, quick-service restaurants, and newsstands.

He moved quickly down the stairs to the lower level of the station and drifted over toward track 112, where Mount Vernon trains arrived and departed. He made sure no guard was looking, and disappeared through the gate.

Down on the platform, he hurried around the U-shaped space at the end of the tracks. He made his way past sewer pipes to a sloping ramp that led into the depths of the terminal. His movements became quicker, furtive. Overhead, the station was bustling with the comings and goings of travelers. Here in this poorly lighted area the sounds were different: the throbbing of a pneumatic pump, the rumbling of ventilating fans, the trickle of water. Starved cats slithered in and out of the darkened tunnel under Park Avenue.

He continued down the ramp to the foot of an iron staircase and hurried silently up the steps. On the small landing was a heavy metal door. Carefully depositing the suitcase and bag, he fished for the key in his wallet. Nervously he inserted the key. The lock yielded reluctantly and the door swung open.

Inside, it was pitch-black. The musty smell was overwhelming. The intruder brought in the suitcase and shopping bag and let the door close noiselessly. The sounds of the station were only faintly discernible. It was all right.

He fumbled for the light switch and the room became gloomy bright. Dusty fluorescent lamps glared from the ceiling, casting deep shadows in the corners. The room was L-shaped, with layers of gray paint hanging in jagged flaps from the walls. Two ancient laundry tubs were to the left of the door. Dripping faucets had streaked their insides with rust. In the middle of the room, tightly nailed boards entombed a chimneylike dumbwaiter shaft. A door at the right was ajar, revealing a grimy toilet. He knew it worked. He'd come into this room last week for the first time in over twenty years and checked the lights and plumbing.

Against the far wall was a rickety canvas cot, an orange crate next to it. Obviously someone else, sometime, had stumbled onto this room and stayed in it. But the stale dampness could only mean the room had been unopened for months, maybe years.

Until last week, he hadn't been here since he was sixteen, more than half a lifetime ago, when this room was used by the Oyster Bar. Located directly below the Oyster Bar kitchen, the old dumbwaiter used to bring mounds of greasy dishes to be washed in the deep sinks and dried and sent back upstairs. Then dishwashing machines had been installed in the Oyster Bar kitchen and this room was sealed off. But it could still serve a purpose.

When he'd pondered where he could keep Peterson's son until the ransom was paid, he'd remembered this room. When he'd been working here, with his hands swollen from detergents and scalding water, all through the terminal well-dressed people had been rushing home to their expensive houses, or sitting in the restaurant eating the shrimp and clams and oysters he'd have to scrape off their plates, never caring about him at all.

He'd make everyone in Grand Central, in New York, *in the world* notice him. After Wednesday they'd never forget him.

It had been simple to get into this room. He'd found a key in his collection that fitted the rusty lock.

Tonight Sharon Martin and the boy would be here with him. Grand Central Station. The world's busiest railroad terminal. The best place in the world to hide people. He laughed aloud. The peeling walls and sagging cot and leaking water excited him.

Here he was the master, the planner. He'd get his money. He'd close the eyes forever. He couldn't stand dreaming about them.

Eleven thirty Wednesday morning was exactly forty-eight hours away. He'd be on a plane leaving for Arizona, where no one knew him. It wasn't safe for him in Carley. But he'd be safe out there, with the money—and the eyes gone—and if Sharon Martin was in love with him, he'd take her along.

He carefully laid the suitcase on the floor. Opening it, he removed a tiny cassette recorder and camera and put them in the deep left-hand pocket of his shapeless brown coat. The hunting knife and gun went into the right-hand pocket. No bulges showed.

He picked up the shopping bag and arranged its contents on the cot. The coat, scarf, twine, tape, and bandages he stuffed into the duffel bag. Finally he reached for the enlarged photographs. His eyes lingered on them. He smiled.

The first three he hung on the wall, over the cot, securing them with surgical tape. The fourth he studied and carefully put away again. Not yet, he decided.

Time was passing. He turned out the light before opening the door a few inches. He listened intently, but there were no footsteps in the area.

Slipping out, he locked the door and noiselessly descended the metal steps and hurried past the yawning tunnel, up the ramp, around the Mount Vernon tracks, up the steps to the lower level of the station. There he became part of the flow of people, a muscular, barrel-chested man in his thirties, with a stiff, straight carriage, puffy, high-cheekboned face with compressed lips, and pale eyes that darted from side to side. He hurried to the gate on the upper level where the train was leaving for Carley.

NEIL stood on the corner waiting for the school bus. He knew Mrs. Lufts was watching him from the window. He hated that. None of his friends' mothers watched them like Mrs. Lufts did. You'd think he was a kindergarten baby instead of a first grader.

Sandy Parker was in the fourth grade. He got on the bus at this stop too. He always wanted to sit next to Neil. Neil wished that he wouldn't. Sandy always talked about things Neil didn't want to talk about.

Just as Neil climbed on the bus, Sandy came puffing up. Neil headed for a single seat, but Sandy said, "Neil, here are two."

Sandy was bursting with excitement. They'd barely sat down when he said, "We saw your father on the *Today* show."

"My father?" Neil shook his head. "You're kidding."

"No, I'm not. That lady I met at your house was on it too, Sharon Martin. They were arguing."

"Why?" Neil was never sure if he should believe Sandy.

"Because she doesn't believe in killing bad guys and your father does. My dad said that your dad's right. He said that man who killed your mother should *fry*."

Neil turned to the window. He leaned his forehead against the cool glass. Outside, it looked so gray and it was starting to snow. He wished his dad had been home last night. He didn't like being just with the Lufts. They were nice to him, but they argued a lot and Mr. Lufts went out to the bar and Mrs. Lufts was mad even though she tried not to show it in front of him.

"Aren't you glad they're going to kill Ronald Thompson on Wednesday?" Sandy persisted.

" I . . . I don't think about it," Neil said in a low voice.

That wasn't true. He did think about it a lot. He dreamed about that night all the time too. He was playing with his trains up in his room. It was just getting dark out. Mommy was in the kitchen putting away the shopping. One of his trains jumped the track and he switched off the power.

Then he heard the funny sound, like a scream but not a loud scream. He'd run downstairs. The living room was almost dark, but he'd seen her. Mommy, trying to push someone back. She was making awful, choking sounds. The man was twisting something around her neck.

Neil had stood on the landing. He wanted to help her, but he couldn't move. He wanted to shout for help, but he couldn't make his voice work. He started to breathe like Mommy, funny, gurgly sounds, then his knees went all crumbly. The man turned when he heard him and let Mommy fall.

Neil could feel himself falling too. Then the room got brighter. Mommy was lying on the floor. The man was kneeling beside her now; his hands were all over her throat. He looked at Neil before he got up and started to run, but Neil could see his face, all sweaty and scared.

Neil had had to tell all that to the policemen and point out the man at the trial. Then Daddy said try to forget it. Just think of all the happy times with Mommy. But he couldn't forget. He kept dreaming about it and he'd wake up with asthma.

Now maybe Daddy was going to marry Sharon. And Mr. and Mrs. Lufts kept talking about moving to Florida. Neil wondered if Daddy would give him to the Lufts if he got married again. He hoped not. Miserably he stared out the bus window.

THE cab dropped Sharon at the *News Dispatch* building on East Forty-second Street. She went directly to the newsroom, which was already busy with preparations for the afternoon edition. There was a note in her box to see the city editor immediately.

357

She hurried to his small, cluttered office.

He waved her to a seat. "Got your column for today?"

"Yes."

"Any reference to contacting Governor Greene?"

"Certainly. We've still got forty-eight hours."

"Forget it."

Sharon stared. "What do you mean, forget it? You've been right with me all through this."

"I said forget it. The governor called the old man and said that we were deliberately creating sensationalism to sell papers. She said that she doesn't believe in capital punishment either, but she has no right to interfere with Thompson's sentence without new evidence. She said it was our right to campaign to amend the constitution and she'd help us every step of the way, but to pressure her to interfere in one particular case had the effect of trying to apply justice capriciously. The old man ended up agreeing with her."

Sharon felt her stomach twist as though she'd been kicked. Pressing her lips together, she tried to swallow over the constriction in her throat. The editor looked at her closely. "You all right, Sharon? You look pale. Better take a few days off."

"I'm all right."

"File your column and go home. I'm sorry, Sharon. But I can understand the governor's position."

Sharon said, "I understand that legalized murder is not to be protested anymore except in the abstract." Abruptly she got up and left the room.

At her desk, she reached into her shoulder bag and pulled out the article she had worked on most of the night. She tore it into pieces, put a fresh sheet of paper in the typewriter, and began to write. "Society is again about to exercise its recently regained prerogative, the right to kill. Four hundred years ago the French philosopher Montaigne wrote, 'The horror of one man killing another makes me fear the horror of killing him.'

"If you agree that capital punishment should be outlawed . . ."

She wrote steadily for two hours. When she had completed the column, she turned it in, left the building, and took a cab to her apartment on West Ninety-fifth Street.

Riding through Central Park, Sharon watched snow flurries settle over the grass. If this kept up, by tomorrow children would be sledding here. Just last month she and Steve had gone skating at Wollman Rink in the park. Neil was supposed to have come with them. But at the last minute he said he didn't feel well and stayed home. He didn't like her, that was apparent.

As Sharon let herself into the garden apartment in the renovated brownstone, it was obvious to her that Angie, her two-mornings-a-week cleaning woman, had just left. There was a faint smell of lemon polish; the fireplace had been swept, the plants trimmed and watered. As always the apartment offered a restful welcome. Her grandmother's Oriental rug had mellowed into soft shades of blue and red. She'd reupholstered in blue the secondhand couch and chair, a labor of love that had taken four weekends but turned out well. The pictures on the walls she'd selected one by one, in small antique shops, at auctions, on trips abroad.

Steve loved this room. "You have a way with a home," he'd said.

Mechanically she walked into the bedroom and began to undress. She'd try to sleep awhile before driving up to Carley.

It was nearly noon when she got into bed and set the alarm for 3:30. Sleep wouldn't come. She'd been so *sure* the governor would commute Ronald Thompson's sentence. There was no question that he was guilty, but except for an episode when he was fifteen, his record was good. And he was so *young*.

Steve. It was people like Steve who were molding public opinion. His reputation for integrity, for fair play, made people listen to him. Did she love Steve? Yes. Very, very much.

Did she want to marry him? They were going to have to talk about that tonight. Steve wanted so much for Neil to accept her. But Neil was so standoffish, so rejecting. Was it that he didn't like her, or would he react the same way to any woman who took his father's attention from him? She wasn't sure.

Did she want to live in Carley? She loved New York so much. But Steve would never agree to move Neil to the city.

She was just beginning to make it as a writer. Her book was in its sixth printing. Was this the time to get involved in marriage?

Steve. Unconsciously she touched her face, remembering the feeling of those big, gentle hands warming it as he said good-by to her this morning. They were desperately attracted to each other. But how could she accept the uncompromising, stubborn side of him when he made up his mind on an issue?

Finally she dozed off. Almost immediately she began to dream. She was writing a column, but no matter how frantically she pressed the typewriter keys, no impressions were being made on the paper. Then Steve was in the room. He was pulling a young man by the arm. Steve made the boy sit down. "I am so sorry," he kept saying to him, "but it is necessary." Then Steve fastened the boy's arms and legs in shackles and reached for a switch.

Sharon was awakened by the sound of a hoarse voice, her own, shrieking, "No . . . no . . . no!"

3

AT 5:55 the few people in the streets of Carley were hurrying to their cars, heedless of anything except the bitter, snowy night.

The man standing in the shadows near the Cabin Restaurant parking lot was completely unobserved. His eyes constantly roved the area as pelting snow blew in his face. He'd been there twenty minutes and his feet were freezing. Impatiently he shifted and his toe touched the duffel bag at his feet. He felt for the weapons in his coat pocket, and nodded.

The Lufts should be along any minute. He'd phoned the restaurant and confirmed their six-o'clock reservation. After dinner they were planning to see *Gone With the Wind,* which was playing in the Carley Square Theater across the street. The afternoon performance was on now. They were going to the 7:30 show.

He stiffened. A car was turning into the lot. It was their station wagon. He watched as they parked near the restaurant entrance, then waited till they were safely inside before picking up the duffel bag. He cut across the street and hurried behind the movie house.

There were about fifty cars in that lot. He headed toward an old dark brown Chevrolet sedan in the far right corner.

In an instant he had the door unlocked. He slipped into the seat, put the key in the ignition and turned it. The engine purred. With a slight smile he drove into the quiet street. Four minutes later the sedan pulled into the circular driveway of the Peterson home on Driftwood Lane and parked behind a small red Vega.

THE DRIVE from Manhattan to Carley took nearly an hour and a half because of the icy parkways. But Sharon was unaware of the delay. All the way up, she rehearsed what she would say to Steve. "It won't work for us. We don't think alike. . . . Neil will never accept me. . . . It will be easier if we don't see each other again."

Steve's house, a white clapboard colonial with black shutters, vaguely depressed Sharon. The porch light was too bright, the foundation shrubbery too high. She knew that Steve and Nina had lived in this house only a few weeks before her death and that he hadn't done any of the renovating they had planned.

Sharon parked just past the front steps and braced herself for Mrs. Lufts' rapid-fire greeting and Neil's coolness. But this would be the last time. That thought deepened her depression.

Mrs. Lufts had obviously been watching for her. The front door was yanked open as she got out of her Vega. "Miss Martin, it's nice to see you." Mrs. Lufts' stocky frame filled the doorway. Her small-featured face was squirrellike with bright, inquisitive eyes. She was wearing a red plaid coat and boots.

"How are you, Mrs. Lufts?" Sharon had barely enough room to squeeze past her into the house.

"It's awfully nice of you to come," Mrs. Lufts said. "Here, let me take your cape. I love capes. Make you look sweet and feminine, don't you think?"

Sharon set her pocketbook and overnight bag down in the foyer. "I guess so. I've never really thought about it." She glanced into the living room. "Oh . . ."

Neil was sitting cross-legged on the carpet, magazines scattered around him, a pair of blunt scissors in his hand. His sandy hair,

361

exactly the shade of Steve's, fell over his forehead. His bony shoulders stuck out under a brown-and-white flannel shirt. His face looked thin and pale except for the red streaks around the enormous brown eyes that were welling with tears.

"Neil, say hello to Sharon," Mrs. Lufts commanded.

He looked up listlessly. "Hello, Sharon." His voice was quivering, and he seemed so woebegone. Sharon ached to put her arms around him but knew that if she did, he'd only pull away.

Mrs. Lufts made a clicking sound with her tongue. "I'll be blessed if I know what the trouble is. Just started crying. Won't tell me why." Her voice rose an octave. "*Billllllll . . .*"

Sharon jumped, her eardrums ringing. Hastily she went into the living room. "What are you cutting out?" she asked Neil.

"Just some dumb pictures with animals, for school." Neil did not look at her. She knew he was embarrassed to be seen crying.

"Why don't I get myself a sherry and then give you a hand? Want a Coke or something?"

"No." Neil hesitated, then added, "Thank you."

"Just make yourself at home," Mrs. Lufts said. "I got everything on the list Mr. Peterson left, steak and salad makings and asparagus and ice cream. I'm sorry to be rushing, but we want to have dinner before the movie. Bill!"

"I'm coming, Dora." There was annoyance in the voice. Bill Lufts came up the stairway from the basement. "Just making sure the windows are locked. Hello, Miss Martin."

"How are you, Mr. Lufts?" He was a short, thick-necked man in his mid-sixties with watery blue eyes. Tiny broken capillaries formed telltale patches on his cheeks and nostrils, reminding Sharon that Steve was worried about Bill Lufts' drinking.

"Bill, get a move on, will you?" His wife's voice was edged with impatience. "The only time you take me out is our anniversary, seems to me, and I do think you could hurry."

"All right. All right." Bill sighed heavily.

"Have a good time." Sharon followed them to the foyer. "And happy anniversary."

"Wear a hat, Bill. What? Oh, thank you, Miss Martin. Neil, show your report card to Sharon. He's a real bright boy, aren't you, Neil? I gave him a snack earlier, but he hardly touched it. Don't eat enough to keep a bird alive. All right, Bill."

They were finally off. Sharon went back to the kitchen, opened the refrigerator, and reached for the bottle of Bristol cream sherry. She hesitated, then took out a carton of milk. Neil said he didn't want anything, but she was going to make him some cocoa.

While she waited for the milk to heat, she poured the sherry and glanced about. There were crumbs on the counter. The top of the stove needed a good scrubbing. Really the whole house could use a face-lifting.

Steve's property backed onto Long Island Sound. I'd cut all those trees that block the view, Sharon thought, and enclose the back porch— Sharply she checked herself. It was none of her business.

It was not for her to change. The thought of not seeing Steve again filled her with loneliness. This is how it feels to know you have to give up someone, she thought. How does Mrs. Thompson feel, knowing that her only child will die day after tomorrow?

She knew Mrs. Thompson's number. She'd interviewed her when she got involved in Ron's case. That poor woman. She'd been so hopeful when Sharon visited her, then seemed so upset that Sharon didn't think Ron was innocent. But what mother could believe her son capable of murder? Maybe it would help her just to talk with someone who had worked to save Ronald. Sharon lowered the flame under the saucepan, went to the wall phone, and dialed the number. Mrs. Thompson answered on the first ring.

"Mrs. Thompson, this is Sharon Martin. I had to call to tell you how sorry I am, to ask if there's anything I can do."

"You've done enough, Miss Martin." The bitterness in the woman's voice stunned Sharon. "If my boy dies Wednesday, I want you to know that I hold you responsible."

"Mrs. Thompson, I don't know what you mean."

"In all your columns, you have written that there was no question of Ronald's guilt but that that wasn't the issue. It *is* the issue, Miss Martin!" The woman was screaming. "It *is* the issue. Many people know my boy is incapable of hurting anyone. They were working to get him clemency. But you've forced the governor not to examine his case on its own merits. If my son dies, I don't think I'll be responsible for what I might do to you."

The connection was broken. Bewildered, Sharon stared at the receiver in her hand.

The milk was almost boiling in the saucepan. Mechanically she scooped powdered cocoa into a mug. She poured the milk in, stirred it, and started for the living room. The chimes at the front door sounded.

Neil scrambled for the door. "Maybe it's my dad."

Sharon heard him click the double lock with a sense of alarm. "Neil, ask who it is. Your dad would have his key." Hastily she set down the cocoa and sherry on a table near the fireplace.

Neil obeyed her and called, "Who is it?"

"Is Bill Lufts there?" a voice asked. "I have the generator he ordered for Mr. Peterson's boat."

"It's all right," Neil told Sharon. "Mr. Lufts is waiting for that."

He was starting to pull the door open when it was pushed in with violent force, slamming Neil against the wall. Stunned, Sharon watched a man step into the foyer and with lightning quickness close the door behind him. Gasping, Neil fell to the floor. Instinctively Sharon ran to him. She helped him to his feet and, keeping one arm around him, faced the intruder.

Two distinct impressions burned into her consciousness. One was the glittering stare in the stranger's eyes. The other was the long-barreled pistol he was pointing at her head.

"What do you want?" she whispered. Within the crook of her arm she could feel the violent trembling of Neil's body.

"You're Sharon Martin." The voice was a monotone.

Sharon felt a pulse pounding in her throat. There was a persistent soft whistle in Neil's breathing; suppose he was frightened into one of his asthma attacks? She would offer cooperation. "I have about ninety dollars in my purse. . . ."

"Shut up."

The evenly spoken words chilled her. The stranger dropped the large khaki duffel bag he was carrying. He pulled out a ball of

364

twine and a roll of bandage. "Take these. Blindfold the boy and tie him up," he ordered.

"No! I won't."

"You'd better!"

Sharon looked down at Neil. He was staring at the man. His eyes were cloudy, the pupils enormous. How could she help him?

"Sit down!" the intruder ordered Neil.

The child looked beseechingly at Sharon, then obediently sat on the bottom step of the staircase.

Sharon knelt beside him. "Neil, don't be afraid. I'm with you." She opened the bandage and wound it around his eyes.

The stranger was staring at Neil. "Now tie up the boy, Sharon." There was an intimacy about the intruder's command.

Fumbling with the twine, she tied Neil's wrists together, trying to leave the bindings loose enough to allow for circulation.

The stranger cut the twine with a knife. "Hurry up. Tie his feet!"

Quickly she obeyed. Neil's legs were trembling, jerking apart. She wound the twine around his ankles and knotted it.

"Gag him!"

"He'll choke; he has asthma. . . ." The protest died on her lips. The man's face was different somehow, whiter, strained. He was near panic. Desperately she bound Neil's mouth, leaving the gag as loose as she dared. If only Neil didn't struggle . . .

A hand shoved her. She toppled over. The man's knee dug into her back. He pulled her arms behind her. She felt the twine biting her wrists. She opened her mouth to protest, felt a wad of gauze stuffed into it. He yanked a strip of gauze over her mouth and cheeks, knotted it at the back of her head.

She couldn't breathe. Hands slid over her thighs, lingered. Her legs were pulled together; twine cut through the soft leather boots. She was being lifted. What was he going to do to her?

The front door was opened. Cold, wet air stung her face. It was so dark. He had turned off the outside lights. Her shoulders struck something cold, metallic. Then the grating sound of a car door opening. Sharon felt herself falling. Her elbows and ankles took the force of the jolt as she hit the floor. She was in the back of a car.

She heard crunching footsteps retreating. The man must be returning to the house. What would he do to Neil? Sharon tried to wrench her hands free. Pain shot through her wrists and arms. She thought of the way the intruder had stared at Neil.

Minutes passed. Please, dear God . . . Footsteps crunched toward the car. She heard the front right door opening. He must be carrying the canvas bag. Oh, God, Neil was in that bag! She knew it.

He dropped the bag on the floor. Sharon heard the dull thud. He'll hurt Neil. The door closed. Next the driver's door opened, clicked shut. He was looming over her, looking down.

Sharon felt something fall on her, a coat. She jerked her head, trying to free her face from the acrid smell of stale perspiration. The engine started. The car began to move.

Concentrate on directions. The police would want to know. The car was turning left onto the street. It was so cold. Sharon shivered and the cords dug tighter. Stop moving! Be calm. Don't panic.

Snow. If it was still snowing, there might be tracks for a while. But no. There was too much sleet mixed in with the snow. She could hear it on the windows.

The gag was choking her. Breathe slowly through the nostrils. Neil. How could he breathe inside that bag?

The car picked up speed.

ROGER PERRY stared out the window of his living room on Driftwood Lane at the rapidly falling snow. It was a rotten night and it was good to be home. Funny, all day a sense of apprehension had been making him edgy. Glenda hadn't looked well for a couple of weeks. He always teased her that she grew better-looking with every birthday. Her hair, now pure silver, strikingly accentuated her cornflower-blue eyes and lovely complexion. But this morning, when he'd brought coffee to her in bed, he noticed how deadly pale and thin her face looked. He'd phoned the doctor from the office, and they'd agreed that the execution Wednesday must be weighing on her mind. Her testimony had helped convict the Thompson boy.

Roger shook his head. Glenda had had a coronary right after

she testified at the trial. Roger pushed back the fear that another attack might kill her. She was only fifty-eight. Now that their boys were raised, he wanted these years with her. He couldn't do without her. He was glad that she'd finally agreed to hire a daily housekeeper. Mrs. Vogler was to start in the morning and work weekdays from nine till one. That way Glenda could rest more.

Glenda came into the room. She handed him a bourbon old-fashioned and stood companionably beside him at the window.

"Thank you, dear." He noticed that she was sipping a Coke. If Glenda didn't have a predinner cocktail, it meant only one thing. "Chest pains today?"

"Just a few."

"How many nitros did you take?"

"Only a couple. Don't worry. . . . Oh, look at Steve's house! The outside lights are off."

"That's why it seemed so dark to me," Roger said. "I'm positive the lights were on when I came home."

"I wonder why anyone would turn them off." Glenda's voice was troubled. "Maybe you should take a walk over there."

"Oh, I'm sure there's a simple explanation, dear."

She sighed. "I suppose. But what happened has been on my mind so much— Roger, look! There's a car pulling out of Steve's driveway with no headlights!"

"Now you just stop worrying and sit down." Roger's tone was firm. "I'll get some cheese."

Glenda reached into the pocket of her long quilted skirt and pulled out her glasses. Slipping them on, she stared at the dark outline of the quiet house across the road. The car was disappearing down the block into the swirling snow.

4

THE meeting in the conference room of *Events* magazine lasted until 7:10 p.m. The subject was a just released survey. Two out of three of those contacted in the twenty-five to forty age bracket preferred *Events* to *Time* or *Newsweek*. Besides that, the paid circulation was fifteen percent over that of the previous year.

Bradley Robertson, the publisher, stood up. "I think we can all take a great deal of pride in these statistics," he said. "It's not easy to launch a new magazine these days, and I want to say that the creative direction of Steve Peterson the past three years has been the decisive factor in our success."

Riding down in the elevator with the publisher, Steve said, "Thanks, Brad. That was very generous of you."

The older man shrugged. "It was true, Steve. We'll all start making decent money soon. I know it hasn't been easy for you."

Steve smiled grimly. "No, it hasn't." The elevator door opened in the main lobby. "Good night, Brad. I'm going to run. I want to catch the seven-thirty . . ."

"My car's outside. I'll drop you at Grand Central."

Once inside Bradley's limousine, Steve leaned back and sighed.

"You look tired," Bradley said. "This Thompson execution must be getting to you."

Steve shrugged. "It is. Every paper is rehashing Nina's death. I worry how much Neil is hearing in school. I'm desperately sorry for Thompson's mother—and for him too."

"Why don't you take Neil away for a few days?"

"I might do that. It probably would be a good idea."

The car pulled up to the Vanderbilt Avenue entrance of Grand Central. Brad shook his head. "You're too young to remember, but during the 1930s, Grand Central was the hub of transportation in this country. There was even a radio series—'Grand Central Station . . . crossroads of a million private lives.'"

Steve laughed. "Then along came the jet age." He opened the car door. "Thanks for the lift."

Steve walked quickly down into the terminal. He had five minutes till train time and decided to phone home to tell Sharon he was definitely making the 7:30 train. He stepped up to a pay phone and made the call. The phone rang once . . . twice . . . three times. After the fifth ring, he redialed the number.

Still no answer. Where could they be? Suppose Neil had had an asthma attack and had been rushed to the hospital again.

It was 7:29. If he tried to phone the doctor or the hospital or the Perrys, he'd miss his train and wait forty-five minutes for the next one. Replacing the phone on the hook, he raced to the gate. He reached the train as the doors were closing.

At that instant a man and woman passed near the phone he had just abandoned. The woman was wearing a long gray coat. Her head was covered with a kerchief. The man's arm was through hers. Under his other arm he carried a heavy duffel bag.

"AFTER all, tomorrow is another day," Scarlett O'Hara murmured, and the music rose to a crescendo as the picture on the screen dissolved into a long view of Tara.

Marian Vogler sighed as the houselights went up. They didn't make pictures like that anymore. She got to her feet reluctantly. Time to come down to earth. Her pleasant, freckle-spattered face slipped back into worried lines as she walked out of the theater.

The kids all need new clothes, she thought. Oh, well, at least Jim had agreed that she could start that housekeeping job tomorrow. She'd have the kids off to school before driving to the Perrys'. She was a little nervous. She hadn't worked in twelve years.

She emerged from the warm theater into the biting cold. The car was in the parking lot behind the theater. Thank God they'd decided to have it fixed. It was eight years old, but, as Jim said, better to spend the four hundred dollars to get it shipshape than use the same money to buy another man's troubles.

Expectantly she hurried into the parking area. Jim had promised to have supper ready and she was hungry. He'd said, "I'll take care of the kids. Enjoy yourself, Babe, and forget the bills."

His words echoed in Marian's ears as she slowed and frowned. She was sure that she'd parked the car over here. She remembered that she'd been able to see the ad in the bank window: "We want to say *yes* to your loan." She could see the bank window, lighted up now, the ad prominent even through the snow.

Ten minutes later Marian called Jim from the police station. Choking back the despairing tears, she sobbed, "Jim . . . No, I'm all right, but some *creep* stole our car."

As HE DROVE through the thickening snow, he reviewed his time-table. The woman would miss this car soon, and start screaming for the police. By the time they put out a radio bulletin, he'd be far away from the local cops.

To have Sharon Martin in his possession! Excitement made his skin glisten. He remembered the rush of warmth he felt when he tied her up. She had acted scared when he carried her to the car, but he was sure she deliberately nuzzled her head against him.

He was behind schedule. The other drivers on the Hutchinson River Parkway were crawling along. Fools. Afraid of slippery roads, afraid to take a chance, delaying him. He took the Cross County to the Henry Hudson Parkway. The pulse in his cheek started to throb. He'd expected to go through the terminal by 7:00, before the commuter rush was over, so they'd be less noticeable. It was 7:10 when he exited from the West Side Highway and turned into a driveway near Tenth Avenue that wound behind a warehouse. There were no guards here.

Stopping the car, he turned off the lights and got out. He opened the back door and lifted the coat he'd thrown over Sharon. He felt her eyes blazing up at him. Laughing softly, he pulled out a tiny camera and snapped her picture. The sudden flash made her blink. Then he grabbed her shoulders and forced her to lie on her stomach. Quick strokes of the knife sliced the cords on her ankles and wrists.

"Now I'm going to take that gag off, Sharon," he whispered. "If one scream comes out of you, the boy dies. Understand?"

He cut the knotted bandage at the back of her head. Sharon spat out the wad of gauze. "Please," she said. "Neil will suffocate."

"That's up to you." The stranger pulled her from the car and stood her up. She felt snow on her face. She was so dizzy. The muscles in her arms and legs were cramped.

"Put this on." The voice was different now, urgent. She reached out, felt rough material, the coat that he'd thrown over her. She raised her arm. The man pulled the coat around her and thrust her other arm inside.

"Put this scarf on!" It felt dirty. It was so big, woolly. Somehow her fingers managed to knot it under her chin.

"Get back in the car. The faster we move, the faster the boy has that gag off." Roughly he pushed her into the front seat. The khaki bag was on the floor. Leaning down, she ran her hands over the bag, felt Neil's head. "Neil, I'm here. We'll be all right."

Did she feel him moving? Oh, God, don't let him strangle. The stranger got in the driver's seat and started the engine. The car moved cautiously into the street.

They were in midtown Manhattan! The realization helped Sharon to focus. She had to do whatever this man ordered.

They stopped for a red light at the Avenue of the Americas. A patrol car drew up beside them. Sharon watched the young driver glance out the window and their eyes locked. She kept her eyes directly on him, willing him to sense something wrong.

She felt a sharp prodding against her side and looked down. The stranger had the knife in his hand. "If we get followed now, you get it first," he said. "Then the boy."

There was icy matter-of-factness in his tone. The car began to move. The patrol car was directly behind them. Its dome light began flashing. Its siren began blasting. "No! Please . . ." In a burst of speed the patrol car passed them and disappeared.

They turned down Fifth Avenue and made a left onto Forty-fourth Street. Where was he taking them? Forty-fourth wasn't a through street. It was blocked by Grand Central Station. The stranger drove two blocks to Vanderbilt Avenue and turned right. He parked near the Biltmore Hotel, opposite the terminal.

"We're going into the terminal," he said, his voice low. "Walk next to me. Don't try anything. I'll be carrying the bag, and if anybody pays any attention to us, the boy gets the knife." His eyes were glittering. The pulse in his cheek throbbed. "Understand?"

She nodded. Could Neil hear him?

He pushed open his door and stepped out. The street was almost deserted. He's taking us on a train, Sharon thought. We'll be miles away before anyone even begins to look for us!

She became aware of a stinging in her left hand. The antique moonstone ring Steve had given her for Christmas—the raised setting had cut her when her hands were tied. Quickly Sharon slipped

371

the ring off. She just had time to force it down in back of the seat before the door on her side opened.

Unsteadily she stepped onto the slippery sidewalk. The man gripped her wrist, leaned into the car, and picked up the gag and the cords he had cut when releasing her. Sharon held her breath. But he didn't notice the ring.

He bent down and picked up Neil; Neil, who still had the gag on. Neil, who might already be suffocated inside that bag. "Come on!" His hand was at her elbow. He was forcing her to walk with him across the street—a man and woman, anonymous in their cheap clothes, with duffel bag instead of suitcase.

Inside the brightly lit terminal, they stood overlooking the main concourse. The huge Kodak display opposite caught Sharon's eye. It read, "Capture beauty where you find it."

A hysterical laugh threatened to escape her lips. *Capture?* The clock in the middle of the terminal said 7:29. *Steve was catching the 7:30.* He was here right now—in a train that in a minute would be taking him away. Steve! She wanted to shriek . . . Steve!

Steely fingers bit into her arm. "Down here." He was forcing her onto the stairs. Should she try to fall—draw attention to them? No. She couldn't take the chance, not with that burly arm encircling the duffel bag, and that hidden knife so near Neil.

Now they were on the lower level. Over to the right was the entrance to the Oyster Bar. Last month she and Steve had sat at the counter and had steaming bowls of oyster stew. Steve, find us, help us. . . .

She was being pushed toward the left. "We're going down there." Track 112. The sign said MOUNT VERNON—8:10.

Near the gate, Sharon saw a shabby old woman carrying a shopping bag. She was bundled in a man's jacket over a ragged woolen skirt. Thick cotton stockings drooped on her legs. The woman was staring at her. Did she realize something was wrong?

"Keep moving. . . ." They were going down to track 112. The warmth of the terminal was vanquished by a clammy, cold draft. The platform was deserted.

"Around here." He was forcing her to move faster, around the

end of the platform where the tracks terminated, down another ramp. Water was trickling nearby. She heard a rhythmic throbbing sound, a pump. They were in the depths of the terminal. What was he going to do to them? The ramp widened into an area half the size of a football field. To the left, about twenty feet, was a narrow staircase with a railing.

"Over there—hurry up!" His breath was coming in harsh gasps. She scrambled up the stairs to a landing and a metal door.

"Move over." He set down the duffel bag. In the dim light she saw beads of perspiration on his forehead. He turned a key in the lock, pushed the door open, and thrust her inside. She heard him grunt as he picked up the duffel bag. The door closed behind them. He snapped a switch, and fluorescent lights blinked on.

Sharon looked around the filthy room, at rusty sinks, a boarded-up shaft, a sagging cot, an old suitcase on the floor. "Where are we? What do you want with us?" Her voice was a near whisper.

Her abductor didn't answer. Pushing her forward, he hurried toward the cot, laid the duffel bag on it. Sharon dropped to her knees and fumbled with the drawstring. Pulling it apart, she reached for the small, crumpled figure. Frantically she tugged at Neil's gag, pulling it down over his chin.

Neil gasped, clawing for air. She heard the wheeze in his breath. Supporting his head with her arm, she tugged at the blindfold.

"Let that alone!"

"Please," she cried, "he's having an asthma attack. Help him."

She looked up, then bit her lips to force back a scream.

Over the cot, three enormous pictures were taped to the wall.

A young woman running, hands outstretched, looking back over her shoulder, terror stamped on her face.

A blond woman lying by a car, her legs jackknifed under her.

A dark-haired teenager with one hand raised to her throat, a look of puzzled detachment settling into her staring eyes.

YEARS ago Lally had been a schoolteacher in Nebraska. Finally retired, alone, she had come to New York. She never went home.

The night she'd arrived in Grand Central Station was the turning point. Bewildered and awed, she'd carried her suitcase across the enormous concourse, looked up, and stopped. She was one of the few to realize that the sky on the vaulted ceiling had been painted backward. The eastern stars were in the west.

She'd laughed aloud. People glanced her way, then hurried along. Their reaction had delighted her. At home, if Lally were seen laughing by herself, it would be all over town the next day.

She checked her suitcase in a locker, and washed up in the ladies' room, smoothing her shapeless wool skirt, buttoning the thick cardigan sweater. Finally she combed the short gray hair, plastering it damply around her broad, chinless face.

For the next six hours Lally had toured the terminal, taking a childish delight in the bustling crowds. She ate at a counter in a cheap lunch stand, window-shopped in the corridors leading to the hotels, and finally returned to the main waiting room.

The crowds swelled and thinned again. It was nearly midnight when she noticed that one group had stayed a long time—six men and a tiny, birdlike woman, who were talking with an easy camaraderie. The woman noticed her watching them and came over. "You new here?" Her voice was raspy but kind.

"Yes," she said.

"Got any place to go?"

Lally had a reservation at the Y, but some instinct made her lie. "No."

"Well, don't worry. We'll show you around. We're the regulars." Her arm jerked backward toward the group.

"You live near here, then?" Lally asked.

A smile quirked the woman's eyes, revealed decaying teeth. "No, we live *here*. I'm Rosie Bidwell."

In all her cheerless sixty-two years Lally had never had a close friend. Rosie Bidwell changed that. Soon Lally was accepted as one of the regulars. She got rid of the suitcase and, like Rosie, kept all her possessions in shopping bags. She learned the routine— dawdling over cheap meals in the Automat, showers in a public bathhouse, sleeping in flophouses.

Or—in her own room in Grand Central.

That was one secret Lally kept from Rosie. A tireless explorer, she'd become familiar with every inch of her terminal. She climbed the stairs behind the platforms and wandered around the cavernous area between the floor of the upper level and the ceiling of the lower level. She even walked along the tracks of the tunnel under Park Avenue, flattening herself against the wall when a train thundered by and sharing scraps of food with the prowling cats.

She was especially fascinated by the area in the depths of the terminal that the guards called Sing Sing. With its pumps and vents and air shafts and generators creaking and groaning, it was like the very heartbeat of her station. The unmarked door at the head of a narrow staircase in Sing Sing intrigued her. Cautiously she'd mentioned it to one of the security guards, who became a friend. Rusty said that was only the miserable hole where they used to wash dishes for the Oyster Bar and she had no business there. But she'd worn him down until he took her to see the room.

She'd been delighted with it. The musty, peeling walls and ceiling didn't bother her at all. The lights and water worked. She'd known immediately that this place would fill her one remaining need, for occasional, absolute privacy.

"Room and bath," she said. "Rusty, let me sleep here."

"No way! It'd cost me my job." But she'd worn him down on that too, and every once in a while he'd let her spend a night there. Then one day she borrowed his key and secretly had another one made. When Rusty retired, she made the room her own.

Little by little, Lally carried objects up the steps—a dilapidated canvas cot, an orange crate. She began to stay there regularly. That was what she liked best, to sleep in the womblike darkness, in the very depth of her station, to hear the rumble of trains.

She never used her room during the winter. It was too cold and damp. But from May till September she stayed there about twice a week, just infrequently enough so the cops didn't catch her, so Rosie didn't get curious.

Six years passed, the best of Lally's life. She came to know the guards, the paper vendors, the countermen. She even recognized commuters, knew which ones took which trains, at what time.

That Monday evening Lally suddenly felt she couldn't wait any longer to see her room. It had been six months now. Maybe, if it wasn't too cold, she'd even sleep there tonight.

She walked heavily down to the lower terminal. Carefully she moseyed around, watching for policemen. She couldn't take a chance on being spotted going to the room. She was about to drift down to track 112 when her attention was caught by a tattered, scarlet lining drooping below a gray coat.

Lally recognized the coat. She'd tried it on in a Second Avenue thrift shop the week before. There couldn't be two like that, not with that lining. Her curiosity piqued, she studied the face of the woman wearing the coat and was surprised to see how young and pretty she was behind the big scarf.

The man with her was someone Lally had seen around the station lately. Lally noticed the girl's expensive-looking leather boots.

Funny combination, she thought. A thrift coat and those boots. The duffel bag the man was carrying seemed heavy. She frowned when she saw them go down to track 112. There wouldn't be a train for thirty minutes. Why wait on the cold, damp platform?

She shrugged. That settled that. She couldn't go to her room with them on the platform to see her. She'd have to wait until tomorrow.

5

"TALK, Ron, talk, please!" The dark-haired attorney depressed the "record" button. The cassette player was on the bunk between the two seated young men.

"No!" Ron Thompson got up, walked restlessly across the narrow cell. "What good?" The nineteen-year-old's lip quivered. Quickly he brushed a hand across his eyes. "Bob, you did your best. But there's nothing anyone can do now."

Bob Kurner stood up and put his hands on the boy's shoulders. "Nothing except give the governor a reason why she should grant executive clemency, even a stay."

"But you've tried. That writer Sharon Martin—if she couldn't, with all the important signatures she got . . ."

"Damn Sharon Martin!" Kurner clenched his hands. "She loused you up, Ron. We had a *real* petition going, people who know you're incapable of hurting anyone, and she goes screaming all over that of course you're guilty but you shouldn't die. She made it *impossible* for the governor to commute your sentence."

"Then why waste your time if it's hopeless? I don't want to talk about it anymore!"

"You've got to!" Bob's voice softened as he looked into the younger man's eyes. There was a compelling honesty in them. Ron had been planning to go to college; instead he was going to die in the electric chair. Even the two years in prison hadn't made his muscular body flabby. Ron exercised regularly in his cell, but he'd lost twenty pounds and his face was chalk white.

"Look," Bob said, "you *didn't* kill Nina Peterson. If we can just find one piece of evidence to take to the governor, one valid reason to make it possible for her to grant you a stay . . . We've only got forty-two hours."

"You just said she won't commute my sentence."

Bob snapped off the cassette player. "Ron, listen to me. When you were convicted of Nina Peterson's murder, a lot of people felt that you were guilty of committing those two other unsolved murders. You went to school with the Carfolli girl. You'd shoveled snow for Mrs. Weiss. Then after you were arrested there weren't any more murders—*till now.* Ron, two more young women have been murdered in this county in the last month. If we can just come up with something that might suggest a link between Nina Peterson's death and the others . . .

"Ron, I know how lousy this is for you. But you've told me how often you go over that day in your mind. Maybe there's something that didn't seem important, some detail. If you'd just *talk.*"

Ron walked over to the bunk and sat down. He depressed the "record" button. Frowning in concentration, he began to speak.

"I was working after school in Timberly's Market. Mr. Timberly had just told me that he was going to fire me because of the time I needed off for baseball practice. Mrs. Peterson heard him. When I helped her with her groceries, she said . . ."

THE TRAIN PULLED into the Carley station at nine o'clock, forty minutes late. By then Steve's frantic impatience had settled into deep, gnawing worry. Something was wrong. He felt it.

But maybe it was the execution coming up that had him so rattled. Tonight's paper had Nina's picture on the front page, Thompson's picture next to hers. A nice-looking kid. Hard to believe him capable of cold-blooded murder.

Over and over on the train ride, Steve found himself staring at Nina's picture. The reporters had clamored for a photograph at the time of the murder, and he had let them make copies of this one. It had been his favorite, a snapshot he'd taken with the breeze blowing the dark curls around her face and the small nose wrinkled, the way it always was when she laughed. And the scarf tied loosely around her neck. Later he'd realized that was the scarf Thompson had used to strangle her. Oh, God!

Steve rushed off the train and raced down the slippery platform stairs. In the parking lot, he tried to brush the snow from his car. A layer of ice crusted his windshield. Impatiently he opened the trunk and reached for the scraper.

The last time he'd seen Nina alive she'd driven him to the train in her Karmann Ghia. He'd noticed the balding spare on her right front wheel. She'd admitted she'd had a flat the night before.

He'd exploded at her. "You shouldn't be riding on that lousy tire. Darn it, honey, your carelessness will get you killed."

Will get you killed!

She'd promised to pick up the other tire right away. At the station, he'd started to get out of the car without kissing her good-by. But she'd leaned over and her lips had brushed his cheek. "Have a good day, Grouchy. I love you."

He hadn't answered her, or looked back, just ran for his train. He'd debated about calling her from the office, but told himself that he wanted her to think he was really upset. He worried because she was often careless in ways that mattered.

So he hadn't called, hadn't made up with her. And when he got off the 5:30 train that night, his neighbor Roger Perry was waiting at the station to tell him that Nina was dead.

379

Steve had sold Nina's car after the funeral. It was impossible to see it in the garage next to his Mercury. The night she died, he'd walked out to the car. The new radial was back on the front wheel; the balding spare was in the trunk. She'd obviously taken his annoyance seriously. Nina, Nina, I'm sorry.

And then nearly two years of bleak pain until that morning six months ago when he'd been introduced to the other guest on the *Today* show, Sharon Martin. Sharon. She'd made him come alive again. Because of her, the numbness and pain had dissolved like ice gradually melting in a spring thaw. He'd started to believe that he'd been given a second chance at happiness.

The windshield was clear enough. Steve jumped in the car. He wanted to get home and find Neil all right. He wanted to put his arms around Sharon and hold her.

As he turned onto Driftwood Lane, it seemed uncommonly dark. The lights were off at *his* place! Fear tensed his body. He careered down the block. He turned into his driveway and jammed to a halt behind Sharon's car. Racing up the steps, he unlocked the door and pushed it open. "Sharon! Neil!" he called.

In the living room, scissors and papers were scattered on the floor. Neil must have been doing cutouts. An untouched cup of cocoa and a glass of sherry were on the table near the fireplace. Hurrying over, Steve felt the cup. The cocoa was cold. The sense of danger was stifling.

He raced through the kitchen and den, back to the foyer, and noticed Sharon's overnight bag and purse. He opened the hall closet. Her cape was there! What would make her rush out without it? Neil must have had one of those violent attacks.

Steve ran to the kitchen phone. The emergency numbers were listed. He called the doctor's office first. The nurse was still there. "No, Mr. Peterson, we didn't get a call about Neil." He phoned the hospital emergency room. . . . "We have no record. . . ."

He looked at the wall clock. Nine twenty. Nearly two hours since he'd tried to phone home. Where were they? The Perrys'! Sharon might have rushed over there with Neil. Steve turned to the phone again. Please, God, let them be at the Perrys'!

Then he saw the message on the memo board. Printed in chalk. Thick, uneven lettering.

"If you want your kid and girl friend alive, wait for instructions. *Don't call police.*" The message was signed "Foxy."

IN THE Manhattan office of the FBI, Hugh Taylor stood up and stretched. His shoulders and neck were stiff. Pushing fifty and feel like I'm eighty, he thought. It would be good to get home.

Hugh reached for his coat. He'd been so depressed today. He couldn't get that Thompson kid out of his mind. Hugh had been in charge of the Peterson case two years ago. He'd traced Thompson to the motel in Virginia where they nabbed him.

The kid had so persistently denied the murder—even when he knew the only chance of saving his skin was to throw himself on the mercy of the court. Hugh shrugged. It was out of his hands. The day after tomorrow Ronald Thompson would be electrocuted.

As Hugh walked to the elevator, he heard his name being shouted. Hank Lamont, one of the younger agents, rushed down the hall. "Steve Peterson is on the phone—you know, Nina Peterson's husband."

"I know who he is," Hugh snapped. "What does he want?"

"He says that his son and that writer, Sharon Martin, have been kidnapped."

"WHO took those pictures?" Sharon saw that the terror in her voice had startled him. His lips narrowed; the pulse in his cheek quickened. She said, "I mean, they're so realistic."

The rigidity eased. "Maybe I found them."

She remembered the flash that had blinded her in the car. "Or maybe you took them." There was a hint of a compliment.

"Maybe."

She felt his hand touch her hair, her cheek. Don't act afraid, she thought frantically. She was still holding Neil. He began to tremble. Sobs broke under the asthmatic wheezing.

"Neil, don't cry," she implored. She looked up at their captor. "He's so frightened. Cut him loose."

381

"Will you like me if I do?" His leg was pressing against her side as she knelt by the cot.

"Of course I'll like you, but *please.*" Her fingers smoothed damp, sandy ringlets from the small forehead.

"Don't touch that blindfold!"

"I won't." Her voice was placating.

"All right. Just his hands. But I can't have both of you untied. Let go of the boy and lay down."

There was nothing to do except obey. He tied her legs together, then pulled her to a sitting position on the cot. He cut the cords on Neil's wrists. Neil's hands flailed the air. His gasps were staccato-paced, the wheeze a constant, rising pitch.

Sharon wrapped him inside the coat with her. He struggled. "Neil, calm down." Her voice was firm. "Remember what your dad told you to do when you get asthma. Be still and breathe very slowly." She looked up. "Please. Will you get him some water?"

He nodded and went over to the dripping faucet. While his back was turned, Sharon looked up at the posters. Had he killed those women? What kind of madman was he? Why had he kidnapped her and Neil? He had planned this carefully.

Neil choked, then began to cough—a harsh, racking sound. The abductor turned from the sink. When he handed Sharon the cup, his hand trembled. "Make him stop that," he said.

Sharon held the cup to Neil's lips. "Neil, sip this." He gulped the water. "Slowly . . . now lean back." The boy finished the water, sighed. She felt a faint relaxing of the slight body. "That's it."

The captor was leaning over her. "You're a very kind person, Sharon," he said. "That's why I fell in love with you. Because you're not frightened of me, are you?"

"No, of course not. But why did you bring us here?"

Without answering, he walked over to the black suitcase, lifted it carefully and set it down a few feet to the side of the door. Crouching, he opened it.

"What is in there?" Sharon asked.

"Just something I have to make before I go."

"Where are you going to go?"

"I can't talk when I'm working like this. You have to be careful with this stuff."

Sharon's arms tightened around Neil. This insane man was handling explosives. If he made a mistake . . . jarred something . . .

Prayerfully she watched as he worked with painstaking care, watched as the circulation in her legs stopped, as the dampness penetrated her skin.

Finally the man straightened up. "It's all right."

"What are you going to do with that?" she asked.

"It's your baby-sitter. I have to leave you until morning. I can't take any chance of losing you, can I?"

"How can you lose us, if we're tied up alone here?"

"One in a million, someone tries to get in this room while I'm out. So if the door is wired and someone tries to come in . . ."

"How long are you going to keep us here?"

"Until Wednesday. Don't worry, Sharon. Tomorrow night Steve Peterson is going to give me eighty-two thousand dollars. Then Wednesday morning you and I will go away and I'll leave word where they can find the boy."

She could not be hearing this. He came across the room. "I'm sorry, Sharon." In a sudden movement, he yanked Neil from her arms, dropped him on the cot. Before she could move, he pulled her hands behind her. He let the coat slide off before he tied her wrists together.

He reached for Neil. "Don't gag Neil, please," she begged. "If he chokes, you may not be able to get the money—you may have to prove he's alive. Please. I . . . I . . . like you. You're so smart."

He was watching her, considering.

"You know my name, but you haven't even told me yours. I'd like to be thinking about you."

His hands turned her face to him. They were callused, rough. He bent over her. His breath was stale, hot. She suffered his kiss, harsh on her lips, moist, lingering on her cheek and ear. "My name is Foxy," he said huskily.

He tied Neil's wrists and pulled him beside her. There was barely room for both of them lying on the cot. He covered them with

383

the coat. Then he looked at the boarded-up dumbwaiter. "No. I can't take the chance that someone might hear you."

The gags were around their mouths, but not quite so tight this time. The nervousness was building up in him again. With agonizing care he was fastening a slender wire to something in the suitcase and trailing it from there to the door. He was going to string that wire across the door and attach it to the outside. Then if anyone opened the door, the bomb would be triggered!

She heard the snap of the switch, and the dust-shrouded lights flickered off. The door opened and closed noiselessly. The room was desperately dark now, and the silence was broken only by Neil's labored breathing and the occasional rumble of a train.

6

ROGER and Glenda Perry decided to watch the eleven-o'clock news upstairs. Before getting into bed, he opened the front window, for they enjoyed fresh night air in the room. Automatically he glanced over at Steve's house. It was lighted, outside and in. Through the falling snow he could see cars parked in the driveway.

He turned to Glenda. "You don't have to worry about Steve's lights being off. His place is bright as a Christmas tree now."

"He must have company. Thank heaven we're not out tonight. Oh, I am tired." Her expression changed. Her body tensed.

"A pain?"

"Yes."

"Lie still." He went to the night table and reached for the ever-present bottle of nitroglycerin tablets, then watched as she slipped one under her tongue and closed her eyes.

A minute later she sighed. "Oh, that was a bad one. But it's all right now."

The phone rang. Roger muttered, "Some people . . ." He picked up the receiver with a curt yes.

Immediately his tone became concerned. "Steve, is something wrong? Oh, dear God! I'll be right over."

As Glenda stared, he replaced the receiver and reached for her hands. "Neil and Sharon Martin are missing," he said carefully. "I'm going there, but I'll be back as fast as I can."

"Roger . . ."

"Please, Glenda. Stay calm."

He pulled a heavy sweater and slacks over his pajamas and stuffed his feet into moccasins. He was just closing his front door when he heard the telephone ring again. Knowing Glenda would pick it up, he ran out into the swirling snow, across the street, into the Peterson driveway.

He was panting when he hurried up the steps. The door was opened by a trim-looking man with bold features and graying hair. "Mr. Perry. I'm Hugh Taylor, FBI. We met two years ago."

Roger thought of that day when Glenda had been knocked down by Ronald Thompson as he ran from this house, when she'd rushed in to find Nina's body. "I remember." Shaking his head, he went into the living room. Steve was standing by the fireplace, his hands gripped together. Red-eyed and sobbing, Dora Lufts was seated on the couch. Beside her, Bill Lufts hunched forward helplessly.

Roger went to Steve and gripped his shoulders. "Steve, my God, I don't know what to say. How long have they been gone?"

"We're not sure. It happened sometime between six and seven thirty." Steve's voice broke. "They were alone."

"Mr. Perry," Hugh Taylor interrupted. "Is there anything you can tell us? Did you notice any strangers in the neighborhood, strange cars or vans or trucks—anything?"

Roger sat down heavily. Think. There *was* something. What was it? Yes. "Your outside lights were off!"

Steve turned to him. "Bill is positive they were on when he and Dora went out. They were off when I got home. When did you notice them?"

Roger's analytical mind offered a precise timetable. "Your lights must have been on when I got home at quarter of six, otherwise I'd have noticed. Glenda made a cocktail. It wasn't more than twenty minutes later that we were looking out our front window and she remarked that your place was dark." He paused. "Glenda said something about a car coming from your driveway."

"What kind of car?" Hugh Taylor snapped.

"I don't know. I had turned my back to the window."

Roger remembered Glenda's feeling of alarm, how she'd wanted him to walk over here. How much could he tell her? He looked at Steve compassionately. The younger man was outwardly calm, but the bleak look of suffering that had only begun to lighten in these last months was there again, in the gray pallor, in the taut lines around his mouth. "Why don't you have a drink, or some coffee, Steve?" he suggested. "You look pretty shaken."

"Maybe coffee."

Dora looked up eagerly. "I'll make it. Oh, my God. Neil. Why did I have to go to the movies tonight? If anything has happened to that boy, I can't take it!"

Bill Lufts put his hand over his wife's mouth. "For once in your life, shut up!" he barked. Roger realized that Hugh Taylor was studying the couple intensely. Could he suspect the Lufts? No. Never. Impossible.

The foyer chimes began to peal frantically. They all jumped as an agent raced past Roger and pulled the door open.

Glenda stood in the doorway, her hair wet with snow. Her pink wool dressing gown was her only protection against the wind. Her face was marble white, the pupils of her eyes were dilated. She was clutching a sheet of notepaper. Roger ran to her, caught her just before she collapsed.

"Roger, the phone call . . ." She was sobbing. "He made me write it down. He said get it right, or Neil . . ."

Hugh snatched the paper from her hand and read it aloud. "'Tell Steven Peterson if he wants his son and girl friend back, to be in the telephone booth of the Exxon station at exit twenty-two of the Merritt Parkway tomorrow morning at eight o'clock.'"

Hugh frowned. The last word was indistinguishable. "What is this word, Mrs. Perry?" he demanded.

"I could hardly write, he was so impatient. It's Foxy." Glenda's face twisted in pain as she clutched her chest. "He—he was trying to disguise his voice. But when he repeated that name . . . *Roger I've heard that voice.* That man is someone I know."

AFTER HE LEFT the state prison, Bob Kurner phoned Kathy Moore and asked if he could meet her in her office. Kathy was an assistant prosecutor. They'd been going together for three months, and Kathy had become deeply involved in the lawyer's fight to save Ron Thompson.

She was waiting for him with the typist he'd requested. "Marge said she'll stay all night if necessary. How much have you got?"

"A lot," Bob said. "I made Ron go over the story four times. There's a good two hours' worth of tapes to be transcribed."

Marge Evans stretched out her hand. "Just give them to me. I'll start right away."

"Thanks." Bob turned to Kathy. "Did you get those files?"

"Yes, they're inside." He followed her to her cubbyhole of an office. The desk was bare except for four manila folders labeled CARFOLLI, WEISS, AMBROSE, CALLAHAN. "The police reports are on top," she said. "The prosecutor wouldn't appreciate this, Bob. In fact, he'll probably fire me if he finds out."

Bob looked at Kathy. She was wearing dungarees and a heavy sweater. Her dark hair was held back by a rubber band. She looked more like an eighteen-year-old coed than a twenty-five-year-old lawyer. But after he'd been pitted against her in court, Bob never made the mistake of underestimating Kathy. She was a good lawyer, with a keen mind and a passion for justice.

"I know the chance you're taking, Kath. But if we can only find some thread between these murders and Nina Peterson's—our one hope for Ron now is new evidence."

Bob pulled up a chair, and they sat down on opposite sides of the desk. Kathy reached for two of the files. "As of this morning they're calling these last two the Citizen Band Murders."

"How come?"

"Both the Callahan girl and Mrs. Ambrose had CB radios and had called for assistance. Mrs. Ambrose was out of gas and the Callahan girl had had a blowout."

"And two years ago Mrs. Weiss and Jean Carfolli were killed while driving alone at night on lonely roads," Bob said.

"But that doesn't *prove* any connection. After Ron Thompson was arrested, we didn't have another woman killed in the county until last month. Now we have two unsolved deaths. Those CB radios are great to have, but it's insanity for a woman to get on the air and say she's alone and her car has broken down. It's an invitation to every kook who's listening to head straight to her."

"I still say there's a connection between these four cases and Nina Peterson's case," Bob said. "Call it a hunch. But help me."

"I want to. How do we go about it?"

"We'll start with a list: place, time, cause of death, weapon used, kind of car. When we're finished, we'll compare everything with the circumstances of Mrs. Peterson's death."

They began at 8:10. At midnight Marge came in with four sets of Ron's transcripts. "All finished," she said. "You know, listening to that boy is enough to break your heart. I've been a legal stenographer for twenty years and I've heard an awful lot of stuff, but that kid's telling the truth."

Bob and Kathy worked until dawn making line-by-line comparisons. Finally Kathy said, "We've got to quit. I'm due in court at eight o'clock. Any anyhow, I don't want anyone to see you here."

Bob nodded. The words he was reading were blurring in his mind now. Over and over they'd compared the four versions of Ron's account of his activities the day of the murder. They'd concentrated on the time Nina Peterson talked to him in Timberly's Market until he ran panic-stricken from her home. There wasn't a single meaningful discrepancy they could find. "There's got to be something here," Bob said stubbornly, getting up. "I'll take these with me, and the lists we made on the other four cases. I'll compare them with the trial transcripts."

Kathy helped him put the material in his briefcase. His arm encircled her. "Love you, Kath."

"Love you." Weary tears glistened in her eyes.

"If only we had more time," he cried. "It's this damn capital punishment. When, and if, they get the real killer, it will be too late for Ron." He kissed her forehead. "Talk to you later."

In his office, Bob put the kettle on the hot plate. Four cups of instant coffee, strong and black, cleared the sensation of fogginess

388

He glanced at his watch. It was 7:30. He had just twenty-eight hours till the execution. His heart was pounding.

Something was hammering at his consciousness. There is something we have missed, he thought.

Long after the Perrys went home and the Lufts retired to their third-floor room, Steve and Hugh Taylor sat at the dining-room table.

Quietly and efficiently other agents had dusted the house for fingerprints and searched the grounds for signs of the abductor. But the scrawled message was the only evidence to be found.

Hugh studied his methodical notes. "There's a pay telephone in an outside booth at that Exxon station," he told Steve. "We're putting a tap on it as well as on this house and the Perrys' line. When you talk to Foxy, try to keep him on the phone. That'll give us a chance to record his voice and run a trace. Our big break is that Mrs. Perry may remember who he is if she hears him again."

"Do you think she could be imagining she recognized the voice?"

"Anything's possible. But she seems levelheaded and she's so *positive*. Anyhow, cooperate. Tell Foxy you want proof that Sharon and Neil are alive and unharmed, that you must have a message from them on a cassette or tape. Whatever money he asks for, promise to get it, but insist that you'll pay it only when you receive the proof."

"That won't antagonize him?" Steve wondered that he could sound so detached.

"No. It will help ensure that he won't panic." Abruptly Hugh clamped his lips together and picked up his notebook. "How many people knew the schedule of this house tonight—that the Lufts were planning to go out, that Sharon was coming up?"

"Just the Lufts and Sharon and Neil."

"Is there any chance that Neil would have talked about Sharon's coming, to his friends or teachers at school?"

"It's possible."

"I understand that you and Miss Martin were on the *Today* show this morning and that you disagree strongly about capital punishment. How much does that affect your personal relationship?"

"What's that supposed to mean?"

"Only this. As you know, Sharon Martin has been desperately trying to save Ronald Thompson's life. Do you think there's a possibility that this kidnapping is a hoax, that she's hoping somehow to delay the execution?"

"No, no, no! Hugh, I understand you have to look at that angle but please, for God's sake, don't waste your time on it. Sharon would be incapable of doing this to me."

Hugh looked unconvinced. "Mr. Peterson, we've had some mighty unusual people breaking the law in the name of causes these last ten years. I only offer this thought: If Sharon Martin engineered this, your child is safe."

"No," Steve said flatly. "That's impossible."

"Very well. What about your mail—any threats, hate letters?"

"Quite a few hate letters because of my editorial stand on capital punishment, especially with the Thompson execution so near. But that isn't surprising." Steve frowned.

"What are you thinking?" Hugh asked quickly.

"Just that Ronald Thompson's mother stopped me last week. take Neil for antihistamine shots every Saturday morning. She was in the parking lot of the medical building when we came out. She asked me to beg the governor to spare Thompson."

"What did you tell her?"

"I said I couldn't do anything. I was anxious that Neil not hear us talking, so I turned my back to her. She thought I was ignoring her. She said something like, 'How would you feel if it was your only son?' Then she walked away."

Hugh made a note in his book. "We'll check her out." Standing up, he flexed his shoulders. "Mr. Peterson," he said, "try to hang on to the thought that our record of recovering kidnapping victims is good and everything possible will be done. Now I'd suggest that you try to get a few hours' sleep."

"Sleep?" Steve looked at him incredulously.

"Then go up to your room and lie down. We'll be right here and we'll call you if there's any reason."

"All right." Wearily Steve went up the stairs to the master bedroom. After Nina died, he'd refurnished this room. He hadn't wanted to be around the antique white furniture she'd loved so much. He'd replaced the double bed with a twin-size brass bed, selected a color scheme of brown and white. A man's room, the decorating shop had assured him.

He'd never cared for it. It was lonely and impersonal. The whole house was like that. They'd bought it because they wanted waterfront property. Nina had said, "The house has real possibilities. Just give me six months." She'd had two weeks.

The last time he'd been in Sharon's apartment, he'd daydreamed about redoing this house with her. She knew how to make a home charming and restful.

Switching off the light, he lay on the bed and drew up the coverlet. The snow made furry, pelting sounds against the windows.

Steve dozed off into a light, uneasy sleep. He began to dream. Sharon, Neil. They wanted him to help them. He was running down a long hallway. He was trying to get into a room at the end of it. He reached it and threw the door open. And Neil and Sharon were lying on the floor, scarves knotted around their throats and iridescent chalk marks outlining their bodies.

7

HE LEFT Sharon and the boy at about eleven o'clock. It was dangerous to be seen coming up from the Mount Vernon tracks late in the evening, but he reached Vanderbilt Avenue without attracting the attention of the guards. He glanced across the street. A police tow truck was there. Clanging chains were being attached to the shabby brown Chevrolet. They were just about to tow the car away!

Hugely amused, he started uptown. He was planning to make the phone call from a booth opposite Bloomingdale's. During the chilly fifteen-block walk up Lexington Avenue he thought of the pulsing desire he'd experienced when he kissed Sharon. And she wanted him just as much. He could feel it.

He might have made love to Sharon then except for the boy.

Even with the blindfold the eyes were there. Maybe the boy coul
see through the blindfold. The thought made him shiver.

He had decided to phone the Perrys—calling the Peterson hous
directly could be risky.

Mrs. Perry picked up on the first ring. He gave her the messag
in the low, gruff voice he'd practiced. It was only when sh
couldn't get the name that he exploded and raised his tone. It wa
careless of him! But she probably was too upset to notice.

Gently replacing the receiver, he smiled. If the FBI had bee
called, they'd tap the phone in the Exxon station. That was wh
when he called Peterson in the morning, he'd tell him to go to th
booth in the next service station. They wouldn't have time to pu
a tracer on it. He left the phone booth feeling exhilarated, brilliam
and hurried to the Biltmore.

The same sneering night clerk gave him his key. He ordere
dinner and three bottles of beer from room service. Around th
time he always got thirsty for beer.

While he waited for the two hamburgers and french fries an
apple pie, he soaked in the tub. It had felt so musty and cold i
the room. He put on the pajamas he'd bought for this trip.

He tipped the room-service waiter generously. They always di
that in the movies. The first bottle of beer he gulped down. Th
second he had with the hamburgers. The third he sipped, listenin
to the midnight news. There was more about that Thompson kid
"The last possibility of a reprieve from death for Thompson wa
ended yesterday. Plans are being made to carry out the executio
at eleven thirty Wednesday morning." But not a whisper about Ne
or Sharon. Publicity was the one thing he feared.

The girls last month had been a mistake. He just couldn't hel
it. He never cruised around anymore. Too dangerous. But whe
he heard them on the CB, something made him go to them. Th
thought of the girls made him churn inside. Restlessly he switche
off the radio. He really shouldn't . . . it might excite him.

He *had* to.

From his coat pocket he took out the miniature recorder and th
cassettes he always carried. Selecting one, he slipped it in the re

392

corder, got into bed, and turned out the light. Putting the earplug in his right ear, he depressed the "play" button. There was the sound of a car engine, then the squeal of brakes, a door opening, and his own voice, friendly and helpful, as he got out of the Volks.

He let the cassette run until he got to the best part. That he replayed over and over again. Finally he turned off the recorder, pulled out the earplug, and fell into deep sleep, the sound of Jean Carfolli's scream—"Don't. Please don't"—ringing in his ears.

MARIAN and Jim Vogler talked far into the night. Something like despair had seeped into Marian's soul. "I wouldn't mind so much if we hadn't just spent all that money! *Four hundred dollars!* If someone had to steal the car, why didn't they take it *last week* before we fixed it? Arty did such good work on it. And how can I get to the Perrys'? I'll lose that job!"

"Babe, you won't have to give up the job. I'll borrow a couple of hundred bucks and look for another jalopy tomorrow. Someday we'll get caught up on these lousy bills."

"I guess so," Marian agreed.

They were drifting off to sleep when the phone rang. Jim fumbled for it. "Yeah, this is James Vogler. Tonight. Oh, that's good! Where? You're kidding. . . . I know. Right. Thanks." He hung up.

"The car," Marian cried. "They found our car!"

"Yeah, in New York City. It was parked illegally in midtown and the police towed it away. The cop said it was probably heisted by some kids joyriding. We can get it in the morning."

"Oh, Jim, that's wonderful!"

"There's a hitch." Jim Vogler's eyes crinkled. "Babe, can you believe . . . we're stuck with the twenty-five-buck parking ticket and the sixty-five-buck tow charge?"

Marian gasped. "That's more than my first week's pay!" She laughed hysterically.

In the morning Jim took the 6:15 train to New York and was back with the car at 8:55. Promptly at 9:00 Marian turned into Driftwood Lane. In the Perrys' driveway, she pulled up beside a Mercury. It looked like the one she'd noticed in front of the house across the street when she'd come for the interview last week. The Perrys must have company.

She lingered a moment before opening her door. She was a little nervous . . . all that excitement with their old car just when she was starting a job. Well, count your blessings. It was back. Affectionately she patted the seat beside her with her gloved hand.

Her hand stopped moving. She had touched something hard. She looked down and with two fingers tugged a shiny object from where it was wedged between the cushion and the backrest. Why, it was a ring. How pretty—a pale pink moonstone in a lovely gold setting. Whoever stole the car must have lost it.

Well, as far as she was concerned, the ring made up for the ninety dollars Jim had laid out for the ticket and towing fee. She pulled off her glove and slipped the ring on her finger.

It fitted perfectly. Suddenly confident, Marian stepped out and walked briskly to the kitchen door of the Perry home.

THE phone in the outside booth of the Exxon station rang promptly at 8:00 a.m. Swallowing over the sudden dryness in his mouth, Steve picked up the receiver. "Hello."

"Peterson?" A voice so muffled, so low, he had to strain to hear it. "In ten minutes I'll call you at the pay phone of the service station just past exit twenty-one." The connection was broken.

Desperately Steve looked over to the service island. Hugh had driven into the station before him and was standing with the attendant, pointing at one of the tires. Steve knew he was watching him. Shaking his head, he got back in his own car and careered onto the parkway. He saw Hugh jump into his car.

Steve clenched the wheel. This time he'd try to keep Foxy on the phone longer. He'd write everything down. When Steve pulled into the next service station, the public phone was ringing insistently. He raced into the booth, grabbed the receiver.

"Peterson?"

Steve could hardly hear the voice.

"I want eighty-two thousand dollars in tens, twenties, and fifties. *No new bills.* At two o'clock tomorrow morning be at the pay phone on the southwest corner of Fifty-ninth and Lexington in Manhattan. Drive your own car. Be alone. You'll be told where to leave the money."

"Eighty-two thousand . . ." Steve stalled.

"Hurry up, Peterson."

"I'm writing this down. I'll get the money. But how do I know my son and Sharon are still alive? I need proof."

"What kind of proof?" The whisper was angry now.

"A tape, or a cassette. Something with them talking." Was that a muffled laugh? "I must have it," Steve insisted.

"You'll get your cassette." The receiver was slammed down.

"Wait!" Steve shouted. The dial tone. He hung up slowly.

As they'd arranged, Steve drove directly to the Perrys' and waited for Hugh in the driveway. The icy wind made him shiver. Oh, God, was this really happening?

Hugh parked down the block and walked back. "What'd he say?"

Steve read the instructions. The sense of unreality deepened.

"How about the voice?" Hugh asked.

"Disguised, very low. I don't think anybody could identify it. But he promised the cassette. That means they must be alive."

"How about the ransom?" Hugh asked. "Can you raise eighty-two thousand dollars today?"

"Thanks to Neil's mother, I can get the money," Steve said.

"Neil's mother?"

"She inherited seventy-five thousand from her grandmother before she died. I put it in a trust fund for Neil for college. With the interest it comes to just over eighty-two thousand."

"*Just over eighty-two thousand dollars.* Mr. Peterson, how many people are aware of that trust?"

"Nobody except my lawyer and accountant."

"What about Sharon Martin?"

"I don't remember mentioning it to her."

Hugh started to go up the porch steps. "Mr. Peterson," he said carefully, "you have to go over in your mind everyone who knows about that money. That and the possibility that Mrs. Perry can identify the kidnapper's voice are our only leads."

395

When they rang the front-door bell, Roger Perry answered quickly. "Come in. The doctor just left. He thinks Glenda's on the verge of another coronary."

"Mr. Perry, I'm sorry, but we have to ask her to listen to a recording of the first call the kidnapper made this morning."

There was a long pause; then Roger said to Steve, "Glenda refused to go to the hospital because she thought you'd need her. The doctor gave her a tranquilizer. If she just slept for a while . . ."

Chimes were an intrusion. "That's the back door," Roger said. "Oh, the new housekeeper. I forgot."

Hugh spoke quickly. "Introduce me as the doctor. When we leave, send her home. Say you'll call her in a day or two. We may want to check her out."

"All right." Roger hurried to the back door and returned with Marian. Hugh studied the pleasant-looking woman carefully.

"I've explained to Mrs. Vogler that my wife is ill," Roger said. "Mrs. Vogler, my neighbor, Mr. Peterson, and Dr. Taylor."

"How do you do?" Her voice was warm, a little shy. "Oh, Mr. Peterson, do you live across the street?"

"Yes."

"That must have been your little boy I saw last week. He was out front, and he pointed out this house for me. He was so polite." Marian was reaching her hand to Steve.

"I . . . am proud of Neil." Abruptly Steve turned his back to her. Blinding tears stung his eyes. Oh, God . . . please . . .

Hugh jumped into the breach. He shook Mrs. Vogler's hand, careful not to squeeze the unusual ring she was wearing. Pretty fancy to do housework in, he thought. His expression changed subtly. "I think it's a good idea Mrs. Vogler is here today, Mr. Perry. You know how concerned your wife gets about the house."

"Oh, I see. Very well." Roger stared at Hugh. Did Hugh think this woman might be tied to Neil's disappearance?

Bewildered, Marian watched Steve open the front door. Maybe he thought she was too forward, offering to shake hands. Embarrassed, she closed it quietly behind him and, as she did, the moonstone ring made a faint clinking sound on the knob.

HE DIDN'T WANT to be a crybaby, but he couldn't stop it. There was something inside him that kept bothering him. It began that day when Mommy got hurt and went to heaven. He'd been playing with his trains. He never played with them anymore.

The thought of that day made Neil breathe faster. The thick gauze over his mouth made him gag. He was going to cry.

"Neil, stop that." Sharon's voice sounded funny. She must have something around her mouth too. Where were they? It was so cold and smelly here. He didn't remember anything after the man put him in the bag, not until Sharon was pulling him out. He wondered why he didn't remember. It was like when Mommy fell.

He didn't want to think about that. Sharon was saying, "Breathe slowly, Neil. Don't cry. Neil, you're brave."

She probably thought he was a crybaby too. Tonight he'd been crying when she came. It was just that when he didn't eat the toast Mrs. Lufts made for him, she said, "Looks like we'll have to take you to Florida when we go, Neil. Got to fatten you up."

See. That proved it. If Daddy married Sharon, they'd make him go with the Lufts. And he'd started to cry.

Sharon was saying, "In . . . out. Breathe through your nose. You're brave, Neil. Think about when you tell this to your friends."

In . . . out. Sharon's cheek was next to his. She didn't seem to mind that he was squished against her. Why had that man brought them here? He knew who he was. He'd seen him a couple of weeks ago when Mr. Lufts took him to where the man worked. He'd been getting a lot of bad dreams since that day.

His breathing got choky again. "Neil." Now Sharon was rubbing her face against his. "Try to think about when we get out of here. Your dad will be so glad to see us. I bet he'll take us out. You know, I'd like to go ice-skating with you. You didn't come with us that time your dad came down to New York. And afterwards we were going to take you to the zoo."

He listened. Sharon sounded as though she really meant it. He'd been planning to go that day, but his friend Sandy had said that Sharon probably didn't want him and was just trying to make his father feel good by asking him along too.

"Your dad tells me he wants to take you to football games at Princeton next fall," she said. Her voice sounded like a growly whisper. "Your dad's so proud of you. He says you're very brave when you get the asthma shots. He said you never complain or cry."

It was so hard to talk. She tried to swallow. "Neil, when I'm scared or sick, I plan something nice that I know will be fun. I think we should plan a real treat for you. You know, your dad says that the Lufts are really anxious to move to Florida now."

Neil felt a giant fist squeeze his chest.

"Easy, Neil! Breathe slowly. Well, when I saw the Lufts' room and looked out the window, it was just like a painting. Because you can see the harbor and the boats and the Sound. And if I were you, when the Lufts move to Florida, I'd take that room for myself. I'd put bookcases in it and shelves for your games, and a desk. The room is so big you could put tracks all over it for your trains. I had trains when I was little too. In fact, I've got some great Lionel trains that used to be *my* dad's. I'd like you to have them."

When the Lufts move to Florida. Sharon didn't expect him to go with them. Sharon thought he should have their room.

"And I'm scared now and I'm uncomfortable, but I'm glad you're with me and I'm going to tell your dad how brave you were and how careful you were to breathe slowly and not get all choky."

The heavy fist in Neil's chest relaxed a little. Suddenly he felt desperately sleepy. His hands were tied, but he could slide his fingers along Sharon's arm until he found a piece of her sleeve he could hold. Wrapping his fingers around the soft wool, he drifted into sleep.

Apprehensively Sharon listened to the thick wheeze, felt the labored movement of Neil's chest. This room was so freezing, so damp. But at least lying this close together meant their shared body heat gave some warmth.

How long had Foxy been gone? It must be past midnight. Tuesday now. Foxy had said they'd be here till Wednesday. Where would Steve get eighty-two thousand dollars in one day? And why that crazy figure? Why in God's name had he kidnapped them? There was something about the way he looked at Neil. As though he hated him and was frightened of him. But that was impossible.

Had he blindfolded Neil because he was afraid Neil might recognize him? Maybe he was from Carley. When he pushed his way into the house, Neil had *stared* at him. Neil would recognize this man if he saw him again. He must realize that too. Was he planning to kill Neil as soon as he had the money? *Yes, he was.*

A passion of fear and anger made her press closer to Neil. This must be the way Mrs. Thompson was feeling now. This primal need to protect one's young. And Steve must be frantic. He and Mrs. Thompson were going through identical agony.

She rubbed her wrists against the cinder-block wall, but the cords were so tight that her hands took the brunt of the contact.

Those pictures. He had killed those women. Only a madman would take pictures as he murdered. He had taken *her* picture.

That bomb. Suppose someone did come near this room? If that bomb went off, she and Neil and how many others would die? She prayed, over and over, "Please let Steve find us in time."

The pain in her arms and legs subsided into numbness. Neil slept fitfully. It must be getting toward morning. The train sounds were more urgent. Neil stirred and muttered.

He tried to open his eyes and could not. His arms and legs hurt. It was hard to breathe. Then he remembered what had happened. There was a far-off train sound.

A train sound. And Mommy. He'd run downstairs. And the man let Mommy drop and turned to him. And then the man was bending over Mommy, looking all sweaty and scared.

No. The man who pushed the door in last night, who stood over him and looked down at him; he'd done that before. He'd come at him. He'd let Mommy drop and come at him. He'd put his hands out and looked right down at him. And something happened.

The chimes. The chimes from the front door. The man had run away. Neil had watched him run away.

That was why he couldn't stop dreaming about that day. Because of the part he forgot—the scary part when the man came to him and had his hands out and reached down to him.

The man . . . the man who'd been talking to Bill Lufts . . . and

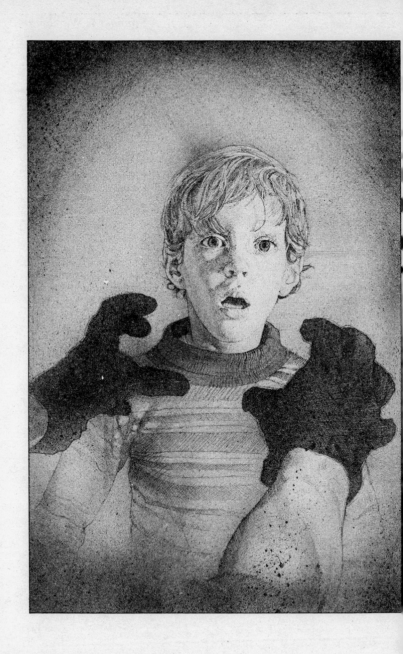

last night had come pushing into the house and stood over him.

"Sharon." Neil's voice was muffled and hoarse.

"Yes, Neil. I'm here."

"Sharon, that man, the bad man who tied us up."

"Yes, dear. Don't be afraid. I'll take care of you."

"Sharon, that's the man who killed my mommy."

8

LALLY *had* to go to her room. It didn't matter how cold it was. She missed it so much. She needed her place to dream.

Years ago Lally would lull herself to sleep pretending that instead of being a homely spinster schoolteacher, she was a movie star coming into Grand Central Station with all the photographers waiting. Sometimes she'd be in white fox when she stepped off the *Twentieth Century Limited;* another time she'd be wearing a silk suit, holding sable skins. After a while the dreams faded and she became used to her lonely life. But when she arrived in New York and began to spend all her time in Grand Central, it was as though she really was remembering her heyday as a star, not pretending at all. Then when she had gotten the key to her room and could sleep, nestled in her station, listening to the faint sounds of her trains, it made everything perfect.

At 8:30 Tuesday morning, armed with her shopping bags, she was heading toward the Mount Vernon track. Her plan was to join the people taking the 8:50, then slip around to her room. On the way she stopped at the Nedicks takeout counter and ordered coffee and doughnuts.

The man ahead of her looked vaguely familiar. Why, he was the one who spoiled her plans last night by going down to the Mount Vernon platform with the girl in the gray coat! Resentfully she watched as he paid for two coffees and rolls and milk, and left.

After leaving Nedicks, she dawdled through the terminal until she was on the platform of the Mount Vernon track. As people hurried into the train, Lally slipped around the last car and turned right. And then she saw him. The man who'd just bought the coffee and milk and rolls. He was disappearing into the throbbing depths of the terminal.

There was only one place he could be going. *Her room.* He had found it! That was why he went down on the platform last night.

Bitter tears welled up in Lally's eyes. He and the girl had taken over her room! Then her lifelong ability to cope rescued her. She'd get rid of them! She'd wait and when she was sure he was out, she'd go into the room and warn the girl that the cops knew they were there and were coming to arrest them. That'd scare them off fast enough.

Lally headed for the waiting room. Don't get too comfortable in there, missy, she thought. You're going to have company.

STEVE, Hugh, the Lufts, and agent Lamont sat at Steve's dining-room table. Hugh consulted the list in front of him. "First," he said, "there'll be an agent here round the clock till this is settled. I think this man Foxy is too clever to call this phone or the Perrys'. But there's always the chance.

"Mr. Peterson has to go down to New York, so if the phone rings, Mrs. Lufts, you answer it. Agent Lamont will be on the extension and we'll be recording it as well. If the abductor does call, you must keep him on the phone as long as possible."

"I'll try," Dora quavered.

"What about Neil's school? Did you phone and report him ill?"

"Yes. Right at eight thirty, just as you told me."

"Fine." Hugh turned to Steve. "Did you reach your office?"

"Yes. The publisher had suggested I take Neil away for a few days until after the execution. I left word I was doing that."

Hugh turned to Bill Lufts. "Mr. Lufts, I'd like you to stay here in the house today. Would anyone find that unusual?"

His wife laughed mirthlessly. "Only the regulars at the Mill Tavern."

"All right, thank you both." Hugh's tone dismissed the Lufts. They went to the kitchen, partially closing the door.

Hugh leaned over and closed it with a thud. "I don't think the Lufts miss much of what's said in this house," he commented.

402

Steve shrugged. "I know."

"You said they've been here two years?"

"A little longer than that. Dora was our cleaning woman. When Nina was killed, I had to have someone to take care of Neil. I suggested that they move into that large third-floor room."

"How has it worked out?"

"Reasonably well. They're both very fond of Neil. But since Bill's retirement the first of the year, he's been into a lot of drinking. They're anxious to move to Florida, and frankly, I'll be glad when they do."

"What's holding them back?" Hugh asked sharply. "Money?"

"No, I don't think so. They've really been staying on as a favor to me. Dora would love to see me remarried so that Neil would have a mother again."

"And you've been getting close to that with Sharon Martin?"

Steve's smile was wintry. "I hope so." Restlessly he got up and walked to the window. The snow was falling again. It seemed to him that he had as much control over his life as one of those snowflakes had over its ultimate destination. He could not wait here, immobilized. He had to *do* something. "I'll get the bankbook and start down to New York," he said.

"Just a minute." Hugh reminded him: "We need to discuss what happens if you don't get a tape of your son and Sharon. Are you prepared to pay the money without the proof?"

Steve considered. "Yes. I won't take the chance of antagonizing him. Maybe he'll leave a cassette somewhere, expecting it to be found, and then if I don't follow through . . ."

"All right. If it hasn't come by two a.m. when he calls you at the Fifty-ninth Street pay phone, you can tell him you didn't get it. If he claims he left it somewhere, it's easy enough to pick it up. Now, do you want to give him real cash? We could get counterfeit money that would be easy to trace."

"I simply won't take that chance. The money in the trust is for Neil's education. If anything happens to him . . ."

"All right. Get a cashier's check from your bank. Then take it down to the Federal Reserve Bank. They'll give you old bills that

403

we've photographed. That way at least we'll have some record. Now there are several precautions I'm going to urge you to take. One, let us rig cameras into your car. After you make contact with the abductor, we may be able to get a picture of him or pick up the license number of the car he's driving. We'd also like to install a beeper device in your car so that we can follow you from a distance. Last, we'd like to conceal an electronic tracer in the suitcase with the money."

"Suppose it's found. He'll know I brought you in."

"Suppose you *don't* put it in and you don't hear another word. That has to be considered. At least the area may be narrowed down if we can follow the kidnapper's trail electronically."

Steve shrugged helplessly. "Do what you have to."

He left his car at the station so that Hugh could pick it up and make the installations, then caught the 10:40 train and arrived at Grand Central at 11:50. His sense of futility and misery deepened as he trudged up Park Avenue carrying a large empty suitcase. Yesterday morning he and Sharon had stood in the falling snow a few blocks from here and he'd held her face in his hands and kissed her good-by. Her lips had been unresponsive, just as he'd been unresponsive when Nina kissed him good-by that last day.

He arrived at the bank. The news that he wanted to withdraw all but two hundred dollars from Neil's account was greeted with a lifted eyebrow. The teller went to consult a senior vice-president, who hurried over to Steve.

"Mr. Peterson, is there any problem?"

"No, Mr. Strauss. I simply wish to make a withdrawal."

"I'll have to ask you to fill out state and federal forms. It's required for any withdrawal that large."

Mechanically Steve scrawled the necessary information on the government forms as the teller made out the cashier's check. The vice-president's face became thoughtful. "I don't mean to intrude, but there isn't any trouble, is there, Mr. Peterson? Perhaps something we can help with?"

Steve took the cashier's check. "No, no, thank you, Mr. Strauss." To his own ears he sounded strained, unconvincing.

404

He next took a cab to the Federal Reserve Bank, where FBI agents were busily photographing the bills that would be exchanged for his cashier's check.

Steve watched unemotionally as the tens, twenties, and fifties were placed in exact rows in his suitcase. *The king was in his counting-house, counting out his money.* Nina used to singsong that nursery rhyme when she was getting Neil ready for bed.

Carrying the heavy suitcase, Steve returned to Grand Central and just missed the 3:05 train. The next train wouldn't leave for an hour. He called home. No further news. His head was aching, and he realized he'd eaten nothing since yesterday's lunch.

He'd go down to the Oyster Bar. On his way he passed the phone he'd used when he tried to call Sharon only twenty hours ago. It seemed a lifetime.

Where were Sharon and Neil? Had they been given anything to eat? Were they in a place with heat? If there was any way possible, he knew Sharon would take care of Neil. Suppose the three of them had spent last evening at home. After Neil went to bed, he was going to say, "Marry me, Sharon. We're good together." She probably would have turned him down. She despised his position on capital punishment. Well, he'd been positive he was right.

The restaurant was nearly empty. The lunch rush was long since over. He sat at the bar and ordered some oyster stew and a drink, carefully keeping the suitcase under his foot.

Last month he and Sharon had met here for lunch. She'd been exhilarated because of the overwhelming response to her campaign to have Thompson's sentence commuted to life imprisonment. "We're going to make it," she'd said confidently. She'd been so happy; she *cared* so much. I love you, Sharon. Had he said it then?

He sat in the Oyster Bar, the bubbling stew untouched, until at 3:55 he paid his bill and went to the Carley train. He didn't notice a man seated in the rear of the car he entered, his face buried behind a newspaper. After he had passed, the newspaper was lowered slightly and glittering eyes followed his progress through the coach with the heavy suitcase.

That same passenger got off at Carley too. He waited on the platform until Steve had entered the parking lot and driven away in the car which now had powerful cameras hidden in the headlights and behind the rearview mirror.

GLENDA Perry slept until one o'clock. The pain had been bad during the night, but she was *not* going to the hospital. They'd sedate her so much that she'd be useless. She couldn't forget that her testimony had helped condemn the Thompson boy. . . .

"He knocked you down, Mrs. Perry?"

"Yes, he was running from the house."

"It was dark, Mrs. Perry. Can you be sure it wasn't someone else running away?"

"Positive. He hesitated in the doorway before he collided with me. The kitchen light was on."

And now Neil and Sharon. Oh, God, let me remember. Foxy. The way he said it. What was the association?

The door opened and she saw Roger look in. "It's all right, dear, I'm awake. Did Steve talk to . . . Foxy?"

Roger explained. . . . "So they only have a few words. Are you up to listening to them?"

"Yes." Fifteen minutes later Hugh Taylor entered the bedroom. Propped up on pillows, Glenda listened intently as he ran the cassette of Foxy's phone call to Steve.

"Oh, it's so low. It's impossible . . ."

The tense expectancy slid from Hugh's face. "Well, thank you for listening, Mrs. Perry." He picked up the recorder.

"No, wait!" Glenda put her hand on the machine. "Can you leave this with me? I *know* the person I spoke to last night. I'm going to try now to retrace everything I've done in the last few weeks. *Maybe* something will come to me."

"Mrs. Perry, if you could *only* remember . . ." Hugh bit his lip as Roger Perry shot a warning glance at him. Quickly he left the room, followed by Roger.

When they were downstairs, Roger asked, "Why did you have me keep Mrs. Vogler here today?"

"We can't let any possibility pass. But she seems all right. Good character, good family situation, well liked. Anyhow, she's got the best alibi of anyone last night and so does her husband."

"Why is that?"

"The cashier saw her enter and leave the movie. Neighbors saw her husband at home with their kids. And sometime after seven o'clock they were in the police station reporting a stolen car."

"Oh, yes. She did mention that. Lucky she got it back."

"Mr. Perry, what do you think of the Lufts? Is it possible that they might be part of this? They're trying to save money. They could have known about the trust fund."

Roger shook his head. "Not a chance. If Dora picks up anything for Glenda at the store, she always makes sure she's given her the exact change. He's like that too—painfully honest."

"Okay. I'll be at the Petersons'. Call if Mrs. Perry has anything to tell us."

Agent Lamont was waiting for Hugh with news. "Last night Mrs. Thompson talked to Sharon Martin!"

"She *what?*"

"The Thompson kid told us. I sent agents to interview him in his cell. They didn't mention the kidnapping. Just said there'd been some threats against the Peterson boy and warned him that if his friends were pulling something, we'd better get their names before they got into deep trouble."

"What did he say?"

"He's clean. The only visitors he's had in the last year are his mother, his lawyer, and his priest. His closest friends are away in college. But he did tell us that Sharon called his mother."

"Did they talk to the mother?"

"Yes. She wasn't home. But they found her in church, praying. Won't believe the kid's going to be executed tomorrow, God help her. She says Sharon called her a few minutes before six. Wanted to know if she could do anything. Admitted she blew up at her. Threatened that she wouldn't know what she'd do to Sharon if the boy dies. What do you make of it?"

"Let's try this," Hugh said. "Sharon Martin is upset by the phone call. She's desperate and calls someone to come for her and the boy.

She's planning a grandstand stunt—make it look like a kidnapping and make Neil a hostage for Thompson's life."

"It's a possibility," Lamont said.

Hugh's face hardened. "I think it's more than a possibility. I think that poor guy Peterson is having his guts torn out because Sharon Martin thinks she can manipulate justice."

"What do we do now?"

"Continue to treat this as a real snatch. And dig up everything we can about Sharon Martin's associates, particularly in this area. If only Mrs. Perry can remember where she heard that voice."

In her room, Glenda was playing the cassette over and over. Helplessly she shook her head and turned off the machine. That wasn't the way to do it. Start retracing this last couple of weeks.

Yesterday she hadn't gone out at all, until Foxy called. Sunday, she and Roger drove to New York and had brunch in the Pierre and went to Carnegie Hall. Saturday, she'd been at the decorator's, she'd had her hair done, and . . . Unconsciously Glenda pushed the button and began running the cassette. Once again the muffled voice filled her ears. "Peterson? In ten minutes I'll call you at the pay phone of the service station just past exit twenty-one."

9

Walking back from the phone booth, Foxy thought about the cassette Peterson had asked for. After he recorded Sharon and the boy, should he do it? Why not?

He went directly to Grand Central. Sharon and the kid were probably hungry. He didn't want her to be hungry. But she probably wouldn't eat if he didn't feed the boy too. Thinking of the boy always made him nervous. A couple of weeks ago he'd almost panicked when he'd seen the boy staring at him from the car. Just the way he did in the dream, those round brown eyes, accusing.

This afternoon he'd take the train to Carley. He'd go to his place and see if there were any messages. Where could he leave the cassette? Maybe Peterson wouldn't pay if he didn't get it.

He had to have the money. It was too dangerous for him to stay in the county now. And everyone expected him to leave.

"Any unexpected departures in this area?" the cops might ask.

"Him? No. He's been complaining about losing the place; begged the old man to renew his lease."

But that was before the last two girls. The CB Murderer, the papers were calling him. If they only knew. He had even gone to the Callahan funeral service. The funeral service! Suddenly he knew where to leave the cassette, where he could be sure it would be found this evening and delivered.

Satisfied, he walked briskly into Nedicks, ordered coffee, milk, and rolls. He didn't want Sharon to think he was unkind.

When he left the area of the Mount Vernon track, he had an odd sense of being watched. His instinct was very good about that. He tiptoed back. It was just one of those old shopping-bag ladies making her way up the ramp to the terminal.

With infinite care he released the sliver of wire that was taped to the door of the room. Gingerly he took out his key, inserted it in the lock, and slipped into the room.

He switched on the fluorescent lights and grunted in satisfaction. Sharon and the boy were just as he had left them. Setting down the package, he yanked the gag from Sharon's mouth.

She seemed very nervous. He didn't want her to be scared of him. "Are you afraid, Sharon?" His voice was horribly gentle.

"Oh, no, not at all. But won't you please take the gag off Neil, and won't you untie us, even just our hands?"

His eyes narrowed. Something was different about her. "Certainly, Sharon." After freeing her hands, he reached for the boy.

The child shrank against Sharon. "It's all right, Neil," she said. "Remember what we talked about."

"What did you talk about, Sharon?"

"Just that Neil's dad would give you the money and you'd tell his dad where to find him. I said I was going away with you but that his dad would be here soon after we left. Isn't that right?"

Foxy's voice was thoughtful, his glittering eyes speculative. "You're sure you want to go, Sharon?"

"Oh, yes, very much. I . . . I like you, Foxy."

"I brought rolls and coffee and some milk for the boy."

"That's very nice of you." He watched as she began to rub Neil's wrists, as she smoothed his hair back from his forehead. He gave Sharon a container of coffee.

"Thank you. Where is Neil's milk?"

He handed it to her, watched as she put it in Neil's hands. "There it is," she said. "Hold on to it, Neil. Drink slowly."

The boy's raspy breathing was irritating, evoked memories.

He brought out the rolls, buttered thickly. Sharon handed one to the boy. "Here, Neil; it's a roll." Her voice was soothing. It was like she and the boy were in a conspiracy against him.

He hadn't taken off his coat because of the cold room. Sullenly he sat down on the orange crate and got out his recorder from his coat pocket. "You're going to make a recording for Peterson."

"A recording?" Sharon tried to think. Was there a chance? Ever since Neil had told her that this man murdered his mother, she'd been even more frantic to get out of here. Tomorrow might be too late for Ronald Thompson as well as for Neil. The memory of her quest to save Ronald tortured her. His mother had been right. By insisting on his guilt, she had helped condemn him. And she had been the one to tell Steve *he* was trying to play God.

Foxy had a gun. She had seen him put it in his coat pocket. If she could get him to put his arms around her, she could reach for it. If she had the chance, could she kill him? She looked down at Neil, thought of Ronald Thompson. Yes, she could kill this man.

She watched as he inserted a cassette in the recorder. "Read this, Sharon." He had a message written down. "Steve, pay the ransom if you want us back. Eighty-two thousand dollars. Don't let it be marked. Go to the phone booth at Fifty-ninth and Lexington at two a.m. in your car. Alone. Don't call the police."

She looked up at him. "Can I add anything? I mean, we had a quarrel. Maybe he wouldn't pay money for me, if I don't apologize. Maybe he'll only pay half the money, for Neil, because he knows I don't love him. But we'll need all the money, won't we?"

"What do you want to say, Sharon?"

410

Did he believe her? "Just an apology, that's all." She reached over and stroked his hand. "What do you want Neil to say?"

"Just that he wants to come home. When I push this 'record' button down, start talking."

She swallowed, and waited until the cassette began to wind. "Steve . . ." She read the message slowly, trying to buy time. Then she paused. "Steve, Neil is going to talk to you now. But first, I was wrong. I hope you'll forgive me." The recorder clicked off.

"That's enough apology, Sharon." He pointed at Neil.

She put her arm around the child. "Neil, talk to your dad."

The wheezing was accentuated by his effort to speak. "Dad, I'm all right. Sharon is taking care of me. But Mommy wouldn't want me to be here, Dad."

The recorder stopped. *Neil had tried to give Steve a message*, had tried to connect their kidnapping to his mother's death.

The man rewound the cassette, played it back. He smiled at Sharon. "Very nice." He put the recorder in his pocket.

"Sharon." Neil tugged at her sleeve. "I have to . . ."

"You want to go to the john, kid?" Foxy went over to Neil, picked him up, and walked into the toilet with him, closing the door. Sharon froze, waiting, but in a minute he was back, carrying Neil under his arm. He dropped him on the cot. The boy was trembling.

"Sharon, you want to?" said her captor. She nodded. He picked her up and took her inside the musty cubbyhole. "There's a bolt up there, Sharon," he said. "I'll even let you put it on, 'cause otherwise the door don't stay shut. But you better come right out." His hand caressed her cheek. "Because if you don't, the boy gets it now." He stepped out, pulling the door closed behind him.

Quickly she slid the bolt. She ran her hands down the walls, along the tank. Maybe there was something here, something sharp.

"Hurry up, Sharon."

"All right." When she started to open the door, the knob felt loose. She tried to twist it off, but she could not wrest it free.

"Come out of there!" Instantly she opened the door, hobbled out, stumbled. He came over to her. Deliberately she put her arms around his neck. Forcing back revulsion, she kissed his cheek, his

411

lips. His arms tightened. She felt the sudden racing of his heart. Oh, God, please . . .

She slid her arms down around his shoulders, his back. Her right hand slipped into his coat pocket, felt metal.

He shoved her backward onto the concrete floor. Her legs buckled under her. Blinding pain shot through her right ankle.

"You're like the rest, Sharon," he screamed. He was standing over her. His face seemed disembodied. The pulse under his eye was throbbing. His eyes were black narrow pits. "You bitch."

Yanking her up, he threw her on the cot and slapped her arms behind her. Pain made blackness close over her. "My ankle."

"Sharon, what happened?" Neil sounded terrified.

With a tremendous effort she bit back a moan. "I fell."

"Like all the others, pretending, lying—but worse, trying to trick me." She felt hands close on her throat, pressing. God . . . help . . .

"No." The pressure vanished. Her head fell backward.

"Sharon, Sharon," Neil was crying.

Gulping in air, she turned toward him. Foxy was at the rusty sink, splashing water on his face. He was trying to calm himself. He'd been about to kill her. What stopped him? There was no way out, no way. Tomorrow when he got the money he'd kill her and Neil. Her ankle was swelling, pressing out against the leather boot. The cords were biting into it. Oh, God, please.

After drying his face with a handkerchief, he came over and methodically retied Neil's hands, put tight gags on both of them. He adjusted the wire from the suitcase to the door. "I'll be back once more, Sharon," he said. "Tomorrow."

He knew if he stayed, he'd kill her. And he might need her again. They might demand more proof that she and the boy were alive.

He waited in the darkness near the entrance to the tunnel until the eleven-o'clock train came in from Mount Vernon. Carefully he slipped around the ventilating shafts to the platform, melting in with the disembarking passengers.

Feeling too restless to sit in the hotel room, he walked west on Forty-second Street, went into a movie and watched three X-rated films. At 4:05 he was on the train to Carley.

He did not see Peterson until he was seated on the train. Fortunately he was buried behind the newspaper, a precaution against being recognized. Steve was carrying a suitcase. It was the money! And tonight he'd have it.

Waiting till Steve had left the Carley station, Foxy then walked briskly through the snow to his place, a shabby garage on a dead-end street. The sign said A. R. TAGGERT—AUTO REPAIRS.

He went inside. There were no messages under the door. Good. The garage was cold and dirty, not much better than the place in Grand Central. He'd certainly always worked in stinking holes.

His dark green Volks Beetle was there, ready to go. It was equipped with a set of license plates he'd changed for a customer a couple of years ago; he'd also filed off the engine number and unhooked and crated the CB radio. He filled the car with gas from the pump in the corner. Installing that pump had been handy for customers—for him too. Easy to cruise around at night. "You're out of gas, ma'am? Why, I've got some right in my trunk. Cars are my business. . . ."

He'd gotten rid of all the other license plates he'd accumulated over six years and extra sets of car keys he'd made. He'd been too nervous to work much the past couple of months. Lucky he'd had that big job on the Vogler car. Just tided him over.

Going into the small room in the rear, he took a battered suitcase out from under the single bed. From an old maple dresser he extracted his clothes and placed them in the suitcase.

He took out his recorder and listened again to the cassette he had made with Sharon and Neil. His other recorder, the Sony, was on the dresser. He put it on the bed, rummaged through his cassettes, and put one on. He just needed the beginning. It only took a minute to transfer that part of the old cassette to the one he was sending to Peterson. Perfect. He wrapped it up. With a red Magic Marker he wrote a message on the package.

The other cassettes and the two recording machines were placed in the suitcase between his folded clothes. He closed and locked the suitcase and carried it to the car. He'd have enough trouble managing the suitcase with the money in the plane cabin. This one

413

and his crated CB radio could go in the baggage compartment.

He opened the garage door, got into the car and turned on the engine. He smiled. "Now for a visit to church and a beer," he said.

"I DON'T believe it," Steve told Hugh, "and you are endangering the lives of Neil and Sharon if you treat this as a hoax."

Just back from New York, Steve was pacing the living room, his hands thrust in his pockets. Hugh watched him with both compassion and irritation. The poor guy had himself in iron control, but he'd aged ten years in as many hours.

"Mr. Peterson," Hugh said crisply, "I assure you we are presuming this is a bona fide kidnapping. However, we believe that Sharon and Neil's disappearance might be directly tied into an attempt to bargain for clemency for Ronald Thompson."

"And I say it isn't! Has there been any sign of a tape or cassette from Foxy?"

"No. I'm sorry."

"Then we can only wait."

"Yes. You'd better plan to leave for New York by midnight. The road conditions, Mr. Peterson, are pretty grim."

"Do you think that Foxy might be afraid to meet me, afraid of not being able to make a getaway?"

Hugh shook his head. "Your guess is as good as mine. We've put a tap on the phone at Fifty-ninth Street, but I suspect that he'll direct you immediately to another phone booth. We'll have agents following your progress unobtrusively. Don't worry. The beeper in the car will let us track you within a few blocks."

Dora Lufts came into the living room. "Excuse me, but couldn't I just fix a club steak for you and Mr. Taylor?"

"Not for me, thank you, Dora. Maybe Mr. Taylor . . ."

"Put on steaks for both of us if you don't mind, Mrs. Lufts." Hugh patted Steve's arm. "Look, you haven't eaten since yesterday. You need to be alert and able to drive and follow directions tonight."

"I guess you're right."

They were barely seated at the dining-room table when the door chimes rang. Hugh said, "I'll get it." Steve wadded his napkin. Was it the cassette? Would he hear Neil's voice . . . Sharon's?

Hugh came back, followed by a familiar-looking, young dark-haired man—Ronald Thompson's defense attorney, Robert Kurner. He seemed agitated. His suit was rumpled as if he'd slept in it.

"Mr. Peterson," Bob said, "I've got to talk about your son."

"What about my son?" Steve felt Hugh's warning glance.

"Ron did not kill your wife. He was convicted because most of those jurors thought he also killed the Carfolli girl and Mrs. Weiss."

"He had a record."

"A *juvenile* record, a single occurrence."

"He attacked a girl before, was choking her."

"Mr. Peterson, he was a fifteen-year-old kid at a party. He got into a beer-drinking contest. When he was absolutely out of it, somebody slipped him cocaine. He has no memory of touching that girl. Ron had the lousy luck to get in serious trouble the first and only time he got drunk. And he had the incredibly bad luck to enter your house right after your wife was murdered."

Bob's voice was trembling now; his words rushing out. "Mr. Peterson, I've been studying the trial transcript. Then yesterday I had Ron repeat over and over again every single thing he said or did between the time he spoke to Mrs. Peterson in Timberly's Market and when he found her body. And I realized a mistake I made.

"Mr. Peterson, your son, Neil, told about coming downstairs when he heard your wife gasping, seeing a man strangle her, and then seeing the man's face."

"Ron Thompson's face."

"No! Here, look at the transcript." Bob pulled a sheaf of papers out of his briefcase. "The prosecutor asked Neil why he was so sure it was Ron. And Neil said, '*It got light, so I'm sure.*'

"I missed that. Because when Ron was going over his testimony yesterday, he said that he rang the front-door bell. Neil didn't say one word about hearing chimes."

"That proves nothing," Hugh interrupted. "Neil was upstairs playing with his trains. They were noisy."

"No. Because he said, '*It got light.*' Mr. Peterson, this is my point. Ron rang the front-door bell. He waited, rang it again, walked around the house. He gave the killer time to escape. That's why the back door was open.

"Ron turned on the kitchen light. Don't you see? The reason Neil saw Ron's face clearly was because the light was coming in from the kitchen. Mr. Peterson, Neil comes running downstairs and sees his mother being strangled. The living room was dark. Only the foyer light was on. Isn't it possible that he went into some kind of shock, maybe even passed out? Then when he comes to, he *sees*, because now the light is coming from the kitchen through to the living room. Neil sees someone bending over his mother, someone tugging at her throat. Ron was trying to get that knotted scarf off. And he realized she was dead, so he panicked and ran. If he were a killer, would he have left an eyewitness like Neil?"

Hugh shook his head. "It's all conjecture. There isn't a scrap of proof in this."

"But Neil can give us the proof, if you will let him be questioned further," Bob begged.

"That's impossible!" Steve bit his lip. He'd been about to blurt out that you can't question a kidnapped child. "Just get out of here," he said.

"No, I won't get out!" Bob hesitated, then reached into his briefcase again. "I'm sorry to show you these, Mr. Peterson. They're the pictures taken of this house after the murder."

"Are you nuts?" Hugh grabbed for the photos. "Where did you get them? They're state's evidence."

"Never mind where I got them. Look at this one. See? The kitchen. The globe isn't on the ceiling fixture. That means the light might have been unusually strong."

Bob thrust open the kitchen door, dragged a chair over to the light fixture, jumped up on the chair, unscrewed the globe. The room brightened measurably. He hurried into the foyer and turned that light on. Finally he switched off the living-room lamps.

"Look into the living room. Now it's perfectly possible to see into it. Now wait." He rushed back into the kitchen and turned off the light. Steve and Hugh sat mesmerized at the table.

"Look," Bob pleaded. "With the kitchen light out, the living room is almost dark. What could Neil see? Not much more than a silhouette attacking his mother. He passes out. *He never heard the bell.* By the time Ron has rung the bell again and walked around the house, the killer is gone. And Ron probably saved your child's life by coming here that day."

Is it possible that boy is innocent? Steve wondered.

Striding into the dining room, Bob said, "Mr. Peterson, I beg you to let Neil be questioned. Please, give Ron that chance."

Steve saw the faint shaking of Hugh's head. If he admitted Neil had been kidnapped, this lawyer would suggest that it was tied to Nina's death. It would mean publicity; it might end the hope of getting Neil and Sharon back safely.

"My son is away," he said. "There have been threats against me because of my stand on capital punishment. I will not divulge his whereabouts to anyone."

"Mr. Peterson, an innocent nineteen-year-old kid is going to die tomorrow morning for something he didn't do!"

"I can't help you." Steve's calm snapped. "Get out and take those cursed pictures with you!"

Bob knew it was hopeless. Jamming the papers in his briefcase, he started to close it, then yanked out the copies of Ron's statements made the day before. He slapped them on the table.

"Read these, Mr. Peterson," he said, "and see if you can find a killer talking. Ron was sentenced to death because this county was shocked by the Carfolli and Weiss murders as well as your wife's. There have recently been two more murders of women in their cars. I swear to God those four murders are linked and I swear that somehow your wife's murder is connected to them. They were all strangled with their scarves or belts. The only difference is that your wife's killer came into your home."

He was gone, slamming the front door behind him. Steve looked at Hugh. "Could he be right about Nina's death?"

"He's a lawyer trying to save his client. Now please, that steak's probably no longer worth eating, but have *something*."

Steve nodded, crumbled a roll. The transcripts of Ron's statement were at his elbow. He started to read the top sheet.

I was pretty down about losing the job, but Mr. Timberly needed someone who could work more hours. I knew that being on the varsity would help me get a scholarship to college, so I couldn't work more. Mrs. Peterson heard Mr. Timberly. She said she was sorry and she asked me what kind of job I'd get. I said I'd done house painting. She told me that they'd just moved and there was a lot of painting to do and asked me to come over later and look at the house. I was putting her groceries in the trunk. I said, "I guess this is my lucky day, bad luck turning into good luck." Then we joked because she said, "It's my lucky day that way too. At least there's room in the trunk for all these darn groceries." That was at four o'clock. Then . . .

Steve stopped reading. Nina's *lucky day!*

The phone rang. Steve rushed to the kitchen extension. Let it be good news—please.

"Mr. Peterson, this is Father Kennedy from St. Monica's Church I'm afraid something quite unusual has happened."

Steve felt his throat muscles close. "What is it, Father?"

"Twenty minutes ago when I went to offer the evening mass, found a package propped against the door of the sanctuary. Le me read what it says. 'Deliver to Steve Peterson at once—life o death.' And your phone number. Could it possibly be some sor of joke?"

Steve felt the clammy sweat in his hands. "No, it's not a joke I'll be right down for it, Father; and please, don't say anything about this to anyone."

When Steve got back to the house half an hour later, Hugh wa waiting with the recorder. As the spool began to turn, for an in stant they heard a muted, rasping sound, then Sharon's voice. Steve paled. She was repeating the message the kidnapper had give him. What did she mean about being wrong? What was he supposed to forgive her for? Neil . . . That was the rasping sound Neil, choked with asthma. Steve listened to his son's halting voice Why did he mention his mother? Why now?

He gripped his fists until his knuckles were white, held them to his lips to push back the sobs that he felt shaking his chest.

418

And then it came. A warm, bubbly voice, melodic, welcoming. "Why, how nice of you," it was saying. "Do come in."

Steve jumped up as an anguished cry broke from his lips.

"What is it?" Hugh shouted. "Who is that?"

"Oh, God," Steve cried. "That's my wife—that's Nina!"

10

AGENT Lamont parked his car in front of the Mill Tavern in Carley. Through the window the dimly lighted interior seemed empty. Just as well—he'd get more chance to talk to the bartender.

He stepped inside. There were four men at the bar. He ambled up, heaved his bulk onto a stool, and ordered a Michelob.

While he sipped it, his eyes flitted from side to side. Two of the patrons were watching hockey on television, and a bald, glassy-eyed executive type was drinking a martini.

The bartender was drying glasses. "Never seen you around here, have I?" he asked Lamont.

"No. Just passing through and remembered my old buddy, Bill Lufts; says he's usually here about this time."

"Yeah, Bill's here just about every night," the bartender agreed. "Last night he was taking his wife out for their anniversary, but it's surprising he's not here tonight, unless she's giving him a lot of flak again. And if she does, we'll hear about it, right, Arty?"

The other drinker looked up from his beer. "In one ear and out the other," he said. "Who wants to listen to that stuff?"

Lamont laughed. "Well, what's a bar for if not to get your beefs out of your system?"

The men watching the hockey game switched it off. "This here's a friend of Bill Lufts." The bartender jerked his head toward Lamont. "Meet Les and Joe."

"Pete Lerner," Lamont lied. "Say, how about everyone having a beer on me?"

An hour passed. Lamont learned that Les and Joe were salesmen in a discount house on Route 7. Arty repaired cars. The bald-headed executive, Allan Kroeger, worked in an advertising agency.

419

Les was giving Joe a ride. They asked for their bill. Arty got up to go. The bartender waved away his money. "This one's on me," he said. "We'll miss you."

"Good luck, Arty," Les said. "Let us know how you're doing."

"Thanks. If it don't work, I'll come back and take the job at Shaw's. He's always bugging me to go with him."

"Why wouldn't he? He knows a good mechanic," Les said.

"Where'ye heading for?" Lamont asked.

"Rhode Island—Providence."

"Too bad you didn't get a chance to say good-by to Bill," Joe commented.

Arty laughed. "Rhode Island ain't Arizona. I'll be back. Well, better get some sleep. Want to get an early start."

Allan Kroeger wove unsteadily toward the door. "Arizona," he said, "home of the Painted Desert." The four men went out together, letting in a blast of cold air.

Lamont studied Arty's retreating back. "That Arty, he a particular friend of Bill Lufts'?"

The bartender shook his head. "Nah. Anybody who can *hear* is a friend of Bill's after he gets a couple of boilermakers."

"I see." Lamont shoved his glass forward. "Have one yourself."

"Don't mind if I do. Lousy night. Kind of gives you the creeps. And that Thompson kid's execution tomorrow."

Lamont's eyes narrowed. "That's what happens when you go around murdering people."

The bartender shook his head. "Most of us can't imagine that kid murdering anyone. But they say some of the most vicious killers are real ordinary on the surface."

"That's what I hear."

"You know, Bill and his missus live at the house of the woman who was murdered. He says the kid still has nightmares."

"It's tough," Lamont agreed.

"Bill says the kid's father will get married again. He's going with some writer—she was coming up last night. But the kid is pretty cool about her. Well, guess I'll start closing up. Want another?"

Lamont considered. He flipped out his badge. "FBI," he said.

420

An hour later he was back at the Peterson house. He conferred with Hugh, then called FBI headquarters in Manhattan. Making sure the den door was securely closed, he spoke softly into the phone. "Hugh was right. Bill Lufts is a bigmouth. Everyone in the Mill Tavern has known for two weeks that he and Mrs. Lufts would be out last night, that Peterson had a late meeting, and that Sharon Martin was expected. The bartender gave me a list of ten regulars. Some of them were there tonight. An Arty Taggert who's pulling out tomorrow for Rhode Island. Seems harmless. Two salesmen—wouldn't waste time on them. Here are the other names."

When he'd concluded, he added, "Another thing. Bill Lufts told that whole bar about Neil's trust fund less than a month ago; overheard Peterson talking to his accountant." He hung up, and walked out of the den. Steve was putting on his coat. It was nearly midnight and time to leave for his rendezvous with Foxy.

LALLY was so upset over the intruders that when she met Rosie in the main waiting room she blurted out the story and immediately was sorry. What if Rosie wanted to share her room?

She needn't have worried. "You couldn't get me near there!" Rosie shuddered. "You know how I hate cats."

"Well, you know me," Lally said. "I love them. Poor things get so hungry. . . . So I figure the two of them's staying there," she concluded, "and I'll scare off the girl when he's out. Maybe you could help me keep an eye on him."

Rosie loved intrigue. She smiled widely, revealing broken yellow teeth. "Sure."

They finished their coffee, carefully putting leftover pieces of the doughnuts in their shopping bags, and headed for the lower level. Somewhat nervously they took up a position near The Open Book display windows. They waited patiently. Then Lally grabbed Rosie's arm. "That's him, see, brown coat, green pants, coming up from the track. Now I can go down," Lally exulted.

Rosie looked doubtful. "Olendorf's on duty. I wouldn't." He was one of the strictest guards. "He keeps looking over here."

But Lally was not to be dissuaded. When she saw Olendorf leave for his lunch break, she slipped down to the platform. She disappeared around the track and hurried down the ramp as fast as her arthritic knees would allow. She'd have the girl out of her room in two minutes.

She shuffled around the sewer pipes. She looked up the staircase and smiled happily. She gripped the railing.

"Where do you think you're going, Lally?" The voice was sharp. Lally let out a frightened cry and turned around to face Officer Olendorf. So he'd only pretended to go to lunch.

She was silent, helpless. A spitting sound came from a shadowy corner and inspiration struck Lally. "The cats!" With a trembling hand she pointed to the moving skeletal forms. "They're starving! I wanted to bring them something to eat." Eagerly she yanked the bits of doughnut from her shopping bag and tossed them out.

The guard's tone was less hostile when he spoke. "I'm sorry for them too, but you've no business here." His glance passed her, eyed the steps, moved upward to the door of her room.

Lally's heart beat wildly. "You got cats home, Mr. Olendorf?" She was moving, willing him to come away.

He hesitated, shrugged, decided to follow her. "Used to, but my wife isn't much for cats anymore."

Back in the waiting room, Lally decided she wouldn't go near her place again until tonight when Olendorf went home.

NEIL knew Sharon was hurt. The man must have pushed her down. The rag on his mouth was so tight he couldn't talk. He wanted to tell Sharon how brave she was to fight that man. He'd been too scared to fight him when he was hurting Mommy.

Sharon had said, "Don't be scared if you hear me talk about leaving you. I won't leave you. But if I can get his gun, maybe we can make him take us out of here. We have to try to save Ronald Thompson."

He knew what Sharon meant. They were going to kill Ronald Thompson for hurting Mommy and he hadn't done it. But Neil said he had. Neil hadn't meant to lie. That was what he was trying to tell Daddy on the message.

422

It was so cold and his arms and legs hurt. But something inside him had stopped hurting. Sharon would figure a way to get them out of here. Or Daddy would come and get them.

He could feel Sharon's breath on his cheek. Being squished against her made him feel better. It was like when he was a little kid and sometimes woke up in the middle of the night with a bad dream and used to get into bed with Mommy and Daddy. Mommy would pull him close and say "Stop wiggling" in a sleepy voice, and he'd go back to sleep all tucked against her.

Sharon and Daddy would take care of him. He wished he could tell her not to worry about him. He'd take long, slow breaths through his nose. He'd think about something nice—the room on the top floor and the Lionel trains Sharon would give him.

"For God's sake, dear, it's nearly midnight. Give it up." Roger watched helplessly as Glenda shook her head.

"No. I'll get it. I know I will. I've been going back day by day, but I still have missed something. Maybe if I tell you . . ."

He knew it was useless to protest. Pulling up a chair close to the bed, he prepared to concentrate. His head was throbbing. Watching Glenda's ashen pallor, he thought of that day when she'd had the coronary. Oh, God, if she knows anything, let her remember, Roger prayed. If Neil and Sharon died and afterward Glenda felt she could have saved them, it would kill her too.

"Roger." Glenda's voice was remarkably steady. "Maybe if you make a diagram of each day, by hours, it will help to point up whatever I'm missing. There's a pad in my desk."

He walked over and got it. "All right," she said. "Let's go backward from last Saturday. . . ."

"Mr. Peterson"—Hugh reached out his hand—"good luck." Hugh and Steve were in the foyer. Steve was gripping the heavy suitcase containing the ransom money.

"Luck?" Steve said the word with wonderment. "I haven't been thinking of luck so much as I have of an old Wexford curse. It's something like this: 'May the fox build his nest on your hearthstone. May the light fade from your eyes, so you never see what you love. May the sweetest drink you take be the bitterest cup of sorrow.' Rather appropriate, isn't it?"

Without waiting for an answer, Steve left. Hugh watched the Mercury pull out of the driveway. *May the fox build his nest on your hearthstone.* God help that guy Peterson. He was coming to the end of his emotional tether. That business of Sharon's imitating his wife's voice had been the limit. And poor Peterson kept insisting it was Nina. What a clumsy way to try to link the abduction to Nina's death. There were a couple of other things. Sharon's request for Steve to forgive her, and Neil saying, "Sharon is taking care of me." Wasn't that the tip-off that this was a fraud? Or was it?

Grabbing his coat, Hugh hoped that John Owens would be able to help them. Hugh was meeting him at FBI headquarters in New York in a couple of hours. Maybe he could make something of the cassette the kidnapper had sent. A retired agent who'd gone blind twenty years before, John had developed his hearing so keenly that he could interpret underlying sounds on recordings with remarkable accuracy.

Hugh had asked Steve about Nina's background: Philadelphia Main Line family, attendance at a Swiss boarding school, and Bryn Mawr College. The information would be enough for Owens to give a pretty accurate opinion whether that voice was Nina's or an impersonation. Hugh had little doubt about the outcome.

THE Merritt Parkway had been sanded, and even though snow was still falling, the driving was better than Steve had expected. At 1:40 he was parked in front of the pay phone opposite Bloomingdale's. At precisely 2:00 a.m. the phone rang. The same muffled, whispering voice instructed him to go immediately to a phone on Ninety-sixth Street and Lexington Avenue.

At 2:15 that phone rang. Steve was told to drive over the Triborough Bridge, take Grand Central Parkway to the Brooklyn Queens Expressway exit; then drive to Roosevelt Avenue, turn left to the end of the first block, douse his headlights, and wait.

At 2:36 Steve turned onto Roosevelt Avenue. A large sedan was parked halfway down the block on the other side. As he passed it, he twisted the wheel, hoping the hidden cameras might be able to pick up the license number; then he pulled over and waited.

It was a dark street. The store windows were protected with gratings; elevated tracks blocked the streetlights.

There was a thump at the driver's door. Steve spun his head around, felt his mouth go dry. A gloved hand was gesturing for him to roll down the window. "Don't look at me, Peterson."

Steve glimpsed a dark coat, a ski mask. A duffel bag was dropped on his lap. He felt sick in the pit of his stomach. This man was not going to take the suitcase with the tracer.

"Open that suitcase and put the money in the bag. Hurry up."

Steve could hear the high-pitched undercurrent in the voice. With fumbling hands he wrenched the packets of money from the suitcase, jammed them into the duffel bag.

"Close it and hand it over. Don't look at me."

Steve stared straight ahead. "What about my son and Sharon?"

The abductor reached in through the window, yanked the bag away from him. "You're being watched, Peterson." The voice was hurried. "Don't leave here for fifteen minutes. If I'm not followed and the money is all here, you'll be told where to pick up your son and Sharon at eleven thirty this morning."

Eleven thirty—the exact minute of Ronald Thompson's execution. "Did you have anything to do with my wife's death?" Steve burst out.

There was no answer. The abductor had slipped away. Across the street a car started. Steve's watch said 2:38.

At 2:53 Steve headed back toward Manhattan. At 3:10 he was at FBI headquarters on Sixty-ninth Street and Third Avenue. Grim-faced agents rushed to his car and began unscrewing the headlights. A somber-looking Hugh listened to Steve's story as they rode up to the twelfth floor. There he was introduced to a man with snow-white hair and dark glasses.

"John has been listening to the cassette," Hugh explained. "From the quality of their voices and a certain echo, he concludes that Sharon and Neil are being kept in a nearly empty, cold room, about eleven by twenty-three feet. They may be near a freight yard; there's a continuing faint sound of trains."

"Mr. Peterson, about the last voice on the cassette." John Owens' manner was hesitant. "By any chance was your late wife's first tongue French rather than English?"

"No. She was raised in Philadelphia—wait a minute! Nina did tell me she'd had a French nurse, that as a young child she actually *thought* in French rather than English."

"Then that was no impostor or mimic. You are correct in identifying your wife's voice."

"All right. I was wrong about that," Hugh said. "But John says that last voice was definitely added to the cassette after Neil and Sharon were recorded."

The phone rang. Hugh grabbed it. "Good. Get right on it!" He slammed the receiver down. "Mr. Peterson, you got a clear picture of the car and license plate. We're tracing it now."

John Owens stretched out his hand in the direction of Steve's voice. "Mr. Peterson, my impression is that your wife spoke while she was opening a door. Are you aware of a particular door with a faint squealing sound when it opens, something like *eerkkk?*" He gave a startling imitation of a rusty hinge moving.

Hugh and Steve stared at each other. It is a mockery, Steve thought dully; it is already too late for everybody.

Hugh answered for him. "Yes, John. That's exactly the way Mr. Peterson's kitchen door sounds."

11

ARTY drove away from the Mill Tavern, a nagging worry sending alarm signals through his body. He'd counted on Bill Lufts being in the bar; he had wanted to pump him. If Bill wasn't there, maybe it was because Peterson had called the cops—or the FBI.

That guy who called himself Pete Lerner, who asked so many questions—he was an FBI agent. Arty knew it. Arizona. That had been a bad mistake. Why did he say, "Rhode Island ain't Arizona"? Probably the guy hadn't noticed, but it had been a mistake.

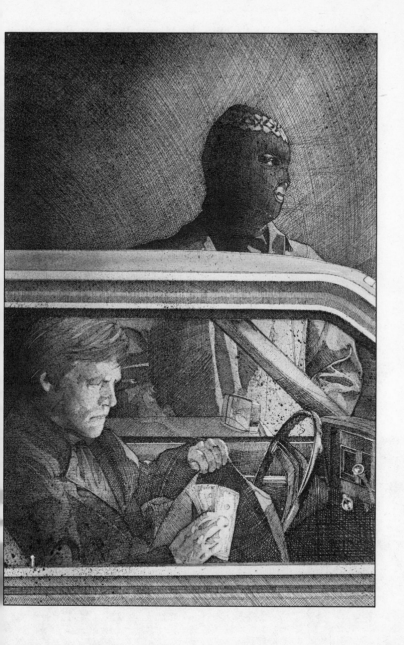

He steered the Beetle onto the Merritt Parkway. Perspiration oozed from his hands. Twelve years slipped away. He was being grilled in FBI headquarters in Manhattan. "Come on, man, the news vendor saw you with that kid. Where'd you take her?"

"I carried her bag out to a cab. She said she was meeting some guy." They couldn't prove anything. But they tried.

"How about the other girls, fella? Take a look at these pictures. You're always hanging around the Port Authority. How many of them did you carry bags for?"

They were coming too close. That was when he drifted up to Carley. Six years ago he'd taken over the repair shop there.

The Merritt faded into the Hutchinson River Parkway. His plan was ingenious. Stealing a car was dangerous. There was always the chance that the owner might come back in ten minutes, that the cops would have an alert before you had gone five miles. So you had to make sure the owner was out of the way—like watching a movie or taking off on a plane.

At 11:20 he drove into a parking lot at La Guardia Airport. He took a ticket from the machine; the gate lifted and he selected a space between a Chrysler and a Cadillac, behind an Oldsmobile wagon. In the midst of them the Beetle was hidden.

He slumped in the seat. Forty minutes passed. Two cars came by, one a flashy red, the other a yellow station wagon. Both too easy to spot. Then a dark blue Pontiac pulled into a spot three rows ahead, and the driver got out with a large suitcase. A few minutes later Foxy saw the man board the bus for the terminal.

Quietly Foxy got out of the Beetle and in quick strides was beside the Pontiac. The second key he tried opened the door. He switched on the ignition. The engine started almost noiselessly; the tank was three-quarters full. Perfect.

He turned off the engine. The guard would be suspicious if he collected on a ticket with less than a couple of hours' parking in this lot. But he had plenty of time. He leaned back, closed his eyes, and Nina's image floated across his mind . . . that first night. . . .

He'd been cruising around, knowing it was too soon after Jean Carfolli and Mrs. Weiss, but he'd seen the Karmann Ghia alongside

428

Route 7 in that lonely spot. The slender body caught by his head-lights. The little hands struggling with the jack. The enormous eyes that looked startled when he pulled over.

"Can I help you, miss? I'm a mechanic."

The worried look disappeared. "Oh, great," she said. "Of all the crazy places to get a flat."

Quickly he changed the tire. He stood up.

"How much do I owe you?" Her purse open, her neck bent. Her breast rising and falling under the suede coat. Class. Something about her that showed it. He reached out his hand to touch her.

A light swung from across the road, illuminated the two of them. A cop car. He could see the dome. "It's three dollars to change the tire," he said briskly, "and I can fix your flat if you want. I'm Arty Taggert; I have a repair shop in Carley on Monroe Street."

The police car pulled up. The trooper got out. "You all right, ma'am?" His look at Arty was suspicious.

"Oh, fine, Officer. I certainly was in luck. Mr. Taggert is from my town and he came along just as I got the flat."

She made it sound like she knew him. What a break! The police-man's expression changed. "You're lucky, ma'am. It's not safe for women to be alone in disabled cars these days."

The cop got back in the patrol car but stayed there watching. "Will you fix the tire for me?" she asked. "I'm Nina Peterson. We live on Driftwood Lane."

"Be glad to." He took the tire and got back in his car, never show-ing that he *had* to see her again. He could tell the way she looked at him that she was sorry the cop had come along too.

So he'd driven away and the next morning she called him. "My husband just gave me what-for about driving on the spare," she said, and her voice was very warm. "When can I pick up my tire?"

He thought fast. Driftwood Lane was in a quiet area. If she came to his place, there'd be no way of getting friendly with her.

"I have to go out on a job right now," he lied. "I'll bring it by late this afternoon, about five." It got dark by five.

"Wonderful," she said. "As long as the darn thing is on the car before I go to pick up my husband at half past six."

Feeling so excited that day, he didn't bother with work. He just showered and dressed and listened to his cassettes. Then he put a fresh cassette in the recorder and labeled it NINA. He made sure his camera was loaded. At 5:10 he left for Driftwood Lane. He parked in the woods next to her house. Just in case . . .

Her car was in the driveway, keys in the ignition. He could see her through the kitchen window, unpacking groceries. The bare bulb made the room very bright. And she was so beautiful in that pale blue sweater, and that scarf knotted at her throat.

He changed the tire very fast, keeping an eye out for signs of other people in the house. Then he turned on the recorder and began to whisper into it his plans for making Nina happy. He went up to the kitchen door and knocked. She ran over, looked startled, but he held up her keys, smiling through the glass. Right away she opened the door, all warm and friendly, invited him in.

She asked what she owed him. He reached up—he had his gloves on, of course—and switched off the light. He held her face and kissed her. "Pay me like this," he whispered.

She slapped him, a stunning slap. "Get out of here," she said, like he was dirt, like he hadn't done her a favor.

He went wild. Like the other times. He reached for her scarf. But she slipped away and ran into the living room. She never screamed for help. Afterward he understood why. She didn't want him to know the child was in the house. But she seized a poker from the fireplace.

Laughing, he put the poker back. Then he grabbed her scarf and twisted it around her neck. Her great brown eyes widened and glazed and accused. She gasped. Her face turned blue.

He was holding her with one hand, snapping the picture, when he heard a choking sound somewhere behind him.

He swung around. The boy was standing in the foyer, staring at him with huge brown eyes that burned through him. The boy was gasping just like she'd been gasping. It was like he hadn't killed her at all; like she'd moved into the boy's body, taunting him, promising revenge.

He started across the room for the boy. He'd make him stop that

430

noise; he'd close those eyes. He bent over the boy. The chimes rang.

Racing into the kitchen, he slipped out the back door. The chimes rang again. He was out through the woods, in his car, back in his shop in a few minutes. He went to the Mill for a beer, was there when news of the murder swept through the town.

He was scared, but he heard later that a neighbor had been knocked down by someone running out of the Peterson house. She had identified him as Ronald Thompson, a local boy who had been seen talking to Mrs. Peterson that afternoon.

Then Thompson was caught at that motel in Virginia and the kid identified him too. Incredible luck. The living room had been dark. The boy might not have seen his face clearly, and then Thompson must have gone into the house.

But he'd started to go for the kid; he'd gotten close to him. The boy must have been in shock. . . . Suppose he remembered someday. The eyes haunted Arty's dreams.

He never went looking for girls after that. Until that night last month when he heard the Callahan girl on his CB saying she had a blowout. Two weeks later he went out when Mrs. Ambrose got on the CB saying she was out of gas.

After these last two, the dreams of Nina came every night. Accusing. Then a couple of weeks ago Bill Lufts drove up to his place with the boy, Neil, beside him in the wagon. Neil stared at Arty. That was when he knew he had to kill Neil. And when Lufts bragged about the trust fund in Neil's name, he'd known how to get the money he needed to leave Carley.

Whenever he thought about Nina, he hated Steve Peterson more. Peterson had been able to touch her without getting slapped; Peterson was a big-shot editor with people to wait on him; Peterson had a good-looking new girl friend. He'd show him.

Then everything came together. The August *Rommel* Taggert plan. A fox's plan. Sharon and Neil would die just at the minute the Thompson kid was executed. Because he was executing them too, and Thompson deserved to die for having interfered that night. If only Sharon didn't have to die; if only she had loved him. . . .

And all those people in Grand Central under tons of rubble.

They'd know how it felt to be trapped. And he'd be free. Soon.

It was time to go. He turned the ignition key in the Pontiac. At 1:45 he paid the tollbooth collector for the ticket he'd taken at the gate for his Volks, and drove out of the airport to a phone on Queens Boulevard. Promptly at 2:00 he called the pay phone opposite Bloomingdale's. As soon as Peterson answered, he directed him to the public phone at Ninety-sixth Street.

He was hungry. In an all-night diner, he gulped down coffee and some toast as he watched the clock. At 2:15 he dialed the Ninety-sixth Street phone and tersely gave directions to Steve. Now for the really dangerous part.

At 2:25 he headed toward Roosevelt Avenue. Ten minutes later he parked, facing the Brooklyn Queens Expressway. It was a good place to make contact. It was exactly six minutes from La Guardia, in case the cops came with Peterson and he had to get away. And the pillars of the elevated tracks obstructed the view.

At 2:36 he saw headlights approaching. Instantly he slipped on the ski mask. Peterson's Mercury swerved right at him. Was he trying to take a picture? Lot of good that would do.

Peterson's car stopped across the street. Foxy swallowed nervously. He had to move fast. He reached for the duffel bag. In his electronics magazine he'd read that in ransom payments suitcases were usually bugged. He wasn't taking any chances.

He crossed the street, rapped on the car door. As the window slid down, he shoved in the duffel bag. In the whispery voice he'd practiced, he told Peterson to put the money in the bag.

Peterson didn't argue. Foxy's eyes roamed the area for cops. He watched Peterson drop the last packet of bills in the duffel bag and told him to close it and hand it over.

"Did you have anything to do with my wife's death?"

The question startled Foxy. How much were they beginning to suspect? He had to get away. He was sweating now, heavy beads of perspiration that soaked his suit. He crossed the street, got back in the Pontiac and floored the accelerator. At 2:46 he was at La Guardia. Ninety seconds later the Pontiac was parked exactly where he'd found it.

He locked the car and hurried to the dark green Beetle. Inside the Volks he opened the duffel bag, switched on his flashlight, and greedily began to count. It was all there. Eighty-two thousand dollars. He reached for the empty suitcase in the back seat and neatly piled the packets inside it. This bag he'd carry on the plane.

At 7:00 a.m. he pulled out of the parking lot and blended with the commuter traffic into Manhattan. He parked in the Biltmore garage and hurried upstairs to his room for a shave and shower.

By 4:00 a.m. it was clear that the one lead they had, the license number of the car the abductor had used, was going sour. The Pontiac was registered to Henry A. White, a vice-president of the International Food Company of White Plains. A quick investigation showed that Mr. White had just left for a skiing vacation.

At 5:00 a.m. Hugh and Steve left Manhattan for Carley. Hugh drove. "What do you make of the Pontiac?" Steve asked.

"It'll probably turn out that White's car was stolen from wherever he left it," Hugh replied.

"What do we do next?"

"We wait. He may release them. He has the money."

"He's covered his tracks so carefully. You don't really expect him to release two people who could identify him, do you?"

"I don't know," Hugh admitted. "If he doesn't let them go, we have to consider giving the story to the media."

Steve stared ahead. "Could publicity panic the kidnapper?"

"I would say so." Hugh's inflection was different, crisper. "What's on your mind, Mr. Peterson?"

The question. Flat. Direct. Steve felt his mouth go dry. It's only a hunch, he told himself. But it may cost Neil and Sharon their lives. Then he thought of what Ronald Thompson had said at the trial: "I didn't do it. She was dead when I got there."

"Hugh, do you remember that Bob Kurner said he thought the murders of those four women and Nina's murder were tied together, that the only thing he couldn't understand was that the others had car trouble and Nina had been strangled at home?"

"Go on."

433

"The night before she was murdered, Nina got a flat. The next morning when she drove me to the train, I noticed the spare was on her car. Remember that transcript Kurner left? Thompson recalled that Nina said something about the groceries all fitting in the trunk."

"What are you saying?"

"Her trunk was small. If she had extra room in it, it can only mean that the spare tire hadn't been put back. That was after four o'clock and she must have gone directly home, because Dora was there housecleaning that day and said Nina drove her home shortly before five."

"Then she and Neil went straight back to your house?"

"Yes, and he went up to play with his trains. Nina unloaded the car. We know she died in the next few minutes. I looked at her car that night. The spare tire was in the trunk. The new radial was back on her front wheel."

"You're saying that someone returned the tire, changed it, then killed her?"

"When else could the tire have been changed except right at that time? And if that happened, that Thompson boy may be innocent. For God's sake, find out if he remembers whether the spare was in the trunk when he loaded those groceries."

Hugh pressed on the accelerator. The speedometer climbed to eighty. The car screeched into Steve's driveway as dawn cut across the somber sky. Hugh rushed to the phone, dialed the prison and demanded to speak to the warden. He told him the story. . . . "I'll hold on." He turned to Steve. "They're shaving the kid now."

"Good God—"

"Yes, I'm here." Hugh listened. "Thank you very much." He slammed down the phone. "Thompson swears the spare was missing when he loaded the groceries."

"Call the governor," Steve pleaded. "Beg her to at least delay the execution."

Hugh was dialing the statehouse. "It's not evidence," he said. "It's a string of coincidences. I doubt she'll postpone it on this."

The governor could not be reached. She had referred all requests for postponement of the execution to the attorney general. He would be in his office at eight. There was nothing to do except wait. Steve prayed, Dear God, they are all three so young . . . please . . .

At 7:35 Bob Kurner's car pulled into the driveway. He stalked in furiously and demanded to know why Ronald had been asked about the spare tire.

Hugh glanced at Steve. Steve nodded. Tersely Hugh explained.

Bob paled. "Do you mean that Mr. Peterson's son and Sharon Martin were kidnapped and you've been covering it up? When the governor knows this, she'll *have* to postpone the execution."

At exactly eight o'clock Hugh reached the attorney general. He spoke for thirty-five minutes, his voice forceful, arguing, pleading. He was still talking when Steve heard the dial tone. Hugh let the phone drop. "The execution's on," he told them flatly.

12

IT WAS so hard to think with the pain shooting up through her body. Her throbbing ankle was still swelling against the boot, against the biting twine. She smothered a moan.

She felt Neil sliding closer to her, trying to comfort her. He would be so like Steve when he grew up. *If* he grew up. She had to get him out of here. She tried to think. . . .

She was drifting away. Time passed. Was it day or night? Muted train sounds . . . Come for us, Steve. "I love you, Sharon . . . I've missed you terribly." Big, gentle hands on her face . . .

Big, gentle hands on her face. Sharon opened her eyes. Foxy was bending over her. With horrible gentleness his hands were running over her face, her neck. He slipped the gag from her mouth and kissed her. She tried to turn her head.

He whispered, "It's all finished, Sharon. I have the money."

She tried to focus on his glittering eyes through the blur.

"You killed Neil's mother. You're going to kill us."

"That's right, Sharon. Oh, I almost forgot." He was unwrapping something. "I'll put this picture up with the others." She looked

435

up. Eyes like Neil's were staring down at her, eyes that were part of a sprawled body with a scarf around its neck. A shriek tore her throat. He was hanging it next to the others on the wall, ritualistic in his exactness. Would he strangle them now?

"I'm going to set the clock for you," he told her. "It will make the bomb go off at eleven thirty. You won't feel anything, Sharon. You'll just be gone. And Neil. And Ronald Thompson."

He was opening the suitcase. She watched as he took out a clock and set it at 8:30. He was setting the alarm for 11:30. Now he was attaching wires to the clock. Three hours.

Carefully he put the suitcase on top of the laundry tubs near the door. The face of the clock glowed across the room.

"Do you want anything before I go, Sharon?"

"Could I . . . would you let me go into the bathroom?"

"Sure, Sharon." He came over, untied her hands, helped her up. Her leg collapsed under her. Black curtains closed over her eyes. No . . . no . . . she could not faint.

He left her inside the dark cubbyhole. She twisted the doorknob around, around. A faint cracking. The handle broke off.

Sharon felt the jagged edge of the metal. She slipped the handle in the deep pocket of her skirt and opened the door. He tossed her down on the cot, retied her hands. She was able to keep them a little separated. The gag was placed over her mouth.

Foxy leaned over her. "I could have loved you very much, Sharon, as I think you could have loved me."

With a quick movement he pulled off Neil's blindfold. Neil blinked, his eyes looked enormous. The man stared directly into his eyes; his gaze slid to the picture on the wall, then back. Abruptly he clicked off the lights and slipped out of the room.

Sharon watched the glowing clock. It was 8:36.

GLENDA's bed was strewn with pages. "No, on the fourteenth I didn't go straight to the doctor. I stopped at the library—put that in, Roger." They reviewed every detail of the past month, but nothing triggered awareness in Glenda of the man who called himself Foxy. At 4:00 a.m. Roger said, "We're so tired we're incapable of thinking. Let's get some sleep." He set the alarm for 7:00.

At 7:00 Roger went down to make tea. Glenda slipped a nitro-glycerin tablet under her tongue and picked up her pad.

At 9:00 Marian Vogler arrived. At 9:15 she came up to see Glenda. "I'm sorry you're not feeling well, Mrs. Perry. I'll concentrate on cleaning the downstairs."

"That would be fine. Thank you."

"I'm just glad to be here, that I didn't have to disappoint you with the trouble we had over the car."

"My husband mentioned something." Glenda's pen was poised.

"It was really awful. After just spending four hundred dollars to get it fixed. Arty's such a good mechanic that my husband said it was worth it. Well, I see you're busy. I shouldn't be gabbing."

The door closed behind her. A moment later Roger came in. Glenda depressed the "play" button on the recorder. The familiar sentence filled their ears: "In ten minutes I'll call you at the pay phone of the service station . . ." She snapped the machine off. "Roger, when did we get my car serviced?"

"A little over a month ago, I think. Bill Lufts took it to that place he recommended."

"Yes, and you dropped me off there when it was ready. *Arty*, that was his name. I noticed his sign said 'A. R. Taggert' and asked if the *A* stood for Arthur, because I'd heard Bill call him Arty.

"Roger"—Glenda's voice rose—"he told me that people started to call him Arty because of the sign A. R. Taggert, but that his name really was August Rommel Taggert. And I said, 'Rommel—wasn't he the famous German general?'

"And he said, 'Yes, Rommel was the Desert *Fox*.' The way he said *Foxy* on the phone the other night— Roger, I swear that mechanic is Foxy and he's the one who kidnapped Neil and Sharon!"

It was 9:31 a.m.

LALLY hadn't slept all night. She was getting sick. There was something inside her winding down. She wanted to get into her room and lie on the cot and close her eyes. She *had* to.

She drifted down with the 8:40 Mount Vernon passengers. It

437

didn't even matter if the man was there. She'd take her chances. Her heavy sneakers padded silently back to the staircase.

Then she heard the muffled sound of a door opening slowly. Her door. Lally shrank behind a generator.

Soft footsteps. He was coming down the metal stairs, the same man. She pressed against the wall. She watched him stop, listen intently, then move toward the ramp. In a minute he'd be gone. If the girl was still in her room, she'd scare her off.

Her arthritic fingers started to pull the key from her pocket, fumbled. It fell with a ping at her feet. She held her breath. Had he heard? There was no sound. She waited ten minutes, trying to calm the pounding of her heart. Then slowly she bent down, felt for her key. It was so dark. She found it and sighed with relief.

Lally was just straightening up when something shivery cold grazed against her back. She gasped as it touched her skin and slipped in, so sharp, so quickly that she barely felt the blinding pain, the warm gushing of her blood as she sank to her knees and slumped forward. As she slipped into unconsciousness, her right fist closed around the key.

At 9:30 an agent from FBI headquarters phoned Hugh Taylor at Steve's home. "We think we have something, Hughie."

"What is it?"

"That mechanic at the bar, Arty Taggert. A guy known as Gus Taggert got picked up hanging around the Port Authority about twelve years ago. Suspect in disappearance of some young girls. His description matches the one you gave us."

"Good work. What else have you got on him?"

"We're trying to check out where he used to live. He had a bunch of jobs in New York, pumping gas on the West Side, dishwasher in the Oyster Bar—"

"Concentrate on where he lived, if he has any family."

Hugh hung up. "Mr. Peterson," he said, "we may have a lead. A mechanic who hangs around the Mill Tavern—"

"A mechanic." Steve's voice rose. "A *mechanic!*"

"Exactly. I know what you're thinking. It's a slim chance, but if someone fixed your wife's tire that day, is it possible she'd have written a check—"

The phone rang. It was Roger Perry shouting that Glenda was positive a mechanic called A. R. Taggert was Foxy.

Hugh slammed down the phone, was about to dial New York when it rang again. "What?"

Steve watched as Hugh started writing on a pad.

Thank you for the money. You have kept your promise. Now I will keep mine. Neil and Sharon are alive. At 11:30 they will be executed during an explosion in New York State. In the rubble from that explosion you can dig for their bodies.

Foxy

Steve stared at the pad. "Who took the message?" he asked.

Hugh's voice was infinitely weary. "He phoned the mortician in Carley who handled your wife's funeral arrangements."

It was 9:35 a.m.

IF THAT old hag hadn't made that noise! Arty was drenched in perspiration. Suppose he hadn't heard her? She must be the one who'd dragged that cot into the room. If she'd found them, they'd have had time to get experts to deactivate the bomb.

He hurried to the Biltmore, where he picked up his car from the hotel garage and drove frantically to La Guardia. The plane to Phoenix left at 10:30.

He returned to the parking lot that he'd left only hours before. He pulled his two suitcases and the crated CB radio out of the trunk, walked swiftly to the bus stop, and took the next courtesy airport bus. The other passengers glanced at him indifferently. Little did they know that he was a clever, wealthy man.

At the American Airlines entrance, a skycap was checking luggage. Arty showed his ticket. The name on it was Renard. That meant fox in French. It was the name he planned to use in Arizona.

"Check all three pieces, sir?"

"Not that one!" He yanked away the suitcase with the money.

Once inside the terminal he made a telephone call. Then he stopped in a cafeteria and ordered breakfast. He was beginning to relax. The thought of the phone call to the funeral home made him chuckle. At first he was going to warn them of an explosion in New York *City*. At the last minute he'd changed it to New York *State*. He could just imagine the cops going nuts now.

Looking into the boy's eyes had been necessary. He wouldn't have to run away from them ever again. . . . Arizona, land of the Painted Desert.

At 10:12 he left the cafeteria, the suitcase gripped in his hand.

At 10:15, as he was passing a phone booth near the departure gate, an idea occurred to him.

Quickly he stepped into the booth, pulled out quarters and dimes, dialed a number. He whispered a message, replaced the receiver, went through the inspection, and checked in without a hitch.

The boarding sign was flashing as he hurried to the plane.

It was 10:16 a.m.

HER clothes felt wet and warm and sticky. Blood. She was bleeding to death. Lally knew it. The man who had taken her room had taken her life. . . . Her room. She wanted to die in it. Maybe no one would find her there. She'd be entombed in the only home she'd ever had, sleeping forever with the comforting sound of her trains. She didn't have long. She had to get to her room.

Aware of the key in her right fist, Lally tried to drag herself up. Something was pulling—the knife was still plunged into her. She couldn't reach it. She began to crawl toward her room. Twenty feet to the staircase. Then the stairs. Could she?

Right hand . . . left hand forward . . . right knee . . . left knee . . . She would do it. She kept in her mind the vision of opening the door, closing it . . . pulling herself up on the cot . . . waiting.

Death would come as a friend, with cool and gentle hands.

THEY are dead, Steve thought. When you are condemned, you are already dead. He was standing by the window. A knot of reporters and television cameras was grouped outside. It was 10:10.

440

"We have an hour and twenty minutes. What have you done about the bomb threat?" he asked Hugh.

"Alerted every major city in the state to stand by for an emergency. An explosion in *New York State*—do you know how many thousands of square miles that covers?"

Agent Lamont came in with Bill Lufts. They were going over his story again. "Mr. Lufts, you've talked to this Arty a lot. Please try to remember—has he ever mentioned wanting to go to some particular place, like Mexico or Alaska?"

Bill shook his head. Arty, a quiet fellow, a good mechanic. Just two weeks ago he and Neil had driven over to his place. Desperately he tried to remember what Arty talked about.

Lamont was furious at himself. He'd been sitting in the tavern buying that guy beers. Like Hughie always said, everything a man does leaves traces. He could see that guy leaving the bar. Arty had made some crack when he said good-by. What was it?

Bill was saying, "Like I tell you, minds his business—"

"Hold on," Lamont interrupted.

"What is it?" Hugh asked the younger agent.

"When Arty left the Mill Tavern with the others, and they said something about his not seeing Bill before he left for Rhode Island—"

"Yeah. And in a pig's eye he's heading for Rhode Island."

"That's what I mean. He said something else, and that advertising guy made a crack—about the Painted Desert. That's it! Arty said, 'Rhode Island ain't Arizona.' Could that have been a slip?"

"We'll find out soon." Hugh barked orders into the phone. "If he's heading for Arizona, we'll get him."

Roger came in, put his hand on Steve's shoulder. "Glenda wants you to come over. Please. We'll go out the back way and avoid the reporters."

A ghost of a smile touched Steve's lips. "I don't intend to avoid them." He opened the door. The reporters raced to him. Television cameras angled to catch his drawn, tired face.

"Mr. Peterson, do you think the kidnapper will carry out his threat to execute your son and Sharon Martin?"

"We have every reason to believe he's capable of doing so."

"Do you think it's a coincidence that the explosion is threatened for the exact minute of Ronald Thompson's execution?"

"I do not think it is coincidence. I think the kidnapper, Foxy, may have been involved in my wife's death. I have tried to reach the governor. I now publicly implore her to delay the Thompson execution. That boy may very well be innocent—I think he is."

"Mr. Peterson, has your position on capital punishment changed in view of your terrible worry over your son and Miss Martin?"

Steve looked directly into the camera. "Yes. I have changed my mind. I say this knowing that it is very unlikely that my son and Sharon will be found alive. But even if their kidnapper is apprehended too late to save them, I have learned something in these past two days. No man has the right to determine the time of death of a fellow human being. I believe that power rests only with Almighty God, and"—his voice broke—"I only ask you to pray to that God that Neil and Sharon and Ronald will be spared this morning." Tears streamed down his cheeks. "Let me pass. . . ."

Quietly the reporters separated. Roger and Hugh ran behind him as he darted across the street.

Glenda opened the door for them, put her arms around Steve. "Let it out, dear," she said quietly. "Go ahead."

"I can't lose them," he cried brokenly.

She let him cry, hugging him as the broad shoulders heaved. If I had only remembered sooner, she agonized. "Steve, you're going to have a cup of tea and some toast. You haven't eaten or slept in two days." Somberly they went into the dining room.

The door between the kitchen and dining room was open and Marian could overhear the conversation. That poor Mr. Peterson. No wonder he'd seemed so rude when she spoke to him. He'd been all choked up about the little boy being kidnapped. Shows you should never judge people.

She took in the teapot. Steve's face was buried in his hands. "Mr. Peterson," she said gently. "Let me fix you a nice hot cup of tea." She picked up his cup. With the other hand she began to pour.

Slowly Steve lowered his hands from his face. The next instant the teapot was flying across the table, spilling a bubbling stream over the flowered placemats.

Glenda, Roger, and Hugh jumped up. Shocked, they watched Steve, who was gripping a terrified Marian's arms. "Where did you get that ring?" he shouted. "Where did you get that ring?"

AT THE state prison, Kate Thompson kissed her son good-by. She stared unseeingly at his shaved head, the slits in the legs of his trousers. She was dry-eyed as she felt his strong arms around her. She pulled his face down. "Be brave, dear."

"I will. Bob said he'd look out for you, Mama."

She left him. Bob Kurner was going to stay until the end. She knew it was easier if she went now—easier for Ron.

She walked out of the prison, along the windswept road to town. A police car came by. "Let me drop you, ma'am."

"Thank you." With dignity, she got in the car. "Would you take me to St. Bernard's, please."

The church was empty. She knelt at the statue of the Virgin. "Be with him at the end. You who gave up your innocent Son, help me if I must give up mine. . . ."

A TREMBLING Marian tried to speak over the dryness in her mouth. The tea had burned her hand. Her finger hurt where Mr. Peterson had wrenched the ring from it.

Mr. Peterson gripped her wrist. "Where did you get the ring?"

"I . . . I . . . I found it."

"You *found* it!" Hugh's voice dripped with scorn. He looked directly at Steve. "Are you positive this is Sharon's ring?"

"Absolutely. I bought it in Mexico. It's one of a kind. Look!" He tossed it to Hugh. "Feel the ridge inside the band."

Hugh ran his finger over the ring. His expression hardened. "Mrs. Vogler, you're coming in for questioning."

"You talked about Arty this morning," Glenda accused. "How *could* you, a woman with children of her own, be part of this?"

Marian thought she was going to faint. The ring wasn't hers. Now they suspected she had something to do with the kidnapping. How could she make them believe her? "Mr. Peterson . . . I want to help. I *did* find the ring. In our car. Our car was stolen Monday night. Arty had just fixed it for us."

Steve looked into the frightened face. "Stolen! *Your* car?"

"Let me handle this, Mr. Peterson." Hugh helped Marian into a chair. "Mrs. Vogler, how well do you know Arty?"

"Not well. He's a good mechanic. I picked the car up from him on Monday. Then I went to the movie. I parked it in the movie lot. It was gone when I got out at seven thirty."

"Did he know you'd be going to the movie?" Hugh asked.

Marian frowned. "Yes, we were talking about it at his place. And then he filled up the car with gas."

"Mrs. Vogler," Hugh said. "*Where* was your car recovered?"

"In New York City. The police towed it. It was illegally parked by some hotel . . . Vanderbilt Avenue!" she cried. "On Vanderbilt Avenue near the *Biltmore* Hotel."

Hugh grabbed the phone and dialed FBI headquarters in New York. He issued orders. "Get back to me fast." He hung up.

"An agent is rushing to the Biltmore with an old mug shot we have of Taggert," he said. "Let's hope they can help."

Tensely they waited. Steve prayed. "Dear God, please!"

The phone rang. Hugh yanked the receiver off the hook, listened, yelled, "Good God, I'm on my way." He dropped the phone. "The room clerk positively identified the picture as an A. R. Renard who checked in on Sunday night. He had a dark green Beetle in the Biltmore garage. He checked out this morning."

"*Renard*—that's French for fox," Glenda cried.

"The clerk has seen him going in and out at odd hours, which could mean he's keeping Neil and Sharon somewhere in midtown."

"We've got no time, no time," Steve cried. "What good will knowing this do?"

"I'm taking the copter down to the Pan Am Building. If we don't get Taggert in time, our best bet is to search in the Biltmore area. Do you want to come?"

Steve didn't bother to answer. He ran for his coat.

Glenda looked at the clock. It was 10:30.

FATHER KENNEDY sat at his desk in St. Monica's rectory listening to the news. No wonder Steven Peterson had been so upset when he came for the package at the rectory last night.

The phone rang. Wearily he picked it up. "Father Kennedy."

"Thanks for delivering the package, Father. This is Foxy."

The priest felt his throat constrict. "What—"

"Never mind any questions. Just call Steve Peterson and tell him I said the bomb will go off at a major transportation center in New York City. He can do his digging there."

The phone went dead.

13

FOXY moved across the waiting area of gate 9 toward the ramp that led to the plane. A presentiment of danger was jangling his nerves. He glanced down at the boarding pass he held in one hand and the black suitcase he gripped firmly with the other.

Sound! That was it. The sound of running feet. Police! He dropped his ticket, vaulted the low divider between boarding area and corridor. Two men were racing down the corridor toward him. Desperately he looked around and saw an emergency exit fifty feet away. It must lead to the field.

But he couldn't run with the suitcase. With only the briefest hesitation, he threw it backward. It thumped against the floor and burst open. Money scattered over the corridor.

"Stop or we'll shoot!" a voice commanded.

Foxy threw open the emergency door, yanked it closed, and wove across the field. He ran around the Phoenix-bound plane. A small service van, its engine running, was near the left wing. The driver was just getting back in. Foxy grabbed him from behind, punched him viciously in the neck. The man grunted and collapsed. Foxy shoved him aside and jumped into the van. Pressing his foot down on the accelerator, he raced away from the plane.

The cops would be following in a car any second. But they'd never look for him in the terminal. He stopped near a hangar, grabbed a requisitions book from the seat beside him, and got out of the van. A door marked AUTHORIZED PERSONNEL ONLY was ahead. Bending over the book, he opened it and went through.

Now his manner became authoritative as he swiftly walked through the terminal, out to the curb, and hailed a cab.

"Grand Central Station," he told the driver. He pulled out a twenty-dollar bill, the last of his money. "How fast can you get there? I gotta make a train before eleven thirty."

"Mister, that's calling it close, but I'll do it. Hang on."

Foxy leaned back. Icy perspiration chilled him. This was Sharon's fault. He should have strangled her yesterday. She had tricked him, pretending to be in love with him. Then trying to get his gun. She was the worst of all of them, the women in the foster homes, in the detention homes, all pushing him away when he tried to kiss them. "Stop that! Don't do that!"

The bomb was too good for her. She had to feel his hands on her throat. He had to look down at her and listen to her beg him not to—then he'd squeeze. He shivered in ecstasy.

If he got into the room by 11:25, he'd have enough time. He'd get away through the Park Avenue tunnel.

They passed through the midtown tunnel. The traffic began to back up at Thirty-eighth Street. The driver whistled. "Mister, looks like some streets are closed off up there."

Foxy tossed the twenty-dollar bill at the driver, opened the door, and slid out. Cops all over the place. Forty-second Street closed off. He shoved his way through. People were talking about a bomb in the station. Had they found Sharon and the boy? The thought brought black fury.

"Stand back, buddy. You can't go any further." A burly policeman tapped his shoulder.

"What's the matter?" He had to know.

"Nothing, we hope, sir. But there's been a bomb threat."

His own phone call! *Threat!* That meant they hadn't found the bomb. Exultation leaped through him. His hands tingled the way they always did when he started to go to a girl and knew nothing could stop him. He spoke smoothly to the cop. "I'm a surgeon. I'm joining the emergency squad in case I'm needed."

446

"Oh, sorry, Doctor. Go right through."

Foxy ran along Forty-second Street, where people were streaming out of buildings, prodded by the urgency of the police bullhorns. "Do not panic. Walk to Third or Fifth Avenue."

It was exactly 11:22 when Foxy reached the main entrance to the terminal. The doors had been wedged open to speed the exodus. A policeman grabbed Foxy's arm. "Hey, you can't go in there!"

"Terminal engineer," Foxy said crisply. "I've been sent for." The cop dropped his arm.

He ran into the station. Grim-faced policemen were searching behind booths. He'd outsmarted all of them! A small group of people was clustered near the information desk. The tallest one, a broad-shouldered, sandy-haired man, was shaking his head. Steve Peterson! Sucking in his breath, Foxy raced across the concourse. He needed only two more minutes. His fingers curled and uncurled as he rushed down the stairs to the lower level. Unchallenged, he ran through the gate to the Mount Vernon platform.

THE news of Foxy's phone call to Father Kennedy reached Hugh and Steve as the helicopter passed over the Triborough Bridge.

"*Major transportation center, New York City,*" Hugh snapped into the phone. "That includes all airports, bus terminals, and railroad stations. Have you started evacuating them?"

Steve's hands were clasping and unclasping. Oh, God, it was hopeless. . . . "May the fox build his nest on your hearthstone . . ."

Hugh hung up the phone. "There's no use kidding. It's bad. We have to assume he's carried out his threat to set that bomb."

Steve's voice was ragged. "Where do you start looking?"

"The main search will be in Grand Central. Remember, he stayed at the Biltmore and John Owens heard trains on that cassette."

"What about the Thompson boy?"

"If we don't get a confession out of Foxy, he's finished."

At 11:05 the helicopter landed on the Pan Am Building. Hugh threw open the door. A thin-faced agent ran over to them. White with anger, he briefed them on Foxy's escape.

"*Escaped?*" Hugh exploded. "Are you sure it was Foxy?"

447

"He dropped the ransom. They're searching the field and terminal for him now. The airport is being evacuated."

"They've got to find Foxy and make him talk," Hugh snapped.

Foxy escaped. Steve numbly absorbed the words. Sharon. Neil. "Steve . . . I was wrong . . . forgive me." "Mommy wouldn't want me to be here." Would that cassette be his last contact with them? The cassette. Nina's voice!

He grabbed Hugh's arm. "That cassette he sent—he must have dubbed Nina's voice on it. Maybe he still has the other cassette with Nina's voice, maybe he has something that would show where Sharon and Neil are."

Hugh spun around to the other agent. "What about luggage?"

"There are two stubs clipped onto the ticket he dropped. But the plane took off about twenty-seven minutes ago."

"Get that plane back!" Hugh shouted. "Have every baggage handler in La Guardia ready to unload it."

Hugh ran to a phone. Rapidly he dialed the warden at the state prison. "We're still trying to locate evidence to prove Thompson's innocence. Have a phone manned to the last second."

He called the governor's office, got through to her private secretary. "Make sure the governor's available and you have a phone open to our guys in La Guardia and another to the prison." He dropped the phone. "Let's go," he told Steve.

The lobby of the Pan Am Building was jammed with people streaming from the terminal. Bomb threat . . . The words were on everyone's lips. As Steve and Hugh pushed through, an urgent voice kept repeating over the loudspeaker: "Leave the buildings immediately. Leave the area . . . leave the area. . . ."

At the upper level information booth, engineers pored over charts and diagrams, issuing rapid-fire orders to search parties. "We've done a fast check on the platforms and we're hitting all the lockers," a supervisor told Hugh. "The bomb squad has distributed bomb blankets. We can count on one of them being ninety percent effective in containing an explosion."

Steve's eyes swept the terminal. The loudspeaker was off now, and the vast area was becoming hushed. He looked at the clock.

Relentlessly the hands kept moving: 11:21 . . . 11:22 . . . 11:23. Distraught, he turned his head. He had to *do* something. His gaze fell on a thick-chested man who was disappearing down the stair-case to the lower level. There was something familiar about him. One of the agents maybe?

The loudspeaker went on. "It is eleven twenty-three. Leave the terminal immediately."

"No! I'm not leaving," Steve said.

Hugh grabbed his arm. "Mr. Peterson, if that bomb goes off, we may all be killed."

Steve wrenched himself free. "Let go of me," he shouted.

IT WAS no use. Her eyes magnetized to the clock, Sharon impatiently tried to jab the broken edge of the handle into the cords on her wrists. Many times she missed, and the metal cut her hand. She could feel the sticky blood. She was beyond pain. But what if she jabbed an artery?

The blood was making the cord softer, resilient. She'd been trying for over an hour . . . it was 10:35. She worked on, her face clammy with perspiration. She felt Neil's eyes on her. Pray, Neil.

At 11:10 she felt the cord weakening. Summoning up a last reserve of energy, Sharon pulled her hands apart. They were free. She shook them to get feeling back.

Leaning on her left elbow, she dragged herself up to a sitting position. Her legs fell over the side of the cot. Raw pain screeched through her ankle. Her fingers trembled with weakness as she worked at the gag. She couldn't undo the knot. Tugging frantically, she managed to pull the gag down. Great gulping breaths of air helped to clear her head. Thirteen minutes.

There was no hope for her. She couldn't walk. She had to free Neil. She yanked his gag off.

And then she heard the sound of something thudding against the door. Was he coming back? Clutching Neil to her, Sharon stared at the door. It was opening. The light switch clicked.

She saw what seemed to be an apparition stumbling toward her— an old woman with sunken eyes, blood trickling from her mouth.

449

Neil shrank against her as the woman came toward them, stared in horror as she slumped down— "Knife in my back . . . help . . . please . . . take it out . . . hurts . . . want to die here."

The woman's head was against Sharon's foot. Sharon saw the handle of the knife between her shoulder blades. She could free Neil with the knife. Shuddering, Sharon put both hands around the handle, pulled. The knife came free. The woman whimpered.

In an instant Sharon cut Neil's bindings. "Neil, run down those stairs! Yell that there's going to be an explosion. Hurry. There's a big ramp. At the train platform, go up the stairs. You'll see people— Daddy will come for you. Get out of this building."

"Sharon," Neil was pleading. "What about you?"

"Just go. Hurry! Run!"

With a beseeching glance at her Neil stumbled out of the room onto the landing. He was so afraid. The bomb. Maybe if he could find someone, they'd help Sharon.

He was at the foot of the stairs. Which way should he go? Sharon said a ramp. That must be it. He raced along it. The tracks were right there. He ran around the platform where the tracks ended

He could hear footsteps coming down a staircase. He tried to yell and couldn't. He had no breath from running. He started up the stairs. He had to tell whoever was coming about Sharon.

Neil looked up and saw the face that had stalked his dreams.

The man's eyes narrowed. He stretched out his hands. . . .

Neil jumped to one side, stuck out his foot. The man sprawled down the last three steps. Eluding the arms that swung out, Neil ran up the steps. He was in a big, empty place. There was no one here. The bad man was going to Sharon.

Sobbing, Neil ran up another staircase. Daddy, he tried to yell. He was on the last step. There were policemen all over. They were all running away. Some of them were pushing another man. They were pushing Daddy!

"Daddy," Neil shouted. With a final burst of energy he stumbled across the terminal. Steve turned, ran to him, grabbed him. . . .

"Daddy," Neil sobbed, "the bad man is going to kill Sharon now— just like he killed Mommy."

A DETERMINED ROSIE was fighting the efforts to put her out. Lally was down in Sing Sing. She knew it. At the information booth Rosie spotted Hugh Taylor, the nice FBI guy who always talked to her. She tugged his arm. "Mr. Taylor, Lally . . ."

He pulled free. "Get out of here, Rosie."

A loudspeaker was ordering everyone to leave. "No!" Rosie sobbed. She watched Hugh wrestle with a tall man.

"Daddy! Daddy!"

Rosie spun around. A little boy was weaving across the terminal. Then the big guy with Mr. Taylor ran past her to the child. She heard the boy say something about a bad man and rushed over. Maybe he'd seen the guy she and Lally were watching.

The boy was crying. "Daddy, help Sharon. She's hurt. And there's a sick old lady . . ."

"Where, Neil, where?" Steve begged.

"A sick old lady," Rosie shrieked. "That's Lally. She's in her room. You know, Mr. Taylor, the old dishwasher room."

"Come on," Hugh shouted.

Steve thrust Neil at a policeman. "Get my son out." He ran after Hugh. Two men with a heavy nylon sheet followed them.

Someone dragged Rosie toward an exit.

THE old woman's moans stopped, resumed, stopped for a longer instant, then began again. Sharon, leaning down, gently patted the tangled hair. Her fingertips smoothed the wrinkled forehead. The skin felt cold. Lally shuddered violently. The moaning stopped.

Sharon knew the woman was dead. And now *she* was going to die. "I love you, Steve," she said aloud. His face filled her mind. She closed her eyes. "Forgive us our trespasses. . . . Into Your hands I commend my spirit."

A sound. Her eyes flew open. Foxy was framed in the doorway. His fingers curved, his thumbs rigid, he started toward her.

HUGH led the way down the ramp to the depths of the terminal. Steve raced beside him. The men carrying the bomb blanket struggled to keep up.

They were on the ramp when they heard the screaming. "No . . . no . . . help me . . . Steve . . ."

Steve felt a tremendous surge of power, a burst of energy. Crazed with the need to reach Sharon in time, he flew past the others. "Steeeeeevvvvveeee!" The scream choked off.

He lunged up a staircase, burst through an open door.

His brain absorbed the nightmarish scene, the body on the floor, Sharon half lying, her legs tied, trying to pull away from the figure bent over her, the thick fingers squeezing her throat.

Steve butted his head into the man's arched back. Foxy sprawled forward. They both fell on Sharon. Under their weight, the sagging cot collapsed and they rolled to the floor. The hands broke loose from Sharon's throat. Foxy stumbled to his feet, crouched. Steve tried to leap up, tripped on Lally's body. Sharon was breathing in choking gasps.

Hugh raced into the room. Cornered, Foxy backed away. His hand found the door to the toilet cubicle. He jumped past it, slammed it shut. They heard the bolt slide into place.

"Get out of there, you crazy fool," Hugh shouted.

The agents with the bomb blanket came in. With infinite care they draped the suitcase with the nylon sheet.

Steve reached for Sharon. Her eyes were closed. He picked her up. Ugly welts were rising on her throat. But she was alive. Holding her to him, he turned to the door. His eyes fell on the wall, on Nina's picture. He hugged Sharon tightly.

Hugh bent over Lally. "This one's gone."

The large hand of the clock was moving to six. "Get out of here," Hugh shouted. "Head for the tunnel!"

They tumbled down the stairs, raced past the generator, onto the tracks, through the darkness. . . .

Foxy heard the retreating steps. He opened the door. Seeing the nylon blanket over the suitcase, he began to laugh.

It was too late for him. But it was too late for them too. In the end the Fox always won.

He reached out to tug the blanket off the suitcase.

A blinding flash, and a roar that hurtled him into eternity.

453

At 11:42 a.m. Bob Kurner burst into St. Bernard's Church, raced up the aisle, and threw his arms around the kneeling figure.

"Is it over?" Her eyes were tearless.

"*Is it over!* Mama, come on and take your kid home. They've got absolute proof that another guy committed the murder, and they've a tape of him doing it. The governor said to get Ron out of that prison *now*."

Kate Thompson, mother of Ronald Thompson, staunch believer in the goodness and mercy of her God, fainted.

Hugh had his arm around a softly weeping Rosie. "Lally saved her station," he said. "And we'll start a petition to put up a plaque for her. I'll bet the governor will unveil it."

"A plaque for Lally," Rosie whispered. "Oh, she'd love that!"

A face was floating somewhere above her. She was going to die and never see Steve again. "No . . . no . . ."

"It's all right, darling. It's all right."

Steve's voice. It was Steve's face she was seeing.

"It's all over. We're on the way to the hospital. They'll fix up that leg."

"Neil . . ."

"I'm here, Sharon." A hand butterfly soft in hers.

Steve's lips on her cheeks, her forehead, her lips.

Neil's voice in her ear. "Sharon, just like you told me, I kept thinking the whole time about the present you promised me. Sharon, exactly how many Lionel trains have you got for me?"

Mary Higgins Clark

Mary Higgins Clark is attractive, vivacious, with an infectious sense of humour. At first meeting she seems hardly the type one would imagine to be a master of chilling suspense. But soon she is talking about her lifelong passion for criminal psychology and criminal justice: "As a kid I loved all the stories of murder trials." She started keeping a journal at the age of seven and has been writing ever since.

Her first novel, *Where Are The Children?*, published in 1975, was a Condensed Books selection and a big best seller. *A Stranger Is Watching* promises to bring her an even wider circle of readers. The book also contains a hint of a happy recent event in Mary Clark's life.

A widow since 1964, Mary has brought up her five children single-handed, not remarrying, she explains, because she has never found someone to be both husband to her and father to her children. Now all that is changed. In August 1977 she spoke of her experiences as a single parent at the American Bar Association Convention in Chicago. There she met Ray Ploetz, an attorney from Minnesota. When Ray was next in New York he took Mary to dinner at the Tavern on the Green, the restaurant where Steve—surely not coincidentally—took Sharon on their first date in *A Stranger Is Watching*. On August 8 this year Mary and Ray were married—and held their wedding reception at the Tavern on the Green.

Mary Clark thrives on a hectic schedule. She is studying philosophy at Fordham University, in New York. She is also working on her third mystery. She and Ray will divide their time between Minnesota, where Ray has a farm; New Jersey, where Mary has a house; and New York City.

A native New Yorker, Mary Higgins Clark has set much of the action in *Stranger* in one of her favourite landmarks, Grand Central Station, which to her is the nerve centre of the big city she loves. Yes, the dingy room under the station *does* exist; Mary has been there.

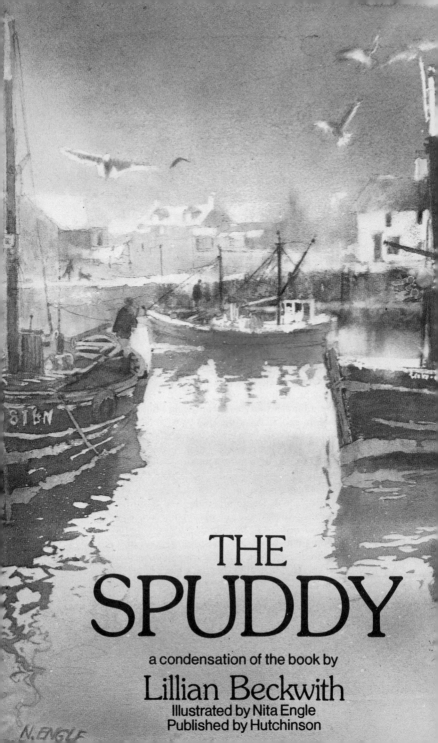

THE
SPUDDY

a condensation of the book by

Lillian Beckwith

Illustrated by Nita Engle
Published by Hutchinson

A boy who cannot speak, a homeless dog and a lonely sea captain touch each other's lives with unforgettable results. When eight-year-old Andy, mute since infancy, was abandoned by his mother, his world seemed truly at an end. Then at Gaymal, the tiny Scots fishing village where he is sent to live, he finds his first friends: the Spuddy, a stray dog who needs no words to understand Andy's devotion to him; and Skipper Jake, a herring fisherman. Running on the moors with the Spuddy, chasing herring on Jake's boat, Andy at last begins to understand the meaning of love and trust. And then, in a dramatic and bittersweet moment, love unlocks some shackle in Andy's heart, giving him the strength to break through the barriers of his own self-doubt.

CHAPTER I

When Joe died, Marie Glenn decided to say goodbye to her home in the brisk little fishing port of Gaymal and take herself off to begin a new life in Glasgow. All she was leaving behind was her husband's dog, "the Spuddy", a thickset grey-black mongrel which he had brought home as a puppy four years previously. He was called the Spuddy simply because Joe had been in the habit of describing anyone who was more than a little astute as a spuddy, and when the dog had begun to display a remarkable intelligence Joe had often found himself saying, "He's a real spuddy, that one." So the Spuddy he had become. Despite his hybridism (Joe used to say his coat looked as if someone had dipped him in a barrel of glue and then emptied a flock mattress over him), the dog had a self-assurance emphasized by an arrogantly held head and a long droop of a setterlike tail which, in his sauntering gait, swung from side to side with the stateliness of an ermine cloak.

The bond between Joe and the Spuddy had never developed into devotion on either side, for though Joe had housed him, licensed him and seen that he was well fed, his feeling for the Spuddy was an absentminded sort of affection. The Spuddy, accepting that he had an owner but not a master, accorded to Joe the forbearing protectiveness he might have bestowed on a child.

Joe had worked as a fish porter down at the pier, and the Spuddy had loyally accompanied him there six mornings of every week. If

459

anything was dropped into the harbour and needed to be retrieved, Joe had only to call the Spuddy's attention to it and the dog would plunge in. Once he had saved a child from drowning and people had said he ought to have a medal, but the town quickly forgot about it.

Apart from the Spuddy's skill at retrieving, he performed two other important tasks on the pier. First, with snarling efficiency he kept all loitering dogs from fouling the boxes of fish waiting to be loaded onto the trucks. His second task was to keep the sea gulls away from the newly landed boxes of fish, a task he performed with boisterous venom, for if there was anything in this world that the Spuddy had learned to hate it was the rapacious gulls. When, among the bustle of landing fish from the boat, the weighing and auctioning, the gulls converged upon the boxes of silvery fresh fish, the Spuddy would be there leaping with lightning snaps and spitting out feathers while he dodged the beaks that jabbed at him from all sides. He was responsible for many damaged wings among the local gulls. Once when he had caught the wing of a great black-back and refused to let go, the gull had somehow managed to pull him over the side of the pier and into the harbour. But the Spuddy had held on, and while the fishermen and fish porters stopped working to watch, the contest continued amid a great splashing of water and a chorus of cries from the spectator gulls. The battle lasted all of five minutes and then the Spuddy, his nose red with his own blood, swam back to the pier steps, leaving the dead blackback floating on the water and the harbour patterned with white gull feathers.

After his owner, Joe Glenn, died, the Spuddy appeared to go into semi-retirement, and though he still visited the pier from time to time, he usually arrived in the late morning, when the boats were at sea and the gulls, either hungry or gorged, had arranged themselves in a white frieze along the roof ridges of the sheds that adjoined the pier. It was almost as if he had called a truce with the birds. He still went home for his meal each day as soon as the clock struck twelve, and he continued to sleep on the porch mat. For Joe's sake, Marie, who had never learned to like the dog, still put the Spuddy's meal out every day. But not for anybody's sake,

460

she vowed, was she going to take him to Glasgow with her, for that was to be her new life.

She had made one or two halfhearted attempts to give him away, but most of the people of Gaymal agreed that dogs were to be tolerated as playthings only until the children were packed off to school. Then the dogs became a nuisance and were disposed of quickly and without compunction.

Effie, one of Marie's neighbours, had summed up the Spuddy's problem with heartless clarity. "What? Give a home to a beast that's as much an accident as a rabbit on the moors? Indeed, if folks is goin' to be bothered with a dog, then they want one that has a decent pedigree so that everyone will know it's cost good money."

Marie accepted the truth of Effie's statement. The fishermen of Gaymal were prosperous and they had to ensure that everything they possessed looked expensive. "You'll just have to have him put away before you go," Effie had insisted. "Give him to one of the boats and get them to weight him and throw him overboard when they're well out to sea."

But Marie, briskly matter-of-fact as she was, recoiled from the idea. "It doesn't seem right, that," she objected. "After all, he hasn't been much trouble. I think the best thing to do is just to leave him here. He's always been kind of independent and I daresay he'll make out."

"If you leave him to wander round, folks will soon get fed up with him an' it won't be long before one of the boats takes him out to make an end of him," Effie told her. "You'd best just give him to the Cruelty an' then he'll be off your mirrd."

"It seems a shame." Marie's voice wavered.

Effie glared at her. "I'm no dog lover," she asserted, "but to my way of thinking it's not so cruel to have an animal put away as it is to desert him after once givin' him a home." She turned towards her own front door. "But I daresay I might just as well save my breath to cool my porridge. You softhearted folks make your own troubles, always takin' the easy way out." The door closed firmly behind her.

Back in her own kitchen, Marie tried to make up her mind

whether or not she was going to ask one of the skippers to dispose of the Spuddy. If she just left him and if what Effie had predicted was true, then he would end up in the sea anyway. But at least, she told herself, when that happened she wouldn't be there.

The furniture van had left. Marie settled herself in the hired car that was to take her on the first stage of her journey, telling the driver she wished to get away as quickly as possible. She gave a nod towards the Spuddy, who was hovering around as if awaiting the invitation to join her. As the car drew away from the kerb, Marie turned to wave to the neighbours who had gathered to see her off. The Spuddy stood watching the car until it disappeared. After a few minutes he climbed to the top step of the empty house and lay down, staring along the street, accepting his plight. The neighbours lingered gossiping for a while before returning to their own homes. The street became quiet except for the mocking echoes of gull cries carried in by a sea wind. The Spuddy's head sank down onto his outstretched paws, but his tobacco-brown eyes stayed wide and reflective, like those of a man mulling over future plans.

WHILE MARIE GLENN was speeding away from Gaymal another car was speeding towards the village. In this car were the driver and a boy about eight years old, who stared out at the passing landscape with wide, inscrutable eyes. The boy's name was Andy, but he could not have told anyone that, for though he was a good-looking boy, well grown and sturdy, with curly fair hair and large eyes the colour of fresh-cut peat, he was completely dumb. When people first saw Andy they tended to exclaim admiringly, "That's a grand-looking boy!" But when they realized he could not speak they would add, "Och, the poor thing's a dummy!" And Andy, whose hearing was at least as good as theirs, winced at their pity. From the time he had been able to understand the speech of adults and become aware of his own affliction, he had begun to feel excluded even from his own parents.

His father was in the merchant navy and was away at sea for long periods, leaving Andy and his mother on their own. But their being together had not brought them close. It was not that his

462

mother displayed any lack of affection towards him; on the contrary, she was at times warmly demonstrative. But Andy had been a beautiful baby, and when he had outgrown the toddler stage and his dumbness had become apparent, she started to feel a sense of outrage that her son should be imperfect. She had taken him to doctors and to specialists, all of whom assured her there was nothing physical to account for Andy's lack of speech, but as time went by and he showed no sign of improvement, her resentment towards him grew, and it was only intensified when he was refused admission to the local school.

She tried teaching him herself, coaxing sometimes for hours on end and mouthing simple sounds for him to imitate, until tears of frustration filled her eyes at his continued lack of response. Seeing her frustration, Andy developed a dread of her lessons, feeling as if he were freezing inside whenever she made him sit down on the stool in front of her and commenced her repetitive mouthing of sounds. It was not so distressing when she taught him other things, like lettering, and he shared her delight when eventually he was able to produce the large misshapen capitals that spelled his name; but having taught him to write his name, her interest in lessons waned until there was only fitful instruction on any subject she found easy to demonstrate, like the hours of the clock and the value of coins.

She had begun to seem frequently distracted, and when she went shopping she left him with a neighbour. Andy knew that his muteness embarrassed his mother and that he was a terrible disappointment to her. He tried hard not to mind that she was away from him so often or that in the evenings when she was home he was usually left to sit quietly drawing in a corner while she entertained her friends.

His mother was thankful for Andy's interest in drawing, and she made sure that he always had an ample supply of materials, but even though she often complimented him on his skill, only his father's praise and criticism were really meaningful to Andy. It was only his father who knew about boats, and Andy almost always drew boats. Great liners, cargo boats, sailing boats, fishing smacks, even dinghies—he drew them all, and when he was not actually drawing boats he drew the moody sea, and wharfs and harbours complete with sea gulls.

He had seen liners and cargo ships when he and his mother had gone to the docks to wave goodbye to his father. He had seen fishing boats and a great variety of other craft when they had spent holidays in Aberdeen with his granny. But now there was no longer a granny in Aberdeen, and the only water he could get near was the pool in the park and the sluggishly flowing river which separated it from the town. But he continued to draw from memory, content in his private world while he listened to the lively chatter that went on around him. Sometimes, looking up, he would think how much prettier his mother was than all the other women in the room and sometimes he wondered if, beneath the gaiety, she was, like himself, longing for his father to come home on leave so that they could all three be together. There came a time, however, when Andy noticed the number of friends being entertained had dwindled, until there were only two or three and finally only one, a man, whom Andy did not much like. When he came his mother insisted on Andy's going to bed.

When the most recent telegram arrived announcing his father's imminent arrival, instead of grabbing Andy's arms and dancing around the room with him, his mother rushed upstairs and began packing suitcases. Coming down again, she said in reply to Andy's look of bewilderment, "I'm going away for a bit." Her voice was strained. She told him not to go out until his father arrived, and added that there was a cold lunch in the pantry. Then she put an envelope beside the clock on the mantelpiece. "See your father reads that when he comes," she told him. She was frowning in an abstracted way and her eyes were bright. As she moved past him Andy put a hand on her arm and looked at her imploringly. "I can't stay, Andy," she said in a tight voice. "It's no good. I just can't stay." His hand slid down to his side. "Be a good boy," she said, giving him a quick hug. The door closed and she was running down the garden path and out to the car where a man was waiting. She did not glance back or wave to her son, who stood forlornly holding aside the curtain, watching his mother go.

Even when his father arrived and enveloped him in a huge hug,

464

Andy did not break down but only pointed to the letter on the mantelpiece. With a quizzical glance at Andy, his father took the letter and sat down to read it. After he had read and reread it he stood up and put a hand on Andy's shoulder. "Your mother's gone away for a wee while," he said thickly. "I daresay she'll be back soon." He didn't look at Andy as he spoke. "Now I'm just going upstairs, and when I come down again we'll put on our best bibs and tuckers and go out somewhere, eh?" He was too distressed to see his son's anxious eyes following him out of the kitchen.

Andy stood desolate. He had wanted his father to talk to him, to admit that his mother had left them for someone she liked better. He wanted his father to share their mutual grief; he felt they should comfort each other. His shoulders sagged. To Andy it seemed that even in this moment of crisis his dumbness was still a barrier; that even his own father accepted that an inability to speak meant a similar inability to understand, or feel or share emotion. Andy wandered into the pantry and looked at the food, but he had no desire to eat. He had no desire for anything—certainly not to go out as his father had promised, because of a fear that if they left, the house and all the other familiar things would not be there when they returned. He went at last and sat on the bottom stair, hugging his knees and listening for a sign of movement from his father.

When his father did come down, determinedly bright and talkative, they went out despite Andy's reluctance, and for the next six weeks of his father's leave they did more things together than they had ever done before. There were trips by rail and by bus, walks in the country, fishing, meals in restaurants, all filling Andy's days with so many new experiences that at night he was too tired to brood for long.

The day came when his father began preparations to return to his ship, and once again Andy was overcome with hopelessness.

"Tomorrow," his father said in reply to Andy's questioning glance. He knelt down and put an arm around the boy. "I've fixed it up for you to go and stay for a little while with your aunt Sarah. You've never seen her, but she's seen photographs of you and she's taken a real fancy to you." He felt the tension in the boy's body and his arm tightened around him. "And there's your uncle Ben. You'll like him. He doesn't draw boats like you, but he builds them. They live at Gaymal, where there are plenty of boats. You'll be able to go down to the pier and draw as many as you've a mind. You'll like that, won't you?"

Andy knew his father wanted him to show enthusiasm, so he managed a faint smile. He dreaded the idea of going to live with strange people even if they were relatives.

"There's a car coming for us tomorrow," his father continued. "I wanted to go with you all the way and see you settled in Gaymal, but my leave's been chopped. The idea now is that this car will take us to the docks where my ship is, and you'll be able to see me go aboard before you set off for Aunt Sarah's." Andy nodded and again forced a smile.

"So off you go to your bedroom and gather up anything you want to take. Mrs. Peake next door is coming in to pack your clothes and things, but you'll be wanting to take your paper and crayons and a good few of your sketches, eh?"

As Andy went slowly up the stairs his father stared after him, asking himself whether it would be more heartrending to have a son who could confide in words his fear and dejection rather than one like Andy, who could only convey it by the slump of his body and the anguish in his eyes.

At the docks, Andy watched his father stride up the gangplank of his ship and turn and wave before he disappeared from sight. Stoically, Andy walked back to the car. The driver talked brightly in an attempt to distract the boy from his grief, but he could see that Andy was taut with pent-up emotion. Fearing he might make some clumsy remark that would crack Andy's control, he lapsed into silence and was relieved when, shortly after five o'clock, they entered Gaymal and pulled up in front of a house three doors away from Marie Glenn's former home.

THE SPUDDY still lay on the top step of the empty house, having returned there after seeking out the dinner Marie had left for him in his bowl beside the coalshed. The Spuddy always waited until the church clock struck twelve before he would start to eat.

466

Always, that is, unless the church clock happened to be slow, for his own sense of time was accurate.

The Spuddy watched the car arrive, as he had watched every activity in the street since Marie had gone. He saw the boy get out and be greeted by a plump, busy little woman wearing a flowered apron over her blue dress. Andy had noticed the empty-looking house and the Spuddy lying there alone, and pulled at his aunt's sleeve while pointing towards the dog. The woman stopped to explain, then shook her head disapprovingly in the Spuddy's direction. She disappeared inside, gesturing to the boy to follow, but Andy paused for a moment and stared at the Spuddy, who returned the stare with a long, interested glance.

ANDY'S FIRST THOUGHT on entering Aunt Sarah's kitchen was how much the room was like its owner, small and clean and bright. There were white curtains at the windows which matched her hair, and just as the fire in the open grate crackled busily, so did Aunt Sarah's tongue crackle as she bustled about. The table was laid for tea.

"You like kippers, do you, Andy?" Aunt Sarah asked briskly, and Andy nodded affirmatively. He had no appetite, but he did not want to risk being questioned by this sharp-tongued little woman. "And so does your uncle Ben," she told him. "They're good kippers we get hereabouts, and I doubt there's better fish in the sea than herring when all's said and done." She put some plates into the oven. "Your uncle Ben will be home any minute now, so you'll just come with me and I'll show you where you're to sleep." She picked up one of his suitcases and started up the stairs. Andy picked up the other and followed.

"There now," she said, opening the door of a small prim room. "How will that do you?" Her mouth closed tightly on the question and Andy missed the smile in her eyes. He looked around and nodded, doing his best to appear grateful. It was a nice enough room, but the unfamiliarity of it almost broke through his control. He was glad when his aunt hurried away, telling him firmly that Uncle Ben liked his meal as soon as he came in, so would Andy please just wash his hands and then come down. He could unpack later. Andy went to the bathroom, splashed his face with cold water until he felt more composed, and went downstairs.

"This is your uncle Ben now," announced Aunt Sarah, and almost immediately the back door opened and his uncle came in. Uncle Ben was tall and spare, with undisciplined grey hair and a roughly shaved, sea-scoured face. On seeing Andy his blue eyes lighted up and he lumbered forward to give him a warm handshake, and he told Andy how welcome he was and how nice it would be for him and Aunt Sarah to have someone young about the place. Aunt Sarah was dishing out the kippers, and just as Uncle Ben appeared to be running out of words of welcome, she ordered them to sit down to their tea.

Andy ate three kippers, or rather there were the remains of three kippers on his plate when he had finished his meal; but when his aunt and uncle weren't looking he had put some of the kipper between two slices of bread and butter and slipped the sandwich into his pocket. He also hid two drop scones.

Since his aunt had explained that the Spuddy had been abandoned, he had resolved that he must try to look after the dog, and he estimated that if his aunt regularly put this much food on the table, he would not have much difficulty.

After tea, while his aunt was washing the dishes, he slipped out into the evening dusk and sped quietly towards the empty house. The Spuddy watched him come. Not knowing for certain whether or not the dog was savage, Andy tore a piece of crust from the kipper sandwich and held it out. Since the Spuddy had eaten his one meal of the day, he was not hungry and displayed no interest. All the same he was intrigued. Children were noisy and excitable and he preferred to avoid them, but the patient, mute overtures of this boy baffled him, and he watched him, making no movement except for a flick of one ear. Andy put the sandwich and the two drop scones on the ground beside the Spuddy and retreated a step or two, but still the food was ignored. He ventured closer again, holding out a hand, palm outstretched, hoping the dog would sniff it, realize it was the hand of a friend and perhaps give it a lick of acceptance. The Spuddy looked at the hand and looked away again. He was not in the habit of licking hands. To Andy the

468

Spuddy seemed to be spurning his offer of friendship. He slumped down on the bottom step in the gathering dark. His head dropped forward on his arms, and his shoulders began to shake with the sobs that had for so long been wanting to escape from his body. Only then did the Spuddy move down to the bottom step and rest a paw gently on the boy's neck, glancing about him as if he were afraid someone might witness his unwonted display of tenderness. He need not have worried. By now it was quite dark and there was no sound in the street until a door opened and Andy heard his aunt calling him.

CHAPTER II

One of the most beautiful boats in the Gaymal fishing fleet was the *Silver Crest*. Her skipper, Jake, was proud of her, as he was of his infant son.

When his son was six weeks old, Skipper Jake's wife announced that she must take the baby home to show him off to her family. Home to Jeannie was her parents' croft in the outer islands. The home Jake provided for her in Gaymal she always referred to as the house. Jeannie was forever making excuses to visit home. In fact, her relatives made so many demands on her time that in the three years they had been married Jake doubted if she had spent more than six months with him. It hurt him that she wanted to be away from him so much, and he had hoped that when the baby was born she would become more attached, if not to himself then to the home he worked so hard to give her.

As he came through from the scullery into the kitchen, where Jeannie was ironing, he was pressing a towel against his newly shaved cheeks, and only his eyes betrayed his unhappiness. There were times when Jake thought he ought to put his foot down about Jeannie's frequent absences, but she was so fair and young and slight and he was so big and swarthy and had such an intimidatingly gruff voice that he was fearful of appearing a bully in her eyes. So he erred on the side of overindulgence, giving her everything she asked for and never complaining of her lack of interest in him.

"Is the baby old enough to travel?" he asked, trying so hard to keep his voice gentle that it sounded almost meek.

"Surely," returned Jeannie as she guided the iron over the sleeves of a tiny jacket. "And after all," she added, "it isn't as if it's the wintertime yet."

Jake went over to the small bed in the corner of the room and, lifting the coverlet, gazed down at his sleeping son. Jake's sad, tight mouth relaxed into a tender smile. Was he going to see as little of his son as he did of his wife? he wondered bitterly. Jeannie had once seemed so shy and desirable with her clear, smooth skin and glossy hair, but soon after they married he noticed her shyness had given way, and though her complexion and hair remained as attractive as ever, he rarely saw her other than as she was now, in slippers and a robe, with her hair in curlers. And he was disturbed that she seemed to do an awful lot of housework on weekends, when he was at home; while he admitted it was nice to have a clean, shining home, he would have preferred it to be a place where he could relax away from the constant swing of the sea, a place where he would be greeted by a neatly dressed wife prepared to share with him the comfort of their own fireside and where a few of the neighbours might drop in late in the evening for a wee dram.

Like most fishermen, he had a strong streak of romanticism, and when he was first married he had dreamed of the weekend respites from the discomfort of the boat: of returning and opening their welcoming door to call, "I'm back, Jeannie!"; of finding her in his arms; of lifting her up and carrying her to the kitchen. But even before he had touched her she had seen the eagerness in his eyes and had rebuffed him. She didn't like that sort of thing. It was soft. Now on weekends he returned either to a listless greeting and the bustle of housework, or else, too frequently, to a house that was clean and shining but was cold and empty, with a note on the table saying, "Have gone home—Mother not keeping well."

At first Jeannie had stayed away only two or three weeks at a time, but then her absences grew to months and he realized that except for financial support there was little she wanted from him. He wondered if she wanted what any man could give her, since

470

island girls had a reputation for cleaving more naturally to their parents than to their husbands.

Gently, Jake replaced the coverlet over his son. He cleared his throat. "I'd like to see a fair bit of the boy, Jeannie."

"And when would you see him anyway," Jeannie taunted, "with you away fishing all week?"

"But, Jeannie! I've to earn money for us, haven't I?" He had to earn much money to keep up with Jeannie's whims. She tired of things so quickly. He reckoned they had bought enough to furnish three homes in the time they had been married. Only he knew how he hated to call out his crew in weather that made other skippers comment, "It's only greed or need that would make a man go to sea on a day like this."

Jeannie shrugged. "Well, I can't help it if I like company. It's what I'm used to."

"Can you not make friends with the other women?" he asked. "They'd be company for you."

"They're not my own folk," she said defensively.

"Aye, right enough they're not," said Jake resignedly. "But all the same I'm sayin' I'd like to see my son growin' up. I'm askin' you not to stay away so long."

"That'll depend on how my father's keeping." Jeannie's voice sparked at him like sticks on a newly lighted fire. "He wasn't keeping so well in my mother's last letter." She thumped the iron down and started to gather up the pile of clothes.

Jake looked at her, dismayed as always by her apparent renunciation of him, but he was too proud and thought of himself as being too inarticulate to plead with her further. He opened a cupboard and took out some tools.

"Which is the shelf you say wants fixin'?" he asked her in a tired voice.

ALL THAT NIGHT the Spuddy lay on the steps of his former home, but when the first fingers of light reached over the shoulders of the hills he got up, stretched himself and sauntered away down the street. Andy, coming out of his aunt's house after breakfast, was disappointed not to see the dog and decided to look for him. And since all Gaymal roads led to the harbour, he eventually found himself on the pier.

He stared in wonder. Andy had visited docks with his father, but those now seemed landlocked and dull in comparison with the spectacle of Gaymal. Here was so much sea, so much sky, colour and movement, that he stood enveloped by the sights and sounds and the smells of the harbour. He forgot his intention of looking for the Spuddy; forgot the ache, the depression of the past few weeks. He even forgot for the time that he was dumb, since there was so much noise that people tended to gesture rather than talk.

Here were boats galore: herring boats landing their catches, launches loading supplies, a lifeboat swinging at its moorings; and at the end of the pier a steamer was hauling up its gangplanks, preparing to leave. Passing fish porters threw Andy friendly grins and he grinned back ecstatically. He picked his way among fish boxes, trolleys, barrels, hoses and ropes, his shoes scrunching on pieces of crab shell or skidding on fish that had been pulped to slime by the wheels of the trucks, until a path brought him into the boatyard where his uncle Ben worked.

As his father had predicted, Andy had taken an immediate liking to Uncle Ben. He wasn't sure about his aunt Sarah, since to him she appeared forbidding with all her scuttle. But Uncle Ben was slow-speaking and smiling-eyed; the little he said was with a gentle voice and comforting words. In his presence Andy experienced the same warm, safe feeling he knew when he was with his father.

The boy found his uncle working on a fishing boat that was winched high on the slip: a boat that had hit a rock and needed to have several planks renewed. She'd been lucky, his uncle told him. If the weather had worsened, the boat could have been totally wrecked and the crew lost. As he was speaking, his uncle's hands were caressing the boat's side with as much tenderness as a mother smoothing a crib sheet over a sleeping child. Andy, who had never before seen anything bigger than a dinghy completely out of the water, was overwhelmed. Standing beneath her and letting his eyes run along the sweep of the hull into the keel, he thought how beautiful she was. Uncle Ben, who had been observing him, took his pipe out of his mouth to say, "Aye, a boat's a beautiful thing, boy."

Andy knew now that he would no longer be content to draw boats; he wanted to go to sea and he wanted to go in a boat just like this one.

The church clock striking twelve reminded them it was time for their dinner, and in the leisurely way of a devoted craftsman Uncle Ben put away his tools. Together he and Andy left the slip, climbed up to the quay and made for home. As they turned into their street the first thing Andy saw was a large van parked outside the empty house, and men unloading furniture from it. Where's the Spuddy? he thought in a panic, and was angry with himself for having forgotten his intention of looking for the dog at the harbour. He dawdled, letting his uncle go in front of him. Andy had assumed the Spuddy would be accessible to further overtures of friendship. But new people meant complications. They might have a dog of their own or they might dislike dogs altogether, and what would happen then? It was at that moment he saw the Spuddy.

The Spuddy had spent the morning doing his usual rounds of the pier and the kipper yard, but when he had heard the clock strike twelve, habit had turned him in the direction of his former home. When he saw the furniture van and strange people going in and out of the house, he slipped around to the back to see if his bowl was in the accustomed place beside the coalshed. It was, but it was empty except for a few drops of rain and the lingering smell of yesterday's food. He licked it, more to assert ownership than for the meat-tainted moisture, but even as he did so a red-haired woman appeared and amid a shrill scream of invective hurled a stone, which hit the path beside him.

Ruffled but with dignity the Spuddy retreated to the other side of the street and sat down to keep an eye on the proceedings. There was a clang against the curb a few feet away from him. It was his empty bowl. The Spuddy was still sitting there, half obscured by the bulky van, when Andy spotted him. He ran and put a gentle hand on the dog's head, crouched down and let his arm slide

473

around the dog's neck. The Spuddy's response was a cursory lick on the ear. Andy, catching sight of the empty bowl in the gutter and guessing why it was there, knew that he had to do something. He retrieved the bowl and, with an encouraging pat on the Spuddy's head, went inside to his dinner. When the meal was over and his aunt had cleared the dishes away, he showed her the Spuddy's empty bowl, mutely asking for scraps.

"Indeed no!" she declared firmly. "I'm not giving you food to take to that dog. If you go tempting him to hang round here, you'll upset the new neighbours, and the more you tempt him to stay, the more likely it's you yourself will be the death of him. Aye, you, Andy," she stressed, seeing his look of consternation. "The woman that's moving into the house was here taking a cup of tea with me this morning and she canna abide dogs at any price. She says if the Spuddy still comes round, her husband's going to complain to the police." She gathered up the tablecloth. "Aye, and then something will have to be done about getting rid of him. The best thing you can do for that dog, Andy, is to keep away from him and make sure he keeps away from you." Out of the corner of his eye Andy saw Uncle Ben nodding sad confirmation.

Dejectedly, Andy tucked the empty bowl under his anorak and went outside.

THE MOMENT Andy saw the Spuddy again his dejection became resolution—if only he could keep the Spuddy fed and unharmed until his father came on leave, he was certain his father would find some way for Andy to keep the dog. He wished, as so often before, that he could correspond with his father, that he could read and write like other children of his age.

Andy approached the Spuddy and, showing him the feeding bowl, enticed the dog to follow him. Before leaving the house Andy had checked the money in his pocket, and money being something his mother had made sure he was familiar with, he reckoned he had enough to buy three days of food for the Spuddy, and today being a Saturday, it was only three days before he was due for another week's pocket money from the sum his father had left for that purpose.

He went to the local shop, where it was relatively easy for him to point to a can of dog meat and a can opener, hand over the money and skip away. Together he and the Spuddy raced towards a promising-looking huddle of sheds within the kipper yard. Watched closely by the Spuddy, Andy set the bowl on the ground, opened the can and tipped out its contents. The Spuddy's glance dropped to the food and his nose twitched. Still without complete conviction, his glance returned to the boy. Andy pushed the bowl nearer, and only then did the Spuddy, with a dignified swing of his tail which Andy interpreted as a thank-you, begin to eat. Crouching with his back against the wall of the shed, Andy smiled.

The next thing he must do, Andy resolved, was try to find a place where the dog might sleep unmolested at night. One of the empty sheds where he had fed the dog was a possibility, but how would he get sacks or some form of bedding to cover the damp-looking earth floor? How was he to mime to strangers his request for bedding for a dog he was not supposed to have? All afternoon the boy and the dog roamed Gaymal, but when teatime came Andy had still found neither bedding nor a cosier alternative to the shed for his companion.

The evening dusk was thickening, and he knew the time had come to leave the Spuddy. Clapping his hands, he gestured towards the kipper yard, but the Spuddy stayed beside him. He tried stamping his feet; he tried dodging and hiding; but the Spuddy was not to be diverted. Feeling like a traitor, Andy at last picked up a stone, and throwing it so as not to hit the dog, he made what he hoped was a menacing rush towards him. The Spuddy was surprised but not deterred. Andy was growing desperate. It was Uncle Ben, coming home from a visit to the barber, who solved the problem for him. "Way back, dog!" he commanded the Spuddy. "Go!" His voice was quietly authoritative and the dog, understanding at last, loped away in the direction of the kipper yard.

The following day was Sunday and Uncle Ben volunteered to show Andy around Gaymal. As they turned the corner into the main road Andy was delighted to see the Spuddy apparently waiting for him, but, unsure of his uncle's attitude towards the dog, he made only discreet signs to the Spuddy to follow them. However, when his uncle took the path that wound up towards the open moors, the Spuddy, increasingly sure of his welcome, began bounding along beside them. Andy glanced anxiously up at his uncle from time to time, but he seemed not to mind the dog's presence and even remarked at one point that he was a "real nice dog" and it was a shame someone didn't take to him and give him a home. But when the time came for them to return for their dinner, Uncle Ben's voice was firm as he commanded the Spuddy, "Get away now! Get away!" Obediently, after a reproachful glance at Andy, the Spuddy turned and went slowly in the direction of the harbour.

After dinner, with the scraps saved from his own plate in his pocket and with the feeding bowl inside his anorak, Andy again set off in search of the Spuddy.

"Be back by four o'clock," his aunt commanded him. "It's church tonight and we have our tea early."

Andy found the Spuddy wandering among the piles of fish boxes on the pier, and when the dog saw Andy he appeared uncertain whether or not to come forward and greet him. After his treatment of the night before and again this morning, Andy could not blame him. He put the scraps into the bowl. Slowly the Spuddy came to investigate and, liking what he found, licked the bowl clean. Andy patted him, wishing he could explain, and in return the Spuddy licked his ear. It seemed they were friends again, but when it was nearing four o'clock and he had to send the Spuddy away, Andy felt sick. He waited until they were approaching the kipper yards before he turned and pointed towards them. He clapped his hands and pointed again emphatically. The Spuddy sat down and made no effort to follow him farther.

ALTHOUGH ANDY wondered miserably if the Spuddy would ever come near him again, his mind was busy with plans as soon as he awoke next morning. He would explore the moors and hills beyond the village, where perhaps he might find a cave. If he could make a good bed for the Spuddy in the cave, he should be safe and snug there during the milder part of the year.

Downstairs, he indicated to his aunt that he would like to take his lunch with him, and she was quick to understand. Uncle Ben wasn't at home for lunch except on Saturdays and Sundays, an arrangement which suited her to perfection, since she always found plenty of housework to do and liked the day to be free of interruptions so that she could get on with it.

Actually the prospect of having Andy around the house for much of the day had worried her at first. But the jolt of concern she had felt when she saw Andy arrive, with his big, watchful eyes shadowed with grief and tiredness, made her realize she was going to find him no cross to bear.

After Andy had gone to bed that night, she had sat down beside the fire opposite her husband, who was reading the paper. Ben looked up and saw that the eyes of his normally brusque, undemonstrative wife were bright with tears. She caught his look.

"Fancy a mother being able to do that to her child, Ben," she said. "Just fancy."

And the normally placid, virtually monosyllabic Ben surprised his wife by saying explosively, "She's a monster, that one!"

Now Aunt Sarah was cutting up a pile of sandwiches for Andy. She added half a dozen cold sausages and a couple of slices of cake and then she went to a cupboard under the stairs. "Here now, Andy," she said, returning with a haversack. Andy watched with pleasure as she put the food and a cup into it. "You'll get plenty of drinking water on the moors," she told him as she helped him to slide his arm through the strap. "There," she said. "Off you go." But again Andy saw only the tight lips and missed the warmth in her eyes. He bounded upstairs, and putting the Spuddy's bowl into the haversack, he thought, This is splendid. Just the thing for a couple of explorers.

Andy was relieved to find the Spuddy waiting. Despite his rough treatment, the dog had after all understood and trusted him as a friend. As Andy walked towards him the Spuddy sat watching, and Andy saw the dog's ears twitch, the tail begin to wave and, most comforting of all, the eyes brighten with welcome. Love and gratitude for feeling wanted surged through Andy. He bent down and let the Spuddy lick his ear before they raced off happily towards the moors.

With the September sun taking the sharp edge off the wind and with the heather springy under his feet, Andy revelled in the space and freedom of the moors. Fearless with the Spuddy for company, he started his quest for a cave, diverted only when he found himself confronting a herd of suspicious-looking Highland cattle or when a rabbit went bounding away from his path. Andy walked on, but before long he noticed that the Spuddy was not following. Andy went back and, patting the dog's head, urged him on. When that had no effect he took off his haversack and laid it on the ground, thinking to examine the dog's paws.

The Spuddy stood up and nudged the haversack with his nose, then sat down and fixed Andy with a hypnotic stare. Andy stared back, whereupon the Spuddy again stood and nudged the haversack. Andy understood that the dog wanted food. He looked at his watch, and seeing that it was five minutes past twelve, he sat down on a convenient thicket of heather, his back against a boulder. He opened the provisions and, putting half the sandwiches and half the sausages into the feeding bowl, placed it in front of the Spuddy, who gave an appreciative wag of his tail.

Once they had eaten, the Spuddy was again eager to follow, and subsequently Andy learned that at twelve o'clock the dog expected to be fed and that he made known his expectations by refusing to obey further orders until he was satisfied.

Continuing his search for a cave, Andy at last came across a low fissure between opposing slabs of rock which leaned together, forming an opening in the shape of an inverted V. He had to go down on his hands and knees and crawl inside, and once there he could only just sit upright, but seeing that it was dry, he decided it would do. He set about gathering autumn bracken and dry mountain grass to make a good bed, and then tested it himself. Finding it tolerably comfortable, he invited the Spuddy to lie beside him; and content yet alert, the Spuddy settled himself down. Andy lay listening to the hissing of the wind backed by the faint murmur of the sea, and his eyes closed.

When he woke, the sun was hovering above the mainland hills, and out at sea he could make out the fishing boats converging on the harbour. It was time to return home, but before leaving he had to convince the Spuddy to stay in the refuge.

It was difficult at first, the Spuddy being determined to follow Andy, but eventually he seemed to understand, and as a reward Andy took out the two pieces of cake from his haversack and put them in the bowl. Then he hurried away, glancing back every so often to make sure the Spuddy was not following. The last time Andy looked back he saw the Spuddy had made his way to the top of a high boulder and there, silhouetted against the evening glow, was watching him leave.

THE NEXT MORNING the Spuddy was waiting for Andy in what was to become their regular meeting place on the main road in the village, and again they made for the moors. When they reached the cave Andy was relieved to see that the Spuddy had used his bed. Andy pointed to the round, nestlike hollow and patted the Spuddy before they carried on exploring, climbing over the shoulders of the hills, stopping sometimes to drink from the sparklingly clear streams, or to paddle or skim stones into the cold, hill-shadowed lochs. There was no difficulty this time in persuading the Spuddy to remain behind when it was time for Andy to return home, though just as he had the previous evening, he insisted on leaping up onto the boulder to watch the boy's departure.

The friendship between the boy and the dog deepened steadily. Every morning the Spuddy would be waiting for Andy, and when they were not roaming the moors and hills they were down at the harbour. For the first few weeks after his arrival Andy had looked every morning to see if the postman had brought him word from his mother—perhaps a postcard like those his father sent him, with lots of x's on the back to let him know she still loved him, but as the weeks became months and there was still no sign from her, he began to accept that either she had forgotten him or she wished him to forget her. If he could not make himself forget her, he did succeed in opening his eyes to the new affection offered him.

In addition to the Spuddy's devotion he had his uncle Ben, who made no secret of the warmth of his feelings; and even Aunt Sarah, whose testiness had at first unnerved him, began to reveal a tender side. She bought him more crayons and paper. She fussed over his

480

health and she began to worry about his lack of education. She had a row with the local schoolmaster when he refused, because of Andy's affliction, to take him into school as a pupil, and when the darker evenings brought long hours indoors she determined that she herself would teach Andy to read and write. Despite a scolding tongue, she displayed not only a natural ability to teach but also an astonishing patience with the boy. The result was that at the end of three months Andy could write to his father the glorious news that if his father wrote a letter in return, he would now be able to read it for himself.

During the day Andy and the Spuddy spent hours down at the pier, mingling with the fish porters and watching the boats. Andy's eye was becoming trained so that he could recognize each boat long before it reached the harbour. He knew most of the crews and was accustomed to being thrown a rope to hitch around a bollard, or even being called aboard to collect the empty pop bottles to take to the grocer with the instruction that Andy could keep the "penny backs" for himself. Andy was glad of the penny backs, because they helped him to buy more food for the Spuddy to augment the scraps he saved. Uncle Ben helped too by saving his own scraps, and if Aunt Sarah ever noticed the total lack of food on her table at the end of their meals, she made no comment.

After a lingering autumn, winter howled in with wild, sharp-toothed winds that scraped the skin like a steel comb. The hills which had been snowcapped became snow-shawled and soon snow-skirted, and fishermen and porters flapped their arms across their oilskinned bodies, trying to keep warm during the minutes of inaction. Andy, snug in the thick sweaters his aunt knitted for him and in the "oilies" she had bought for him, began to worry anew over the Spuddy. The cave was too exposed to make good sleeping quarters during the winter, and when one cold but dry morning he noticed the Spuddy's coat unaccountably wet, he went up to the cave to investigate. To his dismay he found that the bed he had made for the Spuddy was wet, and when he pressed his hand into it, he found that the ground underneath it was little more than a bog. He gathered more bracken, but the bracken itself was wet after the winter rain, and though the Spuddy seemed content enough to

481

stay there, Andy could not sleep that night, worrying about the problem of shelter for his friend.

A few nights later there was a heavy blizzard, and Andy found the Spuddy waiting for him in snow that was up to his belly; his ears were drooping and snow from the last flurry was still melting on his coat. When he tried to follow Andy he stumbled, and Andy knew the dog was sick. In desperation he resolved to somehow persuade his uncle Ben to help find a safe, warm place for the Spuddy to sleep. Down at the boatyard, Uncle Ben watched Andy's passionately expressive mime with complete understanding, and after feeling the dog's hot nose, he led them to the far corner of the workshed where there was a great pile of wood shavings and cotton waste. Andy looked at his uncle gratefully and began to arrange a nest. Even before he had finished, the Spuddy stepped into the centre of the hollow, turned around twice and settled himself down. For three days the Spuddy hardly stirred from his new bed but lay there showing little interest in anything, even food; and Andy, fearing his friend might die, rarely left the boatshed except at his uncle's insistence.

On the fourth day the Spuddy got up out of his bed to greet Andy, and on the sixth day Andy was overjoyed to find the Spuddy waiting for him in their usual place on the road. It was as well that the Spuddy had new quarters, for now that winter had come in earnest, Aunt Sarah had forbidden Andy to go up on the moors alone. He and the Spuddy confined their wanderings to the harbour or to the fields around the village, and when evening came Andy would escort the Spuddy to the boatyard and his warm bed.

CHAPTER III

For Skipper Jake and the crew of the *Silver Crest* the fishing season had proved a disastrous one. It had begun with a broken con rod in the engine, which kept them tied up at the pier for close on two weeks, and when that was repaired there had followed a run of bad luck which included fouled nets, a seized winch, and gear damaged during a heavy storm. When at last they managed to get a good spell at sea, they found the herring shoals elusive, and *Silver*

Crest was arriving in port with a meagre catch which necessitated their turning around right after unloading, and going back out, perhaps snatching only two hours' rest out of the twenty-four. Once one of the highest earning boats in the port, she had dropped to one of the lowest, and the crew were bothered by the superstition that the bad luck dogging them might yet bring worse catastrophe. But Jake dismissed their fears. Despite discomforts and disappointments, he would allow nothing to affect his driving ambition to catch fish—more and more fish to earn more and more money. And since Jeannie, his wife, was away from home visiting her parents, Jake was also goaded by loneliness—loneliness and the recurring pain in his stomach that only hard work or deep sleep could dull.

Before he had met Jeannie, Jake, like most Gaymal fishermen, had been a heavy drinker, spending all his weekends ashore in the local hotel bar downing whisky after whisky, and when the pain had first started he had drunk even more whisky in the hope of alleviating it. Eventually it had driven him to see his doctor.

"You'll have to keep off the drink," the doctor warned after examining him. "I can give you medicine, but medicine can't fight the damage the whisky's doing you."

Jake had intended to heed the doctor's warning, but Gaymal offered only two places where an unmarried man ashore for the weekend could find company and relaxation. Those were the bar and a district up at the back of the kipper yards known locally as Chinatown, where the itinerant "kipper lassies" had their quarters. Not being by nature a wenching man, he had settled for the bar and continued his drinking. Continued, that is, until Jeannie had come into his life.

From the day he had first seen her behind the counter in the local paper shop he had wanted her for his wife. Her smallness and primness delighted him. She was about half his age and he wondered if she would think him too old for her, so he was astounded and delighted when she responded to his tentative approaches.

The change Jeannie had brought into his life had been at first dramatic. In her company he found it easy to stifle the urge to drink, and during their courtship and the early weeks of their marriage and even during her first two or three absences from home, Jake steadfastly renounced his visits to the bar, with the result that not only was his stomach pain less constant but his whole body reacted with a renewed vitality. When Jeannie's visits to her parents became more frequent and more prolonged, Jake, disillusioned and hating the emptiness of the house at weekends, relapsed into his former ways, drinking himself into a confusion of thought that he hoped he might mistake for happiness.

IN THE EARLY hours of a Monday morning after just such a weekend, Jake, grey-faced and bloodshot-eyed, came down to the *Silver Crest*. The crew glanced at him with concern, but they waited until the boat had put to sea and Jake was in the wheelhouse before they commented.

"A drink's a drink," burst out the youngest member of the crew indignantly. "But the skipper's killin' himself with it."

"It's that wife of his that's killin' him," supplied another. "She knows fine he goes on the sauce whenever she's away from him. But she won't stay, not her."

"It's a bloody shame!" still another exclaimed. "He's a damn good skipper an' I don't like to see him made so little of by a woman." He frowned. "Particularly now he has the child."

It was the oldest member of the crew who corrected him. "It's herself has the child."

As he spoke there was an ominous clanking. The engine slowed, then ceased altogether. They rushed up on deck to see the skipper coming out of the wheelhouse.

"Take the boat!" he shouted at the man nearest to him. "That blasted engine's done the dirty on us again." He ran quickly down to the engine room.

"That's it, then," the old man observed to the others remaining on deck. "Our bad luck's not done with us yet."

After an hour or so of wrestling with the engine, Jake managed to coax enough power for them to labour back into port, where an engineer was waiting for them on the pier. Together he and Jake inspected the engine while the crew wondered gloomily how long they were going to be delayed. The engineer came up on deck followed by a glowering Jake. "Not before midnight," he was saying. "Not a hope." As one man the crew set off in the direction of the bar.

For Andy also the day had begun bleakly. That morning Aunt Sarah had told him of a new schoolmaster in Gaymal, a master who was not only willing but anxious to have Andy as a pupil, and it had been arranged that he was to start school the following week. His delight at the news was immediately overwhelmed by dismay: if he had to go to school every day, what would happen to the Spuddy? His misery intensified when, calling in at the boatyard, he found an apologetic Uncle Ben, who warned him that his boss was insisting that the workshed where the Spuddy slept must be cleaned out before the end of the week. There was to be no bed for the Spuddy at the boatyard anymore.

Pottering around the pier, wrestling with his problems, Andy was there to witness the unexpected return of the *Silver Crest*, and anxious to know the cause of it he rán down to watch her tying up. Of all the boats coming in and going out of the harbour Andy thought the *Silver Crest* the most beautiful. Empty or loaded, she rode the sea as easily as the gulls or as serenely as the swans he used to see on the river near his home. She was the boat he most wanted to be allowed to sail in and yet, despite his admiration and despite the fact that he was welcome aboard every other boat in the harbour, Andy had never set foot aboard the *Silver Crest*. First, owing to the poor fishing season *Silver Crest* had rarely been in the harbour for more time than it took to unload. Second, Andy was afraid of Skipper Jake and his rough voice—ever since the day Andy had been sitting on a fish box sketching the *Silver Crest* on the back of a letter to his father, and Jake, ignorant of Andy's affliction, had bellowed at him, "Away an' tell Bobbie I'm wantin' him down here! You know Bobbie? The little fellow with the red hair?"

Andy nodded.

"Aye, then get him. Quick as you can, boy."

Gaymal children accepted that on the pier they were commanded to do things, and Andy ran to find Bobbie, but when the man saw it was the *Silver Crest* Andy was pointing to, he turned away.

"I'm not going," he told a crony. "I'm supposed to be catching a train in half an hour and if Jake gets ahold of me, I might just as well wave it goodbye."

Andy returned to the *Silver Crest*.

"Well, did you find him?" Jake asked.

Andy nodded.

"Is he comin', then?"

Andy shook his head.

"Why isn't he comin'?"

Andy stared at Jake helplessly.

"What's wrong with you, boy?" Jake demanded. "Is it deaf, daft or dumb you are?"

Andy turned and ran quickly from his contempt. Jake climbed onto the pier hoping to spot another likely messenger, and the first thing he saw was the sketch Andy had been making of the *Silver Crest*. He picked up the drawing and studied it. Fancy a stupid kid being able to draw as well as this. He turned the paper over and saw Andy's painstaking printing. "Dear Dad," he read. "This is the boat I like best in the harbour. She is called *Silver Crest* and I think she is beautiful."

Jake wished he had not been so rough with the boy, and going back aboard, he placed the paper carefully between the leaves of a magazine in the wheelhouse, thinking that the next time he saw Andy he would return it to him and at the same time tell him how good it was.

It was three weeks later when one of the crew came across the drawing and commented on it.

"Och, I put it in there to give back to some kid that was on the pier doing it. I sent him to get Bobbie for me that day you lot skinned off ashore, and he came back without him and not a word as to why." Jake's voice was scornful. "Proper little gaper he was, just standin' there an' sayin' nothin'. I shouted at him he must be dumb or somethin'."

"Did he have a dog with him? The one that used to belong to Joe Glenn?" asked one of the crew.

"Aye, I believe he did," Jake admitted.

"Aye, then right enough he is dumb." The man turned away from his skipper's stricken face.

486

Later, Jake learned Andy's story from the crew, and he decided to try to make friends with the boy. To see if he could make some recompense for the hurt he had so unwittingly inflicted.

THE OPPORTUNITY came when the *Silver Crest* limped back into port with the seized engine, and Andy, curiosity overcoming caution, was waiting on the pier with the Spuddy. When the crew had gone off to the bar and the engineer was leaving, Jake hailed Andy, holding out a paper. Andy went slowly up to him.

"Did you do this?" Jake asked as gently as he could, and when Andy replied with a nod he said, "It's good. I like it." He turned the paper over. "I read this too," he confessed. "Is it true you think this is the nicest boat in the harbour?" Andy released a nervous smile. "Aye, I think so too, boy," Jake admitted proudly. "Are you comin' aboard?" he invited. Andy's expression was eloquent. "Come on, then, an' take a look over her."

Andy climbed aboard with the Spuddy.

"Hey!" Jake objected. "I didn't invite that dog. Away you go!" The Spuddy looked questioningly at Andy before obeying the command. The next moment Andy was also ashore, beside the dog.

"What's all this?" Jake asked. "I thought you were keen to see over her." Andy put his hand on the Spuddy's head. "O.K., O.K.," Jake yielded. "He may as well come too." Andy and the dog jumped back aboard and followed Jake into the wheelhouse, down into the hold, through to the engine room and finally into the forecastle, where Jake put on the kettle.

"You get mugs an' rolls an' butter an' jam out of there," he instructed, pointing to a locker. "I daresay you won't say no to a bite to eat."

Andy did as he was told. He had never before eaten any sort of meal aboard a boat, and when Jake had made the tea and they sat on the lockers to eat and drink while the boat swayed to the tide, he was blissfully happy. He had got over his fear of Jake, and Jake was glad of having to entertain the boy and so shorten the hours he would otherwise spend brooding over his misfortunes. All the same, he was finding conversation solely by means of questions difficult to sustain, and for much of the time they ate in silence.

Jake watched Andy giving the Spuddy a piece of every roll he took for himself.

"Does the Spuddy sleep in your room at home?" he probed. Andy shook his head.

"In the kitchen? No? In a kennel outside?" Andy continued to shake his head. "Hasn't he got a place to sleep, then?"

Andy covered his eyes, anguished by the reminder of his problems, but the tears seeped through. Jake saw them and moved closer to the boy. "I suppose you'd miss the Spuddy too much if I suggested he could be a sea dog?"

Mystified, Andy looked up.

"Here on *Silver Crest*," Jake explained. "Why not? Lots of dogs go on boats. He'd have a good berth with me an' the crew. There's always plenty of gash food aboard, an' there'd be a cosy bunk for him down here in the fo'c'sle. But"—Jake gave Andy a doubtful glance—"maybe you wouldn't like to be parted from him so much."

Andy stared steadfastly at Jake. He was grateful to him, but his heart plummeted as he thought how lonely life would be without the Spuddy. Then he remembered about school and how he would be unable to look after the dog all day. He didn't know what to do. He couldn't be parted from the Spuddy now. They needed each other too much.

"You'd see plenty of him at weekends," comforted Jake. He thought, If I get the chance and my son when he's older wants a dog, any sort of a dog, he shall have it sooner than I'll see him suffer like this lad's suffering. Aloud he said, "If you fancied comin' out fishin' with us, you could come whenever you liked."

Andy knew what he ought to do, but he could not bring himself to do it. He stood up and, nodding his thanks to Jake, started up the ladder from the forecastle.

"Think on what I've said, now," Jake called after him.

It was bitterly cold, with a biting wind that seared Andy's cheeks, as the boy and the dog once again made for the moors. The preceding autumn had lingered late and winter had followed its example. They reached the cave and Andy slumped down beside it. This was no place for a dog in such weather. The rock roof was dripping wet and the wind had scattered the bedding. He stared straight ahead, and the Spuddy, coming to lick his face, continued licking at the salty tears. Andy pulled the dog close and buried his face in the rough coat. Then he got up and gestured to the Spuddy to follow him.

They went first to the boatyard, where Andy saw that already the Spuddy's bed had been cleared away to make room for lengths of timber. Out of a cupboard Uncle Ben took the dog's bowl and handed it to Andy. Andy and the Spuddy went purposefully down to the harbour.

Jake was still aboard the *Silver Crest*. He heard the thud of feet on the deck and opened the forecastle hatch. "Come on down, boy," he invited.

Obediently, Andy, followed by the Spuddy, went down into the forecastle. Swallowing hard, Andy reached out and, taking Jake's hand, placed it on the Spuddy's head and held out the bowl.

Jake understood. When he spoke his voice was even gruffer than usual. "I'll look after him for you, boy," he promised. "And I'll not let him forget you."

Andy knelt down and put his arms around the Spuddy's neck.

"You'll want to see where he's goin' to sleep," Jake said. There were eight bunks in the forecastle of the *Silver Crest* and Jake cleared out the lower of two which were obviously not used for the crew. He extricated a couple of spare blankets from a locker and stuffed them into the bunk.

"That's your bunk, mate," he said to the Spuddy. The dog only looked at him. "You'd best tell him to get into it," Jake said, and Andy told the Spuddy in the special sign language the dog now understood so well. Reluctantly the Spuddy got into the bunk. Gently, Andy stroked him, and the forecastle was quiet except for the slapping of the water against the boat.

"Aye, aye," said Jake awkwardly. "Likely he'll miss you, but I daresay he'll settle down."

Andy placed the Spuddy's bowl beside the bunk. The dog had come to accept that wherever Andy placed his bowl, there was his home. But when he saw what Andy had just done, he looked at him with an expression that the boy knew was incredulity. Biting his lips hard, Andy turned away and went quickly up the forecastle steps. The Spuddy jumped out of the bunk, but Jake held on to his collar. The dog struggled until Andy turned and made a repressive gesture. When Andy reached the deck, Jake too climbed the steps and stood in the hatch, blocking the exit. Imprisoned, the Spuddy barked—a single sharp bark of protest.

"See you Saturday," said Jake. "An' don't forget, if your aunt an' uncle aren't against it, you can come with us whenever you have a chance." Jake wished there were more he could do to comfort the boy. He stood watching while Andy ran along the pier and faded into the gathering dusk without once stopping to look behind him.

CHAPTER IV

The Spuddy and Jake assessed each other for a few moments. Then the dog began to investigate the forecastle thoroughly. After having stayed at Andy's bidding in the cave on the moors and then in the shed at the boatyard, he could now trust the boy not to desert him. And after having for so long mingled with the fishermen, he knew instinctively he could trust Jake. All he had to do was to settle himself down until morning, when this man would open up the hatch and let him out to find Andy. He went to the bunk Andy had shown him and sat beside it. Jake came over to him.

"That's your bunk, mate," he told the dog again. "An' remember, on a boat a man's bunk is a man's bunk—he swaps with nobody." He snapped his fingers over the bunk and obediently the Spuddy jumped in. "There's three things you have to learn aboard this boat an' you'll have to learn them quick because nobody's goin' to have time to teach you. Are you listenin'?" The Spuddy's ears pricked and he cocked his head on one side. "The first is, this is your home from now on until your pal can find you a better one. The second is, I'm your skipper from now on, an' the third is, like I've told you, this is your bed from now on."

The Spuddy, discerning the note of companionship in Jake's voice, thumped his tail against the blankets, and the expression in his eyes as he watched Jake was one of perfect comprehension. He nuzzled the blankets into position and with a grunt settled down to sleep.

490

When the bar closed, the crew returned to the *Silver Crest*. "What's he doin' aboard?" they asked, seeing the Spuddy.

"Ship's dog," replied Jake laconically.

"Where's the kid, then?" asked the youngest crewman, recognizing the dog, and when Jake gave a brief explanation they murmured small pretended grumbles and said they hoped he would not be responsible for another run of bad luck.

"Not that one." Jake spoke with conviction. "There's somethin' about that dog that makes me think he's goin' to be our mascot."

It was two o'clock in the morning before the engine was repaired satisfactorily and the *Silver Crest* was ready for sea. Until they were well out of port the skipper ordered that the Spuddy should be shut belowdecks, but once Jake thought it was safe he went down to the forecastle and, threading a length of rope through the Spuddy's collar, took him up on deck. The night was dark, and although the Spuddy had never before been to sea, he knew the sound and smell of it so well he was not afraid when Jake led him along the deck to the wheelhouse. There, Jake shut the door and sat down, his hands on the wheel, his eyes fixed on the bow of his boat as it cleaved through the heaving sea.

"You may as well be here with me, boy," he told the Spuddy. "You an' me, we've got to get used to each other's company."

So the Spuddy stayed with Jake in the wheelhouse until it was time for Jake to be relieved, when they both returned to the forecastle and their individual bunks. When daylight came and the Spuddy was allowed on deck without a rope, the dog was worried because they were so far from land, and he roamed up and down from bow to stern, hoping he might find Andy. When he was tired of roaming the deck, he went back to his bunk and lay listening to the sound of the crew's voices as they ate and talked.

That night *Silver Crest* ran into an enormous shoal of herring, so that they came back to port gunwale-deep with their load. The crew were jubilant that their run of ill luck had ended. "Didn't I tell you he'd be our mascot?" Jake reminded them.

The following two nights they again ran into large shoals. "He's worth his weight in steak," asserted the cook, as if daring anyone to question the sudden increase in the butcher's bill.

491

By the time Saturday morning came the Spuddy was just beginning to get used to his life as a ship's dog, to his warm bunk, to the good wholesome food plus the titbits provided by the grateful crew; but when the boat tied up at the pier and he saw Andy waiting for him, he bounded ashore to greet him ecstatically.

"I'll leave his dinner for him," called the cook as the boy and the dog raced off up the pier.

Andy felt a slight twinge of resentment at that. He was sure it was understood between him and Jake that except for his bunk aboard the *Silver Crest* the Spuddy was to be his alone at weekends, to care for as hitherto. The cook's words seemed to imply that Andy might neglect to feed the dog, whereas Andy had come with a haversack stuffed full of food. Aunt Sarah, now that she knew there was little likelihood of the dog's hanging around the house and annoying the new neighbours, had willingly set aside a "Spuddy pan" in which she not only boiled up house scraps but also added rough pieces of meat bought cheaply from the butcher.

It was a damp day, chafed by a gusty wind but with a hint of sun beyond the lowering clouds; a day when the moors echoed with muted gull cries, and the streams, swollen after a night of rain, foamed peaty brown over the tumbled rocks. Andy plodded on, disturbing flocks of black-faced sheep and shaggy hill ponies that watched suspiciously as he and the Spuddy climbed towards a sheltered corrie overlooking a great chasm of fallen stone. Reaching it, he lay flat on his stomach and the Spuddy lay quietly beside him. Andy loved to come to the chasm not only because of the tales Uncle Ben told of its being haunted, but because he liked to be awed by its sheer size and desolation. And sometimes, if he lay quite still, he was lucky enough to catch a glimpse of one of the elusive hill foxes that had their earths among the chaos of tumbled stone that formed the chasm's floor, or perhaps see one of the equally elusive golden eagles launch itself from its perch on a crevice of the sheer rock face.

The day passed quickly, and when it was time to return, Andy and the Spuddy went aboard the *Silver Crest*. The two were used to evening partings and now the Spuddy quickly accepted that he must stay aboard. With his two front paws resting on the sternpost, he watched until Andy was out of sight and then he slid under the half-open hatch, jumped down into the forecastle and stretched out on his bunk. The following morning when Andy came to the quiet Sunday harbour, where the massed boats lay at rest and the strangely silent gulls were ranged along the roofs as stiffly as a church congregation, he saw that the Spuddy was waiting for him in exactly the same position, as if he had been there all night.

As usual they made for the moors, the bulging haversack on Andy's back. Again in the evening, though earlier because it was Sunday and Andy had to accompany his uncle Ben and aunt Sarah to church, he saw the Spuddy back to the *Silver Crest*. But tonight the parting was more prolonged, because Andy knew it would be another week before he and the dog could be together again.

LONG BEFORE DAWN, Skipper Jake and the crew came aboard and soon the Spuddy heard the approach of other crews, and the harbour began to fill with the sound of throbbing boat engines; of voices shouting greetings, warnings and reminders, while one by one the boats nudged their way out of the crowded harbour towards the sea.

As a member of the crew of the *Silver Crest* during the week and as Andy's faithful companion at weekends, the Spuddy began to know a contentment he had never before experienced, and he did his best to show his appreciation. On the boat, when he saw the catches of herring coming aboard, the obvious excitement of the men affected him and he raced from stem to stern, careful to keep out of everyone's way, yet making sure he was sharing in the activity. Before long he was so anxious to help that he would grab at the net ropes when the men were hauling and, bracing himself, would pull with every ounce of muscle in his body. "We've got ourselves a dog and a half," the crew complimented one another.

One night after a succession of good catches the *Silver Crest* appeared to have lost the shoals, and while the men searched the seas in vain, the Spuddy spent his time running restlessly around the deck or else sitting wistfully in the bow staring into the night-black water. Suddenly he began to bark excitedly. It was the first time since he had been to sea with them that he had been heard to bark, and Jake was puzzled.

493

The dog stood with his two front feet on the bow while he peered down into the water and his tail wagged ceaselessly. Jake eased the throttle and the youngest member of the crew came aft, pulling on an oilskin.

"What's wrong, Skipper?"

"See what's botherin' the Spuddy," Jake shouted. "He's behavin' kind of queer, as if he can see or hear somethin'." The man went forward, and as he reached the bow the Spuddy's tail thrashed vigorously while he continued to bark. The young man knelt beside him, concentrating on the sea. The cook came aft to join Jake.

"What's excitin' the dog?" the cook asked.

"Damned if I know," admitted Jake.

The man in the bow stood up and, turning, gave a wide negative sweep of his arms. "He can't see anythin' seemingly," said the cook.

Jake throttled the engine down to a murmur, and handing over the wheel to the cook with the instruction to steer in a wide circle, he went out on deck and listened and looked intently. A minute later he was back in the wheelhouse.

"Go an' tell them to stand by to shoot the nets," he snapped. "It's my belief that dog's tryin' to tell us there's herrin'."

Flashing him an incredulous glance, the cook rushed forward to pass the command. An hour later they were hauling in their loaded nets while the Spuddy looked on smugly. Later down in the forecastle the crew looked at one another in amazement. "How did he do it, d'you reckon? By smell or by sight or by hearin'?"

"It's enough that he did it," the oldest crew member declared. "What we must wait an' see now is, can he do it again?"

The Spuddy not only did it again and again, but he became such a reliable herring spotter that if he showed no interest in the area they were searching for fish, they knew there was little likelihood of finding any there. In Gaymal, when the stories got around, the Spuddy became a star, and though there were some fishermen who at first refused to believe in the dog's ability to detect the presence of herring, the *Silver Crest*'s consistently good catches were irrefutable evidence of his powers. Soon even the most sceptical of the fishermen tended when at sea to keep the *Silver Crest* close company.

Andy was thrilled when Jake told him on Saturday afternoon of the Spuddy's faculty for herring spotting. They had all three been down in the forecastle of the *Silver Crest*, where, to Andy's delight, it had become more or less a habit for them to meet when he and the Spuddy had returned from their walk. While Jake talked of fishing and of the strange things that sometimes came up in their nets, they would sit beside the stove drinking the skipper's peculiar brew of strong tea sweetened with condensed milk. Even the Spuddy now drank the tea when it was poured into his bowl, and Andy wondered if the dog, like himself, drank it only because he would not risk hurting Jake's feelings by refusing it.

"Aye," Jake had said, rubbing the Spuddy's head fondly. "It was the best thing you ever did for me, letting me take your dog aboard." And Andy, who was not unaware of Jake's drinking bouts and of his loneliness, looked down at the strong hand resting on the Spuddy's head and at the dog's eyes regarding his skipper, and at that moment his last trace of resentment at having to share the Spuddy vanished.

AS THE MONTHS went by, the Spuddy became a cherished and indispensable member of the crew of the *Silver Crest*. In addition to herring spotting he had resumed his war with the gulls, racing along the deck and leaping with snapping jaws at any gull that dared to swoop too low, thus protecting the catch at unloading time. And except for falling overboard one pitch-black night while the skipper and crew were too busy hauling to notice, he did nothing that would cause them concern. That night the Spuddy had been really frightened, but sensibly he had fought the sea to swim around the boat to the side where the nets were being hauled, and gripping the footrope of the net with teeth and legs, he clung on. It was not until the incredulous crew saw him being hauled in with the net that they realized how near they must have been to losing him. Jake's fear had erupted into a flash of anger and he swore at the Spuddy vehemently, ordering him down to the forecastle. But later Jake laughed to himself, thinking of the dignified Spuddy looking so utterly ridiculous being hauled aboard along with a load of herring. Jake called the dog back to the wheelhouse to give him a teasing and patting, but after that he always made sure the Spuddy was shut safely in the forecastle when they were hauling, and he never dared tell Andy of the incident.

There was no doubt, the *Silver Crest* was a happier boat after the Spuddy became its mascot. Jake was glad of his companionship, glad too of the dog's apparent need of him. It was good to be needed, Jake mused, remembering his last meeting with his wife. He had tied up the *Silver Crest,* given his crew a week's holiday and gone to visit her at the home of her parents, in a final attempt to persuade her that her rightful place was at home in Gaymal with him.

Jeannie had seemed pleased enough to see him, but his son, now a toddler, had to be coaxed into recognizing him. When, towards the end of the week, he broached the subject of her return, Jeannie had been at first evasive and then impatient. Couldn't he see for himself her mother was getting frail and needed to be looked after? Jake had tried to convince her of his own need of her and of his longing for his son, but though she had promised to come back soon and spend more time with him, he knew the promise was an empty one. She would never leave him in the accepted sense, for an island girl never "left" her husband; she would retreat from him, slowly but inexorably.

Meantime, Jake's thwarted affections were given to the Spuddy, whose own feelings for his skipper had deepened from trust into much the same devotion as he felt for Andy. There was a difference, though. Andy was his beloved companion, and because the boy was young the Spuddy regarded him as a charge to be protected. But Jake with his quiet strength fulfilled the Spuddy's need for a master who would protect him.

IT WAS about three months after the Spuddy had joined the crew that Andy at last achieved his ambition to go to sea in the *Silver Crest.* A spell of settled weather coincided with a school holiday, and after making a few fussy provisos Aunt Sarah had given her permission. Since it was to be a midnight start it was decided, to Andy's great joy, that he would go down to the *Silver Crest* at his usual bedtime and sleep aboard. So it was that one tranquil Sunday evening when the moored boats lay black against a sea that was stippled with starlight, Andy found himself boarding the *Silver Crest* to be greeted by Jake and the surprised and delighted dog. Together they went below, and Jake pointed to the bunk above the Spuddy's.

"That one's yours," he said, and showed Andy how to line the bunk with blankets so that he would be snug. Jake also showed him how to light the galley stove, and when the kettle had boiled and they had made tea, they sat drinking it in the quiet of the cabin as the Spuddy looked from man to boy and panted happily.

"Now, boy, it's kippin' time," said Jake. Taking off his boots and his jacket, he slid into his bunk, realizing as he did so that it was the first Sunday night for months that he had gone to bed sober.

Climbing into his bunk, Andy took off his own boots and then lay savouring the atmosphere of the man's world which now enclosed him, exulting in the sway of the boat and the trilling of the sea against the planking. He told himself he did not want to sleep but only to close his eyes against the glow of the lamp.

He was shot into wakefulness by the thud of seaboots on the deck above his head, and he rolled out of his bunk as the forecastle hatch was slammed back and one by one the crew came down. Still somewhat bemused with their weekend excesses, they stowed their gear. They woke Jake and went back on deck, and soon afterwards the engine clanged to life and settled to a steady throbbing. Andy pulled on his boots and stood peering out of the hatch. In the light from the masthead he watched the mooring ropes being coiled neatly on the deck. He felt the *Silver Crest* push away from the pier and heard the water splashing against her stem. Jake stayed in the wheelhouse while the men came back to the forecastle, where the cook brewed tea and the crew lighted cigarettes and pipes. The forecastle quickly became stuffy with smoke and Andy was full of yawns.

"Why don't you get back to your bunk like your pal there?" asked the cook, indicating the Spuddy, who was still stretched out luxuriously while keeping half an eye on the activity. "When we start fishin' there'll be plenty of time for you to come up on deck an' watch us."

But Andy was too tense to sleep. Putting on his oilskins, he prepared to join Jake. After the stuffiness of the forecastle, the cold, as he stepped on deck, smote him sharply. The Spuddy moved surely beside him, but Andy's feet were unsteady and he was glad to hold on to the mast and the coamings of the hatches as he scrambled his way to the wheelhouse.

Jake opened the door. "Not got your sea legs yet," he observed. Andy smiled wryly. "Never mind, it won't take you too long an' you're best to be practicin' in the dark to begin with." He made room for Andy on the seat beside him, and the Spuddy settled at their feet. The boy stared out through the window of the wheelhouse, and as his eyes accustomed themselves to the darkness he began to pick out the masthead lights of other boats bound for the same fishing grounds.

Jake looked down at him. "Enjoying yourself so far?" Andy smiled. "Like to take the wheel for a bit?" Andy, hardly able to believe his ears, took over the steering of the Silver Crest while Jake rolled and lighted a cigarette. The cook appeared, bringing steaming mugs of tea and thick wads of bread spread with butter and jam. Jake took the wheel again while Andy ate.

"Shouldn't be too long before we find somethin'," he said after they had been under way for about two hours. "There was herring here last week, so likely as not they'll be here yet." He throttled down the engine, then opened the wheelhouse door. The Spuddy shook himself into alertness. "He knows fine what's happenin' now," Jake explained to Andy, "an' if he doesn't show any interest, we'll not shoot our nets."

But the Spuddy did show interest. Going to the bow of the boat, he stood looking down into the water, and to Andy it seemed that he was also listening intently. The Silver Crest speared on, and as the crew began to come up on deck, fastening their oilskins and pulling on their sou'westers, there was a pale promise of dawn touching the horizon. Suddenly the Spuddy's tail began to wag and he started to bark.

"O.K., now!" shouted Jake to Andy. "You can stick your head out of the hatch there an' watch, but see that you keep that dog down below." Andy did as he was told.

The engine slowed. "Stand by!" Jake yelled, and then, "Shoot!"

Andy stood in the hatchway, stunned by the spectacle of the great pile of nets emerging from the hold and streaming out over the side while one of the crew busily tied buoys onto the rope warp. There seemed to be miles of net and he wondered whether they would ever get it all back aboard again.

"O.K.," said Jake as the last of the nets went out. The engine was slowed until she was just ticking over. And before long the skipper gave the order the crew were waiting for. "Haul!" he commanded crisply.

If Andy had been impressed by the sight of the nets going out, he was spellbound when they began to come in again. As the men strained at the ropes, heaving and hauling and shaking the nets, and the quivering stream of herring poured onto the deck and down into the fishhold, he could only gape. What a story he would have to tell his father next time he wrote! He was still standing enthralled after the last of the nets were in and the crew had finished tidying the deck, and was startled by Jake's voice telling them to go and get their heads down for an hour.

He looked at Andy. "What about you, boy? You could do with a bit of sleep yourself." Andy shook his head. He had only just realized that dawn had spread over the sky and that a metal-bright sun was groping its way through a throng of morning clouds. He followed Jake into the wheelhouse, determined that no part of the homeward journey should be wasted in sleeping.

The cook came aft with more tea and bread and jam, and while Andy ate he watched the sea, ruffled now by an early breeze and flecked by sunlight. He saw the bow spray threaded with rainbows and heard the gulls pleading for a taste of the catch. The Spuddy heard the gulls too and was quick to station himself on deck.

"They'll not come near," Jake assured Andy. "Not while he's here. Though there's nothin' they'd like better than to best the Spuddy. See now," he said as one of the blackbacks tried swooping low over the deck. Andy tried to watch, but his eyes would not focus. Turning around to catch Andy's expected smile, Jake saw that he had fallen asleep, his head against a corner of the wheelhouse and a half-eaten slice of bread and jam still held in his hand.

IT WAS NOT UNTIL HIS next holiday that Andy was again able to spend the night aboard the *Silver Crest*, and that night Jake had cause to be grateful for the presence of both Andy and the Spuddy. They had sailed early on the Thursday morning, making for fishing grounds some hours away. The sea was grey and restless, sending up great sheets of spray to break over the bow of the boat as she ploughed into it, and Andy was glad he had now got his sea legs so that his body responded easily to the motion. When they reached the fishing grounds they had hardly shot their nets before a storm came, making it necessary for them to haul and run with their meagre catch to the nearest harbour.

As was their custom when in port, Jake and the crew repaired to the local bar, leaving Andy and the Spuddy in charge of the boat. Andy, tired after the early start, was soon fast asleep. The Spuddy, however, always mistrustful of strange harbours, elected to remain on deck. Jake was the first to return. He was halfway down the slimy harbour steps when the Spuddy, waiting eagerly to greet him, saw him slip and fall into the water not far from the *Silver Crest*.

Even in the harbour the sea was tempestuous, and Jake, who could not swim and who was encumbered with oilskins and heavy thigh boots, would have stood little chance of survival had he not managed to grasp one of the fenders. Immediately the Spuddy pranced around the deck, barking frenziedly and waking Andy, who stumbled up from the forecastle to find out what was the matter. The Spuddy showed him where Jake was still clinging on, and Andy lay flat on the deck behind the gunwale and put down a hand for Jake to grasp. He found his reach too short, so that as the boat reared and the water surged, his hand was tantalizingly a foot above the fender. He next half slid, half crawled along the deck to find a rope, but the Spuddy had decided on his own course of action. Still barking frenziedly and ignoring the danger should he misjudge the distance, he leaped from the deck of the heaving *Silver Crest* to another boat, where he had every crew member aboard coming up on deck to demand, "What the hell's the matter with that bloody dog?"

Fortunately some of the crew realized from the Spuddy's behaviour that something was wrong, and following him back to the

Silver Crest, they saw Andy's desperate struggles to catch hold of Jake. Within minutes Jake was safely back in his bunk, wrapped in blankets and plied with whisky to "kill the cold." When the other crew had returned to their boat Andy stoked up the forecastle stove and made coffee. He stirred condensed milk into hot water and poured a liberal quantity into the Spuddy's bowl. Then he went to Jake's bunk and, pulling the blanket away from his face, indicated the hot coffee.

Jake raised himself on an elbow. "No, no. Thanks, boy, all the same," he mumbled sheepishly.

The Spuddy, hearing the skipper's voice, came and reared up beside the bunk. Jake roughly grasped a handful of the dog's shaggy coat and looked at Andy. "You're a real pair of mates! I would have been a goner if it hadn't been for you two."

The next morning the storm still raged, and skipper and crew slept in. Andy saw to the stove, made his breakfast and took the Spuddy for a walk around the harbour. Returning, he met the bleary-eyed crew just going ashore.

"We're away to have a quick look round the shops," they told Andy. "Comin' with us?" Andy shook his head. He knew Jake would be alone and he was anxious to get back to the boat.

Aboard the *Silver Crest* Jake was up and pouring himself a mug of tea. "So you're back from your wanders," he greeted Andy. "Will you have a cup?" Andy got his mug from the locker and also put out the Spuddy's bowl. Jake filled them both and pushed the tin of condensed milk towards Andy.

"Well, it was a bad do last night," he admitted with a shamefaced smile. "But I'm none the worse, thank God."

Noticing that Andy's eyes were steadily fixed on him, Jake wondered if he was expected to again express his appreciation of his rescue. He was fumbling for suitable words when Andy went over to his bunk and rummaged beneath the mattress. The boy took out a well-stuffed folder, which he laid diffidently on the table in front of Jake. Carefully, Jake opened the folder and saw many drawings of the *Silver Crest*. Something in the boy's attitude made him realize how honoured he was, and he felt a sudden stab of emotion at Andy's trust in him.

"These are great," he said with clumsy admiration. Andy beamed at him. Jake looked up. "These are beautiful, Andy," he enthused.

Still beaming, Andy slid onto the bunk beside him and together they inspected the drawings.

CHAPTER V

Another year passed, during which Andy's father came home on leave three times, and so reassuring was his son's appearance that he was able to return to sea contented. Though he had kept Aunt Sarah informed of his divorce and his wife's subsequent remarriage and departure for Australia, he hadn't mentioned the subject to Andy, partly because he did not wish to mar their infrequent holidays together and partly because he hoped that avoidance of the subject might help Andy to forget more quickly.

At first Andy had wanted his father to tell him about his mother, but it was so long now and she had rejected him so completely that he did not wish to think about her. His life was too full for brooding. He had school, he had an affectionate home with Uncle Ben and Aunt Sarah, and he had the Spuddy and Skipper Jake and the *Silver Crest*. By now he had become accepted by the boat's crew as ship's boy and joined them whenever he could, but he had not been lucky enough to go on one of their longer trips lasting several days.

One Saturday morning when the spring holiday was approaching, Andy was elated to hear Jake say, "We're aimin' to land at a different port next week, so it'll be a kind of longish trip. I'll speak to your uncle Ben about you comin'."

Andy's response was a broad smile, which cut itself off as he remembered his father was due home on leave next week. But Andy was sure his father would understand. He wouldn't want him to miss this trip, he told himself, and anyway since his father's leaves always lasted at least three weeks there would be plenty of time for them to be together when Andy returned.

The spring holiday came with unspringlike wet and cold and sleet, and when the *Silver Crest* speared out to sea at first light on Monday morning, Andy was glad to be able to share the shelter of the wheelhouse with Jake and the Spuddy. The crew were suffering from sore heads and Jake was miserably aware of his own hangover and of the pain stabbing at his stomach. Hunched over the wheel, he scowled at the tossing sea as he steered for the thick grey horizon.

The cook came aft, ducking his head against the spray and sleet. "Are you goin' to get your head down, Skipper?" he asked, reaching for the wheel.

"Aye, I'll do that," replied Jake. "It's not much of a day, so how about makin' for that Rhuna island of yours, seein' you're always tellin' us how sheltered it is in this wind? We could lie to in the bay for a while until we see what the weather's goin' to do. You can pilot us through the passage yourself."

"Aye, aye, Skipper," agreed the cook.

Jake spoke to Andy. "You'd best get some kip yourself, boy, while you can. If we're fishin' tonight, you'll not get a chance."

Obediently, Andy went to his bunk, where he lay listening to the heavy thump of the boat into the seas, the scrunch of the waves and the smacking of spray on the deck.

He woke to the noise of the chain rattling through the fairlead as the *Silver Crest* dropped anchor in Rhuna Bay. He slid quickly out of his bunk and went on deck to stand shivering in the wind. Rhuna Bay, hugged by two arms of jagged land, was relatively quiet, though the waves were fussing and hissing around the black rocks, and the wind in the boat's rigging had a high-pitched note of menace. Andy could see the low grey stone croft houses set close to the shore, and beyond them, where the land rose to meet the hills, he discerned drifts of brown and black cattle grazing on the tawny grass. Skipper Jake, who had been up on deck to supervise the anchoring, paused to glare at the livid sky above the plump grey clouds before returning to the forecastle, where, his face taut with pain, he threw himself into his bunk.

Andy, aware of his own sea appetite, joined the rest of the crew in a meal of bacon, eggs and sausages. Just as they were finishing they heard a boat scrape alongside, and the youngest crew member went up to investigate. He returned a few minutes later with two middle-aged men dressed in what Andy took to be their Sunday clothes. The cook was quick to recognize the men, and when they had exchanged a few sentences in Gaelic, he translated. "They're sayin' there's a weddin' on today. One of my relatives it's supposed to be too."

There were questioning murmurs from the rest of the crew. "Aye, an' they're after askin' us over an' take a wee dram with them an' wish the bride an' groom good luck." The cook's expression was eager. "How about it, boys? Just for an hour or two?"

All the crew liked the idea of going ashore for an hour, and when they woke Jake he not only agreed to let them go but insisted they take Andy with them.

"You may as well take the Spuddy too, Andy," Jake said, dragging himself out of his bunk to watch them leave. "A run ashore won't do him any harm."

But surprisingly, when the time came for the Spuddy to jump into the dinghy, he refused. Even when Andy tried coaxing by patting the seat beside him, the Spuddy did not yield. Andy noticed a slight quiver passing through the dog's body, and thinking he might be sick, he stood up in the dinghy intent on climbing back aboard. But the youngest crew member pulled him down.

"You can come to the party instead of goin' for a walk, Andy. You'll fairly enjoy yourself," he asserted. Andy still looked troubled, but by now the dinghy was pushing off.

Jake was glad to be left alone. An hour's quiet and he was confident he'd be himself again. The anchor was good, the sea was quiet enough in the bay, and even though the crew were ashore, Jake trusted them to keep an eye open for anything going amiss. He went back to his bunk to collapse in a stupor of pain. The Spuddy, having watched the dinghy reach the safety of the shore, followed his skipper to the forecastle and stretched out in his own bunk.

Some time later Jake was roused by the Spuddy's sharp, insistent barking. He was out of his bunk in a second. "What the hell?" he asked himself, recognizing by the motion of the boat that something was wrong. "The bloody anchor's dragged," he muttered, consternated, and stumbled on deck to be met by a blinding blizzard.

Close at hand he could hear the noise of breakers, muffled by the snow but still far too loud. She was almost ashore! He rushed to start the engine. Where in hell's name were the crew? Why hadn't they noticed the change in the weather? Once the engine began to throb confidently, his mind could grapple with the next problem. The anchor! Dismissing the possibility of trying to get it aboard himself, he ran forward to cast off the anchor chain. That was a loss the crew could pay for, he thought grimly, as he raced back to the wheelhouse and put the engine in gear.

He tried to peer through the blizzard for a sign of the dinghy bringing out the crew, but the snow was impenetrable, obliterating everything beyond the outline of the boat. Cautiously, Jake began to dodge the *Silver Crest* towards the entrance of the bay while cursing himself for having relied on the cook to pilot them through the narrow Rhuna passage. What was it he'd said to avoid? Remembered snatches of forecastle talk rushed confusedly through his mind and Jake recalled with mounting panic something about there being a couple of rocks, submerged at high tide and well out beyond the coast to the west of the island. Just how far out must he steer to avoid them?

He was shouting curses now; cursing himself, the cook and the snow. How near was he coming to the entrance of the bay? How soon could he risk turning? Gradually he became aware of a sharp lift to the sea and he heaved a sigh of relief, knowing that he must be approaching open water. Resolving to turn westward rather than risk the hazardous passage between Rhuna and the mainland, he headed the *Silver Crest* directly into the seas, revving up the engine to combat the rapidly worsening conditions. Despite the cold, his body was running with sweat; his hands, even his arms, were shaking as he clutched the wheel, and he found himself no longer shouting curses but murmuring prayer after fervent prayer as the boat leaped and plunged.

The crash as she came down on the rocks flung Jake to the deck while the mast came hurtling through the top of the wheelhouse. For a moment he lay stunned, blood welling from a great gash on the side of his head, and then he was desperately struggling to his feet to slam the engine into full astern. The propeller raced uselessly, and as the sea tumbled away he saw that the *Silver Crest* was caught amidships by two great fangs of rock that were holding her

506

above the water like a priest holding up a sacrifice. Jake moaned. Why hadn't he gone out more before turning? How had he so badly misjudged his distance from the shore? The bloody snow! His stomach burned with pain and he clutched at it as he retched onto the deck.

Staggering forward, he clung on as another mountainous sea smashed itself over the rocks, and then all Jake was conscious of was the thundering water and the screams of his boat as she keeled over and the sea and the rocks began rending her apart.

Gasping, he lay on the tilting deck, his hands gripping the capping, while the realization that his boat was doomed soaked into his brain as pitilessly as the chill sea soaked into his weakening body. He glimpsed the rocks again spiking through the snarling water; grasping, greedy rocks. Jake's breath came in sobbing coughs. They'd got his boat and now they wanted him. Those rocks, they wanted him all right. The thought hammered at him repetitively, and he thought of his wife who didn't want him and of his infant son who didn't need him.

Suddenly he remembered the Spuddy. Where was he? Could he still be down in the forecastle? Gulping and gasping, Jake pulled himself along, hanging on to the fallen mast only to find that the seas were breaking through the forecastle hatch. Then he saw the Spuddy.

When the mast had fallen the dog must have come up from the forecastle and have been trying to reach him in the wheelhouse, and he lay now, his hindquarters pinned down by the wreckage. The Spuddy's mouth was open and he might have been howling, though Jake could hear nothing above the savagery of the sea.

"All right, Spuddy!" he panted. Slithering and clawing his way along the deck, he at last managed to insert his shoulder under the mast and heaved with all his remaining strength. The effort was enough to release the Spuddy and the next sea did the rest, washing the dog into the water. Relieved, Jake saw that he could still swim. The Spuddy might stand a chance of getting ashore alive. A dog's chance. No more. In the next instant he perceived the Spuddy was trying to turn to swim back to him.

"No, Spuddy! No!" Jake's voice came out in a rasping shout.

"Ashore, Spuddy! Skipper's orders!" Through a thinning swirl of snow Jake caught a glimpse of land. He retched again and slowly his hands released their grip of the boat.

BACK IN RHUNA, the crew, caught up in the gaiety of the wedding, failed to notice the passing of time and the threatening storm. Even Andy was too entranced by the old fiddler's playing to give a thought about getting back to the Spuddy. He had seen a few snow-flakes whirling about, but the house in which they were being entertained was tucked in behind the hill. It was not until the time had come for them to return to the boat and they had rounded the shoulder of the hill that they became aware of the full force of the blizzard. When they reached the shore they were concerned to find that the sea was breaking so viciously over the shingle it was impossible to launch the dinghy.

Andy could not hide his anxiety, but the crew, feeling guilty over their inattention to the weather, tried to reassure themselves that there was nothing to worry about. When the tide ebbed there'd be a chance to launch the dinghy, they consoled themselves. And this blizzard couldn't last long, surely; not coming down as thickly as it was.

They accepted the hospitality of a cottage near the shore, where they drank tea and smoked and bit their fingernails and stared at the snow-masked windows. It was almost dark before the blizzard ceased and the sea was calm enough for them to get out the dinghy, but there was no *Silver Crest* in the bay.

"She must have started draggin' her anchor an' so he thought he'd best get out of it," suggested the youngest member of the crew.

"I daresay that's the way of it," agreed the cook.

"In that case he'll soon be back to pick us up," said the oldest, and they clustered around the dinghy, kicking at the shingle, stamping their cold feet, flapping their arms, smoking, muttering, and all the time staring out across the bay, willing the lights of the *Silver Crest* to appear around the point. The wind died to a frosty calm and a full moon rose, polishing the dark rocks against the snowy collar of the bay, and still the men waited on the shore, refusing the proffered warmth of the cottage. When the dawn came and there

508

was still no sign of the boat, the crew and some of the crofters walked out to the point to scan the sea. What they saw impaled on the jagged rocks sent some of them for help while others hurried to search the rocky shores.

WHEN THE SEA had flung the Spuddy on the sandy inlet between the rocks on Rhuna's west coast, it was the top of the tide, and after dragging himself out of reach of the water he lay quite still. All through the night, oblivious of the thrashing surf and the pain of his crushed body, he waited for the peace he knew would not be long in coming.

At dawn, he lifted his head, as if for one last look, and saw lying just above the now calm water the body of his skipper. He tried to move, digging his paws into the sand, and laboriously, shuddering every now and then with pain, he dragged himself down until he was beside Jake. As he nuzzled under the cold hand that had given him so many rough caresses, his tail lifted and dropped once and his breath came out in a last long moan.

Man and dog were still lying together when the search party found them. Gently they moved the body of the Spuddy aside while they lifted Jake onto a makeshift stretcher and carried him away. When they had gone, Andy, accompanied by his father, who had been told on his arrival in Gaymal of the wreck and had hitched a lift on the first boat out to Rhuna, reached the place where the Spuddy lay. Andy's father let the boy go down to the shore alone, and he saw Andy bend down and tenderly rest his hand on the dog's wet body. He saw him go then to where the shattered bow of the *Silver Crest* had been washed ashore; saw him run his hand down the curving stem as he might have run it along the neck of a favourite horse; saw him return to the Spuddy and kneel beside him in the sand.

Then he turned away so as not to witness his son's grief, and crouching behind a rock he looked up at the gulls as they circled low over the shore, listening to the laughterlike mutterings of a couple of blackbacks, the loud, harsh screams of the herring gulls. Thinking he heard a human shout, he looked around him to see who might be coming.

He stood up. The shout seemed to be coming from the direction of the shore, but he knew there was only Andy down there. Andy and a dead dog. He looked more intently. The shout was unmistakably coming from the shore.

"No! No!" it was saying over and over again, and as Andy was shaking his fists at the low-swooping gulls his mouth was forming the word no, and the sound was without doubt coming from it.

The father stood in dazed unbelief while he watched Andy pull some cord from his pocket, tie one end of it around a boulder and the other around the Spuddy's neck. He saw him drag the dog into the water, and fearful of what might happen, he bounded down to the shore, calling, "Andy! Andy!"

But Andy paid no attention. He knew he had to do this last service for his friend. He couldn't let the enemy gulls ravage the poor dead body that could no longer defend itself. He must get the Spuddy out to deep water—deep enough to be out of the way of the gulls and where the boulder would ensure that he would be carried out to sea by the next tide. As his father splashed through the water Andy let go of the Spuddy. He grasped the hand his father was holding out to him.

"Andy!" rejoiced his father as they waded ashore. "You spoke. Did you know?"

Andy's hand went to his throat. "No!" he said, not answering his father's question but still shouting at the gulls.

"But you spoke again then. You really did," his father insisted.

"Yes," said Andy experimentally, and feeling the strange throbbing that had begun in his throat, he said yes and no over and over again as together he and his father climbed out of the bay and tramped back across the snowy moors.

510

Lillian Beckwith

Shortly after the outbreak of World War II, Lillian Beckwith was seeking a quiet place in which to recuperate from a bout of illness and decided to visit the Hebridean Islands, off Scotland. It was a visit which stretched into almost twenty years, and gave her a chance to indulge a lifelong curiosity about back-to-nature living.

Settling on one of the lesser islands, Miss Beckwith became a crofter—a small tenant farmer. Remembering those times, she says now, "I learned the hard way. If I shirked peat cutting in the spring, I'd be cold in winter. The land was so poor that it was virtually impossible for the crofters to have a surplus to dispose of. When, in the early days, I naïvely asked if I could buy some of their produce, they responded by giving me generous sacks of peat or hay or potatoes, refusing any suggestion of payment. It was their way with ignorant strangers and ensured that I didn't have the cheek to ask again."

Although Hebridean life was hard, there were always the rewarding aspects: "impossibly beautiful scenery" and the great satisfaction of living at one's own chosen pace. Through the years, too, Miss Beckwith came to know fishermen such as those portrayed in *The Spuddy*, and she worked on a series of stories about life in the Hebrides, a selection of which was published in Condensed Books under the title of *Incredible Island*. She feels now that isolation played a large part in her decision to write. Sometimes there was simply no one to talk to, so she put down on paper what she wanted to say.

In 1961 Miss Beckwith married Edward Comber, an artist, and they moved to the less remote but no less enchanting Isle of Man, still as close to the sea as possible.